VOLUME 2

T0366729

WOMEN'S HISTORY IN GLOBAL PERSPECTIVE

VOLUME 2

PUBLISHED WITH THE
AMERICAN HISTORICAL ASSOCIATION

WOMEN'S HISTORY

IN GLOBAL PERSPECTIVE

Edited by Bonnie G. Smith

UNIVERSITY OF ILLINOIS PRESS

URBANA AND CHICAGO

© 2005 by the American Historical Association
All rights reserved
♾This book is printed on acid-free paper.
Printed and bound in Great Britain by
Marston Book Services Ltd, Oxfordshire
1 2 3 4 5 C P 5 4 3 2 1

Library of Congress Cataloging-in-Publication Data
Women's history in global perspective, volume 2 /
edited by Bonnie G. Smith.
p.   cm.
"Published with the American Historical Association."
Includes bibliographical references and index.
ISBN 0-252-02997-6 (cl. : alk. paper)
ISBN 0-252-07249-9 (pbk. : alk. paper)
1. Women—History. I. Smith, Bonnie G., 1940–
HQ1121W88585   2005
305.4'09—dc22   2003024938

Contents

Introduction

BONNIE G. SMITH

These volumes testify to an exciting new stage in teaching women's and gender history: the development of a global perspective on the past. For several
centuries scholars in the West have produced world history textbooks, including those of Johann-Christophe Gatterer (1761) and Johann Gottfried von
Herder (1784–91). These usually began with the appearance of the human
species as an advance over animal life, followed by what can be called a Christian trajectory that saw other civilizational groups in relationship to the unfolding of Judeo-Christianity. There were also parallel efforts by earlier historians of women—Lydia Maria Child's *History of the Condition of Women* (1835)
is just one among many possible examples—to investigate the experience of
the world's women.

As imperialism, debates over the slave trade, more rapid communication
and transport, and global trade itself brought people into greater contact with
one another, histories of women in the Middle East, China, Africa, and elsewhere poured from the pens of amateur scholars in the nineteenth and early
twentieth centuries. The professionalization of history and the cataclysmic wars
from 1914 on curtailed some of those efforts. More recently, the vast new evidence of global connectedness has revived the imperative to better understand
the world, especially the worldwide history of women. These volumes are
devoted to surveying the most recent findings on women and gender in the
hope of bringing teachers at all levels a practical introduction to the new data,
historical issues, and historiographical debates from all regions of the world.

The volumes are part of the evolution of women's history since the 1960s,
and many authors of these chapters were pioneers in that development. The
1970s revived and professionalized the study of women's past, particularly in
the form of social history, in which the experience of women as workers, mothers, outcasts, prostitutes, and homemakers took center stage. Historians of
women during these and subsequent years quantified many aspects of wom-
en's past, often looking at such new issues as the female life-cycle. Investigations of the workplace and the household were primary, but there were also

forays into issues of reform and women's participation in great national events such as war. In addition to concern for class as a determinant of women's experience, the women's history written in the 1970s and 1980s brought the study of race to the fore. Work in this field focused on difference and incommensurability, especially as it traced African American women's unique past as slaves, reformers, and free workers. One culminating moment in this development was the appearance of a groundbreaking biographical dictionary, *Black Women in America: An Historical Encyclopedia* (1994).

During the mid-1980s, gender theory emerged to reorient and even contest the path that women's history was taking. In brief, this theory proposed looking at masculinity and femininity as sets of mutually created characteristics shaping and even producing the lives of men and women. It replaced, or at the very least challenged, ideas of masculinity and femininity and of men and women as operating in history according to fixed biological determinants. Many established historians who observed the emergence of the history of women thought it belonged more appropriately to natural history. Women's history, some believed, had to be told in conjunction with the history of the family and women's biology. Gender history changed all that. By removing these categories of men and women from the realm of biology, it made a history possible.

For some, the idea of "gender history" was but another term for women's history, but serious students of gender theory transformed the ways in which they approached writing and teaching about men and women. To some extent it may be hypothesized that the major change gender theory offered was to problematize the study of men, making them as well as women gendered historical subjects who operated in a culturally constructed universe of symbols developed around the issue of gender. The leading proponent of gender theory, Joan W. Scott, pointed to the ways in which the operation of gender produced hierarchies of meaning and value, which were part of the operation of power in the world. The subsequent investigation of gender in history took on an enhanced variety of subjects under the expanded mandate of gender theory.

As these developments continue to play themselves out in the form of important new scholarship, the last decade of the millennium vividly highlighted the need for more global and comparative perspectives in teaching and scholarship. World and global history appeared more insistently in the curriculum of schools and universities, owing to the rapid unfolding of world events such as migration, communication technology, wars, and increased global trade. Because of the expanded subject matter teachers had to convey, attention to women and gender dropped by the wayside. This material was seen as secondary to the more important subject matter of global politics directed by men or of global economic systems such as the Silk Road or routes on the

Indian Ocean. In the first forays of a new world history, as in the earlier text-books in German universities or Arnold Toynbee's extension of their paradigm, women were rarely to be seen. Even when making an appearance, it would be to extend an earlier paradigm. Books introduced unique topics—footbinding, for example—to point to the barbaric treatment of women outside the (Christian) West. This situation had to be changed, many educators felt.

In the midst of the development of a modern version of world history in the academy, activists from around the world were also at the forefront of high-lighting the importance of a fresh, global perspective in women's and gender history, and their insights contributed to developing the new scholarship on women and gender in global perspective. Almost two centuries ago, Lydia Maria Child's work on women in various parts of the world was born of her commitment to abolitionism, and it allowed her to see slavery as part of a world system—a perspective reborn in the decades since World War II. More recently, the international meetings of women connected with second-wave feminism inspired participants, especially those from Central and South America, Africa, and Asia, to insist on a more encompassing and diverse global perspective. Issues taken as normative by U.S. and West European feminists had little rele-vance from the vantage point of activists in Africa, South Asia, and Latin Amer-ica. Outside the prosperous northern tier of countries, family, work, politics, and nation had different meanings and entailed different political strategies. Gender was multiply constructed, non-Westerners maintained. Western igno-rance and U.S. dominance were called into question during these meetings, and an entire system of scholarly priorities and values was thrown into ques-tion as well. Nowhere was that more evident than in the study of history.

The dissolution of the Soviet Union and the collapse of state socialism in Eastern Europe and Central Asia have also challenged the orientation of traditional historical research in the United States. As scholarship on women and gender emerged from that region, it raised an alternative array of histor-ical questions, particularly concerning democratization, the free market, and citizenship. In what was euphemistically called "the transition," women sud-denly found themselves without jobs and without the social services that had provided health care for them and their children. Following free-market val-ues meant unemployment for women, and belief in women's equality was equated with a failed and often brutal socialist system. Women's inequality became prized in these countries because of its association with American and West European success, inspiring bursts of feminist activism from women in the post-Soviet world. As nongovernmental organizations sponsored women's and gender history programs in Budapest and Moscow, scholars and activists used the insights of Western scholars and devised many new questions of their own, often contesting the would-be hegemony of U.S. feminists and their

3

scholarly concerns. Historians in Eastern and East Central Europe helped shift attention to issues of citizenship and democratization as global processes. East European scholars have helped their counterparts elsewhere address issues of historical evidence and feminism from a fresh point of view.

These events alone have shown that a global perspective calls for examining the past from more than one point of view. Beyond that, however, questions of what constitutes world history and global studies still remain open to zestful debate. World history has had many metamorphoses and will probably have many more. Orthodoxies have come and gone while the field of knowledge about women and gender in world history has expanded exponentially. For some, a global perspective has meant examining and integrating the history of all countries except the United States. According to this view, global history is best taught by specialists in the Chinese, African, or similarly non-U.S. fields. Others have seen global history as best when it additionally excludes Europe, which is perceived as so hegemonic in historical narrative that studying it irremediably distorts attempts at understanding the global past. In these two versions of global history, such a history means "the rest" and has led to a much-criticized pedagogy. While Americanists and Europeanists have focused on relatively specialized scholarship and teaching, specialists from outside those fields have been charged with teaching the world in its entirety.

In contrast, this book and the two that accompany it try to integrate both North America and Europe into the global perspective in the belief that such inclusion is necessary for a holistic history that encompasses the world. Similarly, the most innovative textbooks in the field have increasingly rejected this strategy. The initiator of the volumes, the Committee on Women Historians of the American Historical Association, envisioned a wide-ranging series that would make available the insights and information from recent scholarship from *all* geographic regions. Moreover, it aimed for inclusive topical chapters that would bring into play women's experience of such large-scale institutions and movements as the nation-state, feminism, and religion from around the world and that would be written by specialists in a variety of geographic fields. We see the virtues of inclusiveness, for example, in a chapter on work, which establishes discernible patterns, topics, and analytical themes that can unify the study of work in many parts of the world over the centuries. Material on women in the United States and Europe helps establish those themes and patterns, but it does not dominate the analysis. More important, the global sweep of an analysis of work prevents the omission of the United States and Europe from distorting our understanding. Instead, the centrality of gender to the organization, remuneration, and conditions of work globally comes into true focus.

Because of the vast amounts of potential historical coverage in both topical and geographical volumes, the distinguished authors to these books have been ruthlessly selective, providing usable models to teachers who also must prune their classroom presentations. Understanding that there are many world religions, a chapter on religion, written by a specialist in North Africa, has focused on Islam, Christianity, and Judaism while omitting other systems of belief that are treated in other chapters and volumes. Regional and national presentations of women's and gender history are also pared to the most central and useful topics and themes. These are not necessarily uniform across the volumes because each region's history and central concerns differs. A chapter on China, for example, provides a detailed overview of the family system as a prelude to the more general treatment of women and gender in Chinese history. The early history of Latin America, in contrast, brings into play the impact of contact on indigenous women and on the evolution of gender. The author of an early history of North America emphasizes the interaction and diverse lives of the multiple ethnicities there, offering excellent material for teachers wishing to establish a background to the complex gendering of North American history.

Several classroom uses are intended for this volume and those that accompany it—and we stress again the practical intent of these overviews. First, they allow more material on gender to be introduced into the study of any particular area of the world. The regional volumes are designed to help teachers and students of Chinese history or Latin American history, for example, learn more about the gendered aspects of that history and add the history of women to their understanding. Women are present in the evolution of classical Chinese thought and in the nation-building processes of modern Latin America. The regional histories provide an overview of women's history from around the world and can enrich the gendered component in national and regional courses.

A second step, one that has shaped world history courses, is to encourage comparisons among the historical experiences of women from various continents, regions, nations, and religious traditions. The topical chapters on family, religion, race, and ethnicity and other basic subjects allow nearly any course to have a comparative gendered component. Critical insights develop when the study of such phenomena as nationalism or work contains material on women and gender. Material from this volume and volume three, however, also allows for comparative study and teaching.

As mentioned earlier, women's activism has led to seeing history in a more inclusive, comparative manner. That activism brings to light still another perspective on globalism that involves thinking about the very nationalist bias of women historians in the United States in the writing and conceptualization of history. A substitute way of thinking considers the histories that crossed borders. Transnational women's movements parallel such contemporary phenomenon as global migration, multinational corporations, global communications, and transnational ruling structures like the World Bank. These developments, however, have been accompanied by new findings in world history that suggest the enduring nature not of nations but of global contact.

A surprising constancy, going back tens of thousands of years of global migration, cultural exchange, and the spread of disease and epidemics, opens new vistas for the history of women and gender. Among these phenomena are women's relationship to overland and overseas trade, their variegated participation in migration and diasporas, and their contributions to culture, both nationally and internationally. Women throughout time have been part of regional and transregional slave systems and international prostitution; they have also participated in international movements against slavery and forced prostitution. The transregional spread of religion has involved women and, simultaneously, often has been a highly gendered process.

The chapters in this book and Volumes 1 and 3 include material that allows teachers to focus on the place of women and the role of gender in the transnational aspects of world history. Various components of women's work have implications beyond national and regional borders, and information on their labor appears in chapters on race and work, among others. Women's relationship to world religions and philosophical systems appears in multiple chapters, including most of the regional chapters and topical ones. Women's transnational activism is also prominent, especially in the investigation of feminism and nationalism. All three books are intended to encourage gendered study in the exciting evolution of world history as it comes to examine processes that operate across current national and regional boundaries.

A "global perspective" allows for several different approaches to women's and gender history in the classroom. First, it can mean simply bringing to the fore historical material from most of the discrete areas of the globe—what might be called a "civilizational approach" that many teachers find important. Reading the two volumes of regional chapters will provide an overview of women's history from around the world and permit teachers to enrich the gender component in national and regional courses. It also permits cultural literacy in women's history that is worldwide. A second step in developing a global perspective would be to encourage comparisons among the historical experiences of women from various continents, regions, and nations. The topical chapters on family, religion, race and ethnicity, and other subjects allow courses based on a topical approach to have a gender component. Many teachers find that organizing a course by topic allows for clear organization that students can follow. Insights develop when a study of such phenomena as nationalism or work contains material on women and gender. If the study of women and gender has helped transform historical study, we believe that there is still more to be done—namely, using multiple strategies to open a still wider window on the historical world.

As historians of women struggle to meet the need to inform students and themselves more broadly about both global processes and pressing international issues, the sheer mass of information in the ever-expanding historical field seems overwhelming. The chapters that follow provide economical coverage of basic themes and facts. In the face of our current information overload, however, the greater danger is to continue to claim only marginal importance for issues of women and gender and omit any coverage at all. In the face of great world events and the need to understand major cultural influences, women's importance can appear to shrink. The chapters also demonstrate a distinctly opposite historical world in which issues of gender and the presence of women have been pivotal to political, economic, and cultural development.

From the opening salvos of this book to its final chapters there are perils to accurate understanding if women's experience and the construction of gender are omitted from the historical account. Both have been central to the development of nationalism, the economy, and religious life, and individual regions and nations have mobilized both women and gender to advance political and economic agendas.

Responsible and accurate historical understanding depends on considerations of women and gender, and these volumes seek to provide a usable overview of the latest issues, central facts, analytical tools, and current scholarship. In sponsoring this volume, the one ahead of it, and the one following, the Committee on Women Historians of the American Historical Association seeks to enrich the connection of all teachers and students to the vital world of women's and gender history.

1

Women in Ancient Civilizations

SARAH SHAVER HUGHES
AND BRADY HUGHES

Women in Ancient Global History

This essay examines the lives of women in ancient civilizations from three perspectives. The first focuses on women's importance in prehistory. The second describes common characteristics of women's productive work and legal status in literate societies. The third introduces the importance of women's reproductive functions both to their self-esteem and as a source of potential power in society. The essay presents a descriptive discussion by region of those people whose gender histories in the ancient period are known. The conclusion suggests some bases for comparing women's status in various ancient societies.

The thesis of this essay is that women have been both victims and victors rather than having been universally subordinated in patriarchal societies everywhere. But even this dyad of victors and victims is too simplistic. Women's historical lives, even within the most explicitly patriarchal societies, were seldom affected exclusively by male power. Rather, age, class, marital status, freedom or slavery, fecundity, ambition, and physique all contributed to the texture of life. Focusing too narrowly on aspects of male power may obscure domains in which female power existed, whether in the home or in society.

Although the complexity of gender in global history has only recently begun to be systematically explored, it is evident that women's political and social subordination to men was typical in most literate civilizations of the classical period. Less certain is whether patriarchal legal institutions were modified or ignored by customary practices in some eras, regions, or classes. Furthermore, the literate, generally urban, and imperial civilizations included too few of the world's population to assume they represent the status of all women. Nevertheless, these literate civilizations of western Asia and North Africa, South Asia, East Asia, and the northern Mediterranean are all necessarily the focus of this essay. Little research has been published on women in the nonliterate civilizations of these regions. Excluded from this essay is discussion of ancient women in the regions of northern Europe, Central Asia, sub-Saharan Africa, and what are now called the Americas, where monographic studies on ancient women either have not been written or the published sources in English are insufficient.

REDISCOVERY OF GLOBAL HISTORY AND WOMEN'S HISTORY

Although rediscovery of global history and women's history occurred at about the same time in Western scholarship, until recently these were parallel scholarships whose tracks occasionally crossed but did not converge. World history, developing from the histories of states, surveyed political, military, economic, intellectual, and sometimes social changes within regional frameworks. Distancing themselves from the grand theorizers of earlier generations, historians of the 1970s and 1980s initially approached comparative history gingerly. Long-distance trade, epidemics, and migration were typical of the topics studied, considering long-term historical developments as more complex than the rise and decline of empires or cultures. Yet this new global history tended to omit actual people—even the famous men of older narratives—in favor of broad, impersonal but implicitly masculine forces, for the bias of Western culture suggests that if no gender is specified, the ideas and activities are those of men.

In contrast, women's history was very personal, but it was long preoccupied with the individuals and politics of the West. When origins of gender beliefs were sought, the search was limited to the ancient history of western Asia and Europe. Since the 1990s the focus has shifted, however, and histories of women in many, but not all, parts of the world have proliferated. But this history is usually pursued by area specialists and with little comparative analysis. Comparative history has entered women's history mainly in scholarship about the period from the 1950s to 2000. As the absurdities of women's exclusion from economic development programs accumulated in scholarly literature and field reports, a global framework appeared in contemporary women's studies. Concern with differences of class, sexuality, and ethnicity among women in Western societies also broadened speculation about global differences. Convergence of women's and world history, although desirable, requires recognition of the separate development of the disciplines during a period of more than thirty years.

The "new" women's history arose from an international, Western women's movement composed of feminists from many fields. This history has always been consciously interdisciplinary and has consistently engaged with theories of human and social development, where ideas flow freely between disciplines, especially anthropology, sociology, literature, and history. In this "new" women's history, gender is a fundamental analytic concept (as important as kinship, class, ethnicity, or the state) in which *gender* does not merely refer to a simple male-female dyad. Rather, biological differences between men and women are shown to have social meanings so various and changing that the notion of universal male and female characteristics is more misleading than useful. By assuming that gender is a social construction whose meaning cannot be presumed at any time in any society, scholars have discovered that some cultures have complex gender patterns that do not draw sharp boundaries between male and female.

What happens when very different cultural constructions of gender collide? From the invasion of the Americas to the partition of Africa, European colonialism has provided a fertile field for studying how conflicts over gender formed a core of resistance to domination as well as a rationalization for conquest. Kathleen M. Brown suggests considering "the relationship between gender and colonialism" as "cultural encounters . . . occurring along gender frontiers." Such gender frontiers were not distinct from economic, linguistic, political, or religious confrontations; rather, they pervaded these aspects of culture, with each society defining its gender categories as "natural." Brown concludes that "the struggle of competing groups for the power that comes with controlling definitions of 'the natural' makes gender frontiers a useful concept for understanding colonial encounters."[1] For the ancient world, scholars know little of those crucial gender encounters along the frontiers between Greece and Persia, Egypt and Nubia, China and Japan. Instead, scholars are trying to define what these societies called "natural" in differentiating gender among their own people.

ORIGINS OF THE SOCIAL CONSTRUCTION OF GENDER IN PREHISTORY

Patriarchy is a central concept in the history of women. Historians seek its beginnings, although it is unlikely that there was one universal origin. Yet the world's first known civilizations with written records were more or less patriarchal. Historians thus must familiarize themselves with the scholarship of archaeologists and anthropologists who have investigated the prehistoric Neolithic Age (7000–3000 B.C.E.), when humans turned from gathering and hunting to agriculture.

Western scientists and social scientists have sought to formulate general explanations for the differences that societies create around issues of gender. Primatologists compare behaviors of various animals with that of humans, seeking the origins of gender differences in distant evolution. Archaeologists look among the ruins and artifacts of lost antiquity. Biologists consider how chromosomes, hormones, reproductive organs, and musculature shape social patterns. Psychologists search for distinctive "female" or "male" behavior patterns, and anthropologists compare how cultures variously constructed gender. But so far there is no simple universal biological, prehistoric, or historical pattern to explain patriarchy's origins. A trajectory seems clear, even in Western traditions, only when much is omitted. Patriarchy may not have prevailed universally everywhere, although it is evident in the records of literate, dominant world civilizations (women in these societies are discussed later in this essay).

Older stereotypes described pre-agricultural societies as naturally patriarchal. Men killed animals while women stayed in the camp, taking care of children, cooking food, and curing skins to be made into clothes. These stereotypes were challenged, however, by anthropological field studies of similarly organized contemporary societies that reported that women gathered roots, nuts, and leaves and trapped small animals. The food women gathered sustained families, rather than the meat of male hunters, whose production was erratic. Anthropological field studies of contemporary gathering and hunting societies also reported that although men and women had separate traditional tasks, they were organized in an egalitarian system. Assuming that Neolithic societies were similar, a feminist interpretation of foraging communities stresses the importance of women's gathering to their families' sustenance, their participation in some hunting activities, existing patterns of shared child care, and relative gender equality. What is important is that both women and men participated in producing vegetable and animal foods. Societies depended on productive labor by most adults, but they usually divided it into male and female tasks.[2]

Some researchers have sought to develop the concept of a universal matriarchy, which many nineteenth-century writers, including Friedrich Engels, believed existed before patriarchy. Some feminists suggest a prehistoric, Neolithic time when the widespread worship of goddesses reflected women's temporal power. Links can be made between female figurines, fertility, the importance of motherhood, and belief in goddesses. But generalizing further to explain a global social structure, or the Neolithic power relationships between women and men, is contrary to the evidence of decades of research. Scholarship of archaeologists, anthropologists, and historians illustrates the complex ways in which humans have divided social functions and power by gender rather than stages of dominance of women over men or of men over women.

An example by Gerda Lerner may clarify this discussion. In 1986 Lerner published *The Creation of Patriarchy,* which quickly became a key book in the field of women's history.[3] Limiting her scope to Western civilization, she found that patriarchy existed in archaic states before the written records she studied. She described a process of establishing patriarchy in Mesopotamia between 3100 and 600 B.C.E. During that time men's control and exchange of women's sexual and reproductive capacity became the basis of private property. After commodifying women in their own families or clans, the rise of military elites associated with developing states led to the increasing enslavement of women. Conquered men were killed, while women were enslaved. Women of the conquerors' families were then further devalued because any woman could potentially become an enslaved captive. Yet even after women had become sexually and economically subordinate to men, their prestige as shamans, healers, and priestesses (as represented by worship of powerful goddesses) remained strong until imperial kings subordinated the goddesses to male gods, often as wives of the gods. Patriarchy triumphed when the Hebrews developed monotheism. Hebrew women were excluded from access to the covenant of males in a religion that allowed worship of only one male god.

This western Asian subordination and marginalization of women, Lerner argued, became one of the founding metaphors of Western civilization. Lerner knew this thesis was specific to Western civilization, but she hoped it was applicable to other civilizations as well. But instead of one universal pattern of subordination, there are many historical patterns of gender, even in the Mediterranean region. Focusing on legal restrictions on women, Lerner saw one pattern. Another pattern emerges from looking at women's work, which is the focus of the following section.

Women's Work in Ancient Societies

In many societies the labor necessary to sustain life is divided according to gender. Biology dictates that women perform the reproductive labor of childbirth. Social customs determine who cares for children after early infancy, especially after weaning, and who is responsible for the infirm and the elderly. Societies also shape the allotment of the tasks men and women do to produce goods and services. Sometimes gender rules of work are rigid, with stern taboos prohibiting one sex from any participation. Women, for instance, have been banned from metalsmithing in many African and Asian societies. More often, such rules probably have governed customary daily life more loosely, with changes possibly occurring as demography or technology shifted the balance of resources.

PRODUCTION OF GOODS AND SERVICES

Particularly striking in ancient societies is women's economic importance. Consider the production of human necessities—food, clothing, and shelter—and think of their immense value in preindustrial civilizations. Although women's daily labor in growing, processing, and cooking food appears to have been such an accepted universal cultural reality, it is difficult to find documents describing this essential work. In some ancient societies, building and repairing housing also fell to women in the division of labor. Today, most Americans assume that household labor means what they know of vacuuming, laundry, cookery, and child care. In this context it is hard to imagine the physical effort or the significance of earlier women's domestic labor in gathering and growing crops; processing and cooking food; spinning threads, weaving cloth, and sewing and laundering clothes; marketing crop and craft surpluses; and nursing, educating, and comforting children.

Despite older interpretations that claimed that men discovered farming, women were often the primary gatherers in foraging societies because they knew where and when plants grew as well as their sun and water needs. Women, therefore, were better equipped to develop agriculture. In her work *Women in Prehistory,* Margaret Ehrenberg explains:

> One of the most momentous changes in the history of the human species was surely the domestication of plants and animals—the invention of agriculture. . . . The transition from foraging to farming would have made profound differences to nearly all aspects of the lifestyle of prehistoric women and men. Rather than moving around in search of food, the discovery of agriculture allowed, or perhaps necessitated, a sedentary lifestyle. . . . The discovery of farming techniques has usually been assumed to have been made by men, but it is in fact very much more likely to have been made by women. On the basis of anthropological evidence for societies still living traditional foraging lifestyles and those living by simple, non-mechanical farming, taken in conjunction with direct archaeological evidence, it seems probable that it was women who made the first observations of plant behaviour, and worked out, presumably by long trial and error, how to grow and tend crops.[4]

Women performed a substantial amount of farm labor in most ancient societies, whether agriculture was done with a hoe or a plow. After food was grown, it was both processed and cooked in the home.

Try to visualize cooking food for a family of eight the way women did in the ancient world. Erase from memory supermarkets, delis, refrigerators, microwaves, electric or gas stoves, and ovens. The materials to be prepared might be grain still in the husk, roots of turnips, taro or potatoes, or sandy vegetable leaves. And if there was meat, such as rabbit or squirrel, the animal had to be skinned and cleaned first. Jane I. Guyer has angrily protested the underestimations of the time women spend cooking:

> Cooking is a true universal; it is different in kind from other tasks. Cooking must be one of the earliest manifestations of the superior imagination of Homo sapiens. It exists in every known society, regardless of the general level of technical and social complexity, and the nature of the resource base. Without a shadow of a doubt, cooking as a task must be the greatest single consumer of human time, effort, and routine attention, even in the most technologically advanced of societies. . . . As a consumer of female labor time, it surely outstrips nursing and child care since cooking is a life-long occupation regardless of child-bearing status. Girls often take part in cooking before puberty, childless women are not exempt, and cooking does not become a redundant activity at menopause.[5]

Perhaps the single most arduous daily task for ancient women was carrying water, because few were fortunate enough to live near a water source. In some Canadian Indian societies women held the task of choosing the campsite; in doing so, they were probably expected to shorten their journeys for water.

In addition to bearing almost sole responsibility for cooking, ancient women largely produced the clothing of humans, from harvesting raw fibers or skinning small animals to carrying out all of the intermediate steps of production for a finished product. The process was easily broken down into separate steps, most of which could be spliced into "downtime" within the household. Under hand manufacture in ancient cultures, women dominated the early stages of producing thread from cotton, flax, hemp, wool, feathers, or silk—the tedious processes of cleaning, carding, and spinning. Full-time weaving could be men's or women's work, but part-time weaving was almost always women's work. The importance of discerning gender patterns in textile production might seem obvious, but this work, like much of women's labor, is often not even reckoned in counting the wealth or product of an economy. Little research has concentrated on women's economic activities in the ancient world—in part because sources are scarce. Another reason is the difficulty of valuing household production and consumption. The domestic work that women undertook for their own family members was essential to any society's survival. Women's household production, however, included such tasks within the domestic realm as making cloth or tanning leather for sale that today would be done outside the household.

Women's weaving has had the most attention in the existing scholarship, particularly in Chinese and Egyptian history, perhaps because textiles entered market transactions. Monarchs levied taxes on home-woven fabrics and sup-

15

ported "factories" where women wove linen or silk, which the courts used to opulently display their power or in exchange for armed allies. Textiles constituted so much of the value and volume of international trade throughout the ancient era that such trade cannot be discussed without considering Chinese silks or Egyptian linens. One enduring problem in the scholarship is determining the gender of those who produced the fabric. If weaving was done in a domestic setting, as was Chinese silk, women were most likely the main producers. But if weaving became so important that factories were built, the workers may have been men *or* women. Exports of Indian textiles were large, but gender divisions of production within the ancient caste system have not been investigated. Even when all possibilities of male weaving are weighed, the available evidence indicates that women dominated cloth production for both home and market use in the ancient world. In some cases, as in Egypt, production could be so high that textiles were the second largest export after agriculture.[6]

In most ancient societies women worked in service industries. Many women prepared food and drinks, such as beer, for sale at markets or cooked in other families' homes. Midwives, wet nurses, maids, morticians, and mourners were other categories of women's employment. Entertainment often featured female dancers and musicians. Prostitution also depended on women workers. Female doctors, in addition to midwives, appear in numerous records. Priestesses also appear in temple documents of polytheistic peoples. Even when these occupational categories are named, however, there is no evaluation of women's contributions to the production of goods and services. Nowhere is this omission more significant than in agriculture, where women's daily labor, and sometimes management or ownership of farms, tends to be overlooked. When no explicit accounting of women's contributions to production and marketing is given, the implicit conclusion is that the economy was a male realm.

Slavery could be found in nearly every ancient civilization. Women may have constituted the majority of ancient slaves; they certainly were crucial to slave systems. The type of slavery found in the American South before emancipation is only one of several possible forms. In ancient societies, female slaves were commonly household workers whose treatment could range from sadistic torture to becoming a family member by bearing heirs. Some female slaves were taught skills. In societies from Mesopotamia to Greece, which secluded elite women, female slaves performed essential tasks that could only be accomplished in public: cultivating and harvesting crops, drawing water, or doing marketing or errands. Most prostitutes in classical Athens and Rome were slaves. Both male and female slaves worked outside in fields and with animal herds. Female slaves were not exempted from heavy labor in construction or mining. Male slaves were often soldiers, merchants, and government officials—even the highest officials. Slaves of both sexes could be sacrificed in religious or funeral ceremonies. The slave concubine achieved her highest station as queen mother if her son became a kingdom's ruler.

REPRODUCTION OF SOCIETY

Women were vital to the ancient world, for without their daily labor, supplies of food, water, and clothing would have disappeared. The embers of household cooking fires, spindles and looms, water jugs, as well as hoes, marked women's often unacknowledged work. Could the caravans of the silk route have set forth from China if its women had not paid their family taxes in silk yardage? If it seems remarkable that work done by the female half of ancient populations has been ignored, is it not more peculiar that women's truly unique capacity—childbearing—has also been either omitted from history or denigrated by the designation of child care. This is a modern judgment. Men in the ancient world primarily valued women, according to their laws and speeches, as machines to produce children—male heirs and female baby-makers. Women esteemed themselves as mothers. Among many feminine roles, reproduction was among the most important to both sexes and to society. In times of high mortality and short life spans, female fertility could determine the very existence of any people. Most children were born to married couples. In ancient civilizations, almost every free person married and was expected to have children. The average number of children per woman varied, of course, but in ancient Roman society it has been estimated that a woman had between five and six children. Multiple births did not necessarily produce large families because about half of all infants died before they reached age ten.[7]

Patrilineal societies gave considerable importance to a son's marriage for maintaining family ownership of its property through grandsons who would eventually inherit and continue to worship the family ancestors if that were vital in the culture. Such societies placed a very high value on the production of children in a marriage, but only the wife was blamed for infertility. In many societies, to provide the essential heir in childless marriages, a husband divorced one wife to marry another. A divorced woman might face a life of disgrace and poverty. In societies in which life-long marriages were traditional, a second wife or a concubine could be the solution to a couple's infertility—for those with enough money.[8] In other patrilineal societies, however, there are indications of valuing women's independence: if male adultery was punished, if wives had the right to divorce, or if widows could remarry without loss of status.

In matrilineal societies, families invested inheritance rights in their daughters, but this does not mean that women necessarily held property rights or political power. Ancestry could be traced through females, whose brothers or husbands exercised dominant social powers. Those matrilineal societies in

17

which land rights and crop ownership were also vested in women offered women high status. In ancient civilizations mothers were responsible for their daughters' education until they married and for their sons' education at least until they were five. Often this early socialization was publicly recognized as essential for the society's strength.

Male social control of female sexuality made women victims. What does the desire for control tell about a society? Some societies required that brides be virgins upon their first marriages. This premium on virginity often meant very early marriage ages for girls and a disparity between the ages of the bride and groom. Virginity at marriage was also paired historically with concern for a wife's chastity. Often such societies kept adult female family members in seclusion, and women had the low status equivalent to that of dependent children. Seclusion of women had as one of its goals control of women's sexuality. Another goal was to enforce class lines between those who were "respectable" and those who were not. In classical Athens, China, Japan, Mesopotamia, and Persia, women from elite families were generally restricted to their homes. Elite married women who could afford slaves seldom left their houses; when they did so they were veiled or enclosed in a curtained cart or sedan chair. Sumptuary laws in some societies prohibited lower-class or slave women from wearing veils.

In most cultures today, governments control permission to divorce a spouse. In the ancient world, legal limitation of divorce might be minimal, as in the Late Roman Republic, where divorce required only that one of the partners tell the other to leave. In divorces based on incompatibility, the husband frequently had to return his wife's dowry, but he kept the children. Either partner might be allowed to remarry, and he or she frequently did. Disposition of the dowry and custody of children, as well as permission to divorce, are key measures of women's status in the ancient world.

In most ancient literate civilizations widows who inherited some of their husband's property had much to fear from their husband's relatives. Concerned for the loss of family property to her new husband, male relatives often tried to prevent the widow's remarriage. Some societies required a widow to marry one of her husband's male relatives (called a "levirate marriage"). In religions that prohibited divorce, even young widows might not be allowed to remarry. Widowers almost always could remarry, however.

Although historical demographers have seldom written about the ancient world, students of women's and family history should be aware that ancient life expectancies were shorter, and reproductive rates were higher than those in modern industrial societies. In recent studies of prehistory, some specialists have speculated that in foraging societies with life expectancies for both men and women of less than twenty years, gender roles had to be flexible, with everyone doing almost all tasks, including those traditional for the opposite gender. If only mothers (rather than fathers or other adult members of society) could care for their children, the society could not generate enough children to perpetuate itself. That conclusion was established when evidence of permanent camps could not be found, meaning that everyone was mobile during daylight hours. Children under the age of five could not keep up with such a group, and mothers would have to carry them. But a mother could not carry both an infant and a toddler while foraging effectively. This meant that mothers who had a life expectancy of less than twenty years could not produce and care for the two children necessary to reproduce the population. If every adult, regardless of gender, shared care for children after weaning, mothers might have a second child before they died. Given the size of the bands, men would have had to have helped with child care or the population would have disappeared.

Another demographic example from Roman society helps explain how women could take independent actions in a society that legally required every woman to be the dependent of a man (father, husband, or guardian). Because men married late and fathers died about the time their daughters married, daughters were often able to have complacent guardians appointed to them who allowed the daughters to do as they pleased.

Women in Ancient Literate Civilizations

Although oral histories, archaeological findings, and new translations expand knowledge of the women of sub-Saharan Africa, northern Europe, what are now the Americas, Southeast Asia, and Pacific Oceania to some centuries before 1500 C.E., the thinness of the sources and literature in antiquity (even within the most generous definition of that period) suggests that these regions should enter women's global history in a later era—for the time being at least. It is possible that future research will open unexpected sources for understanding gender in the preliterate societies of these regions. Scientific analysis of fingerprints or DNA traces, for instance, may reveal the gender of basket makers, potters, or metal workers, and further analysis of gender in origin myths may cause reconsideration of perspectives on cultures and states. Translation and publication of written documents or monument inscriptions from Axum, Ethiopia, and Meroë; from the frontiers of Rome's European provinces; from the Mayan, Olmec, or Zapotec cultures; or from Java, Thailand, or Vietnam may eventually fill the present void in knowledge of gender roles before about 800 B.C.E.

For the world's literate ancient civilizations discussed in this section, serious research into the social history of women began only recently. Even where archival documents are relatively plentiful, as in China or Egypt, modern translations and interpretive essays began to appear only since the 1980s. A complete description of women's lives in any ancient society, however, cannot be extracted from published research (except, perhaps, for Rome). Monographs tend to be on narrow topics, whether upper-class women in one city in a specific time period, applications of a society's marriage laws, or the biography of a female ruler. Nevertheless, there is no better way to understand the subtleties of the ancient world than to read these essays. What follows is a summary of scholarship on women's histories in western Asia and North Africa, South Asia, East Asia, and the northern Mediterranean.

WESTERN ASIA AND NORTH AFRICA

Western Asian and North African civilizations, with written records from before the second millennium B.C.E., have the oldest translated documents on women. Three cultures within the area—Mesopotamia, Egypt, and Israel—have traditionally been considered key sources of civilization. But despite the extensive research that has been done on these societies for more than a century, the paucity of scholarship focused on women is surprising.

MESOPOTAMIA

In the existing world histories, the distinct ancient societies of western Asia are customarily collapsed into the category of Mesopotamia. Sumer is the collective name given to the third-millennium B.C.E. city-states between the Tigris and Euphrates Rivers, now part of Iraq. Sumerian is the name of their language, written in cuneiform from the fourth through the second millenniums B.C.E. Sumerian cuneiforms were subsequently used by successor Mesopotamian states of Akkad, Assyria, and Old Babylon. The city-states of Sumer frequently fought each other as well as several external enemies. The first leader to unify the region around 2350 B.C.E. was an outsider, Sargon of Akkad, whose conquests stretched from the Persian Gulf to the Mediterranean. It seems probable that endemic regional warfare both enhanced the status of male soldiers and institutionalized enslavement of captive women and children.

Gerda Lerner stresses the importance of Mesopotamian women in *The Creation of Patriarchy*.[9] She marshals evidence about early patriarchal practices in a compelling narrative that discusses slaves as well as aristocrats as she traces the beginning of veiling and seclusion to the sharp distinction made between respectable free Mesopotamian women and their slave sisters. Lerner reviews historiographic issues, carefully defines terms, and includes valuable analysis, but her examples sometimes appear chosen to support her hypothesis.

Ilse Seibert, in *Women in the Ancient Near East*, discusses such topics as women and the law, marriage, family, women rulers, the harem, and women scribes in an approach designed for general readers.[10] Historians will find her book useful, but it should be used with care, for Seibert draws her evidence from a period beginning with the ninth millennium B.C.E. and continuing to the seventh century C.E. Women's experiences surely must have been more varied than she implies. A short essay covering much of the same material, but with less documentation, is "Women of Egypt and the Ancient Near East" by Barbara S. Lesko.[11] Bernard Frank Batto analyzes a cache of elite women's correspondence with an Assyrian subking from 1790 to 1745 B.C.E. He finds that these women's positions were superior to that of some of their predecessors.[12] Hammurabi's Babylonian laws (ca. 1800 B.C.E.), frequently mentioned in textbooks, were a collection of cases that were supposed to be suggestive for those making judgments rather than a law code. Insights into the treatment of women in the society may be gained by comparing punishments in these cases for the same crime committed on or by people of different statuses or classes, such as the differing severity of punishment for the rape of a slave, a betrothed woman, or a wife.

The dearth of scholarship on women in ancient western Asia is further revealed by the lack of comprehensive modern gender studies among the Assyrians, the Babylonians, the Persians of the Achaemenid Empire in Iran, and the Phoenicians. What is known of Persian women derives from the blame cast upon them for the faults and defeats of the Achaemenid kings by their enemies, the Greeks. Maria Brosius, in *Women in Ancient Persia (559–331 B.C.)*, demonstrates the inaccuracies of Greek stereotypes in a technical analysis of ancient sources, but the scarce Persian documents yield few useful generalizations even about royal women.[13]

EGYPT

More is known about Egyptian women of all classes than of any other ancient society. This may be a result of the fact that for the most part their status was high, and they participated in more public economic and political activities than women in other societies. Egyptian government was centralized, continuous, and militarily secure over much of its nearly three-millennium history before Alexander's conquest in 322 B.C.E. Specialists have focused research on the social history of the New Kingdom dynasties (1550–1070 B.C.E.), when Egyptian armies conquered the people of western Asia to create an empire.

As is typical in many ancient histories, the most is known about elite women, especially those of the ruling family. Strangely enough, authorities do not agree on how the pharaoh's consorts were chosen. Because sometimes his wife was also his sister or daughter, historians have debated how Egyptians defined incest. One explanation of interfamilial royal marriages is the "heiress" interpretation—that royal descent was only through the female line, so that a pharaoh had to marry a royal female to legitimize his claim to the throne. After examining many royal genealogies, Egyptologists now reject this "heiress" theory because pharaohs so often did not have wives from the ruling dynasty.

In the New Kingdom era, queens had important religious responsibilities, which seems natural because queens traditionally were attributed a divine aspect. As a pharaoh's wife, the queen might live on a separate estate, owning other estates and perhaps factories producing perfume or textiles. Both she and the ruler's mother might influence the choice of officials in the government—a fact that gave them considerable power in the state. The New Kingdom had several famous royal women. Ahhotep I, the mother of Ahmose, the founder of the Eighteenth Dynasty, played an important role in driving the foreign Hyksos conquerors out of Egypt. Hatshepsut I, a granddaughter of Ahmose, ruled successfully as pharaoh for ten years. Queen Nefertiti played an important part in the monotheistic religion introduced by her husband, Akhenaten (1353–1335 B.C.E.). Under the Ptolemaic dynasty of Hellenistic Egypt, royal women assumed power far more frequently than in the past. Cleopatra VII, the Egyptian ruler during the era of Julius Caesar and Augustus, is among the most famous women in history. Her various modern literary portraits emphasize her romances, however, more than her political struggle to make Egypt the capital of the eastern Mediterranean.

Compared with women in other ancient civilizations, ordinary Egyptian women led relatively independent lives. Legally they were equal to men, although they were excluded from high government positions and professions. Documents prove that Egyptian women bought and sold property, including land, with the courts' protection. Some women were wealthy. Analysis of court records shows that about one property owner in ten was female. Scholars think that some women could write, but scribes, who made a living charging a fee for writing, had male names. It is likely that women were more often involved in small-scale transactions that did not require a permanent record. Women's labor was essential to Egypt's national economy. Production of textiles, especially linens, was largely in the hands of women. The art of weaving reached a high point in Egypt, and the surviving cloth is considered some of the finest ever produced. Besides clothing and domestic linens, sails for the Nile's vessels were woven on women's looms. Women also manufactured the oils and ointments necessary in the dry desert climate, where thick eye makeup helped catch irritating particles blown in the wind.

Egyptian women's history during the first three Egyptian millenniums, before Alexander's invasion, is the topic of Gay Robins's *Women in Ancient Egypt*.[14] Her survey discussing royal women, marriage, family, work, law, housing, and religion is based on close analysis of ancient documents, art, and architecture. Barbara S. Lesko's short study *The Remarkable Women of Ancient Egypt* (1978) also includes an excellent discussion of women's work.[15] There is no other study as detailed as E. J. W. Barber's *Prehistoric Textiles*, however, which concentrates on the area bordering the Aegean Sea.[16] Barber describes the production of Egyptian textiles so well that even those without an understanding of weaving can follow. Women in the Hellenistic period enjoyed more advantages than their ancestors. In *Women in Hellenistic Egypt: From Alexander to Cleopatra*, Sarah B. Pomeroy focuses on Greek women in Egypt rather than on Egyptian women, so she underestimates the impact of Egyptian customs in changes attributed to Hellenistic influences.[17]

ISRAEL

The history of Jewish women has attracted the scholarly attention of both theologians and historians. Although the story of the creation of Eve and Adam and their expulsion from the Garden of Eden (as told in the book of Genesis) is central to Christian, Islamic, and Judaic justifications of women's subordination to men, scholarship on ancient Jewish women concentrates on the period between the Exodus from Egypt and the founding of King Saul's monarchy in the eleventh century B.C.E. This era of the biblical Judges was when Jewish women had the most active public roles in Hebrew society.

One of several studies of women in the post-Exodus period is by Jo Ann Hackett.[18] She analyzed stories about women in the book of Judges, chapters 3–16, which described events from approximately the twelfth and eleventh centuries B.C.E. For example, Deborah, a prophet and a judge, helped deliver the Israelites from the oppression of the Canaanites. She and Jael were glorified as heroines in this decentralized Hebrew agricultural society. Polygyny existed as did prostitution and intermarriage with surrounding people. Carol L. Meyers goes beyond biblical study in her examination of the period of the Judges.[19] Meyers recognizes that urban elite males of a later era wrote the restrictions placed on women in the Torah. She concludes that such men were unlikely to have paid much attention to the rural pioneers who came to the arid West Bank of the Jordan River at the end of the trek from Egypt. Relying on archaeological, anthropological, and sociological evidence, Meyers found an agrarian society without classes living in small groups of families, working very hard to survive in a harsh climate. Women and men had to depend on each other's work simply to exist. Her conclusion is that these Jewish women had a rough equality with men in status and in contributions to society and their families. They were strong and significant in Jewish society.

King Saul's monarchy, established by about 1000 B.C.E., brought this era to an end. Conquests of the Hebrews by the Assyrians and Babylonians meant that after 586 B.C.E. they adjusted to survival within foreign cultures. With brief exceptions, self-government was no longer possible. One notable exception was the reign of Queen Salome Alexandra (76–67 B.C.E.), the only woman known to rule the Jews. Leadership usually fell to male religious elites, who generally cooperated with the dominant political power. Religious distinctions were enforced to emphasize separation from the larger society and to maintain a viable subculture. Marriage outside the Jewish community was discouraged by excluding non-Jewish wives and their children from membership in the religion. Worship turned from public sacrifices made at the temple to services involving the reading of the law. It became necessary to produce a satisfactory written version of the law. This was done in the middle of the fifth century B.C.E., while the Jews were under the control of Babylon. This is the version of the Tanakh (Old Testament) that is used today.

Two scholars have summarized the position of women in the Tanakh, a subject of great interest to both Jewish and Christian feminists. The most accessible study is by Phyllis Trible, but it is relatively brief.[20] Phyllis A. Bird provides more detail.[21] Both scholars list the restrictions placed on women by Hebrew patriarchal society, but they also point out numerous examples of Jewish women who overcame these social limitations. Gerda Lerner criticizes both Bird and Trible, however, for arguing that men and women were essentially equal. She finds women in ancient Hebrew society "in servile, submissive, and subordinate roles." For Lerner, the Old Testament shows a gradual restriction of women's public and economic roles, a lessening of their religious functions, and an ever-increasing regulation of their sexuality as Jewish tribes moved from confederacy to statehood.[22] Judith Hauptman, one of the first female professional teachers of the Talmud, illustrates the changing position of Jewish women in later centuries by explaining how rabbis modified biblical restrictions to conform to changing social standards and to protect women while keeping men in a dominant position.[23]

SOUTH ASIA

The Indian subcontinent's oldest known civilization developed in the third millennium B.C.E. along the Indus River, a region that today is mainly within the borders of Pakistan. Archaeological research has revealed little about the women who lived in Indus city-states such as Harappa and Mohenjo-Daro. Scholars of women's history have instead focused on the subsequent era that began with the Aryan invasions of the subcontinent and the societies from which Hindu culture developed.

INDIA

Current interest in women's history for most ancient civilizations began in the 1970s. Indian civilization is an exception, however. Western scholars have been interpreting Indian women's history for more than two hundred years. The earliest writers sought to justify British colonial rule by proving that Indian moral deficiencies were so great that Europeans, in this case the British, had to civilize the subcontinent by transforming Indian society into a European clone. James Mill, an employee of the East India Company, is characteristic of those sentiments. Writing in 1817, Mill asserted that Indian society had not substantially changed since the Aryan invasion of 1600 B.C.E. and that Indian society was primitive, immoral, and "rude." For Europeans, the one important test of a society's level of civilization was the status of women. "Among rude people women are degraded; among civilized people they are exalted," wrote Mill. "Nothing can exceed the habitual contempt" that Indian men had for their women, he concluded.[24] Mill's evidence included the fact that Indian men did not share meals with their wives, they embraced child brides, and women practiced sati.[25]

Nineteenth-century opposition to these British scholars came from a number of European Sanskrit scholars: the Orientalists. Working from the similarity of Sanskrit, classical Greek, and Latin, Max Muller developed the thesis that Europe and India shared a common lost past. Indian women's history was presented as a positive model by Clarisse Bader in a book first published in 1867. Bader asserted that European women should learn from the ancient Aryan civilization in which women had "a sense of duty dominating all affections, a feeling of respect for the family life, a love for one's neighbor, a charity, including even animals in its tender effusion, a spirit of sacrifice, presenting a nearly Christian atmosphere."[26] Bader approved of sati for some widows: "Yes, for the wife who loved her husband, it was ineffable happiness to rejoin him in another life. But for her who had been the victim of an unhappy union, for her, who still in childhood, could hardly comprehend the grief of widowhood, and even for her, who attached to the memory of her husband, yet felt weak at the idea of death, what a frightful prospect! What a barbarous obligation!"[27]

The Orientalists argued that the years following the nomadic Aryan invasions were the golden era of Indian history, especially for women. That period (1600–800 B.C.E.) is usually called the Vedic period, termed so after the four volumes of religious hymns (the Vedas) that have survived. Some recent scholars of Indian history would agree with A. S. Altekar that the condition of women during the Vedic period was "fairly satisfactory."[28] Julia Leslie notes that Indian women in this period could receive religious education and conduct ritual sacrifices.[29] Ellison Banks Findley proves that as late as around 600 B.C.E. women were recognized as Vedic scholars.[30] During the Vedic period, women lived in extended families and married in their midteens, having participated in choosing their husbands. Monogamy was preferred, but polygamy and polyandry are both mentioned in the surviving written material. Male offspring were especially welcome. Widows performed symbolic suicides, usually at their husbands' funerals, and frequently married their dead husbands' brothers.

The Indo-European Aryan invaders classified people by occupational groups: warriors (Kshatriyas), priests (Brahmans), merchants (Vaishyas), and cultivators (Sudras). They called the groups *varnas,* which the Portuguese translated as "castes." Only the Sudras were prohibited from making sacrifices to the Aryan gods. Soon *jati* (subgroups) formed, based on specialized occupations, and over time the subgroups developed rigidity. Membership was inherited, marriage choices were limited to families in the same subgroup, and members could eat only with others in their subgroup. In northern India these invaders brought slavery. At first most slaves were females. Uma Chakravarti assumes that their main work was herding animals because the proportion of female slaves decreased when the Aryans switched to agriculture.[31] Women's work increasingly became the hard labor of household production. Details of Indian slavery are complicated, as one might expect of an institution more than three millennia old. By the time of the first Mauryan ruler at the end of the fourth century B.C.E., nine different types of slavery existed, including debt bondage.

Women's rights deteriorated after the Vedic period. No one has been able to prove why this happened. Scholarly interest has focused on women's exclusion from performing Hindu rituals, which was in effect by 500 B.C.E. There are conflicting explanations for this exclusion. A. S. Altekar argues that Aryan males began giving their non-Aryan (Sudra) wives roles in the rituals. Brahmans reacted by excluding first the non-Aryan wives and then all wives from participating in these rituals. Uma Chakravarti and Kumkum Roy object to this explanation, calling it racist.[32] Julia Leslie thinks that women's exclusion resulted from intentional mistranslation of the Vedas by male scholars, as the rituals became more complicated and as the requirement for property ownership was more rigorously enforced at a time when women could not own property.[33]

The falling age of marriage for Indian women is another illustration of their loss of rights. In 400 B.C.E. about sixteen years was a normal age for a bride at marriage; between 400 B.C.E. and 100 C.E. it fell to pre-puberty; and after 100 C.E. pre-puberty was favored. These child marriages also affected women's religious roles. Because girls married before they could finish their education, they were not qualified to perform ritual sacrifices. Furthermore, wives' legal rights eroded. As child wives, they were treated as minors. Then their minority status lengthened until they were lifetime minors as wards of their husbands. Finally, women were prohibited any independence and were always under men's control: their fathers, husbands, or sons. By 100 C.E. Hindu texts defined women with negative characteristics, stating, for example, that women would be promiscuous unless controlled by male relatives. While Indian women were losing their independence, Indian men continued to glorify their wives and mothers. A wife was the essence of the home, a man was not complete without a wife, and sons were expected to respect their mothers more than their fathers. As Romila Thapar sums up these contradictions, "The symbol of the woman in Indian culture has been a curious intermeshing of low legal status, ritual contempt, sophisticated sexual partnership, and deification."[34]

One of the causes for this deterioration of women's rights and independence was the increasing rigidity of Hinduism under the influence of the Brahmans. By 600 B.C.E. sects were springing up that opposed Brahman power and ostentatiously omitted some of the Hindu essentials, such as priests, rituals and ceremonies, animal sacrifices, and even caste distinctions. Jainism and Buddhism are two of the sects that have survived. They were especially attractive to women. Jainism, the older religion, gained prominence with the efforts of its last prophet, Mahavira, who lived at the end of the sixth century B.C.E. Jains sought to live without passion and to act "correctly." One could achieve liberation only by living within a monastery or nunnery. Women who sought to join a nunnery found that the Jains had no membership restrictions. Many women entered and found new and exciting roles that were for the first time open to them. Today there are about two million Jains, mostly in India. Little other than short biographies of exemplary individuals has been published in English about Jain women.

Mahavira's contemporary, Gautama Siddhartha (the Buddha), began the religion that eventually spread throughout Asia. Among studies of Buddhist women, the early years have been a focus of interest. While Buddhism had no priests, it relied on celibate monks, who were initially homeless, except in the monsoon season, and had to beg for their necessities as they spread their ideas. The Buddha was reluctant to allow women to become nuns. He refused even the women in his family who sought to become nuns until he was reminded repeatedly by his aunt and his disciple Ananda of his stated principle that anyone could attain enlightenment. The Buddha then reluctantly accepted women followers, and they, like monks, eventually lived in their own self-governing celibate monasteries.

Uma Chakravarti describes Indian society in the sixth century B.C.E., when the Buddha lived. Buddhism's growth was encouraged by the changing economy, political consolidation, and new socioeconomic categories.[35] Julia Leslie provides details on the dominance of the monks.[36] Janis D. Willis tells of the Buddha's decision to allow women to become nuns.[37] She explains that over the centuries male leaders became fearful of religious women and increasingly derogatory toward them. Buddhist monks had much more respect for wealthy female lay benefactors. Leslie suggests that their gifts may have been significant in sustaining the religion in India during difficult times. I. B. Horner analyzes the roles of both nuns and lay women in Buddhism.[38] Much less is known of the history of these nuns after Buddhism's first hundred years. Nancy Auer Falk finds that nuns remained a significant religious force in India from the time of the Buddhist emperor Ashoka in the mid third century B.C.E. through the period of the northwestern kingdoms of the Kushanas in 240 C.E. After that, the nunneries declined, although they remained in existence until the ninth century C.E.[39] Today there are few Buddhists in India.

The collection of women's writing edited by Susie Tharu and K. Lalita covers the entire period of Indian women's history.[40] Their general introduction to the first volume and the introductions to individual sections provide brief historical summaries, while the translations of women's literature from various Indian languages, particularly those of the south, offer a wider perspective on the subcontinent's cultural past.

EAST ASIA

Written records in Chinese have been dated as early as the sixteenth century B.C.E. However, evidence of women's lives appears with the writings of the philosophers beginning in the ninth century B.C.E., but it remains scarce even in the lifetime of Confucius. Because relationships between family members were important to the followers of Confucius, they were the first to describe the ideal roles for women of all classes. Reliable Japanese records with significant references to aristocratic women date from the third century C.E., but little is known about other women until later dates. Historical records of Korea's societies begin with the emergence of the Three Kingdoms of Koguryo, Paekche, and Silla in the early centuries of the common era, but scholarship on ancient Korean women is not yet available in English translation.

CHINA

Modern scholarship on women's history in ancient China concentrates on elite women of the ruling dynasties. Almost nothing is known of non-Han Chinese women's lives. Little modern history has been written in English on the ordinary women of the millennia before the tenth century C.E. Sung dynasty. Little interpretation has been done on the ideological roots of Chinese gender practices that belong to the ancient period that includes the introduction of Confucian, Taoist, and Buddhist beliefs to Chinese civilization.

For Chinese women the ideas of Confucius (551–479 B.C.E.) have been most influential. There is little mention of women in his *Analects*. His neo-

Confucian interpreters corrected this omission, however. They made explicit men's desire for a woman's subordination to her family, her husband, and her sons. For example, Lieh Nu Chuan (also known as Liu Hsiang, 80–87 B.C.E.) wrote *The Biographies of Eminent Chinese Women,* in which he included 125 biographies of women from the peasant class to the emperor's wife, taken from prehistoric legends to the early years of the Han dynasty.[41]

Although the purpose of these biographical sketches was to provide moral instruction in the passive ideals of Confucian womanhood, translator Albert Richard O'Hara's analysis of the women's actions reveals their influence on events that were important to them. The traditional Chinese interpretation of the genre is evident in one of the best-known biographies, that of the widowed mother of Mencius (Meng K'o, or Meng-tzu), whose stern supervision and self-sacrifice were shown to have shaped her son's character and philosophy. This tale drives home the point that a woman's highest ambitions should be fulfilled indirectly through the talents of her sons. Pan Chao, a female scholar in the first century C.E., wrote *The Seven Feminine Virtues* as a Confucian manual for girls' behavior. Its prescriptions of humility, meekness, modesty, and hard work continued to be copied by generations of young women until the twentieth century. Nancy Lee Swann recognized Pan Chao's significance as the first female historian and translated her writings in 1932.[42]

Three scholars' articles on women of classical China concentrate on imperial and elite women. The studies of women in imperial families focus on women's access to political power, ranging from their domination of the choice of future empresses to the struggles of male courtiers to prevent the natal family of an empress from usurping the royal lineage. Melvin P. Thatcher's essay "Marriages of the Ruling Elite in the Spring and Autumn Period" (770–453 B.C.E.) considers elite women before the influence of Confucianism. Thatcher finds that most subsequent Chinese aristocratic marriage practices were already established, except that the ruling elite could then have more than one primary wife, and divorce was easy and frequent.[43] Jennifer Holmgren, in exploring imperial marriage practices from the Han to the Ming dynasties, argues that in the classical dynasties royal princesses exercised significant political power on a day-to-day basis. Unlike their brothers, who were exiled in remote provinces, daughters of the emperor, whether single or married, had access to the palace, where they advanced their own interests and those of their husbands. Yet in China as in western Asia, a princess might also be sent as a wifely pledge of alliance to a distant ruler's court.[44] Patricia Buckley Ebrey, in her essay "Shifts in Marriage Finance from the Sixth to the Thirteenth Century," notes that as the prestige of aristocratic clans declined and the influence of men with high bureaucratic rank rose, there was a corresponding increase in the value of the wedding gifts exchanged by families of newlyweds.[45]

Occasionally, imperial women seized power to govern when acting as regent for an underage emperor. Usually regents exercised this power cautiously behind the scenes because there was much opposition to women's open governance. Two famous empresses ruled openly, however, and sought to transfer royal descent to their own natal families. The first, Empress Lu, violated every canon of Confucian femininity. The widow of Gaodi, the first Han emperor (ruled 202–195 B.C.E.), Empress Lu acted swiftly and brutally to eliminate competitors at court during the near-fifteen years of her rule as regent for her son, her grandson, and another adopted infant grandson. By retaining power until her death in 181 B.C.E., she expected that her own nephews would succeed her. Instead, a civil war over the succession ended the period of peaceful prosperity, low taxes, and lessened punishment for crimes that had made her reign popular with the Chinese people. Five hundred years later, Empress Wu (Wu Chao, ruled 690–705 C.E.) became China's second female monarch. Married to Emperor Kao-tsung (ruled 649–83 C.E.), her strong personality enabled her to assume a substantial role in governing in 660 because her husband was often ill. When Kao-tsung died, Wu Chao was named regent for the young emperor. Like her predecessor, Empress Wu retained office by ruthlessly killing her opponents at court. Finally, in 690 C.E. she mounted her own coronation, thus becoming the only woman to officially rule the Middle Kingdom.[46] Confucian historians long denigrated her leadership, but contemporary historians judge her a competent ruler whose people were content. She encouraged government employment of men passing the national examinations. As a Buddhist, she supported monasteries. Empress Wu raised the status of women by extending a mother's mourning period to equal that for a father. Her foreign policy was expansionistic. Her personal rule wavered as she aged, however, and she could not secure an orderly succession.

The histories of ordinary women's lives before the Sung period (960–1279 C.E.) are little known. Despite the fact that silk production—from the culture of the cocoons to the weaving of the textile—was largely a woman's occupation, Chinese economic history is customarily discussed without reference to gender. It is only for a time well after the classical age that Patricia Buckley Ebrey, in *The Inner Quarters: Marriage and the Lives of Chinese Women in the Sung Period,* has written one of the best examples of the new history of women.[47] She describes the parameters of married women's lives and projects both their perceptions and their participation over the broad social and economic changes of three centuries. She explains women's interests in land and tax reform, commercialization, and urbanization. Ebrey points out that in contrast to the Tang period (618–907 C.E.), when Chinese society was "granting women greater autonomy," the Sung period "has attracted scholars because it was a time when women's situations apparently took a turn for the worse. It is associated with the spread of footbinding and strong condemnation of remarriage by widows." Despite these customs indicating female social subordination, Ebrey argues that women's economic condition was not in fact declining during the Sung period. There is "evidence that women had particularly strong property rights during that period. . . . All women who brought dowries into marriage retained considerable control over their use and disposal as long as they lived, even taking them into second marriages."[48] Of particular interest are the pages tracing the origin of footbinding (the wrapping of a young girl's feet into a permanent, painful, debilitating deformity) to the similar practice of wrapping female dancers' feet. Readers are likely, however, to linger over Ebrey's analysis of commercialization in the economy, especially its impact on women's near monopoly of cloth making. Her final point—that Chinese culture and history "look different after we have taken the effort to think about where the women were"—deserves the attention of those studying the earlier classical period.[49]

JAPAN

The centuries of Japanese history that directly correspond to the classical years of Chinese or Indian civilizations are mostly told through Japanese legends or the remarks of Chinese travelers. Accounts of the rise of the Japanese state begin in the third century C.E. Before 1945, Japanese historians largely ignored women's history because they assumed that women had always been completely subservient to men, confined to the home, and excluded from politics. These assumptions were challenged in the 1960s and 1970s, however, when popular interest in women's pasts increased with the formation of national and local history societies that were focused on women's history. There has been much research published in Japanese since then, although very little has been translated into English.

The first feminist research about Japanese women's history argued that patriarchy had not existed before the eighth century C.E. Before that in Japan, marriage was often matrilocal, women were property holders, and there was a tradition of female shaman leaders. Scholars still debate whether patriarchy was established in Japan as early as the third century C.E. or as late as the fourteenth. It is widely agreed that by 1500 C.E. women had lost most of their earlier advantages. They occupied no formal government offices in the later warrior-dominated state, and they rarely owned property. Furthermore, marriage was mainly patrilocal, and inheritance was patrilineal. In searching for when and how patriarchy was established in Japan sometime between 700–1500 C.E., scholars have examined the extent of female property ownership and matrilocal marriages. Patriarchy is possible when women have these privileges, although complete submission is far less possible.

Female property ownership eroded between the Nara (710–84) and Heian (794–1185) periods. At the beginning of the Nara period, women acquired property as part of the payment for occupying an imperial office, as an inheritance from parents or (rarely) as a gift or bequest from their husbands. From early in the eighth century, women were less frequently appointed to imperial offices, so that source of property disappeared. As elite males began to emphasize patrilineal descent and inheritance through the male line, elite women's property ownership gradually declined. The same trend eventually spread to women in the lower classes, and by the end of the fourteenth century few women owned property.[50] Heian aristocratic women still had considerable wealth, but the rigid conditions of seclusion that propriety imposed on them hindered their control of property. Such women as the writers Murasaki Shikibu and Sei Shonagon, for example, owned separate houses in which they lived before coming to the imperial court. Upon their fathers' deaths such women usually received a share of the family estates, and they may have had additional land holdings. Some empresses had so much property (land was given with the title) that they had to have an administrative council to manage it. The seclusion of all elite women prevented direct administration of their estates, and this necessary reliance on men left them vulnerable to corruption and such dangers as annexation by a neighbor.

Also in the Nara-Heian periods, Japanese society may have had a greater variety of marriage practices than any other society. In a famous article on late-Heian marriage practices, William McCullough lists four practices: (1) the woman lives with the man's family; (2) the man becomes part of the woman's family; (3) the man and woman each have separate residences; and (4) the man and woman live together, apart from their in-laws.[51] Haruko Wakita contends that McCullough's list is too narrow, however. She adds the adopting-a-son-in-law marriage and the wife-visiting-husband, who has several wives. Wealthy men also had concubines. Japanese literature thoroughly examines the psychological damage suffered by the wives in wife-visiting marriages. Wakita summarizes how prevalent forms of marriage changed over time: "[T]he Nara and Heian periods may be seen as a transitional stage in the development of marriage, with a gradual shift from wife-visiting to the adopting-a-son-in-law to the taking-a-wife [virilocal] form of marriage. . . . It is certain that among aristocrats and powerful provincial families, the status of women in the Nara and Heian periods as revealed by marriage and inheritance practices was relatively high compared to later periods."[52]

Most Japanese aristocratic women lived in nearly complete isolation from men, yet they wrote novels and poetry that are among the classics of Japanese and world literature. In fact, the best authors in the Heian period were women, who developed vernacular Japanese while men mostly wrote in Chinese.

Murasaki Shikibu, for example, wrote *The Tale of Genji*, a novel ranked among the great works of world fiction. Another female author, Sei Shonagon, kept a journal that has become famous as *The Pillow Book*. Her often-caustic comments in this journal illuminate the lives of those within the imperial court. Poets whose works are still valued flourished among the women of the court. Many of the twenty books of collected classic Japanese poems, called *Kokinshu*, were written by women.[53]

These women all wrote under the handicap of complete seclusion. The only adult male eyes that could see them with propriety were those of their fathers, husbands, or lovers. Sitting behind screens, curtains, blinds, or shutters, the women flirted, gossiped, and conducted their extensive business affairs. Even while traveling, they remained behind the curtains of ox carts. Despite this restricted environment, women's independence and self-confidence are displayed in their writing. Wealthy female members of the court spent their time amusing themselves and engaging in complex personal intrigues. Girls who were expected to become members of the court were carefully educated in calligraphy, music, and poetry.

In Japan's early states, women often ruled. During the 1950s, scholars found that women held the emperorship in the first century and a half of imperial rule (592–770 C.E.) as frequently as men. The power of these empresses (called "female emperors" in Japanese historiography) has often been denigrated by critics who claimed that the women did not rule but were only dowager queens acting as regents for their underage sons. Research by E. Patricia Tsurumi confirms that most of these women were indeed regents at some point. Nevertheless, six empresses ruled alone, with Empress Suiko reigning for thirty-six years (592–638 C.E.). In actions reminiscent of China's Empresses Lu and Wu, these Japanese monarchs seized power when their husbands died, sometimes by appointing themselves emperor without consulting the Council of Notables. If a crown prince died, for example, an empress might not appoint a successor. When one female emperor abdicated, she placed her daughter on the throne. Japanese empresses often patronized Buddhism.[54] In subsequent centuries the royal public power of both female and male emperors declined, but the matrilineal tendency in Japanese politics continued, albeit in disguised form. During the ninth through the eleventh centuries, for example, the matrilineal Fujiwara clan maintained a dictatorship of Japan even though a male emperor remained on the throne. Visible political power was completely in male hands while a system of extraordinary complexity obscured the invisible matrilineal power of Fujiwara women.

Emperors in the Fujiwara period tended to resign when they were barely thirty. If an emperor was reluctant to resign to become a Buddhist monk or to simply resign, the Fujiwara chancellor encouraged him to do so. The crown prince, who had already been given that title, was typically a minor when he ascended the throne, and his powers would be exercised by a regent. Traditionally, the young emperor's mother and grandmother were influential in choosing the regent, and because both of them were Fujiwaras, often daughters or sisters of the chancellor, the new regent was usually the old chancellor. The Fujiwaras then arranged for the young emperor to marry another Fujiwara consort. When this couple had a male child, who could be declared crown prince, a new cycle began. Through much of his life the crown prince actually lived with his mother's (Fujiwara) family. When an empress became pregnant she moved out of the emperor's palace to avoid causing the pollution it was commonly thought that pregnant women brought by their presence on sacred ground. The pregnant empress went to her parent's home to have the baby, who was usually raised by her family. Although Fujiwara men always took the public post of chancellor, Fujiwara women controlled key personal decisions of the clan's marriage politics and presumably were also involved in policy decisions.[55]

As late as the Heian age, Japanese aristocratic parents preferred daughters over sons because status inheritance at that time was matrilineal. Traditionally, male aristocrats married women from their own or a slightly higher social level. Children inherited their status from their mothers, and adopted children received status from their foster mothers. For example, Prince Genji, the hero of Murasaki Shikibu's novel, was the son of the emperor and a concubine. Even though his father was emperor, Genji himself could never become emperor because his mother was not from an aristocratic family. Yet Prince Genji's daughter, whose mother was a commoner, eventually became empress after she was adopted by Genji's aristocratic wife.[56] The rise of a warrior elite and patrilineal dynasties of shoguns during Japan's later medieval centuries of civil war speeded the erosion of aristocratic matrilineal inheritance and of women's power in Japanese government.

NORTHERN MEDITERRANEAN

For many readers, "classical civilization" means Greece and Rome, and these authors of antiquity exemplify the origin of rational human inquiry. Recovery of art, architecture, and literature of these civilizations has been a prestigious endeavor in the West since the Renaissance. The Minoan society of Crete and the first Greek society of Mycenae, both established by about 1650 B.C.E. but rediscovered by scholars only in the nineteenth century, yielded mainly speculation about women. Although the intricate and changing fashions shown in portraits of Minoan women on frescos and clay figurines (analyzed by Elizabeth Wayland Barber) reveal a highly developed textile tradition, the copious documents of later Greek and Roman societies, written mainly by men, reveal much more.[57]

GREECE

Considering all of ancient Greek history, most is known about the women of Athens in the classical period (500–338 B.C.E.). Much Athenian research for that period describes women as living in a model of total patriarchy. It is tempting to argue that the Athenian example was followed everywhere throughout Greece. However, Greek women's experiences did not fall into one pattern. Rather, there were significant variations over time from the archaic (800–500 B.C.E.) to the Hellenistic (323–331 B.C.E.) periods. Diversity existed within the classical period itself, as the relative freedom of Spartan women illustrates. Furthermore, even within classical Athens the patriarchal model is derived more from men's idealization of women's conditions than from historical knowledge of their lives.

Because the Greeks were illiterate through most of the archaic period there is little contemporary written evidence of women's lives. For the most part, interpretations are made from surviving poetry, art, and archaeological findings. The existing fragments of art consist of a few formal statues of clothed young women and drawings on vases and funeral plaques. The interpretation of each type of evidence is problematic for historians, however. Poetry provides glimpses of the Greek mind through mostly male eyes. Sappho, the seventh-century poet of Lesbos, is the earliest female writer known today in world history. By the classical period she was already famous among Greeks, and by the Hellenistic period evocation of her name or poetic style by female or male poets suggests sympathy for women's independence in life and love. Unfortunately, only fragments of Sappho's poems remain today, but her lyrics describe women in religious rites, festivals, and personal relationships with each other. These erotic poems express the mutual feelings between older and younger women involved in lesbian relationships.

Epic poems, especially those by Homer, provide further evidence of women's lives, but scholars disagree about how much of real life can be inferred from Homer's legendary stories of mortals and immortals. On the basis of epic poetry, some classicists conclude that women in the archaic period had more control over important personal decisions than women in classical Athens.[58] Homer's positive depictions of Penelope and Nausicaa, for example, offer one literary interpretation of the Greek male attitude toward women. The profoundly misogynist poets Hesiod and Semonides offer another interpretation: They describe women who are feared and hated as the source of nearly all the evil that might fall upon men.

Classical Greece has long been admired for its political theories, philosophy, science, and the arts. Until recently, Greek social history was largely ignored. Slavery, homosexuality, and subordination of women are topics once dismissed as insignificant but now recognized as important to understanding the culture. In the classical period there were actually many "Greeces," with distinct societies developing in the city-states of Athens, Sparta, and Thebes. Gender patterns varied considerably among these cities. Sparta's aristocratic women, for example, were often left alone to acquire wealth and some autonomy when their mercenary husbands soldiered elsewhere. To some Athenian men such as Aristotle, Spartan women were thought to be despicable, licentious, greedy, and the reason for Sparta's decline.

Aristotle and other Athenian men dominate the discourse from classical Greece. Their male descriptions tell how Athenian society secluded elite women, denigrated and exploited them, and made them the legal dependents of men. Because no women's writings survive, only indirect evidence suggests how Athenian wives escaped their lives of hard work in the isolated, dark rooms that their husbands imagined necessary to preserve their chastity. But as drawn on vases, groups of Athenian women read to one another, spun and wove, shared child care, or talked. Women are shown in public processions and getting water from wells. Bits of documentary records show respectable married women earning their livings as wet nurses, farm workers, and retail vendors. Most records reveal the lives of privileged women, yet many Athenian women were slaves. Exposure of unwanted female babies was one internal source of slaves, for the rescuer of such an infant became her owner. Athenian enslavement of females was exceptional in its celebration of prostitution in literary and artistic records. One explanation for the large number of slave sex workers may be the Athenians' desire to attract sailors and merchants to their port.[59]

Research on women in the Hellenistic period concentrates on Greek women living in Egypt. These women were much more assertive and influential than their sisters in either contemporary Greece or later Rome. Women in the ruling Ptolemaic family often actually ruled Egypt, some as regents, others as queens. Cleopatra VII (69–30 B.C.E.), one of the best-known women in ancient history, guided her country from a tributary position in the Roman Empire into a partnership with Marc Antony that might have led to Egypt's domination of the eastern Mediterranean. Non-elite women had unusual freedom. They owned property (including land), participated in commerce, produced textiles, were educated, and enjoyed careers as artists, poets, and farmers. But some women were slaves. There does not seem to be much interest in the existing scholarship in explaining the disparity between the independence of women in Hellenistic Egypt and the position of their contemporaries elsewhere in the Greek world. Sarah B. Pomeroy's *Women in*

Hellenistic Egypt: From Alexander to Cleopatra, the standard source, is largely grounded on Greek texts and biased against Egyptian culture, in part because of the author's inability to read Egyptian texts in Demotic.[60]

For nonclassicists, medical and scientific texts by Greek and Roman authors are important because of their influence on later Western authors' conceptualizations of women's bodies and health. Such influential men as Aristotle and Galen provide, in the histories of Greek and Roman women in the classical period, some evidence drawn from actual women's lives. Although male scientific thinkers supported male superiority with theories defining biological gender differences, practicing doctors using these arguments with female patients had to provide explanations their clients would accept. Some interpretations try to draw out female self-conceptions from medical case reports.[61]

ROME

As late as the sixth century B.C.E., Rome was dominated by its northern neighbors, the Etruscans. Although no body of Etruscan literature exists, scholars have sought evidence of women's lives from inscriptions and art found in their tombs. Upper-class Etruscan women were more autonomous and privileged than contemporary Greek women. Paintings of husbands and wives feasting together horrified Greek males, who only allowed prostitutes to attend their banquets. Etruscan women were not restricted to their homes as Greek women were and attended the games at gymnasiums. In Italy, all women left votive statues of women in sacred places, probably as a fertility offering, but only Etruscan statues included a nursing child, suggesting an affection for children that paralleled the affectionate touching between couples occasionally shown in their art. Finally, Etruscan women had personal names, in contrast to Greek women, who were known first as their fathers' daughters and later as their husbands' wives.[62]

The Romans did not duplicate the autonomy of women in Etruscan society. Roman women legally were constrained within a highly patriarchal agricultural system organized around clans. A father could kill or sell his children into slavery without fear of legal action. Husbands could kill their wives if they were caught in adultery. Women did not speak in public meetings. They could not buy and sell property without their male relatives' approval. Legally treated as minors, women were first the responsibility of their fathers, then of their husbands, and finally of appointed guardians. Rome was a warrior society and a male republic. Men even dominated the state religion, with the exception of the six Vestal Virgins who served as priestesses. Roman society remained staunchly male until conquests brought wealth to Italy in the second century B.C.E. Changes that accompanied the booty of empire gave women a measure of economic and marital independence that is illustrated by the loosening of legal restrictions against women's property ownership.

The paterfamilias, the oldest male in the family, had complete *manus* (legal control) over his children. In marriage, manus passed from the paterfamilias to the new husband. Among other things, that meant the husband then controlled all of his wife's property. Before the first century B.C.E. some Roman marriages were made without transferring manus to the husband; the wife and her property would remain under her father's control, whose approval was theoretically required for the daughter to buy or sell property. Susan Treggiari explains how this enabled many women to gain control over their property:

> Given ancient expectation of life, it is probable that many women were fatherless for a relatively long period of their married lives. The pattern . . . for the middle ranks of Roman society is that girls married in their late teens and men in their mid- to late twenties. If expectation of life at birth is put between twenty and thirty, then 46 percent of fifteen-year-olds had no father left alive. The percentage grows to 59 percent of twenty-year-olds and 70 percent of twenty-five-year-olds. So there is about a 50 percent chance that a woman was already fatherless at the time of her first marriage.[63]

Upon a father's death, manus was transferred to a guardian, and women began to choose as their guardians men who agreed with them. By the later years of the Roman Republic, therefore, many women bought and sold land as they pleased. Rome's expansion contributed to this change as it fueled a growing market in real and personal property.[64]

In the third century B.C.E., Rome began two centuries of conquests that eventually placed most of the land surrounding the Mediterranean under Roman administration or in the hands of client states. Roman wives farmed while citizen-soldiers of the Republic were on campaigns, sometimes for more than a decade. Successful wars enriched a Roman elite who accumulated estates worked by male and female slaves as small farmers sold their lands and moved to the city with their wives and children. Elite Romans, both men and women, possessed large estates, luxurious urban houses, much rental property, and many slaves. By 50 B.C.E., Rome had a population of approximately one million. Slaves poured into Italy after successful campaigns, when the defeated enemy was enslaved. As the Romans conquered country after country, they brutalized the captured women, enslaving many. Ruling queens in subdued countries were inevitably replaced with either indigenous male elites or Roman officials. Queen Boudicca of Britain, for example, led a revolt that ended in her death in the first century C.E. Queen Zenobia of Palmyra's invasion of the empire in the third century C.E. was so well organized that Roman authors praised her. Cleopatra of Egypt committed suicide when her plan to make Egypt a regional partner of Rome failed.

Roman women did not publicly speak in the Forum (where men debated civic affairs), with the notable exception of Hortensia in 43 B.C.E. She was the spokesperson for a demonstration of wealthy women who protested taxation without representation for civil wars they did not support. Elite women usually indirectly influenced political decisions through networks of politicians' wives. During the civil wars of the first century B.C.E., wives of some tyrants even made temporary political decisions. On a wider scale, middle-class and elite women took advantage of the turmoil at the end of the Republic to acquire businesses, as analysis of Pompeii shows. Prostitution flowered in Rome with the inflow of slaves, both male and female. A small part of the elite lived in the self-indulgent luxury that became famous in literature. In a brief period of two generations at the end of the first century B.C.E., Roman elite women eschewed children and family responsibilities for a glamorous and self-absorbed life of parties and lovers. In this period men and women were openly adulterous. This "café society" flourished in the chaos of civil wars that nearly destroyed the prestige of the elite and killed or exiled many of them.[65]

This era of chaos ended during the reign of the emperor Augustus (ruled 27 B.C.E.–14 C.E.), who sought to stabilize Roman society in part by reducing women's freedoms. Women were criticized for adultery, wearing too much makeup, having immodest dress and conduct, and especially for refusing to have children. Augustus procured laws that intended to remove control of marriage and reproduction from the family and allow the state to regulate marriage and reproduction. He attempted to penalize women between the ages of twenty and fifty and men over the age of twenty-five who did not marry and have children by denying them the right to inherit wealth. Furthermore, women were not to be released from male guardianship until they had three children. The Augustan laws made the state the regulator of private behavior and attempted to raise the birthrate of citizens while accepting some of the social changes that had modified the patriarchal society of the old Roman Republic. Augustus sought political support from conservative males by decreasing the autonomy of women who had less political influence than men.

Comparing Women's Status in Various Societies

As discussed earlier, the major literate civilizations of the ancient world were patriarchal. Later records from preliterate societies of the ancient period indicate that women in such societies could be more independent and have a higher status (for example, in many Southeast Asian and African societies). An appearance of universal subordination of women results from focusing only on early literate civilizations while ignoring the lives of women in nonliterate societies.

In the twentieth century, individual choice in personal relationships has replaced family selection of spouses in many societies, although arranged marriages persist in some cultures. In the ancient patriarchal world, however, the family chose spouses for their daughters and sons. Women lived with few civil rights in male-dominated societies. In interpreting ancient women's lives, scholars are faced with two contradictory images. The harsh portrayal is that women were sold by their fathers or brothers to husbands who abused them and that they were considered to have the intellectual capacity of a child, perpetually dependent on a male. Alternatively, some documents reveal women who were loved by their parents, husbands, and children. These women could use the love and affection of their male relatives to gain personal advantages that society would legally deny them. More likely, both explanations accurately reflect aspects of women's lives. Women negotiated a daily balance of gender power in personal relationships, often ignoring disadvantageous laws or ritual regulations, but those laws and regulations could also fall with terrible force on any woman in the ancient patriarchal world.

On a higher analytical level, Ida Blom, a Norwegian historian, notes that there is a wider meaning to these societies' constructions of gender to favor males:

> Applying gender as an analytical tool—not stopping at analyzing women's oppression but also continuing to locate their strengths and their participation in class, caste, and ethnic hierarchies—yields important knowledge as to how societies functioned. Such analysis reveals that every area of society, be it the family, the workplace, or the political arena, is gender-structured. Inheritance rules, divisions of work and of authority, beliefs as to psychological characteristics of an individual, even political power relations are structured around dichotomies of gender.[66]

Women could benefit personally from marriage terms negotiated for them. A husband's payment for his bride might not represent her purchase; rather, it might secure her future. In a major marriage (the highest status polygamous marriage or the only monogamous marriage) gifts could be given to families or to the newly married couple. But recent studies find that wedding payments often represented the couple's share of their families' estates or that part or all of the gift was destined to be used by the new husband and wife rather than being a payment to her parents.[67]

Discussion of brideprice as the purchase of the wife's labor and sexual services implies that her family relinquished protection of her. Whether that happened, as could be the case in China, or whether a wife's family maintained any contact with her was a determinant of her status in her marital household. The daughter who could ask her family for help in a crisis held a superior position. In some societies the father could arrange a divorce for a daughter who was mistreated. Among wealthy or powerful families, marriages often represented an economic-political alliance between families, with the wife providing the necessary liaison. Friction with, divorce of, or death of a spouse in such marriages therefore created a potential crisis for both families.

If the prenuptial agreement or tradition gave a wife ownership of property, it could provide valuable independence for her. Examination of a wife's control of her dowry can be a clue to this right. It is important to go beyond accepting as fact the laws on dowry, to find out what was actually happening. Women often found ways to get around the laws. In most societies a wife's dowry and personal property constituted her safety net in case her husband abandoned or divorced her or if at her husband's death she inherited little. Her property could include land, but women owned farms less often than personal property. Her wealth was usually in luxury items, small enough to be locked in a trunk or cabinet to which only she had the key. Such items could be jewelry, clothes, linens, and rugs. In prosperous families, women also owned slaves. If women could sign contracts without a male's approval for the sale of products or making loans, that, in itself, is an indication of independence in the ancient world. Women who could administer a business on their own were more likely to be found in wealthy societies with considerable commerce. Even when they were isolated and secluded, some women still conducted businesses.

Many women in the ancient world, however, did not own their bodies or their children. In most societies hired maids and slaves were considered to be sexually available to the male members of the master family. At the opposite extreme, in crowded cities female slaves were denied motherhood as a means of population control. Women sold into prostitution by their families or captors did not own their bodies. Even among free women, a husband often had the right to kill his wife's newborn child or abandon the baby in a designated public place.

Students who examine legal systems to compare women's general status or specific punishments of a crime such as adultery should be wary of simple conclusions. Punishments frequently cited in sources were not always laws; rather, they were suggestions to guide local elders in making decisions. Penalties could vary according to the victim's class. In patriarchal societies, a father might kill or sell as a slave a daughter who lost her virginity, and a husband might be allowed to kill a man found in bed with his wife—sometimes the wife also. But these punishments were not invariably imposed. Societies usually did not have penitentiaries for long incarcerations, so punishments might include material restitution, disfigurement, exile, enslavement, or death. Just as contemporary legal scholars prefer to interpret law by discussing cases and judgments involving the specific violations, so, too, must historians when these are available.

Women citizens seldom had the right to speak in public debates, although many elite women found other ways to influence public actions. Greek and Roman women who were silenced in the Agora and the Forum, for example, used their family connections to pursue influence. Kinship systems also provided women the means for direct political power. In Mesopotamian kingdoms and in Egypt, royal women's administrative and diplomatic abilities were recognized. These women often represented their families as temple priestesses. Politically powerful women also appear in China and Japan. Reigning queens and empresses are both legendary and historical figures. Some, like Amazon Queen Penthesilea or Assyrian Queen Semiramis, may be mythical. But Pharaoh Hatshepsut of Egypt, Empress Lu of China, Empress Koken of Japan, and Queen Zenobia of Palmyra were powerful monarchs. Still, the formal office women actually held in ancient monarchies was less frequently that of ruling queen than of dowager queen, acting as regent for an underage male, the future king. Many female regents ruled competently for years, although they are often omitted or slandered in political histories written by men. Some regents, such as Hatshepsut of Egypt and Empress Wu of China, usurped the throne to reign openly. These women's exploits brought them out of the obscurity usual for regents, although Empress Wu's cruelty in pursuit of power is also revealed. If rulers were supposed to be men, a reigning queen might assume the male insignia and clothing of the office, as did Hatshepsut (1473–1458 B.C.E.) because to do so was less disturbing to her public than admission that a woman ruled.

Women's history since the 1980s has focused more on the families of ordinary women than on the kin of monarchs. More studies are needed of the informal power of princesses who married into important allied families, of queen mothers who used their prerogatives in China and Egypt, of concubines whose sons contended for succession, and of wealthy women who were influential in religions, cults, and charities. Comparing regimes shows how widely royal women exercised political power within the privacy of palace households to decide succession to the throne. Studies of early modern polygamous regimes, such as that of Ottoman Turkey, show how complex these politics could be.[68]

Successful and powerful rulers, not all of whom were male, refute simple theories that women were uniformly subordinated to men in ancient civilizations. Although it is hazardous to draw generalizations across class lines, other evidence indicates that even within gender patterns that seldom granted women equality there were wide variations among women and among different time periods.

Having surveyed the situations of women in the literate civilizations of the ancient world, it is well to remember that they may have experienced more subordination to men than women living in stateless, nonliterate societies. Many anthropological studies of people who lived during the twentieth century suggest turning the nineteenth-century theory of women's status as a measure of civilization on its head so one would look for gender equality and democracy among the preliterate, less-stratified, and independent people of the world. Global gender studies are necessary to establish the comparative importance of other factors: warfare, motherhood, transmission of property, religion, slavery, and productive work in fixing women's status. When the outlines of how gender affected family structures, economies, war, and ideologies are better known, perhaps it will be easier to theorize about why women appear less often in public offices, why they could be excluded from priesthoods, and why they lacked the formal education necessary to create a volume of literature equivalent to that of men.

Notes

1. Kathleen M. Brown, "Brave New Worlds: Women's and Gender History," *William and Mary Quarterly*, 3rd ser., vol. 1, no. 2 (April 1993): 318–19. This is a fine guide to gender literature of the European, African, and American frontiers from 1500 to 1800.

2. Sandra Morgen, ed., *Gender and Anthropology: Critical Reviews for Research and Teaching* (Washington, D.C.: American Anthropological Society, 1989). A useful section appears in Kevin Reilly, ed., *Readings in World Civilizations*, vol. 1: *The Great Traditions*, 2d ed. (New York: St. Martin's Press, 1992).

3. Gerda Lerner, *The Creation of Patriarchy* (New York: Oxford University Press, 1986).

4. Margaret Ehrenberg, *Women in Prehistory* (Norman: University of Oklahoma Press, 1989), 77–78.

5. Jane I. Guyer, "The Raw, the Cooked, and the Half-Baked: A Note on the Division of Labor by Sex," Working Paper no. 48 (Boston: Boston University, 1981), 5.

6. Elizabeth Wayland Barber, *Women's Work: The First Twenty Thousand Years: Women, Cloth, and Society* (New York: W. W. Norton and Company, 1994.)

7. Tim G. Parkin, *Demography and Roman Society* (Baltimore: Johns Hopkins University Press, 1992), 92.

8. Jack Goody, *The Oriental, the Ancient, and the Primitive: Systems of Marriage and Family in the Pre-industrial Societies of Eurasia* (New York: Cambridge University Press, 1990).

9. Lerner, *The Creation of Patriarchy*.

10. Ilse Seibert, *Women in the Ancient Near East*, trans. Marianne Herzfeld (Leipzig: Edition Leipzig, 1974).

11. Barbara S. Lesko, "Women of Egypt and the Ancient Near East," in *Becoming Visible: Women in European History*, 2d ed., ed. Renate Bridenthal, Claudia Koonz, and Susan Stuard (Boston: Houghton Mifflin, 1987), 41–78.

12. Bernard Frank Batto, *Studies on Women at Mari* (Baltimore: Johns Hopkins University Press, 1974).

13. Maria Brosius, *Women in Ancient Persia (559–331 B.C.)* (New York: Oxford University Press, 1996).

14. Gay Robins, *Women in Ancient Egypt* (Cambridge: Harvard University Press, 1993).

15. Barbara S. Lesko, *The Remarkable Women of Ancient Egypt* (Berkeley: B. C. Scribe Publications, 1978).

16. E. J. W. Barber, *Prehistoric Textiles: The Development of Cloth in the Neolithic and Bronze Ages with Special Reference to the Aegean* (Princeton: Princeton University Press, 1991).

17. Sarah B. Pomeroy, *Women in Hellenistic Egypt: From Alexander to Cleopatra* (New York: Schocken Books, 1984).

18. Jo Ann Hackett, "In the Days of Jael: Reclaiming the History of Women in Ancient Israel," in *Immaculate and Powerful: The Female in Sacred Image and Social Reality*, ed. Clarissa W. Atkinson, Constance H. Buchanan, and Margaret R. Miles (Boston: Beacon Press, 1985), 15–38.

19. Carol L. Meyers, *Discovering Eve: Ancient Israelite Women in Context* (New York: Oxford University Press, 1988). The Torah is the first five books of the Tanakh, the Jewish Holy Scriptures. The Tanakh is called the Old Testament by Christians.

20. Phyllis Trible, "Woman in the OT," in *The Interpreter's Dictionary of the Bible: An Illustrated Encyclopedia*, supp. vol., ed. Keith R. Crim (Nashville: Abingdon Press, 1976), 963–66.

21. Phyllis A. Bird, "Images of Women in the Old Testament," in *Religion and Sexism: Images of Women in the Jewish and Christian Traditions*, ed. Rosemary Radford Ruether (New York: Simon and Schuster, 1974), 41–88.

22. Lerner, *Creation of Patriarchy*, 177.

23. Judith Hauptman, "Images of Women in the Talmud," in *Religion and Sexism*, ed. Ruether, 184–212. The Talmud's sixty-three volumes contain commentary on Jewish law and the Tanakh.

24. Quotations from James Mill, *The History of British India*, cited in *600 B.C. to the Early Twentieth Century*, vol. 1 of *Women Writing in India: 600 B.C. to the Present*, ed. Susie Tharu and K. Lalita (New York: Feminist Press at the City University of New York, 1991), 46.

25. "Sati" means "a virtuous woman," and the phrase "to commit sati" is incorrect. The "practice of sati" describes her immolation on her husband's funeral pyre.

26. Clarisse Bader, *Women in Ancient India: Moral and Literary Studies*, trans. Mary E. R. Martin (original French publication, 1867; Varanasi-1, India: Chowkhamba Sanskrit Series Office, 1964), viii–ix.

27. Bader, *Women in Ancient India*, 67–68.

28. A. S. Altekar, *The Position of Women in Hindu Civilization: From Prehistoric Times to the Present Day*, 3d ed. (Delhi: Motilal Banarsidass, 1963), 25.

29. Julia Leslie, "Essence and Existence: Women and Religion in Ancient Indian Text," in *Women's Religious Experience*, ed. Pat Holden (Totowa: Barnes and Noble Books, 1983), 89–112.

30. Ellison Banks Findley, "Gargi at the King's Court: Women and Philosophic Innovation in Ancient India," in *Women, Religion, and Social Change*, ed. Yvonne Yazbeck Haddad and Ellison Banks Findley (Albany: State University of New York Press, 1985), 37–58.

31. Uma Chakravarti, "Of Dasas and Karmakaras: Servile Labour in Ancient India," in *Chains of Servitude: Bondage and Slavery in India*, ed. Utsa Patnaik and Manjari Dingwaney (Madras, India: Sangam Books, 1985), 35–75.

32. Uma Chakravarti and Kumkum Roy, "In Search of Our Past: A Review of the Limitations and Possibilities of the Historiography of Women in Early India," *Economic and Political Weekly*, April 30, 1988, WS2–WS10.

33. Leslie, "Essence and Existence."

34. Romila Thapar, "Looking Backward in History," in *Indian Women,* ed. Devaki Jain (New Delhi: Ministry of Information and Broadcasting, Government of India, 1978), 6.

35. Uma Chakravarti, *The Social Dimensions of Early Buddhism* (Delhi: Oxford University Press, 1987).

36. Leslie, "Essence and Existence."

37. Janis D. Willis, "Nuns and Benefactresses: The Role of Women in the Development of Buddhism," in *Women, Religion, and Social Change,* ed. Haddad and Findley, 59–86.

38. I. B. Horner, *Women under Primitive Buddhism: Laywomen and Almswomen* (1930; repr. Delhi: Motilal Banarsidass, 1975).

39. Nancy Auer Falk, "The Case of the Vanishing Nuns: The Fruits of Ambivalence in Ancient Indian Buddhism," in *Unspoken Worlds: Women's Religious Lives in Non-Western Cultures,* ed. Nancy Auer Falk and Rita M. Gross (New York: Harper and Row, 1980), 207–25.

40. Tharu and Lalita, eds., *Women's Writing in India.*

41. Albert Richard O'Hara, trans., "The Position of Woman in Early China, According to the Lieh Nu Chuan," in *The Biographies of Eminent Chinese Women* (Washington, D.C.: Catholic University of America Press, 1945).

42. Nancy Lee Swann, *Pan Chao: Foremost Woman Scholar of China, First Century A.D.: Background, Ancestry, Life, and Writings of the Most Celebrated Chinese Woman of Letters* (1932; repr. New York: Russell and Russell, 1968).

43. Melvin P. Thatcher, "Marriages of the Ruling Elite in the Spring and Autumn Period," in *Marriage and Inequality in Chinese Society,* ed. Rubie S. Watson and Patricia Buckley Ebrey (Berkeley: University of California Press, 1991), 25–57.

44. Jennifer Holmgren, "Imperial Marriage in the Native Chinese and Non-Han State, Han to Ming," in *Marriage and Inequality,* ed. Watson and Ebrey, 68–96.

45. Patricia Buckley Ebrey, "Shifts in Marriage Finance from the Sixth to the Thirteenth Century," in *Marriage and Inequality,* ed. Watson and Ebrey, 97–132.

46. Diana Paul, "Empress Wu and the Historians: A Tyrant and a Saint of Classical China," in *Unspoken Worlds,* ed. Falk and Gross, 191–206.

47. Patricia Buckley Ebrey, *The Inner Quarters: Marriage and the Lives of Chinese Women in the Sung Period* (Berkeley: University of California Press, 1993).

48. Ebrey, *Inner Quarters,* 5–6.

49. Ibid., 271.

50. Haruko Wakita, "Marriage and Property in Premodern Japan from the Perspective of Women's History," *Journal of Japanese Studies* 10 (1984): 77–99.

51. William McCullough, "Japanese Marriage Institutions in the Heian Period," *Harvard Journal of Asiatic Studies* 27 (1967): 105.

52. Wakita, "Marriage and Property," 87.

53. Ivan Morris, *The World of the Shining Prince: Court Life in Ancient Japan* (New York: Alfred A. Knopf, 1969); Kenneth Rexroth and Ikuko Atsumi, trans. and eds., *Women Poets of Japan* (New York: New Directions, 1977).

54. E. Patricia Tsurumi, "Japan's Early Female Emperors," *Yuho* 1, no. 1 (1980): 49–54; E. Patricia Tsurumi, "The Male Present versus the Female Past: Historians and Japan's Ancient Female Emperors," *Bulletin of Concerned Asian Scholars* 14 (1983): 71–75.

55. Morris, *World of the Shining Prince,* 48–52.

56. Ibid., 207–8.

57. Barber, *Prehistoric Textiles,* 311–57, 394–95.

58. Elaine Fantham et al., eds., *Women in the Classical World: Image and Text* (New York: Oxford University Press, 1994), 10–55.

59. Eva C. Keuls, *The Reign of the Phallus: Sexual Politics in Ancient Athens* (New York: Harper and Row, 1985), 1–5; Fantham et al., eds., *Women in the Classical World*, chs. 2 and 3.

60. Pomeroy, *Women in Hellenistic Egypt.*

61. Fantham et al., eds., *Women in the Classical World*, chap. 6, especially the bibliography.

62. Larissa Bonfante, "Excursus: Etruscan Women," in *Women in the Classical World*, ed. Fantham et al., 243–59.

63. Susan Treggiari, "Divorce Roman Style: How Easy and How Frequent Was It?" in *Marriage, Divorce, and Children in Ancient Rome*, ed. Beryl Rawson (New York: Oxford University Press, 1991), 31–32.

64. Jane F. Gardner, *Women in Roman Law and Society* (Bloomington: Indiana University Press, 1986).

65. John K. Evans, *War, Women, and Children in Ancient Rome* (New York: Routledge, Chapman, and Hall, 1991).

66. Ida Blom, "Global Women's History: Organizing Principles and Cross-Cultural Understandings," in *Writing Women's History: International Perspectives*, ed. Karen Offen, Ruth Roach Pierson, and Jane Rendall (Bloomington: Indiana University Press, 1992), 139.

67. Jack Goody has made an extensive study of brideprice and dowry in *The Oriental, the Ancient, and the Primitive.*

68. Leslie P. Peirce, *The Imperial Harem: Women and Sovereignty in the Ottoman Empire* (New York: Oxford University Press, 1993).

2

Women in East Asia:
China, Japan, and Korea

SUSAN MANN

Standard textbooks on world history, even those with detailed sections on East Asian culture, offer teachers little in the way of material or guidance on gender relations in China, Japan, and Korea. Specialized textbooks treating East Asia or even the separate countries are little better. True, the subject *women* appears often in newer textbooks. But women are most likely to appear visually (in illustrations with brief captions) or anecdotally (in vignettes describing "famous" women, many of whom might better be described as "infamous"). Moreover, women's appearance as an index topic connotes their special role: deviations from a narrative in which the unmarked subject is male.

Historians of East Asia may excuse this by arguing that we are the victims of our sources. Pictorial representations of women are often easy to find, especially in genre paintings, book illustrations, or other works depicting everyday life. Textual evidence, by contrast, is limited. China's standard histories, for example, rarely mention women outside the obligatory chapters on "exemplary women" (a subject discussed below). When women do appear in Chinese historical narratives, they tend to be "state-topplers," seductive or menacing figures who usurp power from legitimate male rulers or corrupt vulnerable young emperors. In Japan, writing by and about women dominated the literature of early periods only to disappear with the rise of warrior culture in the twelfth century. And Korean histories tend to follow Chinese conventions, especially after the thirteenth century with the embrace of Confucian models of governance appropriated from China. Before that time, surviving records speak of women in oblique terms, leaving historians to tease out information about gender relations.

Meanwhile, teachers and students in North America are left struggling to place women in East Asian history, especially in accounts of ordinary life: in the home, in the economy, in religious and spiritual practice, and in creative work—writing, performing arts, and visual arts. Such topics as sexuality and marriage; childbirth and childrearing (including abortion, infanticide, and other aspects of reproductive behavior); socialization and gender roles; and courtship and romantic love present students with cross-cultural issues that invite discussion and provoke critical thinking. Now, moreover, all of these subjects receive attention in standard accounts of western European history and in the history of the Americas.

Ironically, the absence of women and gender as categories of analysis in East Asian textbooks has become more than a simple problem of historiographic omission—it reinforces cultural stereotypes that a broad education ought to challenge. At worst, it invites students and teachers to think that East Asian women have been oppressed, silenced, suborned, or marginalized more than those in Euro-North America.

Using materials in this essay to integrate women and children into historical narratives, teachers can humanize and familiarize people and places that students may otherwise be inclined to treat as backward, remote, or exotic. And by showing how gender relations are constructed in historical context, teachers will help students develop a culturally informed understanding of value systems different from their own—enhancing students' ability to communicate respectfully with one another—and read about other cultures— in their own diverse society and in the global environment they now inhabit.

Topical Approaches to the Study of Gender in East Asia

The narrative structure of standard world and area history textbooks is generally antithetical to the use of gender as a category of analysis, but few teachers have the time or resources to rewrite the books. They can, however, integrate gender issues into the classroom through topics keyed to textbook narratives, to generate discussion or support student research on women or gender-related issues.

FAMILY SYSTEMS

By distinguishing the family systems of China, Japan, and Korea at the outset, a teacher can stress that cultural differences underlay all of the apparent cultural continuities that make East Asia a coherent "region" from the viewpoint of historians in Euro-North America.[1] A focus on family systems has three great advantages for teachers. First, it levels the playing field between West and East, enabling students to think comparatively about what a family is and how co-residence varies across time and space. Second, it immediately dramatizes the remarkable differences in Chinese, Japanese, and Korean cultures. And, third, it places women squarely at the center of any historical narrative. (Within China itself, great variations across regional space make it difficult to generalize about a single family system, but for our purposes we will treat it as such.)

To some extent, generalizing about family systems forces teachers into an artificially ahistorical and at the same time teleological mode. It is almost impossible, for example, to describe a family system in the premodern period without calling it the "traditional" or the "premodern" family system. A compromise is to speak of the "historical family system" of each of these cultures when offering the descriptions that follow. Notice, too, that family systems must be contextualized in the larger system of social stratification and mobility that characterizes each society.

The normative kinship system in late imperial China was patrilocal, patrilineal, and patriarchal. A bride was supposed to move in with her husband's family at marriage, descent and property rights passed through men, and the senior man in every kinship unit wielded formal ritual authority over all members.

This joint family structure, with more than one married couple in at least one generation but with partible inheritance (property divided equally among sons), created unique tensions in the patriarchal organization of the family. It pitted brother against brother and sister-in-law against sister-in-law as offspring looked ahead to the day when the father would die and the estate would be divided. Women were blamed for the conflicts that precipitated division of the family corporate estate. It was said to be women's "narrow-mindedness" and "petty jealousy" that caused otherwise filial sons to abandon the corporate dwelling in the selfish interests of their own conjugal units.

A popular rendition of the imperial Sacred Edict gives this eighteenth-century example of the pressures that could drive a man to pick fights with his brothers, throw filial obligation and brotherly duty to the winds, and force an unseemly premature division of the family property:

> But forsooth, you love to listen to what your wives have to say, and perceiving that there is some reason in their talk, you listen until before you are aware of it you believe them. The wife of the elder brother says to him, "How lazy, how prodigal, your young brother is! You laboriously make money to keep him, and he still finds fault: are we his son and daughter-in-law, that we ought to yield him the respect due to a parent?" The wife of the younger brother will also say to him, "Even if your elder brother knows how to make money, you have made money too; you do just as much as he does in the home: if

you hire a labourer by the year, even he has not such hard toil. But his children forsooth, they are children, buying this, that and the other to eat—can it be that our children are not fit to live?"[2]

The importance of male heirs to carry on the line, maintain the family estate, and continue the sacrifices to the ancestors led to a marked preference for male offspring that produced male-heavy sex ratios in most parts of the country. Among the rich, this preference might produce large offspring sets as families strove to maximize the number of men who would survive to the next generation. Among the poor, it encouraged female infanticide and neglect of daughters. During the Qing period (1644–1911), cases of wealthy families drowning female babies were reported by one official in Guangdong province.[3]

Historical demographers are now showing that female infanticide was patterned by region and by class as well as by temporal cycles (drought, flooding) in the Qing period. New research is pointing to the possibility that Chinese parents strategized to achieve a certain balance in their offspring sets, to ensure the survival of a male heir and also limit the number of surviving sons and allow for the possibility of rearing at least one daughter. It is important to note, too, that female infanticide was routinely condemned by the Qing government and its officials, whose injunctions provide some of the most reliable written evidence of the practice. One study portrays female infanticide as a "functional equivalent of family planning" that might account for a "substantial portion of the decline in population growth in nineteenth-century China."[4]

In spite of the preference for sons and the tensions in the joint family system, a woman's position in the Chinese family was often a function of her age and status. The new bride might face a demanding mother-in-law determined to retain her son's affection and monopolize his loyalties. The bride of a younger son also had to contend with rival sisters-in-law who might resent her carefree status as a young and childless woman. The youngest women were the most likely to be alienated from the goals of the patrilineal descent system. Even in her own natal family, a daughter might be made to feel like unwanted or damaged goods; as late as the 1980s, baby girls in Hong Kong's New Territories were often given names like "Little Mistake."[5] The young mother of a son, however, could look ahead to the time when she in turn might preside over a large household full of sons, grandsons, and dutiful daughters-in-law. And so, with age, her allegiance gradually shifted until finally, as a mother-in-law herself, she became one of the patriarchal family's strongest advocates.

With respect to property rights, the historical position of women in the Chinese patrilineal descent group is less clear. Women's rights to property appear to have changed over time, and they varied so widely from place to place that it is difficult to generalize. According to the statutes of every dynasty beginning with Tang (618–906), property was to be inherited by all male children born to wives and concubines. The Yuan (1279–1368) code stated specifically that property was to be divided equally among all sons; in Ming (1368–1644) and Qing times, illegitimate sons could claim a half-share of property. Women, by contrast, had at best limited rights to property, at least as defined by the law. Even the Chinese dowry system was always a form of indirect dowry in that some or most of the assets were passed from one family to another as dowry and then returned to the bride's family as bridewealth. In Qing times, a woman had no legal title to property and no power to dispose of family property. Even though a Qing woman could inherit under unusual circumstances (for example, if no rightful male heir was living), women—unlike men—were never seen as co-owners of the family estate. Property rights that women did enjoy, by late imperial custom, were limited to the dowry. Even then, "as late as 1918, the Supreme Court maintained that the wife's own property was subject to the husband's authority."[6]

Marriage in late imperial China was early and, for women, virtually universal. Historically, demographers have noted that the Chinese marriage pattern differs from Western models in that marriage, for women, was not delayed by the necessity of establishing a separate household because offspring lived with their parents. In addition, after medieval times few women took to monasteries as an alternative to marriage. Only chaste widows (that is, women whose husbands had died and who refused remarriage) enjoyed a celibate life culturally sanctioned by Confucian norms. Early and universal marriage does not appear to have produced birthrates as high as demographers would project; the reasons for that are now being studied and debated.[7]

All sons joined in common worship before the spirit tablets of their ancestors, acknowledging that a descent group was a living entity; filial sons continued to care for the spirits of their deceased parents and grandparents as their souls required (lest they become wandering ghosts and come back to reproach or even possibly harm the living). Elaborate mourning rituals defined the relationship between each family member and his or her relatives, and that status, in turn, gave each person his or her position in the rites of ancestor worship. Women were honored in the ancestral rites as wives and mothers (and, backward through time, as grandmothers, great-grandmothers, and great-great-grandmothers in the male line). Their role in the sacrifices themselves, however, depended on the scale of the ceremony. Women played an active role in domestic ancestor worship, caring for the shrines in the home and conducting the ordinary daily rituals of lighting incense, but only men were present at the formal sacrificial rites in the lineage ancestral halls. In ritual, women always addressed themselves to their husbands' ancestors, while after death these same women were worshipped as part of the family they had served in life.[8]

By contrast with China, Japan's earliest historical records describe a bilateral family system where duolocal and uxorilocal residence was common, with polygyny widespread in the aristocracy itself. Scholars believe that patrilineal principles were more influential at the court among the aristocracy, but even there patterns of residence make the historical Japanese family system far less patrilineal than its Chinese counterpart. Early records, for example, show married couples residing at the home of the bride. They also might live separately for the first few years after marriage, or until the birth of the first child, with the husband making "night visits" to his wife before she moved into the groom's family home. In polygynous marriages, the husband made night visits to his different wives separately, and duolocal residence remained the norm throughout the marriage. Readers of *The Tale of Genji* will find these practices described in detail.[9] After the Heian period (794–1185), the rise of warrior culture seems to have shifted the family system in the direction of patrilocal residence and increased emphasis on patrilineality, a pattern that intensified in Japan's core areas surrounding Kyoto and Tokyo through the modern period. In rural Japan, by contrast, family practices resembling those of earliest times were still surprising ethnographers and observers during the nineteenth century.[10]

Despite the vigorous promotion of Confucian values by the Tokugawa shogunate (1600–1868), Chinese models of kin relations had little influence beyond the families of the samurai elite. In the prevailing stem-family system, parents designated one heir and the remaining offspring were cut loose from the family and sent off to make their own way in the world. There they often became part of the town populations whose explorations of sexuality were the stuff of novels and short stories by writers like Saikaku.[11] It should be noted, also, that a daughter might be kept at home and a son-in-law adopted to produce an heir in the next generation. Up to 15 percent of marriages in rural Japan during the Tokugawa period were uxorilocal marriages of this type.[12]

The enduring difference between China's joint family system and Japan's stem-family system had profound implications for gender relations on the eve of the modern period. In Tokugawa Japan, for instance, marriage for women was not universal, and only samurai women were cloistered. Unmarried women beneath the samurai class moved freely outside the home, often employed in entertainment (as geisha in the castle towns or at inns as cooks or chambermaids), protoindustry (for example, sake brewing), or as maidservants in upper-class households. These are the same women who set the scene for Saikaku's fiction and for the woodblock prints featuring beautiful women during the Tokugawa period. Commoner women also traveled—to visit natal families, to participate in pilgrimage, or to bathe in the hot springs.[13]

Although divorce was nearly unknown in the Confucian-influenced samurai class of the Tokugawa period, commoner divorce rates were high. One study of villages near Osaka shows a divorce rate of at least 15 percent.[14] Women could even initiate their own divorces through rituals at special temples.

Some commoner women took vows as Buddhist nuns, and they also participated as writers and readers in the *shingaku* (heart learning) movement of the eighteenth century. When women migrated in search of work they tended to marry later; also, many married women continued to work for their parents until their mid- to late twenties or even later before moving to a husband's home. Women in commoner families of the Tokugawa period also remarried far more frequently than in China, where remarriage was scorned by Confucian teachings. Even among wealthy peasants who otherwise observed at least some Confucian teaching, if only in the breach, divorce and remarriage rates were high. Moreover, a Japanese widow was not the ward of her deceased husband's parents. She was often in a position to negotiate a status satisfactory to herself by considering propositions from both her natal and her marital families.[15]

The historical family system in Korea was originally of bilateral descent, in which heredity and residence shifted freely between the patriline and matriline. This family structure emerged in a larger system of social stratification that sharply divided the hereditary aristocracy, identified by the use of Chinese surnames, from a servile mass of nameless commoners. The Korean family, like its Japanese counterpart, was a stem-family system but distinguished from Japan's by two features: first, strict male primogeniture (as opposed to Japanese custom that favored flexibility in the naming of an heir, depending on the father's age and the son's potential); and, second, strict consanguineality (as opposed to the flexible Japanese use of fictive and other constructed kin ties).

Striking similarities between the early Japanese and Korean family systems dramatize the impact of Confucian values and ideologies the Korean court adopted from China and forced upon the Korean aristocracy beginning in the Chosŏn era (also referred to as the Yi dynasty, 1392–1910). The values and ideologies embraced by Korea's elite after the fourteenth century were drawn primarily from records of the rituals and writings of Song dynasty (960–1279) officials and scholars in China. They focused on the educational system, on training and recruitment for government office, and on the reorganization of the government bureaucracy in conformity with Chinese models. As a result of the tension between the Chinese notion of merit and the Korean class structure, Chinese values promoting success through the examination system opened the door to upward mobility for many commoners in Korea during the eighteenth and nineteenth centuries as the economy grew and resources accumulated in new hands.[16] But the impact of Chinese institutions on the position of Korean women was overwhelmingly negative.

53

Ironically, and in striking contrast to the situation in Japan, where neo-Confucian ideologies had at best a limited effect on family organization and family practice, "the family was the aspect of Korean society most markedly transformed by the process of Confucianization."[17] Slowly, under the influence of Confucian ideology and with the strong backing of the Korean court, Chinese models replaced the kinship practices of the Korean family system. Uxorilocal marriage, the naming of women as household heads, burial rites in which men were interred in the sacred space of their wives' families, listing of daughters and sons in strict order of birth and without regard for sex, remarriage by widowed and divorced women—practices central to Korea's indigenous family system—were anathema to Confucian ritualists. All showed signs of eroding under Confucian influence as early as the end of the fourteenth century. By the late fifteenth century, Korean women were being told to study Confucian books for women stressing the importance of separation of the sexes and seclusion of women in the inner quarters. Female inheritance of property, the last of the Korean kinship customs to disappear under the onslaught of Confucian influence, had virtually ended by the middle of the eighteenth century.

The definitive study of the transformation of the Korean kinship system and of women's status under the influence of Chinese neo-Confucian ideology is Martina Deuchler's *The Confucian Transformation of Korea*. In a chapter entitled "Confucian Legislation: The Consequences for Women," Deuchler shows how the Confucian "civilizing project" in Korea, lasting more than 250 years from 1392 to the middle of the seventeenth century, targeted women and made them its central focus.[18] Women were singularly important to the Korean court's campaigns promoting Confucianization because the husband-wife bond was understood in Confucian thought to lie at the core of all human relationships. The husband was responsible for the "outer" realm of work and service, and the wife for the "inner" realm of domestic life. This was the basis of the Confucian principle of "separation" of the sexes into two complementary spheres.

At the time of the most aggressive Confucian intrusions into Korea, the widespread elite practice of plural marriage was a central problem in the Korean kinship system. By failing to distinguish a primary wife from all others, plural marriage created havoc in patrilineal descent. Without a clearly designated primary wife, no accurate ranking of offspring was possible. These rankings were essential to the proper performance of ancestral rites, not to mention the recording of genealogical data and naming heirs to title and property. One can only imagine the chaos that erupted in Korea's upper-class households when the husband was required by law to select one of his many wives as the primary consort whose offspring would have privileges above all others. Among the many disasters attending such decisions was the hardening of class lines defined by marriage alliances because it became customary practice (and later legal imperative) to select primary wives from the ranks of the emerging Chinese-style literati elite, leaving those of lesser status to lower rank in matrimony. After the legalization of the distinction between primary and secondary wives in 1413, married women who were not primary wives occupied an insecure status; their social rank was low, and their position in the husband's family depended almost exclusively on the birth of a son.[19] This and other strains resulting from the internal stratification of wives in elite families pitted married women in the same household against one another and created strife among offspring who grew increasingly conscious of their different statuses determined by the position of their respective mothers.

Ironically, the lowly status of secondary sons (that is, of sons born to secondary wives) in Korean society had no counterpart in China. In the Chinese kinship system, the single primary wife was the ritual mother of all sons born to her husband. By contrast, Korean sons were all stigmatized (or valorized) by their mothers' class and status. Sons of the primary wife remained members of *yangban* (literati) elite, but sons of a secondary wife were excluded, by virtue of their marginal background, from the rituals of their father's descent line. Moreover, they were barred from sitting for civil service examinations and thus from taking public office.

Having clarified that particular line of demarcation, Confucian lawmakers at the Chosŏn (Yi) court went on to other matters: disparaging as un-Confucian the Korean practice of uxorilocal residence (it was widely preferred in Korean families that a woman give birth and rear young children in the home of her natal family, often in the company of her husband who moved in too); pressuring brides to move in with their husbands as soon as possible; banning intermarriage between matrilateral cousins; and revising the mourning system to degrade the importance of matrilateral kin. Didactic books for women modeled after Chinese classics (including a translation of the complete "Four Books") stressed obedience to a mother-in-law, proper ritual preparations and performance, strict separation of the sexes, mastery of proper women's work (especially embroidery), and so on. Women accustomed to traveling about freely, visiting temples and friends or scenic sights, were now banned from the streets during the daytime.

The most dramatic loss for Korean women whose status was transformed by Confucian codes was that of inheritance claims. By the middle of the Chosŏn period (the end of the seventeenth century), the eldest son was recognized as the legitimate ritual heir of the family headship, a status that in turn gave him de facto control over corporate lands that provided the income to underwrite ritual costs. This shift toward a kind of primogeniture was a devastating blow to what remained of the power of women in the Korean family system. It is main-ly in the elaborate *kut* rituals conducted by female shamans, which continue in contemporary Korea, that we can locate remnants of a family system that once consigned authority and control over ritual and property to sons and daugh-ters alike. In modern Korea, as in the past, "Women's rituals . . . highlight a distinctive and persistent feature of Korean family organization: the acknowl-edged autonomy of houses and the positive powers of matrons within house-holds and as links between kin groups." As a result, the contemporary Korean family in effect houses "two traditions under one roof."[20]

ECONOMIES AND ETHNICITIES

Rice agriculture flourished in East Asian societies, especially following China's economic revolution of the twelfth and thirteenth centuries, which introduced double- and even triple-cropping of rice in temperate and tropical zones, pro-ducing surpluses that made rice the staple of upper-class diets and the founda-tion of agrarian commerce. Francesca Bray calls rice economies "skill-oriented" (rather than "mechanical") technologies because they require ever-higher skill levels to continually increase productivity and support growing populations on scarce land. By contrast with models of development identified with the histo-ry of northwest Europe and the United States, rice economies depend on "im-provement in the application of human skills rather than the substitution of machinery for labour, and require a low level of capital investment."[21]

Beyond skill, rice economies foster particular social relationships because of the need for in-person supervision (especially of water control and labor during planting and transplanting); the need for intervillage cooperation net-works (for water control, crop watching, and labor sharing); and the efficien-cy of small plots and decentralized distribution and marketing systems (in turn a function of the value added by close personal supervision of small units work-ing at maximum efficiency). In this production system, returns on education are extremely high, reflected directly in high productivity.

The skill-oriented rice economies of East Asia fostered a work ethic that students of European history might be invited to compare with the Weberian Protestant ethic. Individuals did not work for themselves but for the family— and not simply for the family in the present but to honor parents and ances-tors by building a future for progeny. For instance, in late imperial China— where hereditary rank and privilege were almost nonexistent and open mobility (both up and down) was the rule—family strategies stressed hard work and fru-gality, high educational achievement, and skillful investment of capital for all male offspring.

Women, too, had a work ethic. Marriage was nearly universal for wom-en, meaning that daughters were all socialized to work hard to become good daughters-in-law. Before industrialization, skill in rice economies also translated into skills for women as "good mothers" who could train their children properly. Among the upper classes, where learning and writing (and, especially in China, competence in civil service examinations) were the paths to upward mobility for young boys, women provided their sons' earliest instruction. In preparation for this, they themselves learned to read, write (using a brush and forming elegant calligraphic characters), paint, and play genteel musical instruments (the koto in Japan, the *zheng* or zither in China). Confucian medical texts proposed theories of in utero education, in which a woman's reading, thoughts, and daily habits might have a positive influence on the male fetus growing in her womb.

Because of the different values in the family systems of China and Japan, the place of women in the work economies of East Asia varied through space and time. In China, where footbinding signaled freedom from heavy manual labor and enhanced the marriageability of cloistered women, Confucian values exhorted women—regardless of class—to eschew work in the fields where they might come into contact with men and instead to remain indoors, spinning, weaving, and embroidering. In Japan as well, doubtless due to the influence of Confucian teachings among the upper strata of rural villagers, wealthy peasant women did little or no agricultural labor. But most Japanese farm women in Tokugawa times worked alongside men in the fields, often at wages half or less than what men were paid except at peak season.

The gender division of labor in peasant households may have been sharper in late imperial China than in Tokugawa Japan. One study shows that Tokugawa farm men and women traded tasks pretty much interchangeably. Most strikingly, records show men sharing responsibility for child care, cooking, and cleaning. By the same token, women in the Tokugawa economy performed in many job sectors dominated in China by men. There are accounts, for instance, of Japanese women working in commercial agriculture, in household and shop protoindustrial labor for the market, and in the "tertiary" service sector in towns and trade fairs. A dramatic indication of the implications of women's earning power is Thomas C. Smith's finding that sex ratios (determined mainly by sex-selective infanticide) were more equal in areas where these service sectors (or female off-farm labor markets) were more highly developed. In Kyoto and Osaka, female entrepreneurs were important managers in merchant family business operations.[22]

In sum, it appears that values stressing female seclusion, characteristic of China's joint family system, were far less important in Japan's stem families, where female labor was readily deployed. In rural Japan, young men and women sojourned from home to work. Village custom sent young women off the farm to work for a year or two before marriage, and the earliest factories in the Meiji (1868–1912) industrialization program were filled with female workers. In Japan, in part because of the family system, *dekasegi* (going out to work) was part of the coming-of-age experience of hundreds of thousands of rural young women. Whereas in the Tokugawa period a woman who went out worked close to home, usually within her own district or certainly within her own domain, after the Meiji Restoration women traveled great distances to reach the new mills, responding to the government's calls for workers. Many, perhaps the majority, sent money home to parents; others supported children or themselves in the wake of divorce or for want of a family.[23]

By contrast, in China Confucian values discouraging women from working outside the home may have contributed to a shortage of female labor that constrained China's early industrialization.[24] During the decades when Meiji factories were employing thousands of women in light industry, producing cotton, silk, and other consumer goods, China remained committed to a program of heavy industrialization (mainly weapons and shipbuilding). China's light industry did not begin to develop until nearly the turn of the century, when complaints about the difficulty of luring women outside the home—and debates about the propriety of doing so—presented a sharp contrast to the Meiji government's successful appeal to samurai families to send out their girls to work for the patriotic building of the nation.

In Korea, industrialization did not begin until after 1910, when Japanese colonial rule developed Korea's economy as part of a broad plan for the expansion of the empire. Most investments were channeled toward heavy industry, to complement programs for agricultural development in Taiwan. Part of this plan involved the forced mobilization, and in some cases relocation, of rural women to factories or fields. Some transition to factory labor was under way in the final years of the Yi dynasty's reform efforts, just before Japan established its protectorate in 1905. The Japanese colonial government established several textile factories in Korea and deported many Korean women to work in Japanese factories as well. During the 1920s, as female workers moved into factories throughout East Asia, they presented a stark contrast with the handful of "modern girls" who studied abroad, wore Western clothes, and idealized "love marriage," dramatizing the competing cultural claims that created turmoil in the social relation of the sexes across the region.[25] "Confucian" values exalting the importance of female manual labor and "good wives" and "wise mothers" were reinscribed in the modernization rhetoric of the Meiji industrialization in Japan and later throughout East Asia. Although scholars have sometimes described these values as part of the effort to modernize, their roots reach deep into Confucian teachings appropriated from China and embedded in the rice economies of the region.

RACIAL AND ETHNIC GROUPS

Research on gender and ethnicity in East Asia is still in its early stages, but suggestive findings of limited studies show that in East Asia, as elsewhere, ethnic difference illuminates otherwise masked aspects of gender difference. In China, research on the non-Han people who conquered China from the steppe regions to the north and west has shown that the common practice of the levirate (marriage of a widow to the younger brother or nephew of her deceased husband) influenced the rise of what came to be known as the "chaste widow cult" in late imperial China. Although "widow chastity" (that is, a widow's vow to kill herself to follow her husband in death or to refuse remarriage in order to remain in service to her deceased husband's parents throughout her own life) came to be regarded as a Confucian virtue, it gained recognition as a custom during the Mongol Yuan dynasty when the Mongols encouraged it as a compromise between their own preferences and the Chinese aversion to a levirate. Ironically, then, what has been regarded as a quintessential Han Chinese practice arose mainly as a result of interaction with non-Han people.[26]

Among minorities within China proper, two groups stand out for their size and political significance: the Muslims and the Manchus. China's Muslim communities comprise descendants of Arab, Persian, and Turkish traders who came to China as early as the seventh century, took Chinese wives, and reared their offspring as Muslim.[27] As the "Hui people," China's Muslims are considered an officially protected minority group under current government policy. From about the middle of the seventh until the late fourteenth century, all Muslims—regardless of ethnicity—were treated as foreigners and expected to live apart in their own communities and preserve their own dialects, dress, dietary laws, and religious practices. Beginning in Ming times, however, the government made Sinification of minority people one of its goals, and the Muslim population was forbidden to retain its own dress and languages. Meanwhile, the Ming government cut off China's Muslim-led overseas trade ventures, and China's Muslim minority became increasingly isolated from Muslim communities outside. Chinese Muslims began to speak Chinese, use chopsticks, and take Chinese surnames.

Despite a seventeenth-century reform movement that revived many Muslim customs, China's Muslims remained heavily influenced by their host society and culture. Chinese Muslim women by the early twentieth century did not observe purdah, although some limited veiling was known in Xinjiang province in the northwest. Although most Muslim records omit references to footbinding, it was apparently practiced by some families; how widespread the custom was, no one knows. It is unclear whether the absence of purdah and the adoption of footbinding dates from Ming Sinification policies. It is said, in any case, that the first Ming emperor's wife had "large feet." Chinese Muslims were also influenced by Chinese culture in that divorce was relatively uncommon and concubinage was also rare (except in the northwest, among the wealthiest families).

In many respects, Chinese Muslim women exhibited an unusual degree of independence, particularly in worship. In the Qing period they had their own mosques as well as their own female religious leaders, called *ahung* (from the Persian *akhund*, "to instruct"). Women's mosques have been identified in the cities of Hankou, Kaifeng (where they made up more than half the total in 1921), Nanjing, Beijing, Shanghai, Shenyang (in Manchuria), and Tianjin; in the provinces of Shandong and Shanxi; and on Hainan Island off the coast of Guangdong. A seventeenth-century Chinese Muslim prayerbook gives explicit directions for modifying the five daily prayers for female worshippers. Women were to pray with their arms and legs close to their bodies (unlike men, who were supposed to open up and spread out their hands, knees, and feet as they knelt). This action, likely representative of classical Confucian prescriptions governing women's lives, symbolized that they must confine their activities to their homes.

Muslim women's isolation in Chinese society stemmed not, however, from Confucian constraints but rather from the fact that Muslims considered pork—a staple of the Han Chinese diet—unclean. Because social interaction in Chinese society centered on commensality, Muslims tended to associate with other Muslims. Similarly, Muslims believed that their homes, dress, and kitchens were cleaner than those of the Chinese majority. Finally, as a further mark of social distinction, Chinese Muslims followed the traditional Islamic preference for marriage of daughters to patrilateral parallel cousins (father's brother's sons)—a custom regarded as anathema by most Han Chinese, among whom marriage between individuals who so much as shared the same surname has historically been taboo.

Manchus, Hakkas, and tribal minorities have also received some attention from historians of China interested in gender relations. Although the Manchu family system, like that of the Han Chinese, was patrilineal, Manchu custom gave women considerable power, especially as mothers, and maternal relatives exercised more power in the Manchu family than was usual among the Han Chinese. Manchu women were forbidden to bind their feet. And within the Chinese imperial family, at least, mothers—especially as regents or as empress dowagers—were powerful figures who ruled "from behind the screen" that customarily kept women invisible in the imperial court. The Qianlong Emperor once surprised Jesuits at his court by inquiring whether France had ever had a female ruler. Their unbound feet notwithstanding, the majority of Manchu women became subject to constraints of Han Chinese norms, including chaste widowhood, during the Qing period. But the women of the Manchu elite at the capital Beijing drove carts at horse races and went out to private theater parties, "the only women in the capital permitted formal public socializing."[28]

Among minority groups in China proper, Hakka women have received considerable attention for their unbound feet and their active involvement in physical labor of all kinds outside the home. New historical research argues that the distinctive gender relations within Hakka communities in China were the result of patterns of migration and sojourning in the late imperial period. The Bai and other minority communities in the southwest, whose gender relations have been a perennial subject of curiosity among Han Chinese, have been analyzed more recently by Chinese anthropologists who consider their matrilineal or bilateral descent systems, uxorilocal residence patterns, and generally more egalitarian gender relationships to be legacies of earlier matriarchies. On Taiwan, preliminary research on relationships between aboriginal populations and the Han Chinese who colonized Taiwan also offers some insight into successive colonial regimes and their treatment of aborigine people, starting with the Dutch in the seventeenth century and continuing with the Japanese at the end of the nineteenth.[29]

Historical Overview

Chinese historians liked to illustrate the lessons of the past by telling stories of individual lives, which they offered up for praise or blame. Women's lives, like men's, appear in Chinese biographical collections from earliest times, starting with *Lienü zhuan* (*Biographies of Women*) compiled by Liu Xiang (77–6 B.C.E.). These stories, many of which became staples in the repertoire of popular culture throughout East Asia, are not so much tales of exemplary virtue as they are witty and lively sketches of smart, resourceful, clever, and (in one chapter) wicked women, illustrated in their deeds and words as mothers, wives, and—in a few cases—state-topplers. Only as the dynasties passed did models for womanly behavior shift away from these early examples, ultimately to be replaced in late imperial times by myriad, often repetitious, accounts of women who committed suicide in the name of chastity or dedicated their lives to serving their parents-in-law as celibate widows. Thus the changing character of female biography offers suggestive evidence of changing norms governing women throughout Chinese history.

In addition to biographies of women, the classical texts of Confucianism expounded norms for womanly behavior invoked by statesmen, scholars, and philosophers—and eventually satirized by writers of fiction and drama—through the ages. Confucian classical scholars identified two fundamental precepts that governed women's ideal place in the kinship and political system—precepts general enough to accommodate change over time. First, women must "follow thrice"—that is, a woman's place of residence was with her father's family before marriage, with her husband's family after marriage, and with her son's family in widowhood. Second, human affairs were divided between inner and outer realms, defined by a strict gender division of labor. The inner realm was the sphere of women's activity; the outer the sphere of men's. Men and women were ideally expected to remain fastidiously separate to underscore the significance and importance of this distinction; women presided over the household as men presided over the government. Women were not to ask questions about public affairs just as men were not to concern themselves with household management. In the formal organization of government, similarly, women held no power. They could not sit for the civil service examinations through which men competed for positions in the government bureaucracy, and they did not rule as empresses.[30] Legal codes, compiled in every dynasty from the Tang onward, gave juridical force to classical assumptions about women's place. The law defined a woman's position in the larger society in terms of her relationships within the patrilineal family, and here again, important changes in the law accommodated changes in the cultural and societal context through time.[31] In late imperial times, these classical injunctions were invoked and reinterpreted to restrict women to lives confined by home and family.

These same classical norms were to have a profound impact on gender relations among the Korean ruling class and the Japanese samurai elite after 1600, and to some degree they continue to shape norms of female behavior and gender relations in parts of contemporary East Asia. Of course, Chinese classical norms by no means describe women's real behavior in an absolute sense. They do, however, reflect values that were taking nascent shape in the earliest days of the Chinese empire. Probably the early growth of bureaucracy in China and the effort to curb the hereditary power of feudal houses that threatened the imperium (especially through kinship ties, by marriage, with the imperial throne) had a lot to do with the early separation of men's and women's spheres—a separation associated with the rise of capitalism in Euro-North American societies. Chinese women most definitely did not stay out of politics, however. Nor has it ever been the case that widows deferred to their sons in matters of judgment or domination—despite the many popular interpretations of the phrase "thrice following." The historical record is much more complicated.

The outline of women's history that follows is centered on China. Chinese influence on Japan and Korea waxed and waned over the centuries, but

Chinese norms affecting gender relations had a specific and clearly document-ed impact on Japanese and Korean societies at particular points in time.

CHINA'S EARLY IMPERIAL PERIOD: HAN THROUGH TANG (206 B.C.E–906 C.E.)

The female scholar Ban Zhao (Pan Chao, born circa 45–51, died circa 114–120 C.E.), a member of a prominent court family during the Han period and herself an accomplished historian, wrote the first of what was to become a whole genre of "Confucian" didactic works for women. Her *Nüjie* (*Lessons for Women*), usually interpreted as injunctions to demure and submissive conduct, has recently been reinterpreted as a Daoist strategy manual advising vulnera-ble palace women on how to navigate the treacherous waters of court poli-tics.[32] This new reading of an old text is just one sign of the ways in which gender history has begun to influence Chinese history as a whole.

In the Qing period, *Nüjie,* in its orthodox Confucian interpretation, was canonized as one of the imperially authorized "Four Books for Women" that constituted required reading for the daughters of all upper-class families. But that was a later time, when urban print culture and the growth of a new audi-ence of female readers revived interest in writings by and about exemplary women of the past and when Ban Zhao's portrait, and portraits of other famous women from myth and history, were published in illustrated collections of "beautiful women."[33] Such recurrent "re-readings" of women's place in histo-ry caution us not to reify or create timeless images of Chinese womanhood.

The fall of the Han in 220 gave way to a prolonged period of disunity (the "Six Dynasties" era) lasting nearly four centuries (220–589). Tribal people from the steppe conquered China's northern plains, and their leaders inter-married with elite Chinese families to constitute a ruling "Sino-barbarian" aristocracy, as historians used to call it. South of the Yangzi River, meanwhile, refugees resettled under a series of "southern" dynasties ruled by houses that considered themselves more purely Han Chinese.

Early consciousness about ethnic difference appears to have promoted awareness about gender difference as well. Aristocratic women in the North, for example, were active in society and politics. They rode horseback for sport, lobbied for official posts for their sons, and lodged public protests on behalf of spouses who had been wrongly accused of political crimes. Perhaps because of the combination of high political visibility and "barbarian" blood, these aristocratic ladies of the "northern dynasties" were portrayed by later Chinese historians as scheming and jealous by nature.[34] Following his Han Chinese sources, an eminent American historian described one "typical northern wom-an" of the period as "harsh, puritanical, a fanatical monogamist, a sharp and economical household manager; she was also meddlesome, vindictive, and insanely jealous." Not surprisingly, the son of this particular woman, the future emperor Sui Yang Di, married a *southern* princess who was more pleasingly described as "studious, literary, and of compliant disposition" and who was said to have been much esteemed by her henpecked father-in-law.[35]

This suggestive record casting upper-class women of the Six Dynasties period in two molds—the scheming barbarian and the genteel southerner—has yet to be examined carefully by historians. The barbarian model, which embodies everything that later elite writers came to despise and fear in women, is appropriately associated with non-Han people, whereas southern women like Sui Yang Di's princess embody Confucian virtues and preserve Confucian values. Similarly, southerners exiled below the Yangzi treasured and nurtured the teachings of Confucius in an era when barbarians had overrun the ancient capitals on the North China plain.

The Six Dynasties period is also important to gender history because Taoist philosophy and Buddhist monastic culture flourished in an age when Confucian imperial institutions were under siege, producing an ambience where women shone as intellectuals and savantes. Although some conservative Confucian families in the South tried self-consciously to preserve the traditional teachings of the classics, many alienated members of the southern aristocracy in exile converted to religious Taoism. In these Taoist circles, a kind of salon culture developed that drew men and women together in private homes and mountain retreats to share sprightly and often fanciful conversation about neo-Taoist and Buddhist scriptures. The freedom to come and go enjoyed by many upper-class ladies of the time prompted a complaint from the scholar and alchemist Ge Hong (283–343):

The ordinary women of today have stopped their work of weaving silk. They have laid aside their activities of making cap tassels. Instead of spinning hemp, they trip and dance through the market place. They neglect to oversee the cooking in the home, but cultivate social relationships with friends and relatives. When the stars come out they light torches and hurry on their way without pause. Their attendants are so numerous that dazzling light fills the roads. The hubbub caused by their maids, messengers, clerks, and bodyguards is just like that in a market place. The indecent jokes told along the way are truly shocking and contemptible. Sometimes they spend the night at other homes; sometimes they return to their own homes foolhardily at night. They make excursions to Buddhist temples and watch people fighting and hunting. They climb mountains and go down to the banks of the rivers. They go beyond the district borders for occasions of offering congratulations or condolences. They pull open their carriage curtains and take in all the cities and villages [they pass through]. They drink from wine cups along the road. They play music and sing as they go along.[36]

Many scholars drawn to these salons later joined Buddhist monasteries, and so did their daughters. Repartee from fifth-century salons has been preserved in a text called *Shishuo xinyu* (*New Worldly Sayings*).[37] One story recounts an exchange between the philosopher Xie An (320–385) and his wife, known only as Lady Liu. The lady would allow her husband only to glimpse her female attendants as they danced and performed on musical instruments lest, as she said to her spouse, the sight "undermine your great virtue." This story was elaborated in texts of later years as Lady Liu continually foiled Xie An's plans to fill his apartments with concubines and female entertainers. At length, his nephews lined up in his support, and, not to be outdone by a wife skilled in Confucian rhetoric, they recited passages from the classic *Shijing* (*Book of Poetry*) about the virtuous wife who disdained jealousy. Lady Liu would have none of that. "Who wrote those poems?" she asked. "The Duke of Zhou," was the reply. "Well then," she sniffed, "he was a man, so of course he wrote like that. We can be sure we'd have heard something different from the Lady of Zhou."[38]

Lacking the system of official government supported schools for the northern aristocracy, southern families in exile turned increasingly to education in the home. Thus, "Men sought to marry educated women from scholarly families so they could share the responsibilities of instructing the children," and "This demand for literate and well-read wives made families more conscientious about providing their daughters with an education equal to that of their sons."[39] Because family prestige, as well as livelihood, depended on education, families carefully sought the best-educated brides for their sons; some women learned special arts for which their families were particularly noted. Besides the standard *Analects* and *Classic of Filial Piety*, women taught their children calligraphy, music, literature, composition, manners, and religion. The competition for accomplished women was so intense that young brides feared a match with a man who might be intellectually inferior.

Buddhist nunneries in the South, many patronized by the southern courts, also enrolled ladies of the court and the aristocracy for training in the scriptures. The most noted nuns gave public lectures that drew thousands of laywomen. Literacy rates among the nuns of this time appear to have been high. Of the sixty-five biographies in the *Biographies of Nuns*, only twelve make no mention of the ability to read and write. Some noted southern women in this era also became Taoist adepts. Wei Huacun, for example, received revelations from immortals who appeared to her after she had demonstrated her fidelity to Taoist discipline. When she was a child, Wei Huacun's father provided all the Taoist classics. After mastering those, she built a separate dwelling for herself on her parents' property and ate nothing but flaxseed, considered an elixir that would prevent aging. Although her parents finally forced her to marry, she remained celibate. Her ascetic life of devotion, in defiance of the demands of parents and spouse, won Wei Huacun a loyal following in her lifetime and a place in the Taoist pantheon after her death. In the society of the North, meanwhile, a few exceptional women obtained appointments at official government schools, where their influence reached a still wider audience.[40]

Reunification from 589 to 906, under the Sui and Tang dynasties, marks the early peak of Chinese influence in the emerging civilizations of Korea and Japan. It is worth stressing here that the prevailing modes of gender performance and gender relations in China during this period were unique, a legacy of the Six Dynasties. They bear little resemblance to the "Confucian" gender relations that came to characterize the late imperial period. Chinese society in Tang times was broadly divided into three classes that persisted until the early Song: the super-elite of the capital area (the "great Hebei clans"); the scholar-officials (locally prominent families, sometimes dubbed the "prefectural aristocracy"); and the commoners. All these groups were endogamous, but the Hebei clans were particularly well known for exclusive endogamy, and most prominent families preferred to exchange brides with only a small, select group of equal status. Circles of eligible brides were determined by consulting genealogies specially prepared to assist families and matchmakers in arranging proper marriages.[41] This concern with exclusive class endogamy extended to the imperial family. All high-ranking imperial consorts were chosen from the great aristocratic clans, whose members as a result had undue influence at court:

> [T]he imperial family was . . . enmeshed in a complex web of marriage alliances with the great aristocratic families of the metropolitan area. Although the palace women lived in seclusion in their own section of the palace, guarded and administered by eunuchs, this seclusion was very lax compared with later times. Upper-class women in T'ang times enjoyed a great degree of independence, and there is no doubt that the palace ladies remained closely in touch with their own relatives and with society outside the palace.[42]

To a striking degree, elite gender relations of the same kind prevailed in the early Japanese court at Kyoto. Recent scholarship has stressed, moreover, the importance of female chieftains in the early history of the Japanese polity, arguing for a "social paradigm of gender complementarity" in early concepts of Japanese rulership. This is most notable in accounts of the queen Himiko, who ruled as a "paramount" in her own kingdom, as the chief of a maritime regime, and as an enchantress whose mastery of the "spirit way" ensured bountiful rice harvests for her people.[43]

The tilt toward complementarity or bilaterality sets the Japanese kinship system apart from the Chinese from the beginning. Bilateral residence and inheritance appear in the earliest Japanese classical texts. In the Heian period, in the words of one scholar, "marriages were easily formed and easily broken," polygamy was "common," and "husbands and wives regularly lived apart or lived with the wife's family." Preference in inheritance was given to close female, rather than distant male, relatives, especially daughters. Even after the Kamakura period (1185–1333), laws show that wives regularly inherited from their husbands. For several generations during the thirteenth century, "unmarried women and women as widows had the potential to dominate their families" because of their access to control over "landed officerships," titles conveying control over property, some of which could be alienated or bequeathed to heirs. These relationships are described in detail, with translations of actual legal cases, in *Lordship and Inheritance in Early Medieval Japan: A Study of the Kamakura Sōryō System.*[44]

Gender relations in Japan's courtly culture were also affected by the divide between men, who wrote in classical Chinese, and women, who wrote in the vernacular. Shikibu Murasaki, the female author of *The Tale of Genji*, one of the world's greatest novels, is the best-known master of early Japanese prose, but other genres written by women, especially diaries, provide a view of the world in that period entirely constructed in a language written by women. There is no counterpart in China's elite culture for this gendered use of language because men and women alike were expected to master the formal poetry and prose styles of Chinese. A similar contrast applies in Korea, where the vernacular *han'gŭl* became women's written language after its introduction in the fifteenth century, leaving classical Chinese the domain of elite men.

The Pillow Book of Sei Shōnagon is a cranky, witty, often devastatingly cutting and yet acutely sensitive volume of random observations, jotted down daily by a high court lady of the Heian period (early eleventh century) and provides endless amusement for students seeing the world through Shōnagon's eyes. Gossipy court politics at its most outrageous, Shōnagon's diary also shows the combination of independence and vulnerability that made the lives of court women the subjects of intrigue and political maneuvering. Shōnagon can be assigned in conjunction with *The World of the Shining Prince* or with portions of *The Tale of Genji* to underscore the importance of women's writing and help students grasp the complex family politics of the powerful Fujiwara regents who controlled the imperial throne at the time. Among other things, students will see that Fujiwara women were married to heirs to the Japanese throne and that by custom pregnant empresses returned to their natal homes to give birth. This can facilitate discussion of customs surrounding nuptial residence, early (pre-Buddhist) beliefs in birth pollution, and control over the child socialization of future rulers.

We know little about the lives of commoner and "mean" women in this early period of East Asian history. In China, a few courtesans won fame, notably the poet Xue Tao, who was forced into slavery by poverty following her father's death and became an "official entertainer" in the quarters of a high-ranking official. Xue Tao was admired by the leading male poets of the day, and is even said to have drafted documents for her patron masters. Her extraordinary talent as a writer (she is said to have published more than five hundred poems, fewer than a hundred of which survive) was recognized in the early Qing period, when eighty-nine of her poems were reprinted in the nine-hundred-volume *Collected Poems of the Tang Dynasty*, which was compiled by imperial decree.

The two most famous women of the Tang period, by contrast, are infamous: the woman who ruled as Emperor Wu and the imperial concubine Yang Guifei. Each made her mark as a symbol of the problems caused by women's influence in government. Yang Guifei, the favorite of the emperor Ming Huang of Tang, has entered history as a femme fatale or state-toppler, who, in an archetypal tale of seduction, diverted the emperor's attention from the affairs of state and so (allegedly) caused the famous mutiny that drove him into exile in 755–756, the An Lushan rebellion. The Emperor Wu based the legitimacy of her rule not on the Confucian classics but on passages in a Buddhist sutra that prophesied the emergence of a pious woman ruler who would preside over a world empire seven hundred years after the death of the Buddha. She also proclaimed herself an incarnation of the Buddha of Light and of the Future, the Maitreya. Buddhism, spreading from China to Japan and Korea in this period, found female patrons in both cultures.

Women of the Tang aristocracy appear formidable in the images left to us. Paintings and small mortuary statues of aristocratic medieval women show full-figured ladies with up-swept hair astride horses or standing erect and dignified, wearing loose-fitting gowns with empire waists that fasten in front in a manner still preserved in the classical gowns worn by Korean women—representative of an aristocratic style set by northern conquerors in the Six Dynasties period.

A female deity, the Queen Mother of the West (Xi Wang Mu), worshipped as the special patron deity of female Taoist priestesses and adepts, is another emblem of the unique gender relations of this period. She was the guardian of "singing girls" (the conventional name for courtesans and prostitutes in this era because virtually all were trained to sing and dance as well as offer sexual services) and of dead women. Neither a dutiful daughter, nor an obedient wife, nor a self-sacrificing mother, she was not sought after by married or pregnant women as was the Bodhisattva Guanyin in later times. Instead, she, too, invokes the legacy of earlier dynasties—a rich mythic heritage that identified female goddesses with water, rain, wind, and rainbows; with water spirits (dragons, frogs, fish, and serpents); and with images of yin that were powerful, gorgeous, and full of the promise of immortality for mortal men. And though her attributes included the peach of immortality—a potent fertility symbol that simultaneously signifies "the vulva, the breast, and a baby's round bottom"— in her fertile aspects she represented cosmic, not human regeneration.[45]

In both Japan and Korea during the centuries before 1300, the influence of Chinese models of gender relations appears limited and is seen mainly in sporadic attempts to increase the power of patrilineal descent lines seeking to control the central government. In fact, it was not Confucian influence but the rise of warrior culture that contributed to what appears to be a decline in the status of Japanese women beginning in the twelfth century. The new ethos emphasizing the personal loyalty of armed retainers to a lord, the *bushidō* (warrior way), displaced the importance of marriage alliances as a political strategy and reduced the influence of women in the political arena. In Korea during the same period, sparse records point to a similar tilt away from bilateral kinship relations and toward patrilineality, especially with the growth of Chinese influence in elite culture. Early Chinese records comment on "free choice" marriage in Korea and describe with disapproval women singing and dancing together late into the night.[46] Although, beginning in the tenth century, Chinese influence began to erode these indigenous patterns of gender relations within the ranks of the hereditary elite, the aggressive transformation of the family system that accompanied the embrace of Confucian values in Korea under the Yi dynasty was still several centuries away.

THE SONG AND YUAN DYNASTIES, 960–1368

In China during the tenth through the twelfth centuries, by contrast with Korea and Japan, women are easy to spot in historical records. "Palace ladies" formed a veritable bureaucracy of their own within the imperial precincts; women of "gentry" families presided over household budgets and even managed the estates of the growing new elite of local society. Working women in cities and market towns provided labor and services for the economic revolution of the period. In the palace, women distinguished themselves as regents (ruling on behalf of a deceased spouse or a minor heir), consorts, courtesans, concubines, and female bureaucrats or staff administrators. In the households of gentry families, and in the homes of working-class commoners, women of the Song period emerge as household managers, clothmakers, and religious devotees who had lively spiritual and devotional lives.[47]

The Song dynasty legal code and ritual practice preserved many of the prerogatives women enjoyed in earlier times. Evidence from Song law, for example, suggests that a Chinese woman's ties to her natal family remained important under the law, as they had during the medieval period. The Tang code had stipulated that even a daughter who married out could inherit property if all other heirs had died; an unmarried daughter could also inherit the family wealth if her parents and brothers had died. In Song times it was still possible for an unmarried daughter to inherit the property of her natal family provided all other heirs were dead. During the Song period a woman retained control over her dowry throughout her marriage; it was her property, to be passed on to her children, and it could follow her into a second marriage or be returned to her natal family. Because of this, as one scholar remarks, "The status of elite women as widows on the [Song] marriage market was relatively high."[48]

In the economy as well as in the law, women's status in Song times appears relatively high. The rapid urbanization in Song times, fed by massive migration and commercial growth (partly the result of the introduction of early-ripening rice into southern wetlands), opened an enormous labor market for women. For example, it is during the Song that we learn (from fiction, poetry, and accounts of urban life) of women running restaurants, serving a lively prostitutes' and courtesans' quarter, and selling fish and vegetables. In the affluent cities of the Song, wealthy families employed scores of concubines, maids, cooks, dressmakers, and singing and dancing girls to serve and entertain guests. In Hangzhou, one Song source records that "the middle-class and poor families did not care about getting sons. But when a girl was born, she was deeply loved and given good care. Once she grew up to be a woman, she was taught, according to her beauty and ability, arts and skills so that she would be ready to be picked up by the scholar-official [families that needed her for] entertainment or service."[49]

An eleventh-century Chinese handscroll depicting the city of Kaifeng just before it fell to invaders from the North China Plain offers a glimpse of urban life in Song China; an eighteenth-century copy of the scroll is available on CD-ROM.[50] While viewing the handscroll, students can read accounts of life a century later in the southern city of Hangzhou, to which thousands of exiled Han Chinese retreated when the imperial capital was relocated to the south after 1122. For a lighter view of the era, students can read a hilarious contemporary short story entitled "The Shrew," from a storyteller's prompt book, which recounts the trials of a family coping with a loquacious and unruly daughter-in-law whose sharp tongue is obviously the product of too much education. These accounts may be found in Patricia Buckley Ebrey's *Chinese Civilization and Society: A Sourcebook* and supplemented with Jacques Gernet's *Daily Life in China on the Eve of the Mongol Invasion, 1250–1276*, which is also based entirely on primary sources.

The new economic opportunities offered to women outside the home during the Song commercial revolution may have been one of the threats that inspired Song neo-Confucian philosophers to adopt increasingly conservative views of women's place—particularly with respect to female chastity and widow remarriage. The writings of the neo-Confucian philosopher Cheng Yi, recorded by Zhu Xi in his influential exegesis of neo-Confucian beliefs, stressed that to a wife, her husband must be as heaven; that like a loyal minister, a faithful wife would never serve two lords; that, when it came to remarriage, even though a widow faced the threat of starvation, "to starve to death is a minor matter; to lose one's virtue is a matter of the utmost importance." All evidence indicates that women continued to remarry in the Song period, however; Cheng Yi's doctrine did not have its fullest impact until after the Song.

Increasingly, therefore, scholars are viewing the Mongol Yuan dynasty as a critical turning point in the status of Chinese women, most notably regarding dowry and widowhood. The Mongols who conquered China in 1279 and made it part of their world empire had marriage practices that differed markedly from the Chinese, particularly with respect to inheritance (a wife received a portion of her husband's patrimony during his lifetime, while younger sons did not inherit until both parents had died). The Mongols also practiced polygamy, and they gave brideprice rather than dowry. Under Yuan rule, the chief reason for honoring women shifted from filial piety—especially the obligations of a daughter to her parents in mourning—to wifely fidelity. For example, in *Song shi* (*History of the Song Dynasty*), compiled in 1345 under Mongol rule, chaste wives defending their chastity against rebels, brigands, and foreign soldiers dominate the biographies of women. And by late imperial times, the entire paradigm for womanly virtue had shifted to the ideal of faithful widowhood as service to aging parents-in-law; a woman's filial obligations were transferred from her own parents to her husband's.[51]

The Mongol (Yuan) period was critical to shifts in women's status for other reasons: the ravishing of Chinese women by Mongol invaders increased concern about cloistering women, and also about female chastity, in the population at large. And as members of the Chinese male elite began to emphasize their genteel scholarly attributes, to distinguish themselves from the barbarian Mongol ruling elite, Chinese women responded by creating forms of bodily adornment that stressed their own womanly qualities, especially the fashion of tightly bound feet, which set them apart from non-Han women.[52] The earliest remark about footbinding by a foreign observer was made around 1324 by a contemporary of Marco Polo, who noted in his travels in North China that "with the women the great beauty is to have little feet; and for this reason, mothers are accustomed, as soon as girls are born to them, to swathe their feet tightly so that they can never grow in the least."[53]

Whether or not Mongol influence on women's status in China is corroborated by further research, all scholars agree that a marked shift in values associated with womanly behavior occurred sometime during the twelfth and thirteenth centuries. Whereas in Tang times, equestrian women with their own rights to property enjoyed wide freedom of public movement and remarried without penalty or criticism, by late imperial times (1400–1900) elite women were restrained on all fronts: confined to the domestic realm by bound feet and social custom, barred from inheritance except in the most extreme circumstances, and scorned if they attempted to remarry.

It is striking here to note that the most powerful Chinese influence on the culture and society of Japan came during the medieval period, especially the early Tang (618–ca. 750) when the status of Chinese elite women was high—comparable, certainly, to that of the palace women in Nara and Kyoto. By contrast, Chinese cultural influence in Korea peaked in the late imperial period after 1400, when the status of elite Chinese women had declined markedly. Thus Chinese culture offered very different models of gender relations to the two societies over which its ideals of civilization held sway until the nineteenth century. It is also worth noting that the changes in women's status associated with the Mongol conquest of China, especially the spread of cloistering and footbinding and the rise of a chaste widow cult, did not recur in Japan, which fought off Mongol invaders. Japan's military victory over the Mongols was part of an emerging consciousness of Japan as a divinely protected land that was older than, and in some ways superior to, Chinese civilization.[54] To what extent this self-conscious contrast between China and Japan affected Japanese gender relations remains to be studied.

By contrast, the Mongols' successful invasion of Korea reduced the Korean king to a "son-in-law" of the Yuan imperial house, forced to take Mongol princesses as consorts and to send the crown prince to reside as hostage at the Yuan court in Peking before assuming the throne. Meanwhile, within Korea itself aristocratic families took advantage of the weakened central government to ingratiate themselves in the service of the Yuan court as interpreters, tribute-bearers, and retainers. They used this power to create vast estates in the countryside where laborers took refuge as virtual slaves to escape government taxes and conscription.[55] As a result, the century of Mongol domination in Korea had the unintended consequence of passing the Korean throne to the arms of the forces within China that overthrew the Yuan and established the Ming dynasty.

Korea's Yi or Chosŏn dynasty embraced China's Confucian culture as a model for reducing the power of the great families and consolidating the hegemony of the central government with the support of a Confucian-style literati elite comprising the yangban aristocracy. To the Mongol invasions we therefore owe the subsequent "Confucian transformation" of the Korean family system and its dramatic restructuring of gender relations in Korean culture and society. One of the earliest steps in that direction was the creation in 1446 of a new Korean writing alphabet, han'gŭl, which used twenty-eight letters to convey the sounds of vernacular Korean. That had the immediate effect of dividing the writing world into two: those who composed in classical Chinese—limited to the male literati elite—and those who wrote and read han'gŭl—literate peasants and soldiers, entertainers and monks, and women of the upper classes. In a stroke, as it were, women's voices had been removed from the official documentary record. The Yi court's subsequent persecution of Buddhists also eliminated the influence of Buddhist beliefs and institutions from the court, relegating their religious practice in Korea to a women's domain that was one step removed from the center of power.[56]

THE POST-MONGOL AGE, 1368–1911

The history of gender relations in the post-Mongol age belongs to a separate chapter in East Asian history. In China, the period is referred to as the "late imperial" era, comprising the Ming and Qing dynasties. The historical record on Chinese women for this period is rich. Two monographs, Dorothy Ko's *Teachers of the Inner Chambers: Women's Culture in Seventeenth-Century China* and Susan Mann's *Precious Records: Women in China's Long Eighteenth Century,* treat women. Urban print culture after the sixteenth century catered to a reading audience that featured women in fiction and drama as well as in didactic literature. The great commercial revolution of the seventeenth century provoked radical new currents in Confucian thought, stressing the significance of the individual mind as the source of all good and all knowledge and affirming the potential for sagehood in all individuals, male or female. Belief in the "unity of the Three Teachings"—Buddhism, Taoism, and Confucianism—popularized the worship of Taoist and Buddhist deities that were accessible to women, especially the Bodhisattva Guanyin. Lectures on the Three Teachings drew crowds of both men and women, as described in a passage from an early-seventeenth-century novel entitled *The Romance of the Three Teachings:* "The faithful men and women of the town all came to celebrate: old and young, loud and quiet, worthy and ignorant. There was a troop of women: Aunty Chang from Father's side, Aunty Li from Mother's side, Madam Wang—fat and thin, dressed in black cotton or hemp, tall and short, flower-footed and big-footed, painted and powdered—each in a class by herself. They were all coming and going, pressing and crowding: altogether it was quite lively."[57]

The great cities of Ming times, particularly the southern capital at Nanjing, attracted wealthy men who came to trade or to sit for the provincial examinations. Elite courtesans served the country's best and brightest as they

73

took respite from the pressure of the tests. Here is a seventeenth-century description of the view from the pleasure boats on the Qinhuai River near the examination halls:

> Nowhere else in the empire is there the profusion of lanterned boats of the Ch'in-huai [Qinhuai] river. Strung along both banks are ten miles of river mansions with richly carved and painted balustrades and beautifully worked silk window curtains. There, when guests protest they are drunk, their host says they cannot yet go home. Boatmen plying back and forth point out for their passengers, "The famous courtesan So-and-so lives here at such-and-such riverside mansion. Having the number one provincial graduate is what she considers worthy of her."[58]

Prostitutes served men in "even the most lowly districts," according to another seventeenth-century observer. In Beijing seven copper cash could buy an hour in bed with a woman who would parade nude before her customers to solicit their business.[59] Poetry and fiction in Ming times celebrated the pleasures of the flesh and the romances between glamorous courtesans and fledgling scholars, caught between their awareness of society's moral code and their own passion. The consequences for women's culture of the urban print revolution and the so-called cult of *qing* (passion) are the subject of Dorothy Ko's *Teachers of the Inner Chambers.* Collections of songs sung in the pleasure quarter—many of them comic and spiced with punch lines, almost all celebrating erotic adventures—were published by noted writers. Titles such as "The Hundred Most Beautiful Courtesans of Suzhou" spoofed Confucian values, as did the joke books whose stock characters included sophisticated brides and intimidating wives.[60]

Li Yu's pornographic novel *The Prayer Mat of Flesh,* published early in the seventeenth century and styled satirically as a didactic tale, begins with a chapter admonishing the reader that although sex in moderation is life-enhancing and restorative, this is true only with one's wife or concubine. Prostitution and adultery bring disaster. The novel describes in detail the sexual exploits and adventures of its hero, a young man named Not Yet Spent whose two goals in life are to become the greatest genius of his age and to marry the world's most beautiful woman. In that sense the hero, who eventually comes to grief as his misadventures catch up with him, is a parody of the hero of the romantic novels popular in the same period, in which the young-man-genius falls in love with the lovely beauty, goes on to marry her, achieves success in the civil service examinations, and all live happily ever after. In Japan at about the same time, the capital's Yoshiwara district offered the same kinds of social and cultural entertainments, mixed with sexual allure, for the samurai elite. The most famous geisha of the Yoshiwara were known and admired by connoisseurs in China. In token of their ability to distract men from their official responsibilities, these women were known in Japan as *keisei,* a Japanese reading of the Chinese term for "state-toppler."[61]

Profusely illustrated sex manuals depicting coital positions and offering advice to lovers—for instance, explaining the differences between techniques required for procreation and those more suited to recreation—were printed widely in Ming China and in Tokugawa Japan. Men were advised to sit down with their lovers and turn the pages of these manuals together before having intercourse. A Chinese manual of 1566 explained that sex for pleasure accomplished two things: It could strengthen the man's vital essence and benefit the woman's health by stirring her yin essence. This was contrasted with sex to conceive a child, which was not to include foreplay or variation in positions but should be done directly and solemnly, in "spirit of humble devotion." It was considered important for men to "conserve the vital essence." The same manual includes a table giving the number of times men at various ages could safely afford to ejaculate per week and per month. What role coitus interruptus or reservatus played in birth control in China is a subject still unexplored. A preferred method of lovemaking (for men) was to refrain from ejaculating while bringing a female partner to orgasm so that he could absorb "her vital yin essence." To make a woman conceive, men were advised to have intercourse during the first days after menstruation and to take care that man and woman reached orgasm simultaneously.[62]

During the late Ming, ideals of masculine and feminine beauty appear to have shifted once more. Early Ming paintings and illustrations favor the Tang-Song style: full-figured, plump women with round faces and middle-aged, bearded men. Woodblock prints and illustrated manuals show women wearing wide trousers secured with a cord around the waist, hems tucked in under stockings; a broad brassiere that fastened front or back was sometimes kept on during lovemaking. A short jacket, buttoned down the front and with a high, fitted collar (mandarin style) was worn over the trousers. On top of the jacket, women wore several long-sleeved robes of materials and patterns to suit the season and their class. The ends of the sashes that tied the robes trailed down their fronts. If an additional, shorter jacket was worn, it fastened in front with bands tied with an elaborate bow. Small brocade bags filled with incense were suspended from the sash, and handkerchiefs and other small toilet articles were tucked inside the sleeves of the inner robes. By contrast, later Ming work leans toward slender figures. Young men without beards, moustaches, or whiskers had, by the Qing, shed even the musculature popular among athletic young Ming males in favor of delicate, pale features, narrow shoulders, and a demeanor suggesting sensitivity and dreaminess. Women followed the same trend in Qing times and appeared to be frail, with thin, long faces, flat chests, and narrow hips. They wore gowns instead of pants and were pictured leaning delicately against balustrades and maids. Shifts in fashion during the late Ming await further study. After the Manchu conquest in 1644, the styles of the Lower Yangzi region became the vogue throughout the empire.[63]

Upper-class women were voracious readers and consumers of books in late Ming and Qing print culture. They read medical handbooks that gave advice on pregnancy and childrearing, cookbooks, guides to letter-writing and household management, and, of course, spiritual texts. New editions of classical women's instruction books were reprinted with illustrations. Didactic literary works in classical style, such as the *Analects for Women* published in the Tang and the *Nei xun* (*Instructions for the Inner Quarters*) published early in the Ming period, were issued for more erudite families. Groups of twenty to thirty women would gather to discuss the classics in "clubs" much like those favored by male literati. And some new books, the most famous of which were modeled after Liu Xiang's and Ban Zhao's early works, targeted a relatively low-brow audience—the young women of commoner families who now had access to a teacher and a family library and needed some guidance in an age of pornographic novels and sex manuals. Jingles and illustrated guidebooks were published for semiliterate and illiterate women.[64] Women went out to work, too, joining men in occupations where they worked side by side, taking cotton thread they had spun to market, braiding sandals, knotting hemp, and weaving cloth.

The late Ming has been singled out as an era when basic tensions related to the spread of female literacy and the growth of a small market economy worked against increasingly constrictive Confucian mores.[65] The tensions were manifested in a vigorous debate about the roles and status of women during the eighteenth century under the subsequent Qing dynasty. Following generations of conquest and warfare that destabilized much of China from 1620 to 1680, the period from 1683 to about 1820, often called "High Qing," was an era of peace, prosperity, and growth that fostered new debates about the nature and direction of social change. Jonathan Spence's *Death of Woman Wang* stresses the hardships of the dynastic transition (1644–ca. 1683), hardships felt most keenly by women, on whom starvation, warfare (rape and pillage and the attendant suicides that were demanded of honorable women), and bereavement took the heaviest toll.

In Qing times three phenomena mark the history of Chinese women: the state cult promoting women's virtue, especially virtuous widows; the explosion of literature on families and family improvement; and the critical discussion about women's place that developed among eighteenth-century literati as part of the "Movement for Han Learning." Perhaps because the Qing rulers were foreigners (Manchus), they went to unusual lengths to demonstrate their zealous commitment to Confucian ideals. That meant, among other things, a strong preference for using moral suasion rather than coercion as a means of enforcing social norms. Early Qing emperors developed the imperial Sacred Edict into a document that had to be read monthly at public meetings, a direct message from the emperor himself exhorting his "children," the people, to be filial to their parents, neighborly to their neighbors, and so on. To provide real incentives for good citizenship, early Qing rulers followed their Ming predecessors in offering special imperial rescripts or certificates of merit to honor especially outstanding examples of moral virtue. For men, that meant honoring filial sons, upstanding citizens such as philanthropists, and loyal officials. For women, it meant rewarding fidelity to spouse.

In the early Qing, the dominant role model for wifely fidelity—selected from the historical repertoire of model women—was the faithful widow. The Qing government also rewarded women who died resisting rape. It harshly forbade widow suicide, with some notable results. An imperial award included not only a piece of calligraphy reading "chaste," signed in the emperor's own hand, but also fifty ingots of silver to help pay the costs of enshrining a woman's tablet in a local temple to honor model women. In some cases, a grand stone archway was constructed, on which were inscribed, with felicitous phrases and appropriate documentation, the names of many women so honored. To qualify for the award and inclusion on the archway, a woman had to be widowed young (before the age of thirty) and remain celibate at least until the age of fifty.

In keeping with the constraints implied by the chaste widow cult, the eighteenth-century high Qing was a boom period for the publication of instructional books for women. Widely read books for women in the eighteenth century included the "Four Books for Women," self-consciously named as a counterpart to the Confucian "Four Books" that male scholars had studied since Song times as they competed for examinations. The Four Books for Women consisted of Ban Zhao's *Lessons for Women;* the so-called *Analects for Women,* written in the Song period; the *Precepts for the Domestic Realm,* attributed (questionably) to a consort of the Ming emperor, Renxiao; and the *Rules for Women, Explained with Details,* also written in the Ming, ostensibly by the mother of the compiler of the collection. Female readers were advised that they should "not look around while walking, not open the lips while talking, not shake the knees while sitting, not sway the skirt while standing, not laugh aloud when feeling happy, and not talk loudly when angry. Whether inside or outside, men and women should gather in different groups. Women should not peep over the wall and not go beyond the garden. When going out, a woman's face must be covered."[66]

The formidable influence of Ban Zhao as a model in the eighteenth-century publishing craze for women's didactic literature had a paradoxical effect. On the one hand, it produced an outpouring of instructions focused on the four womanly virtues first elaborated by Ban Zhao herself in her *Instructions:* proper virtue, speech, bearing, and work ("work" referring to spinning, weaving, and especially embroidery, the mark of refinement). On the other hand, it also led to a rising interest in female literacy and education because marriageable young women all had to be able to read the right books. Still more contradictory in the history of Chinese women was the appearance of such satirical novels as *Flowers in a Mirror,* written in the early nineteenth century by Li Ruzhen, who used his fiction to criticize both concubinage and footbinding.[67]

To some degree, all of these tensions surrounding the status and roles of elite women are apparent in Japanese and Korean cultures during this same period. In Japan, the influence of Chinese norms for gender relations seems to have been confined mainly to the samurai elite in the castle towns of the Tokugawa period. Elsewhere, in merchant, artisanal, and farm families, including the households of landlords, positive messages about female education meshed nicely with the relatively bilateral tilt of the Japanese stem-family system. Other more oppressive features of the Chinese Confucian norms affecting women—bans on widow remarriage, for instance, and strict ideas about cloistering women in the home—were largely ignored, as was the custom of footbinding. Japanese publishing houses put out scores of new didactic works instructing women in how to behave properly. One of these, the *Onna daigaku* (*Greater Learning for Women*), attributed to the Tokugawa neo-Confucian scholar Kaibara Ekken (1629–1713), has been translated into English. The term *onnarashisa* ("womanly" or "womanlike") moved from the domain of performing arts—where it referred to actors who played women's roles—into a moralistic discourse premised on an essentialized female identity. At the same time, cultivated women as *bunjin* (literati) won fame through their published poetry and the circulation of their paintings. A handscroll assembled from the paintings and calligraphy of twenty-two mid-nineteenth-century female literati displays their artistry and learning.[68]

In Korea, Chinese hegemony after 1392 produced a marked decline in the relative status of women. A Korean counterpart of the female writer is known to us as the author of *The Memoirs of Lady Hyegyŏng,* a collection of four autobiographical narratives by an eighteenth-century Korean court lady. Lady Hyegyŏng's husband, an heir to the throne, was put to death by his own father, who locked him in a rice chest, where he suffocated after eight tortured days. This horrible death is merely the background for JaHyun Kim Haboush's sensitive contextualization of the tragic remaining life of Lady Hyegyŏng, who defied the Confucian conventions of her day and refused to commit suicide. Instead, she remained alive to protect the interests of her son, despite her own extremely vulnerable position. Not only is the historical and cultural testimony of the document an invaluable window on the time, but the writing itself—

being in Korean han'gŭl as opposed to classical Chinese—underscores the uniqueness of the document, a true woman's voice describing events in a man's political world. Haboush's elegant introduction explains the beauty of the language, the particularity of the genre, and the extraordinary human emotions that inspired this remarkable text.

Thus the eve of the nineteenth century found China, Japan, and Korea on very different trajectories with respect to women and gender relations. In China, debates about the more oppressive aspects of Confucianism were sharpening, especially among the elite in the Lower Yangzi, the most commercially developed region. In Japan, educational opportunity, encouraged by Confucian policies of the shogun's rule, broadened literacy for both men and women in local schools, while inheritance practices continued to free women as well as men for migration and occupational mobility in the growing commercial economy of the castle towns.[69] By contrast, Confucian influence had eroded much of the power women had previously enjoyed in family and political systems among the elite of Korea. In the mid-nineteenth century, as all three societies faced the military and economic incursions of European powers, only the Japanese government seized the initiative to shut out European colonial claims and declare an independent new nation with specific goals for building a "modern" polity that included educating women and putting them to work outside their homes.

During the first three decades of the Meiji period (1868–98) the abolition of the old class system and the creation of a new, emperor-centered government opened all kinds of opportunities for women. Fostered by the "enlightenment" ideology of liberal reformers, these included both education and jobs along with somewhat contradictory programs to promote female gentility and maternal responsibility. Even a mild self-critique of concubinage crept into reformers' rhetoric.

To some extent, these Meiji enlightenment programs were class-based opportunities that drew poor young women into factories while the well-off sent their daughters to school. The growth of political parties and constitutional study societies opened a space for female activists, who took to the lecture circuit to call for women's voting rights during the popular rights movement. Extensive translations of materials from the Meiji Restoration Enlightenment journal *Meiroku zasshi* and from other writing of the period make it possible to study urban life during the restoration decades (especially the last quarter of the nineteenth century) using primary sources, together with visual aids and sources on material life gathered from illustrations in textbooks and other sources.[70]

Women's political activism in Japan was abruptly curtailed in 1889 with the promulgation of a constitution that limited the franchise to propertied males. This was quickly followed, in 1890, by legislation that barred women from political meetings. The suppression of women's political voice culminated in 1898 with the Meiji Civil Code, which made universal a "samurai" kinship system that was strictly patrilineal, with ownership of property conveyed exclusively through primogeniture and limited to male heirs.[71]

To legitimize the new political environment, the Meiji government campaigned to promote the slogan "good wives, wise mothers" as the guiding principle of its gender policies. The slogan aimed to educate women as future mothers of the nation's voting citizens—a goal that became increasingly important after the growth of the postwar Japanese women's movement—but especially as future workers who would strengthen the nation. By focusing on women as wives and workers, the Meiji government was able to mobilize women for productive labor in agriculture and fill its new textile mills with female workers, who outnumbered their male counterparts by a ratio of 6 to 1.[72] Meiji policy was also aggressively pro-natalist, attacking traditional means of birth control, particularly the practice of sex-selective infanticide that was widespread in rural Japan during the Tokugawa period, and promoting high birth rates, especially after the losses in the 1905 war with Russia.[73] In her study of nationalism and rural Japanese women, Mariko Asano Tamanoi makes the point that *hataraki*, the term invoked by the state when mobilizing rural women to work, refers to both productive and reproductive labor.

In Korea during the same period, educational opportunities for women emerged primarily in Christian, especially Roman Catholic, missions. Women were drawn to Catholicism particularly because of affinities with Catholic mysticism and ritual drawn from their own shamanistic religious beliefs. Christianity became the most influential force in the education of Korean women during the late nineteenth century, a forum in which to examine the problem of inequality in gender relations through the tenets of religious faith. Korea's earliest feminist leaders, as in China and Japan, were men influenced by Western values. But Korea's first women's rights organization, Changyanghoe, was organized in 1898 under the leadership of upper-class widows. It was followed a year later by another women's rights group, the Yo-u-hoe (Association of Women Friends), established to protest concubinage.[74]

After Japan's 1905 victory over Russia, Korea became a Japanese protectorate, annexed within five years as a Japanese colony. Colonial occupation severely restricted the activities of Christians in Korea. New women's organizations, which flourished briefly between 1905 and 1910, were disbanded under the colonial regime, and the women's nationalist activities that continued went underground, sometimes with the support of the Christian church. The Patriotic Women's League, Korean Patriotic Women's Society, and at least one socialist women's organization survived underground.[75] From the beginning, in other words, as elsewhere in East Asia, the rise of feminism in Korea was inextricably linked to Korean nationalism. Early women's organizations in Korea solicited funds to pay off debts to Japan aimed at forestalling further colonial inroads. The March First movement of 1919, like its counterpart May Fourth movement in China the same year, brought female teachers and students to the streets to protest Japanese imperialism.[76]

While the Meiji success story was being written and Japan's influence in East Asia grew unabated, China's Manchu rulers attempted unsuccessfully to "enrich the country and strengthen the army" by a belated series of reforms that collapsed in the Revolution of 1911. Korea became caught between the competing demands of Japan's own rising expansionist agenda and China's defensive quest to retain its traditional sphere of influence. In retrospect, changes in the status of women in all three societies are clearly tied to the success of the nationalist programs with which they quickly became identified. Although women in Korea, China, and Japan were repeatedly forced to subordinate their own quest for political, social, and economic equality—itself a "modern" goal—to the aims of state-builders seeking strong military and economic systems, there can be little doubt that "Confucian" values supporting the power of mothers, the importance of education, and the significance of writing and publishing to a fully realized human existence (regardless of sex and gender) positioned women in all three societies to pursue "modern" goals aggressively. The context in which they pursued these goals, however, was radically different.

The course of the nineteenth century, in sum, put Chinese women and Japanese women on opposite trajectories. In China, the Opium War in 1842 had been followed a decade later by the Taiping Rebellion, which devastated China's Lower Yangzi heartland—the area that was at the forefront of educational and cultural opportunities for women during the eighteenth century. These events provoked a conservative response that slowed the pace of change in gender relations during the last half of the nineteenth century. By contrast, in Japan the Meiji government, founded in 1868, proclaimed women's education one of its foremost goals, anticipating by nearly half a century the promotion of similar programs in China. Japan's dispossessed samurai elite sent its own women into the factory workforce as part of the early industrialization drive, while in China respectable women stayed at home. Finally, Korea's own national agenda was put on hold when Japan annexed it in 1905, and it became part of the Japanese colonial empire in 1910, sealing the fate of an emerging reform movement in which feminists were active and driving it underground.

The conservative forces mobilized to resist changes in women's roles in China during the last half of the nineteenth century were catalyzed by the Taiping Rebellion. The earliest Taiping followers included large numbers of a subethnic minority group called the Hakkas, whose women were well known in the South because they did not bind their feet and worked side by side with their men in the fields. Perhaps because of this distinctive role of women in Hakka society, the Taiping ideology and its egalitarian vision included ideas about gender that contrasted sharply with many norms of the Han population. Taiping women, for instance, had a claim on land distribution although the share of land allocated to women may have differed from that given to men. According to the Taiping land system, "Land is to be distributed according to the number of persons [in a family], irrespective of sex," and "Men and women shall receive land on reaching the age of sixteen."[77] Taiping soldiers included all-female battalions whose members wore turbans on their heads, climbed cliffs barefoot, and were reputed to be more ferocious and braver than their male counterparts. The Taipings established their own civil service examination system in territories under their control; women were allowed to compete in special examinations. Women also held office, both in the army and in the government, of the Taiping kingdom.

Things were not as equal as they seemed, however—close examination of evidence about the role of women in the Taiping movement suggests that "egalitarianism" was not precisely the Taiping agenda. Taiping women who held official posts were often the concubines of the leaders to whom they reported. Most infamous is the extensive evidence that the Taiping leaders freely took captured women as sexual partners while insisting on a puritanical monogamous or (in some periods) celibate ideal for the rank and file. The Taipings' own policies toward women were enforced to some degree in the areas they occupied, with sometimes disastrous consequences for local residents. According to one diarist's account:

> The rebels came originally from the mountainous regions, and their womenfolk were used to farming, weaving, dyeing, and so forth. They did not realize that the women of Chin-ling [i.e., Nanjing] were not used to doing work like this. Thinking that whatever they [their women] could do the others could do too, they ordered them [the women of Chin-ling] to do their own share of the work in carrying rice, pounding grain, felling bamboo, digging ditches, carrying bricks, harvesting wheat and grain, carrying salt and water, and other such work. Since their bound feet made working hard for these [Chin-ling] women, they were ordered to loosen the bindings on their feet. They [the Taipings] did not realize that their feet would not grow again once they had been bound. For this reason, the Taipings were called ruthless.[78]

Reactions of the Lower Yangzi Han Chinese elite against the depredations of the Taipings could well have been conflated with a movement to valorize Han customs such as footbinding and female seclusion at the expense of other values associated with women's culture during the eighteenth century.

To further complicate this scene, the entry into China of foreign Christian missionaries after 1860 was accompanied by the opening of orphanages and schools devoted to the special care of women and girls. The Treaties of Tianjin, signed in 1858 with Britain, France, Russia, and the United States, granted missionaries the right to enter China's interior, and the Sino-French Treaty gave Catholic priests in particular freedom to preach and practice their religion anywhere in China and granted Chinese subjects freedom to convert to Christianity without punishment. Protestant missionaries quickly moved to claim similar privileges under the most-favored-nation agreement. Improving the status of women in China was one of the foremost goals of all missionaries, who condemned concubinage and female infanticide, discouraged converts from accepting arranged marriages, and launched campaigns against footbinding.

Criticism of footbinding was not new, of course. Chinese critics were writing outspoken attacks on the custom from the early nineteenth century. When formal organizations sponsored by foreigners (such as the Natural Foot Society, founded in Shanghai in 1895) began crusading in earnest, they were riding the crest of a reform movement that already had a sympathetic ear among educated Chinese.[79] Abandoned by the upper classes, the practice of footbinding rapidly lost its appeal among the urban working classes, among whom women's feet had never been so tightly bound because economic necessity required that they be able to move about to work.

The famed utopian reform leader Kang Youwei led a campaign to abolish footbinding in Guangdong Province in 1882, an action apparently triggered by his refusal to bind his eldest daughter's feet or perhaps by his revulsion at the memory of his sister's experiences.[80] Kang founded a society for the abolition of footbinding in Canton in 1894. His most compelling argument for ending footbinding was summed up in his famous 1898 reform proposals: "All countries have international relations, so that if one commits the slightest error the others ridicule and look down on it. Ours is definitely not a time of seclusion. Now China is narrow and crowded, has opium addicts and streets lined with beggars. Foreigners laugh at us for these things and criticize us for being barbarians. But there is nothing that makes us objects of ridicule so much as footbinding."[81] Foreign leadership may not have been critical in the movement to end footbinding in China. But as a result of the foreign presence, and the anti-imperialist sentiments it inspired in the Chinese elite, reform-minded Chinese men were able to appeal to a rising nationalistic consciousness to win support for their campaigns to abolish footbinding.

Where female leaders appear in early Chinese reform organizations, they almost invariably are inspired to action by foreign contact. But "foreign" does not necessarily mean "Western." Study in Japan was the critical experience for many young women who went to Tokyo as students on China's new education abroad programs. There they joined the Encompassing Love Society, which took as its guiding principle "the rescue of two hundred million women, the recovery of their original rights and the encouragement of their consciousness of the nation, so that they may fulfill their natural role of women citizens." The main way to do this, members agreed, was to work single-mindedly for women's education. The twenty female students in Tokyo who gathered for the organization's first meeting referred to each other as "women comrades." Like the handful of other women's organizations founded in the first decade of the century, this one was patriotic in its inspiration. Raising female literacy rates and economic skills to serve the nation were the goals of the few women leaders with education, many of them Christian converts. An article in the women's journal *Alarm Bell* argued that China's weakness in the international community was in part caused by the weakness of women. Men, whose energies could be devoted wholly to patriotic causes, were slowed and distracted by the necessity of supporting wives and families. The Women's Educational Protection Association, founded by a Cantonese feminist named Zhang Zhuzhun, took as its heroines Harriet Beecher Stowe and Florence Nightingale. *Uncle Tom's Cabin* was translated into Chinese, and its author lauded in the Chinese press during these years.[82] Upper-class women founded philanthropic organizations to assist victims of the North China floods in 1906 and 1907 and to lead campaigns to abolish opium smoking; nationalistic women's associations led boycotts of foreign goods and campaigns promoting the use of China-made products.

Finally, particularly in Japan and Shanghai, a few Chinese women became involved in radical revolutionary activity. The most famous of these was Qiu Jin, who was martyred in 1907 when she was captured and executed by Qing authorities following an abortive coup launched from the school where she and other revolutionaries had been working underground.[83] Two accounts of the life of Katō Shidzue, one autobiographical (*Facing Two Ways: The Story of My Life* by Baroness Shidzue Ishimoto) and the other a 1996 biography (Helen M. Hopper's *A New Woman of Japan: A Political Biography of Katō Shidzue, Transitions: Asia and Asian America*), show the linkages between the feminist movement in Japan and in the United States during the early part of the century. Katō traveled to New York and befriended Margaret Sanger, making the transition from the role of "good wife, wise mother" to "new woman" and political activist lobbying for women's reproductive rights.[84] Contrasting accounts of the lives of a radical woman in Japan (*Reflections on the Way to the Gallows: Rebel Women in Prewar Japan*, edited by Mikiso Hane) and a working-class woman in China (*A Daughter of Han: The Autobiography of a Chinese Working Woman* by Ida Pruitt) convey some of the complexity of that era for women.

THE TWENTIETH CENTURY

The end of the Qing and the eve of the Republican revolution in 1911 presents a complex picture of Chinese women, their position in the larger society in flux. Foreign influence, through Japanese schools and reform organizations founded by women with a foreign education, brought the ideas of Ellen Key to China. To create a strong nation, good wives, and wise mothers was the first essential. At the same time, the demands of a growing infant industry called on the labor of increasing numbers of women, as cottage industrial workers in the home, under contract to brokers, and in the new factories of the treaty ports and smaller cities. In some areas, like the silk-producing regions of Guangdong, women workers had fared well enough in the late Qing period to support themselves and their families and to use their income to delay or even refuse marriage. These young women, who purchased other young girls as adopted daughters to care for them in their old age, formed vegetarian sisterhoods and sometimes joined in lesbian marriages. Their example has been touted by some Western feminists as the ultimately successful rebellion against the Chinese family system. In any case, these women represent a very small regional minority in China; probably one whose customs were influenced by non-Han people at some earlier point in their history.

The study of Chinese women invites a comparison of the impact of capitalist and communist government policies on "traditional" family forms and gender relations. In China under Mao Zedong's revolutionary government, oppression of women by men was seen as an additional tyranny exclusively affecting women, which entitled them to special policies and protections during the transition to communism. Subscribing as they did to the Engelsian notion that women's economic status prefigured their political and social status, China's first communist leaders focused on getting women out of the home and into the workforce.

These policies had many unintended consequences and often succeeded for the wrong reasons. Women's status improved rapidly in urban areas, for example, in part because public housing available in cities enabled many women to live apart from their in-laws, freeing them to make their own reproductive decisions and enabling them to control more of their own income. The result was a fall in the birthrate and a rise in women's employment opportunities that gave Chinese women wage-earning power superior to that of U.S. women, by comparison with their menfolk.

By contrast, in rural areas where housing was still supplied by the family and where women working outside the home were subject to criticism by elders who disapproved of their mingling with men, younger women's status did not improve as rapidly, and their reproductive behavior remained largely under the watchful control of mothers-in-law.

These important differences between women in the cities and women in the countryside of China during the 1950s, 1960s, and 1970s laid the groundwork for the very different impact of the one-child family policy introduced aggressively by the reform government that acceded to power after Mao's death. In cities, the one-child policy was an almost immediate success because by the time of its initiation most women had long since voluntarily limited the size of their offspring sets to one or two children. Many other factors were also at play, of course, including the difficulty of finding good child care; the burdens of transporting children through cities where overstrained buses or bicycle transportation was the norm; and the double burden of full-time wage work and full-time housework. But in the countryside the government's effort to limit births, even with permitting two children to all rural families, had often dire consequences for women, caught as they were between the demands of local officials pressured to meet their "birth quotas" and the expectations of in-laws bent on seeing at least one son mature to carry on the family line. When the reform government also issued new laws permitting families to contract for land and keep the surplus produced on it, demands for labor and the expectations for childbearing young daughters-in-law skyrocketed.

The collision course between reform policies limiting births and reform policies promoting family farming in China's countryside resulted in tragic stories of forced late-term abortion, spousal abuse, and female infanticide, which revived among the customs of the countryside with brutal speed during the high tide of the birth control program. In the 1990s, as the policy waxed and waned and affluence permitted more and more couples to pay the fines required to escape the birth quotas, new problems presented themselves. Among these, one striking outcome is the possibility of sex-selective abortion, increasingly available through the (illegal) use of ultrasound and amniocentesis to determine the sex of a baby in utero.[85]

If the Chinese government for a time became what some scholars have referred to as a "biostate," regulating women's bodies by monitoring menstrual periods and allocating pregnancy permits, other East Asian modern states have also promoted policies affecting women's bodies and reproductive decisions. Recent campaigns have sought reparations for women coerced into sexual service for the Japanese military in Korea and Taiwan during World War II who are now willing to come forward, bringing the policies into the public eye.[86]

With respect to medicine and the law, state policies affecting women and their reproductive decisions have posed problems throughout East Asia. Policies of communist (China and North Korea) and capitalist (Hong Kong, Japan, South Korea, and Taiwan) regimes, often as an unintended consequence, have produced extreme differences in the social relation of the sexes. The impact of these policies is also compounded by the aftermath of British colonialism in Hong Kong, European "semicolonialism" in China's treaty port culture, and Japanese colonial occupation in Korea and Taiwan. These subjects are receiving considerable attention from a new generation of scholars studying postcoloniality.

In postcolonial South Korea, women have continued to confront the legacy of centuries of defense against foreign invasion by Mongols, Chinese, and Japanese as well as generations of recent colonial domination, which have sustained a masculinized rhetoric celebrating "righteous soldiers." South Korean family law since the end of the colonial period has been strongly patrilineal, in contradiction to the "formal gender equality" stipulated by the South Korean constitution.[87] As in Taiwan and other East Asian capitalist societies—and unlike the situation in China before the Communist Party's reform era—South Korean women have been well represented in the workforce, but their earning power is about half that of men, and they are concentrated in jobs customarily reserved for women, especially clerical work. Research on Taiwan, Japan, and Korea, and the continued problems women face in the Chinese family under socialism both before and after the current reform era, suggest that the relationship between economic development, earning power, and independence for women is not a simple one regardless of the political or economic system under which women live.[88]

In sum, East Asia has been the scene of some of the world's most dramatic state-directed efforts to transform gender relations: the "Confucian transformation of Korea" after the fourteenth century was no less dramatic than the Communist revolution that reshaped the lives of women in both China and North Korea. In between, the Japanese Meiji Restoration stands out as a third wrenching example of state-driven change in the social relation of the sexes in East Asia.[89] The best account of East Asian women's history in the period since the early Meiji is Sharon Sievers's masterly discussion *Women in Asia: Restoring Women to History,* edited by Barbara Ramusack and Sievers.

Notes

1. On family systems, see G. William Skinner, "Family Systems and Demographic Processes," in *Anthropological Demography: Toward a New Synthesis,* ed. David I. Kertzer and Tom Fricke (Chicago: University of Chicago Press, 1997), 53–114.
2. Maurice Freedman, *Lineage Organization in Southeastern China* (London: University of London, Athlone Press, 1958), 22.

3. Bernice J. Lee, "Female Infanticide in China," in *Women in China: Current Directions in Historical Scholarship,* ed. R. W. Guisso and S. Johannesen (Youngstown, N.Y.: Philo Press, 1981), 165, 168.

4. William Lavely and R. Bin Wong, "Revising the Malthusian Narrative: The Comparative Study of Population Dynamics in Late Imperial China," *Journal of Asian Studies* 57 (Aug. 1998): 736–38.

5. Rubie S. Watson, "The Named and the Nameless: Gender and Person in Chinese Society," *American Ethnologist* 13, no. 4 (1986): 619–31.

6. T'ung-tsu Chü, *Law and Society in Traditional China* (Paris: Mouton, 1961), 104, quoted in Rubie Watson, "Women's Property in Republican China: Rights and Practices," *Republican China* 10 (Nov. 1984): 1–12; Kathryn Bernhardt, *Women and Property in China, 960–1949* (Stanford: Stanford University Press, 1999).

7. Lavely and Wong, "Revising the Malthusian Narrative."

8. Freedman, *Lineage Organization in Southeastern China.*

9. Shikibu Murasaki, *The Tale of Genji (Genji monogatari),* trans. Edward Seidensticker (New York: Alfred A. Knopf, 1976); see also Ivan Morris, *The World of the Shining Prince: Court Life in Ancient Japan* (New York: Alfred A. Knopf, 1975).

10. Takao Sofue, "Family and Interpersonal Relationships in Early Japan," in *Religion and the Family in East Asia,* ed. G. A. DeVos and T. Sofue (Berkeley: University of California Press, 1986), 217–26.

11. Saikaku Ihara, *The Life of an Amorous Woman,* trans. Ivan Morris (1686, repr. New York: Directions, 1963).

12. Anne Walthall, "The Life Cycle of Farm Women," in *Recreating Japanese Women, 1600–1945,* ed. G. L. Bernstein (Berkeley: University of California Press, 1991), 54.

13. Joyce Chapman Lebra, "Women in an All-Male Industry: The Case of Sake Brewer Tatsu'uma Kiyo," in *Recreating Japanese Women,* ed. Bernstein, 131–50; Walthall, "The Life Cycle of Farm Women," 42–70; Howard S. Hibbett, *The Floating World in Japanese Fiction* (New York: Oxford University Press, 1959).

14. Walthall, "The Life Cycle of Farm Women," 60.

15. Jennifer Robertson, "The Shingaku Woman: Straight from the Heart," in *Recreating Japanese Women,* ed. Bernstein, 88–107; Walthall, "The Life Cycle of Farm Women," 52, 63.

16. JaHyun Kim Haboush, "The Confucianization of Korean Society," in *The East Asia Region: Confucian Heritage and Its Modern Adaptation,* ed. G. Rozman (Princeton: Princeton University Press, 1991), 84–110.

17. Haboush, "The Confucianization of Korean Society," 98–99.

18. Martina Deuchler, *The Confucian Transformation of Korea* (Cambridge: Harvard University Press, 1992), 231–81; Steven Harrell, "Introduction: Civilizing Projects and the Reaction to Them," in *Cultural Encounters on China's Ethnic Frontiers,* ed. Steven Harrell (Seattle: University of Washington Press, 1995), 3–36.

19. Deuchler, *The Confucian Transformation of Korea,* 267.

20. Laurel Kendall, *Shamans, Housewives, and Other Restless Spirits: Women in Korean Ritual Life* (Honolulu: University of Hawaii Press, 1985), 178.

21. Francesca Bray, *The Rice Economies: Technology and Development in Asian Societies* (Berkeley: University of California Press, 1994), 155, citing Thomas C. Smith, *The Agrarian Origins of Modern Japan* (Stanford: Stanford University Press, 1959).

22. Walthall, "The Life Cycle of Farm Women," 57; Kathleen S. Uno, "Women and Changes in the Household Division of Labor" in *Recreating Japanese Women,* ed. Bernstein, 17–41; Lebra, "Women in an All-Male Industry."

23. Susan B. Hanley and Kozo Yamamura, *Economic and Demographic Change in Prein-dustrial Japan, 1600–1800* (Princeton: Princeton University Press, 1977), 254–55; Mikiso Hane, *Peasants, Rebels, and Outcastes: The Underside of Modern Japan* (New York: Pantheon Books, 1982); Patricia E. Tsurumi, *Factory Girls: Women in the Thread Mills of Meiji Japan* (Princeton: Princeton University Press, 1990), 191–92.

24. Susan Mann, "Household Handicrafts and State Policy in Qing Times," in *To Achieve Security and Wealth: The Qing Imperial State and the Economy, 1644–1911*, ed. J. K. Leonard and J. R. Watt (Ithaca: Cornell University East Asia Program, 1992), 75–95.

25. Miriam Silverberg, "The Modern Girl as Militant," in *Recreating Japanese Women*, ed. Bernstein, 239–66.

26. Jennifer Holmgren, "Observations on Marriage and Inheritance Practices in Early Mongol and Yuan Society, with Particular Reference to the Levirate," *Journal of Asian History* 20, no. 2 (1986): 127–92.

27. Barbara Pillsbury, "Being Female in a Muslim Minority in China," in *Women in the Muslim World*, ed. L. Beck and N. Keddie (Cambridge: Harvard University Press, 1978), 651–73.

28. Pamela Kyle Crossley, *The Manchus* (Oxford: Basil Blackwell, 1997); Evelyn S. Rawski, *The Last Emperors: A Social History of Qing Imperial Institutions* (Berkeley: University of California Press, 1998); Pamela Kyle Crossley, *Orphan Warriors: Three Manchu Generations and the End of the Qing World* (Princeton: Princeton University Press, 1990), 80, quotation on 91.

29. Sow-Theng Leong, *Migration and Ethnicity in Chinese History: Hakkas, Pengmin, and Their Neighbors* (Stanford: Stanford University Press, 1997); Harrell, "Introduction"; Hiroko Yokoyama, "Uxorilocal Marriage among the Bai of the Dali Basin, Yunnan," in *Perspectives on Chinese Society: Anthropological Views from Japan*, ed. M. Suenari, J. S. Eades, and C. Daniels (Tokyo: Tokyo University of Foreign Studies, 1995), 182–90; John Robert Shepherd, *Statecraft and Political Economy on the Taiwan Frontier, 1600–1800* (Stanford: Stanford University Press, 1993).

30. Only two women are considered to have ruled China as emperors: the mythic goddess-ruler Nü Gua and the Emperor Wu of Tang, who usurped the throne and proclaimed her own dynasty. The female ruler of China who is best known in the West, the late-Qing Empress Dowager Cixi (Tz'u-hsi), ruled not as empress but as regent, first for her son and then for her nephew (the Guangxu Emperor was her sister's son).

31. Kathryn Bernhardt, *Women and Property in China, 960–1949*; Chü, *Law and Society in Traditional China*.

32. Yu-shih Chen, "The Historical Template of Pan Chao's Nü Chieh," *T'oung Pao* 82, no. 4–5 (1996): 229–57.

33. Nancy Lee Swann, *Pan Chao: Foremost Woman Scholar of China* (New York: Century, 1932).

34. Lien-sheng Yang, "Female Rulers in Imperial China," in *Excursions in Sinology*, ed. Lien-sheng Yang (Cambridge: Harvard University Press, 1969), 41.

35. Arthur F. Wright, "Sui Yang-Ti: Personality and Stereotype," in *Confucianism and Chinese Civilization*, ed. A. F. Wright (New York: Athenium, 1964), 161.

36. Translated in Beatrice Spade, "The Education of Women in China during the Southern Dynasties," *Journal of Asian History* 1, no. 13 (1979): 33.

37. Translated into English in I-ch'ing Liu, *Shih-shuo Hsin-yü: A New Account of Tales of the World*, trans. Richard B. Mather (Minneapolis: University of Minnesota Press, 1976).

38. Spade, "The Education of Women in China," 31–32.

39. Ibid., 19–20.

40. Ibid., 24, 25, 28–29; Kathryn A. Tsai, "The Chinese Buddhist Monastic Order for Women: The First Two Centuries," in *Women in China*, ed. Guisso and Johannesen, 12; Kathryn A. Tsai, trans., *Lives of the Nuns: Biographies of Chinese Buddhist Nuns from the Fourth to Sixth Centuries* (Honolulu: University of Hawaii Press, 1994).

41. David G. Johnson, *The Medieval Chinese Oligarchy* (Boulder: Westview Press, 1977).

42. Denis Twitchett, "Hsüan-tsung (reign 712–56)," in *The Cambridge History of China*, Vol. 3: *Sui and T'ang China, 589–906, Part I*, ed. Denis Twitchett (New York: Cambridge University Press, 1979), 371.

43. Joan R. Piggott, *The Emergence of Japanese Kingship* (Stanford: Stanford University Press, 1997).

44. Jeffrey P. Mass, *Lordship and Inheritance in Early Medieval Japan: A Study of the Kamakura Sōryō System* (Stanford: Stanford University Press, 1989), especially 15–19, 48–51, quotations on 16 and 49.

45. Suzanne Cahill, "Performers and Female Taoist Adepts: Hsi Wang Mu as the Patron Deity of Women in Medieval China," *Journal of the American Oriental Society* 106, no. 1 (1986): 157; Edward H. Schafer, *The Divine Woman: Dragon Ladies and Rain Maidens* (San Francisco: North Point Press, 1980).

46. Yung-Chung Kim, *Women of Korea: A History from Ancient Times to 1945: Han'guk Yosong-Sa*, written under the direction of the Committee for the Compilation of the History of Korean Women, abridged and translated ed. (Seoul: Ewha Womans University Press, 1982).

47. Priscilla Ching Chung, *Palace Women in the Northern Sung, 960–1126*, Monographies du T'oung Pao, vol. 12 (Leiden: E. J. Brill, 1981); Patricia Buckley Ebrey, *The Inner Quarters: Marriage and the Lives of Chinese Women in the Sung Period* (Berkeley: University of California Press, 1993).

48. Holmgren, "Observations on Marriage," 178.

49. Laurence J. C. Ma, *Commercial Development and Urban Change in Sung China (960–1279), Michigan Geographical Publication* 6 (Ann Arbor: Department of Geography, University of Michigan, 1971), 143.

50. "A City of Cathay," vol. 2 of the series *Treasure the Treasures* (Santa Clara: Lee and Lee Communications, 1998), available at http://www.culturalcafe.com. Although this eighteenth-century version of the original handscroll contains anachronistic embellishments, these do not compromise its value for teachers.

51. Holmgren, "Observations on Marriage."

52. Ebrey, *The Inner Quarters.*

53. Quoted in Howard S. Levy, *Chinese Footbinding: The History of a Curious Erotic Custom* (New York: Walton Rawls, 1966), 48.

54. H. Paul Varley, trans., *A Chronicle of Gods and Sovereigns: Jinnō Shōtōki of Kitabatake Chikafusa* (New York: Columbia University Press, 1980).

55. Ki-baik Lee, *A New History of Korea*, trans. Edward W. Wagner (Cambridge: Harvard-Yenching Institute, Harvard University Press, 1984), 155–62.

56. Deuchler, *The Confucian Transformation of Korea;* Carter J. Eckert, Ki-baik Lee, Young Ick Lew, Michael Robinson, and Edward W. Wagner, *Korea Old and New: A History* (Seoul: Ilchokak for the Korea Institute, Harvard University, 1990), 124–31.

57. Judith Berling, "Religion and Popular Culture: The Management of Moral Capital in 'The Romance of the Three Teachings,'" in *Popular Culture in Late Imperial China*, ed. D. Johnson, A. J. Nathan, and E. S. Rawski (Berkeley: University of California Press, 1985), 198.

58. Willard J. Peterson, *Bitter Gourd: Fang I-chih and the Impetus for Intellectual Change* (New Haven: Yale University Press, 1979), 26.

59. Peterson, *Bitter Gourd*, 143.

60. Patrick Hanan, *The Chinese Vernacular Story* (Cambridge: Harvard University Press, 1981), 89–90.

61. Robert E. Hegel, *The Novel in Seventeenth-Century China* (New York: Columbia University Press, 1981); Cecilia Segawa Seigle, *Yoshiwara: The Glittering World of the Japanese Courtesan* (Honolulu: University of Hawaii Press, 1993).

62. Robert H. van Gulik, *Sexual Life in Ancient China: A Preliminary Survey of Chinese Sex and Society from ca. 1500 B.C. till 1644 A.D.* (Leiden: E. J. Brill, 1961).

63. van Gulik, *Sexual Life in Ancient China;* James Cahill, "The Three Changs, Yangzhou Beauties, and the Manchu Court," *Orientations* (Oct. 1996): 59–68.

64. Joanna F. Handlin, "Lü K'un's New Audience: The Influence of Women's Literacy on Sixteenth-Century Thought," in *Women in Chinese Society,* ed. M. Wolf and R. Witke (Stanford: Stanford University Press, 1975), 13–38. For examples of illustrated women's texts, see Katherine Carlitz, "The Social Uses of Female Virtue in Late Ming Editions of *Lienü Zhuan,*" *Late Imperial China* 12, no. 2 (1991): 117–48.

65. Grace Fong, "Record of Past Karma, by Ji Xian," in *Under Confucian Eyes: Texts on Gender in Chinese History,* ed. S. Mann and Yu-Yin Cheng (Berkeley: University of California Press, 2001), 135–46. Fong's translation of an autobiographical essay by the woman poet Ji Xian (fl. 1650s) is one of the few known extant examples of female autobiography in classical Chinese. With its powerful descriptions of dreams, visions, and personal illness, it reveals the emotional turmoil of a young woman torn between her parents' plans for her marriage and her own spiritual quest. A similar conflict between a young woman's spiritual devotions and her parents' desire for her to lead a "normal" married life is analyzed in Ann Waltner's article on the seventeenth-century Daoist mystic Tanyangzi: "T'an-yang-tzu and Wang Shih-chen: Visionary and Bureaucrat in the Late Ming," *Late Imperial China* 8, no. 1 (1987): 105–33.

66. Marina H. Sung, "The Chinese Lieh-nü Tradition," in *Women in China,* ed. Guisso and Johannesen, 71.

67. Paul S. Ropp, *Dissent in Early Modern China: Ju-lin wai-shih and Ch'ing Social Criticism* (Ann Arbor: University of Michigan Press, 1981).

68. Robertson, "The Shingaku Woman"; Patricia Fister, "Female *Bunjin:* The Life of Poet-Painter Ema Saikō," in *Recreating Japanese Women,* ed. Bernstein, 108–30.

69. Yamakawa Kikue's *Women of the Mito Domain: Recollections of Samurai Family Life,* trans. Kate Wildman Nakai (Tokyo: University of Tokyo Press, 1992) offers a woman's perspective on the end of the Tokugawa era and the beginning of Meiji. The extensive introduction and copious notes by the translator, a noted scholar of the late Tokugawa period, make the book accessible to readers who are unfamiliar with Japanese history, introducing everything from household budgets to childhood education to marriage, divorce, and family relationships. In *The Weak Body of a Useless Woman: Matsuo Taseko and the Meiji Restoration* (Chicago: University of Chicago Press, 1998), Ann Walthall examines the Meiji restoration from the vantage point of a female writer and "peasant activist." The daughter of a village headman, Taseko traveled to Kyoto, the seat of imperial power, early in the 1860s and was on the scene in 1868 when the restoration took place. Her poems and other writings about the politics of the era enable a reader to bridge the gulf between "public" and "private" spheres. Finally, a collection of biographies, including the legendary story of an early shamaness ruler and

ending in the mid-twentieth century, makes available in English short biographies of Japanese women of the past: *Heroic with Grace: Legendary Women of Japan,* ed. Chieko Irie Mulhern (Armonk: M. E. Sharpe, 1991).

70. William Reynolds Braisted, trans. and ed., *Meiroku Zasshi: Journal of the Japanese Enlightenment* (Cambridge: Harvard University Press, 1976); Eiichi Kiyooka, trans. and ed., *Fukuzawa Yukichi on Japanese Women: Selected Works* (Tokyo: University of Tokyo Press, 1988); Susan B. Hanley, *Everyday Things in Premodern Japan: The Hidden Legacy of Material Culture* (Berkeley: University of California Press, 1997); Jūkichi Inouye, *Home Life in Tokyo* (1910, repr. London: KPI Limited, 1985); Edward Seidensticker, *Low City, High City: Tokyo from Edo to the Earthquake: How the Shogun's Ancient Capital Became a Great Modern City, 1867–1923* (New York: Alfred A. Knopf, 1983); Sharon L. Sievers, *Flowers in Salt: The Beginnings of Feminist Consciousness in Modern Japan* (Stanford: Stanford University Press, 1983).

71. Robert J. Smith, "Making Village Women into 'Good Wives and Wise Mothers'" in Prewar Japan," *Journal of Family History* 8 (Spring 1983): 70–84.

72. Sharon H. Nolte and Sally Ann Hastings, "The Meiji State's Policy toward Women, 1890–1910," in *Recreating Japanese Women,* ed. Bernstein, 151–74; Sievers, *Flowers in Salt.*

73. Thomas C. Smith, *Nakahara: Family Farming and Population in a Japanese Village, 1717–1830* (Stanford: Stanford University Press, 1977); William R. LaFleur, *Liquid Life: Abortion and Buddhism in Japan* (Princeton: Princeton University Press, 1992).

74. Kyung Ae Park, *Women and Social Change in South and North Korea: Marxist and Liberal Perspectives,* Michigan State University Working Papers no. 231 (June) (Lansing: Michigan State University, 1992).

75. Kim, *Women of Korea;* Park, *Women and Social Change.*

76. Elaine H. Kim and Chungmoo Choi, eds., *Dangerous Women: Gender and Korean Nationalism* (New York: Routledge, 1998), introduction.

77. Vincent Y. C. Shih, *The Taiping Ideology: Its Sources, Interpretations, and Influences* (Seattle: University of Washington Press, 1967), 47.

78. Shih, *The Taiping Ideology,* 65.

79. Although the nineteenth century is pretty much a wasteland in the study of gender issues in Chinese history, a remarkable resource is available: the translated and annotated autobiography of Zeng Jifen (1852–1942), one of the daughters of the official Zeng Guofan, who was a leader of China's mid-century "Restoration" aimed at economic and political recovery following the Opium War and the Taiping Rebellion. Chi-fen [Zeng Jifen] Tseng, *Testimony of a Confucian Woman: The Autobiography of Mrs. Nie Zeng Jifen, 1852–1942,* trans. T. L. Kennedy (Athens: University of Georgia Press, 1993).

80. Charlotte Beahan, "In the Public Eye: Women in Early Twentieth-Century China," in *Women in China,* ed. Guisso and Johannesen, 215–38.

81. Levy, *Chinese Footbinding,* 72.

82. Beahan, "In the Public Eye," 216, 217.

83. Mary Backus Rankin, "The Emergence of Women at the End of the Ch'ing: The Case of Ch'iu Chin," in *Women in Chinese Society,* ed. Wolf and Witke, 39–66. See also the autobiography of another revolutionary: Ping-Ying Hsieh, *Autobiography of a Chinese Girl,* trans. Tsui Chi, intro. Elisabeth Croll (1943, repr. London: Pandora, 1986).

84. See also Barbara Rose, *Tsuda Umeko and Women's Education in Japan* (New Haven: Yale University Press, 1992), the biography of Tsuda Umeko, founder of one of the

earliest girls' schools in Meiji Japan, and Haru Matsukata Reischauer, *Samurai and Silk: A Japanese and American Heritage* (Cambridge: Harvard University Press, 1986).

85. Elisabeth Croll, *Changing Identities of Chinese Women: Rhetoric, Experience and Self-Perception in Twentieth-Century China* (London: Zed Books, 1995); Harriet Evans, *Women and Sexuality in China: Female Sexuality and Gender since 1949* (New York: Continuum, 1997).

86. On Korea, a special issue of the journal *positions* (Spring 1997) analyzes the problem of "comfort women" impressed into sexual service during the Japanese occupation of Korea. The issue includes articles on gender and colonialism, women and war, and the cultural context of rape and shame in East Asia (which, demonstrably, varies from one culture to another). There is also artwork by victims and an extensive bibliography. For other historical studies of sex work and female entertainers in East Asia, see Gail Hershatter, *Dangerous Pleasures: Prostitution and Modernity in Twentieth-Century Shanghai* (Berkeley: University of California Press, 1997); Seigle, *Yoshiwara;* and Liza Crihfield Dalby, *Geisha* (Berkeley: University of California Press, 1998). A contemporary work is Anne Allison, *Nightwork: Sexuality, Pleasure, and Corporate Masculinity in a Tokyo Hostess Club* (Chicago: University of Chicago Press, 1994).

87. Seungsook Moon, "Begetting the Nation: The Androcentric Discourse of National History and Tradition in South Korea," in *Dangerous Women,* ed. Kim and Choi, 33–66.

88. For Taiwan see Susan Greenhalgh, "Sexual Stratification: The Other Side of 'Growth with Equity' in East Asia," *Population and Development Review* 11, no. 2 (1985): 264–314. For Japan see Mary C. Brinton, *Women and the Economic Miracle: Gender and Work in Postwar Japan* (Berkeley: University of California Press, 1993); Jeannie Lo, *Office Ladies, Factory Women: Life and Work at a Japanese Company* (Armonk: M. E. Sharpe, 1990); and Dorinne K. Kondo, *Crafting Selves: Power, Gender, and Discourses of Identity in a Japanese Workplace* (Chicago: University of Chicago Press, 1990). For Korea see Seung-Kyung Kim, *Class Struggle or Family Struggle? The Lives of Women Factory Workers in South Korea* (New York: Cambridge University Press, 1997); and Kyung Ae Park, "Women and Revolution in North Korea," *Pacific Affairs* 65, no. 4 (1992): 527–43. For China under socialism see Margery Wolf, *Revolution Postponed: Women in Contemporary China* (Stanford: Stanford University Press, 1985); Emily Honig and Gail Hershatter, *Personal Voices: Chinese Women in the 1980s* (Stanford: Stanford University Press, 1988); and Xiaojiang Li, "Economic Reform and the Awakening of Chinese Women's Collective Consciousness," in *Engendering China: Women, Culture, and the State,* ed. C. K. Gilmartin, Gail Hershatter, L. Rofel, and T. White (Cambridge: Harvard University Press, 1994), 360–82. For a comparative project on industrialization and women workers in China and Japan consult Emily Honig, *Sisters and Strangers: Women in the Shanghai Cotton Mills, 1919–1949* (Stanford: Stanford University Press, 1986); Barbara Molony, "Activism among Women in the Taishō Textile Industry," in *Recreating Japanese Women,* ed. Bernstein, 217–38; and Tsurumi, *Factory Girls.*

89. On the Confucian transformation of the family in Yi dynasty Korea see Deuchler, *The Confucian Transformation of Korea.* On the nationalist modernization movement in Meiji Japan and the "samuraization of the family," see Sievers, *Flowers in Salt;* Mikiso Hane, ed. and trans., *Reflections on the Way to the Gallows: Rebel Women in Prewar Japan* (Berkeley: University of California Press, 1988); and Smith, "Making Village Women into 'Good Wives.'" On the family and gender revolution in twentieth-century China see Kazuko Ono, *Chinese Women in a Century of Revolution, 1850–1950,* trans. Joshua A.

Fogel et al. (Stanford: Stanford University Press, 1989); Judith Stacey, *Patriarchy and Socialist Revolution in China* (Berkeley: University of California Press, 1983); Elisabeth Croll, *Feminism and Socialism in China* (London: Routledge and Kegan Paul, 1978); Kay Ann Johnson, *Women, the Family, and Peasant Revolution in China* (Chicago: University of Chicago Press, 1983); and Christina Kelley Gilmartin, *Engendering the Chinese Revolution: Radical Women, Communist Politics, and Mass Movements in the 1920s* (Berkeley: University of California Press, 1995).

Appendix: Working with Standard Textbooks to Integrate Women and Gender into the Curriculum

Of all the standard textbooks on East Asian history, only one provides a comprehensive treatment of the histories of the three main national cultures of East Asia (China, Japan, and Korea): *East Asia: Tradition and Transformation* by John King Fairbank, Edwin O. Reischauer, and Albert M. Craig.[1] The Fairbank text, which in many respects is ideally suited to the study of East Asia, impedes fruitful discussions of women and gender, especially because of its introductory comments about the "authoritarian family system" (16). The Fairbank textbook further compounds problems of omission because the limited treatment of women is dominated by negative information. Such major changes as urbanization, for example, are linked to a decline in the status of Chinese women by associating urbanization with the spread of footbinding (142–43). The narrative thus subtly invites students to imagine a backward culture where women were increasingly oppressed, even in the face of economic development. Because Chinese civilization was hegemonic through much of the region's history, the status of women in China serves as a proxy for ideas about women throughout East Asia. Nor is the reader's attention drawn to the fact that neither Korean nor Japanese women ever professed interest in footbinding.

According to the Fairbankian narrative, it was only the spread of Western-style industrialization, which brought with it new economic opportunities for the young and for women, that caused the breakdown of the old family system (765), thus liberating women slowly from oppressive traditions. Subsequent passing references to the "emancipation" of Chinese women mention the May Fourth and New Culture movements in the second decade of the twentieth century and the new marriage law of 1950 (771, 910). These bits of narrative offer the opportunity to situate changes in the position of women in the cultural context of changes within China. But they mainly describe a society where gender relations change following Western models of individual liberation. This is a model most students will be predisposed to accept unless they are presented with other ways of understanding the situation.

In this same textbook's discussion of Japan, mention is made of the liter-

From *Women's History in Global Perspective, Volume 2,* edited by Bonnie G. Smith. Copyright © 2005 by the American Historical Association.

ary achievements of court ladies writing in Japanese (357), who were not subject to the constraints of Confucian thought embedded in classical Chinese
writing, the favored medium of court nobles. (Teachers should note that this
brief discussion is not even listed in the index under "women," which means
that an interested reader might pass it up entirely.) Japanese women do not
appear again until the Tokugawa period, when the textbook discusses wom-
en in the entertainment quarters of Tokugawa cities, the famous geisha (423–
24, 427). The remaining references to women focus on the expanding opportunities for women's education, beginning in the late nineteenth century
under the modernizing Meiji government (534), with major advancements
resulting from the U.S. occupation following World War II (834). It concludes
by pointing to the promise of university-educated women for the future of
democracy in Japan (855). Again, the implicit model for change is the West.
The chapters on Korea in this textbook do not mention women at all.

In confronting such a textbook, one approach for the teacher is to problematize the false dichotomy between "tradition" and "modernity." That is, a
teacher could use the bound foot in China, the geisha in Japan, and the general absence of women from the entire discussion of Korea to help students
notice that the images presented invite either a negative or a dismissive view
of women in these societies. The teacher could then use materials from the
preceding discussion (on city life in Song China, or the material world of the
household and community, or, in the case of Japan and China, on women's
writing during the centuries after 1600 or earlier) to show how distorted the
textbook-induced image of "tradition" is. Having established that things were
a great deal more complicated than the textbook suggests, the teacher can
then move to a discussion of the changing position of women in the nineteenth
and twentieth centuries, showing how "tradition" informs "modernity."

In Chinese "traditional" society, for example, mothers were extremely
powerful, controlling household accounts, bonding intensely with their sons,
bossing their daughters-in-law, and holding up the moral standard by which
most men were judged. The May Fourth student activists—male and female—
and their successors in China's new culture movement advocated independence for young women, free mate choice, and neolocal residence for young
married couples. They also ridiculed bound feet and lobbied for freedom of
divorce. These "modern" ideas, of course, were extremely threatening to the
status and authority of older women. Meanwhile, many younger women—
having declared their economic independence and freedom from arranged
marriage—found themselves in an economy with no job market for career
women and no moral codes to protect unmarried women's sexual or social
experiments with independent life. So the "emancipation" of women in mod-

ern China becomes a problem with complex and not-easily-defined consequences for women of all ages.[2]

EXAMPLES OF GENDER-FRIENDLY TEXTBOOKS

Within the China field itself, three history textbooks are conducive to the study
of women and gender. The *Cambridge Illustrated History of China*, written and
designed by Patricia Buckley Ebrey, presents more material on women than
any of its counterparts. Ebrey, the author of a prize-winning book on women
in the Song dynasty, brings gender relations and family history into her discussion throughout her chronological narrative, with plenty of allusions to
historical change in notions of physical beauty, ritual status, and fictional
images. Lloyd Eastman's *Family, Fields, and Ancestors* and Jonathan Spence's *The
Search for Modern China* both conveniently begin their narratives in the seventeenth century, which is the point when women as writers enter China's historical record in significant numbers for the first time. All three textbooks may
readily be supplemented with Dorothy Ko's *Teachers of the Inner Chambers*, a
study of women and urban print culture to stress the importance of printing
and publishing for gender relations and especially for elite women.

Spence broaches the subject in his introduction and later ventures to suggest that the Chinese literati's specialized mastery of textual research during
the eighteenth century created yet another tier of stratification within the highly
educated literate elite that probably discriminated against women (11, 105).
This is the sort of observation that one is unlikely to find even in specialized
monographs devoted to the subject of literati culture. On page 39, Spence
mentions that Manchu women were forbidden to bind their feet, offering a fine
window for discussions of gender performance, politics, class, and ethnicity. (See
also page 173, where he notes that Hakka women's unbound feet provided a
powerful association with the Taiping rebel force.) And on page 96, Spence
offers an intelligent summary of the complex implications of skewed sex ratios,
universal marriage for females, and the pool of single poor men.

When it comes to the modern period, however, readers of these three
works will encounter the same problems that plague the Fairbank textbook.
Ebrey presents the twentieth century as a rupture marking a break from "assumptions about women's place in society that had gone unquestioned for
centuries" (279) and invites readers to view the twentieth-century agenda as
one aimed at "liberating women." Apart from a subsequent brief discussion
of the "egalitarian" marriage policies of the Communist Party, her textbook
does not refer to women again, except for a single illustration. On page 209,
Spence appears to place Western women in a vanguard from which they urged
on their backward Chinese counterparts toward enlightenment and improved

ideas about "hygiene, cuisine, and child raising." This same narrative goes on to introduce the physicians Ida Kahn and Mary Stone, both educated at the University of Michigan, as paragons of China's "new woman."

Spence does a considerably better job with the modern era. On page 317 he stresses "May Fourth consciousness" and indigenous influences that radicalized young women of the 1920s. And his discussion of Ibsen's play *A Doll House* and its impact on Chinese audiences, both male and female, offers a nice opportunity to do some cross-cultural comparison (317–18). Entering the Maoist era, Spence shows how (375) women's issues were prominent in Mao's own conception of liberation in the countryside (he saw women subject to four, rather than three, forms of oppression). This opens the way for the discussion of new marriage laws (375–76), which were not new with the communists because the Republican government introduced a new law in 1930. On pages 431–32 Spence weighs the advantages of factory labor for poor rural women in an intelligent assessment of costs and benefits. (This would be a fine opening for supplementary reading in Emily Honig's *Sisters and Strangers*.) On pages 685–87, we have a chance to examine some of the long-term fallout from efforts to improve women's economic position while controlling their fertility in Spence's brief but cogent discussion of the birth planning programs, the one-child family policy, and their costs to women. On page 708, Spence offers a discussion of the continued high cost of marriage and other complications of divorce in more affluent times. Finally, Spence mentions some important women's issues in the reform era, including complaints (neglected in most accounts) about sexual exploitation first voiced by Wei Jingsheng in the democracy movement that began in the late 1970s (663).

Eastman's textbook follows a slightly more anthropological format, with plenty of attention to family structure and family relationships in its early part and intelligent discussion of women's liberation issues in the modern period. This format, too, poses problems. It posits a timeless "traditional" family that is juxtaposed against a dynamic and progressive "modern" family, the latter introduced to modernity by influence from the West.

Because this kind of thinking about non-Western cultures is so deeply rooted in the popular consciousness of most students it is difficult to counteract. One approach would be to stress class difference and focus on elite women and elite families, emphasizing access to education and writing for upper-class women and examining the effects of this on women's roles and status, and on gender relations.[3] Another strategy might be to introduce a unit on work or household production and talk about how economic responsibilities and earning power affect gender relations. The best source for this purpose is Francesca Bray, *Technology and Gender: Fabrics of Power in Late Imperial China.*

Notes

1. John K. Fairbank, Edwin O. Reischauer, and Albert M. Craig, *East Asia: Tradition and Transformation* (1973, repr. Boston: Houghton Mifflin, 1978). The only other standard textbook treating all of East Asia is Rhoads Murphey, *East Asia: A New History* (New York: Addison-Wesley Educational Publishers, 1997). Murphey includes a discussion of family and marriage (159–62). Because he generalizes from the Chinese case to all of "East Asia," however, he erases the cultural and historical diversity emphasized here. More valuable is *Asia in Western and World History: A Guide for Teaching,* edited by Ainslie T. Embree and Carol Gluck (Gurgaon, India: Spring Books, 2004), a dense guide that supplies a great deal of bibliography and conceptual material for treating East Asian cultures in historical perspective. Finally, overviews presented in *The East Asian Region: Confucian Heritage and Its Modern Adaptation,* edited by G. Rozman (Princeton: Princeton University Press, 1991), with contributions by leading scholars in the field, offer concise and intelligent commentaries on topics relevant to gender and history.

2. A marvelous discussion of the complexity of ideas about gender and sexuality in Japan's modern transition is found in Carol Gluck's brilliant essay, "Japan's Modernities, 1850–1990s," in *Asia in Eastern and World History* (ed. Embree and Gluck). A brief treatment of the changes in the Korean family system under the influence of Confucianism beginning in the mid-fourteenth century stresses the costs to women and their status, further complicating the notion that "traditional" family systems in East Asia are oppressive to women. JaHyun Kim Haboush, "The Confucianization of Korean Society," in *The East Asia Region,* ed. Rozman.

3. Joanna F. Handlin, "Lü K'un's New Audience: The Influence of Women's Literacy on Sixteenth-Century Thought," in *Women in Chinese Society,* ed. M. Wolf and R. Witke (Stanford: Stanford University Press, 1975); Dorothy Ko, *Teachers of the Inner Chambers: Women's Culture in Seventeenth-Century China* (Stanford: Stanford University Press, 1994); Susan Mann, *Precious Records: Women in China's Long Eighteenth Century* (Stanford: Stanford University Press, 1997).

BIBLIOGRAPHY OF ADDITIONAL SOURCES

Bray, Francesca. *Technology and Gender: Fabrics of Power in Late Imperial China.* Berkeley: University of California Press, 1997.

Eastman, Lloyd E. *Family, Fields, and Ancestors: Constancy and Change in China's Social and Economic History, 1550–1949.* New York: Oxford University Press, 1988.

Ebrey, Patricia Buckley, ed. *Chinese Civilization and Society: A Sourcebook.* New York: Free Press, 1993.

Gernet, Jacques. *Daily Life in China on the Eve of the Mongol Invasion, 1250–1276,* translated by H. M. Wright. London: George Allen and Unwin, 1962.

Greenhalgh, Susan, trans., intro., annot. *The Memoirs of Lady Hyegyong: The Autobiographical Writings of a Crown Princess of Eighteenth-Century Korea.* Berkeley: University of California Press, 1996.

Hopper, Helen M. *A New Woman of Japan: A Political Biography of Katō Shidzue, Transitions: Asia and Asian America.* Boulder: Westview Press, 1996.

Ishimoto, Baroness Shidzue, with an introduction and afterword by Barbara Molony. *Facing Two Ways: The Story of My Life.* 1935. Reprint. Stanford: Stanford University Press, 1983.

Kaibara, Ekken. *Women and Wisdom of Japan* [*Greater Learning for Women*], translated by Shingoro Takaishi. London: John Murray, 1905.

Kim, Yung-Chung. *Women of Korea: A History from Ancient Times to 1945. Han'guk Yosong-Sa*, written under the direction of the Committee for the Compilation of the History of Korean Women. Abridged and translated edition. Seoul: Ewha Womans University Press, 1982.

Lebra, Joyce Chapman. "Women in an All-Male Industry: The Case of Sake Brewer Tatsu'uma Kiyo." In *Recreating Japanese Women, 1600–1945,* edited by G. L. Bernstein. Berkeley: University of California Press, 1991.

Pruitt, Ida, from the story told her by Ning Lao T'ai-t'ai. *A Daughter of Han: The Autobiography of a Chinese Working Woman.* 1945. Reprint. Stanford: Stanford University Press, 1967.

Ramusack, Barbara N., and Sharon Sievers. *Women in Asia: Restoring Women to World History.* Bloomington: Indiana University Press, 1999.

Rawski, Evelyn S. *The Last Emperors: A Social History of Qing Imperial Institutions.* Berkeley: University of California Press, 1998.

Shōnagon, Sei. *The Pillow Book of Sei Shōnagon (Makura no sōshi),* translated by Ivan Morris. Baltimore: Penguin Books, 1974.

Spence, Jonathan D. *The Search for Modern China.* New York: W. W. Norton, 1990.

Tamanoi, Mariko Asano. *Under the Shadow of Nationalism: Politics and Poetics of Rural Japanese Women.* Honolulu: University of Hawaii Press, 1998.

Varley, H. Paul. *The Weak Body of a Useless Woman: Matsuo Taseko and the Meiji Restoration.* Chicago: University of Chicago Press, 1998.

3

Women and Gender
in South and Southeast Asia

BARBARA N. RAMUSACK

Women in South and Southeast Asia have long been an explicit or implicit presence in the histories of these regions but usually as exotic stereotypes, most frequently as self-sacrificing Hindu widows who performed sati, as delicate Javanese dancers, and occasionally as manipulative political actors. In 1984 Cheryl Johnson-Odim and Margaret Strobel launched "Restoring Women to History" as a collaborative effort to provide alternative narratives that synthesized the scholarship on women in Africa, Asia, Latin America, and the Middle East that burgeoned from the early 1970s to the present. Their project went through many renditions and eventually resulted in four synthetic volumes, which were published in 1999.[1]

Three major developments in historiography on women emerged during this period and now shape our understanding of the lived experience of Asian women. The first was a more sophisticated analysis of gender as a social construct that affected the lives of both men and women. So far, there has been more scholarship on what constitutes femininity than on masculinity. The second development was a questioning of how attention to women and gender as categories of analysis as well as topics to be integrated into a narrative could produce more complex recreations of the past and destabilize established periodizations and paradigms. The third consequence was an explicit analysis of issues of sexuality: heterosexuality, same sexual relations, the relation of sexuality to reproduction and the social structure, prescriptive

sexual roles versus lived sexual roles, and desire and pleasure versus reproductive sexuality.

Women's Roles in South Asian Family Systems

In South Asia as in many other societies, women's identities were closely linked
to their roles within a family structure. The Ramayana and the Mahabharata,
the two major epics of Indian culture that later became influential in cultures
of Southeast Asia, provide variant views of such roles among elite families.

Considered the older epic because its core story is included in the Mahabharata and the shorter at thirty thousand verses, the Ramayana portrays a
kingdom where the king and his sons were attentive to the needs of their
subjects; polygyny was practiced; and daughters, wives, and mothers were subordinate to fathers, husbands, and sons. The heroine, Sita, follows her hero-
husband Rama into forest exile, preserves her chastity when captured by the
evil king Ravana, and walks unscathed through fire to prove her purity after
Rama rescues her and returns to rule his kingdom in Ayodhya. In contrast to
Sita, Rama's stepmother, Kaikeyi, engineers the exile of Rama in order to have
her son enthroned instead of Rama, the designated heir. Her maid had triggered this action by warning her mistress that as her physical beauty fades, and
when Rama becomes king, her position will deteriorate. Thus, when women
intervened in politics, they sought to maintain their personal status and not
the common good. Diverse renditions of the Ramayana provide alternative
views of Sita and Rama, but over the centuries the image of Sita as chaste,
submissive, and loyal to her husband became dominant.

The Mahabharata, which has a vast array of stories within its hundred
thousand verses, portrays faithful wives and also the polyandrous Draupadi,
whose five husbands are the heroes of a great war between cousins for control of a kingdom in the rich agricultural Indo-Gangetic plain. Draupadi's
marriage might be an example of fraternal equity. Some commentators have
attributed it to a misunderstanding. Arjun, one of five brothers, tells his mother that he has found a great treasure (meaning Draupadi). His mother in-
structs him to share his good fortune with his brothers. In this explanation, a
man obeying his mother and not a woman's sexual desires or economic needs
produces a polyandrous marriage. This episode of polyandry appears to be a
survival of the customs of tribal groups in the foothills of the Himalayas who
were not fully integrated into Aryan society that was expanding in the Gangetic
region. Draupadi subsequently challenges one husband's right to gamble her
away in a game of dice, resists the winner's sexual advances, and challenges
her husbands to avenge her disgrace. These differing marriage practices in
all-Indian epics indicate that significant variations in family structure and

marriage patterns had once existed in northern India. Sita rather than Draupadi, however, eventually emerged as the ideal woman in Hindu society, where
a patrilineal family structure helped undergird a hierarchical social structure
that came to be labeled the *varna* (caste) system.[2]

Around 200 C.E. the Manusmriti (Laws of Manu) emerged as a compilation of prescriptive texts that reinforced the dominant position of Brahmans
as the first of the four varnas or classifications of Hindu society. Preserved in
oral and later written formats, the code declared, "In childhood a woman
should be under her father's control, in youth under her husband's and when
her husband is dead under her sons. She should not have independence."[3]
Moreover married Hindu women had no rights to property except for the
stridhan (usually, jewelry and some household goods given by parents when
daughters married). These restrictions could be justified by a misogynous view
that "the bed and the seat, jewellery, lust, anger, crookedness, a malicious
nature and bad conduct are what Manu assigned to women."[4]

A Hindu girl was to be married at age eight to a man of twenty-four, im-
plying that the husband would be secure in his occupation while the wife
would be on brink of puberty and childbearing. The girl was to be sexually
chaste, and a family's honor and status came to be intimately related to the
chastity of its daughters and wives.

Anthropologists and women's studies scholars have argued that early ages
of marriages ensured that girls had limited opportunities for sexual experi-
mentation or liaisons, would be more easily socialized as members of their
marital families in a patrilocal culture, and were useful labor for their marital
families either within the house or among lower varnas in agriculture or service occupations. Thus the Laws of Manu authorized the patriarchal, patrilineal, patrilocal family structures associated with the Aryans, who had slowly
migrated from the Caucasus into northern India beginning around 2000 B.C.E.

Under the Laws of Manu, widows were prohibited from remarrying except for levirate marriages in which they could have sexual relations until a
son and heir was produced. Hindu widows were urged to be sati. This word
has been translated to mean that a widow should remain chaste and faithful
to her deceased husband or that she must demonstrate her chastity by immolating herself on her husband's funeral pyre. The origins of sati as self-immo-
lation have been attributed to situations where women were possibly sacrificed
to preserve family and group honor when male relatives confronted inevita-
ble military defeat. The wars in the Mahabharata, or those between Indians
and the Greek followers of Alexander (third century B.C.E.), and the Rajput
practice of *jauhar* are cited as possible sources. Incidents of jauhar are recorded
in the fourteenth and sixteenth centuries, when Rajput women and children
accepted death by fire to avoid capture and rape by a victorious enemy while

their male relatives fought until death to preserve Rajput honor. Although widow immolation was frequently associated with elite groups in Rajput-ruled areas it also extended to the Gangetic Plain and Bengal, where some non-elite women performed sati.[5]

Eyewitness accounts from European travelers, merchants, officials, and missionaries; popular literature such as Jules Verne's *Around the World in Eighty Days;* and graphic prints, films, and even opera have influenced Western perceptions of sati. Recent scholarship has sought to understand the religious and social ideals that informed the practice and the motivations of women who committed sati. Beginning with an account of sati in 1829 in Bali, where Indian traders had grafted the Hindu tradition onto indigenous practices, Catherine Weinberger-Thomas links sati to two underlying concepts articulated in Hindu texts. One is that the immolating widow is an individual instance of sacrifice that transports the material to the divine realm and immortality. The other is that the husband and wife constitute one entity, and sati ensures their immortal union.[6] Although she praises Weinberger-Thomas for contextualizing sati within the Hindu religion, Wendy Doniger points out the absence of a gendered analysis. The unasked question is why "do not men burn themselves on the pyres of their wives?"[7]

There is much speculation on the motivation of Hindu widows who committed sati, but their voices are, of course, silent. Religious incentives seem critical because the performance of sati was said to be spiritually auspicious for a widow and her natal and marital families. Sati stones and temples came to mark the sites of their immolation and were objects of pilgrimages. Material factors could also be influential. The life of a Hindu widow has been characterized as "cold sati." Because she was deemed to bear some responsibility for her husband's death, religious texts and social customs enjoined Hindu widows to fast, eating only one meal a day; to dress simply, usually in a white sari, and wear no jewelry; in some areas to shave her head; and to avoid auspicious occasions, especially weddings. A few women who escaped emphasize material causes for immolation, for example, in-laws who did not want to support a widow, relatives who sought material benefits from sati memorials, and a lack of relatives or other means of economic support.

The alleged sati of Roop Kanwar in 1987 in Deorala near Jaipur, the capital of Rajasthan state, provoked renewed examination of the relationship of sati to Rajput honor, to rising Hindu fundamentalism within a secular, independent India, and to fundamentalism's reinforcement of a patriarchal family structure that subordinates women to male authority and family honor.[8]

Arab warriors, protecting Arab traders, established an outpost on the western coast of India in the eighth century C.E. By the thirteenth century C.E., Turk and Afghan warriors began to extend political control across the Indo-

Gangetic Plain. Both populations carried a patrilinal, patrilocal family structure that had some similarities to indigenous practices. But Islam extended significant rights to Muslim women. They could inherit property, although in lesser shares than men because daughters inherited half of the share of a son and widows varying proportions, depending on the number of surviving children. Widows were allowed to remarry. Divorced women were entitled to support from former husbands for four months after their divorce and then only if the women were pregnant. Otherwise the Muslim community was enjoined to provide for divorced women.

As sati has been associated with Hindu women in world history textbooks, Muslim women have been symbolized by purdah, the practice of female seclusion. There is much debate over what the Qur'an actually prescribes in verses related to the seclusion of women. Judith Tucker points out that "[a]lthough all women are to 'cover their adornments,' only the Prophets' wives are to seclude themselves and cover their faces in the presence of other men ([Qur'an] 33.32)."[9] Among Muslims in India, the tribal customs of Turkish ruling elites, among whom women had considerate physical mobility, tempered the practice of female seclusion. But as Turkish Muslim states developed in India, those aspiring to elite status were typically more assiduous in the observance of purdah.

Many Indian nationalist leaders and historians ascribed the general practice of secluding Hindu women to the impact of Islam and the desire of Hindu men to shield their women from contact with Muslim invaders. Although there are no specific injunctions in the Laws of Manu advocating the physical seclusion of postpuberty Hindu girls and married women, there is evidence in literary sources such as *The Little Clay Cart,* a Sanskrit play of the late fourth century C.E., that respectable, married women had limited contact with unrelated men, were veiled, and traveled in closed conveyances. Although forms of physical seclusion of women existed in Hindu society before the arrival of Muslims in South Asia, the spread of Muslim political power seems to have intensified the practice as a way of gaining respectable status and positions.

Among both Hindu and Muslim women in South Asia, the two principal aspects of purdah are the veiling of a postpuberty woman's body and face with cloth and the segregation of women in a part of a residence known as the harim or zenana. Still, Muslim and Hindu practices of purdah differed. Muslim women were secluded from unrelated males but not male relatives. Hindu women avoided contact with senior male relatives, especially their fathers-in-law and elder brothers-in-law, as well as unrelated males. The extent of purdah among both Hindu and Muslim women in India varied according to class and region, being more extensive in northern India than southern India and among elite groups than lower economic classes and tribal groups.[10]

Women in South Asian History

THE ANCIENT PERIOD TO 600 C.E.

Until the 1970s, many historians characterized the Vedic period from around 1500 to 800 B.C.E. (labeled as such because the religious hymns known as the Vedas were the primary sources) as a golden age for Indian women. During the nineteenth century, Hindu social reformers countered British censure of what imperialists perceived as the degraded status of Indian women with arguments that women enjoyed high status during the early centuries of Aryan dominance in India. Reformers insisted that female infanticide, early marriage, female seclusion, and sati were accretions that lacked Vedic authority. More recent scholarship agrees that the wives of Brahman men had specific roles in sacrifices, the principal ritual through which Aryans communicated with Vedic gods.[11] Women of the twice-born varnas of Brahmans (priests), Kshatriyas (warriors), and Vaishyas (merchants and artisans) originally could hear the Vedas and a few women composed Vedic hymns. Gradually all women and most men except for Brahmans were excluded from learning the Vedas and the sacrificial functions of Brahman wives were minimized. These subordinated religious roles paralleled and are related to material changes in Vedic society and the tightening of male control of women's sexuality and her reproductive functions.[12]

With the transition of Aryan society from a semi-nomadic existence to agriculture and urbanization, Indian men extended their control over female sexuality in order to ensure patrilineal succession to property (as occurred in many cultures) and maintain the ritual purity associated with high-caste status. Uma Chakravarti has coined the term *brahmanical patriarchy* to describe the relationship between caste and the subordination of women that ensured male control of material resources and maintenance of caste status.[13] Uncontrolled sexual desire of women, especially widows, was thus strictly punished and heterosexuality enforced.[14]

As Vedic society evolved from small republics to more structured monarchies, and political leaders extended their authority and centralized their power, more autocratic forms of household organizations were encouraged in which women were subordinated to male heads. Aspiring kings supported the patriarchal authority of the senior male, whose control was reinforced by his alliance with an external political power.[15] In the late fourth century B.C.E., Chandragupta Maurya created the core of a centralized, bureaucratic empire (320–ca. 180 B.C.E.). Kautliya, his Brahman prime minister, is credited with originating the kernel of the Arthashastra, an amoral guide for rulers. Here women had some rights to property, but the principal function for a wife was to produce sons, and virginity was highly prized. At the same time, courtesans received significant attention.

Courtesans were prominent in Indian society during the Mauryan and the later Gupta imperial eras. First, their business could be a significant source of tax revenue, so the Arthashastra has detailed instructions about the taxes courtesans were to pay and how state officials were to protect them so as to ensure their economic productivity. Second, courtesans could provide civil and military intelligence useful to the state and also report on opinions of at least the elite about current conditions, much as modern pollsters do. Thus the Arthashastra considered courtesans along with many other groups as potential recruits for spying.[16] During the classical age of the Guptas (320–540 C.E.) the image of the generous courtesan was immortalized in *The Little Clay Cart,* and avaricious courtesans and their procurers are sketched in other literature. Beautiful courtesans were considered the ornaments of vibrant urban environments where internal and external trade flourished. Simultaneously, wives were lauded who remained faithful to their mercantile husbands, despite the men's long absences abroad and sexual relations with courtesans and prostitutes.

THE MIDDLE PERIOD, 600–1750 C.E.

In many textbooks Indian history is either divided into ancient, medieval, and modern or Hindu, Muslim, and colonial periods. Arab traders on the west coast of India brought Islam to India during the seventh century. By 711 C.E. there was a Muslim political presence in Sind as well. Turks and Afghans established Muslim states based at Delhi only in the thirteenth century. These regimes depended on the participation of non-Muslims. Moreover, religious allegiance did not determine loyalty because many military conflicts were between regimes whose leaders shared a common religious affiliation. Thus the religions of leaders are inadequate to define a historical period. Consequently, "middle" seems more appropriate than either "Muslim" or "medieval" to designate the era when Muslims established political dominance in north India. The historiography on women and gender during these centuries is limited to the religious and political activities of elite women, with some consideration of the possible impact on those who were not elite.

The roles of women in the Hindu bhakti movement and Sufism within Islam during the middle period have attracted some feminist scholarship. Excluded from participation in the Sanskritic tradition, Hindu women found emotional sustenance in bhakti, or devotional, Hinduism, in which one approaches god directly through love and not sacrifice or knowledge. Bhakti saints spread this message through vernacular poetry. The poems of Antal (ninth century C.E.), the first woman bhakti poet, who called on female devotees to surrender to the Lord Krishna, an incarnation of Vishnu, one of the two major Hindu deities, have been translated from Tamil into English.[17]

The most famous woman bhakti poet is Mirabai (ca. 1498–ca. 1546), whose actual existence is questioned even though the potency of her devotional poetry is widely acknowledged. Like other woman bhakti saints, Mirabai transgressed social and sexual boundaries in her quest for union with the divine. She possibly eschewed sexual relations with her princely husband and then refused to commit sati upon his death, claiming a marriage with Lord Krishna. She spent the remainder of her life in the public sphere, singing hymns of praise, and sometimes invoking erotic symbolism, to Krishna. Mirabai's life has been interpreted as a partially successful struggle against brahmanical patriarchy.[18] It is also a means for lower-caste groups in Gujarat and some parts of Rajasthan to express and criticize their oppression by high-caste groups.[19]

For Muslims, Sufi *shaikhs* (leaders of a Sufi order) proclaimed a mystical path through love to a direct union with God. Although there is scant evidence for female Sufi shaikhs in South Asia, many Muslim women as well as men, including Akbar, the great Mughal emperor, sought religious solace, cures for infertility, and advice about family matters from Sufi advisers and through pilgrimages to the *dargarhs* (tombs) of prominent shaikhs.[20]

During the early decades of the Delhi Sultanate (1206–1526), one remarkable Muslim woman ruled in her own right. Iltutmish, a Turkish slave officer who was sultan from 1210 to 1236, groomed his more capable daughter, Razia, to be his successor in preference to less competent sons. Sources characterize Razia, who ruled from 1236 to 1240, as a war leader and record that she wore male attire and rode an elephant in public. When Razia tried to establish an independent base of power, Turkish military rivals engineered her deposition, and she was eventually murdered in 1240 after an unsuccessful effort to regain her throne.[21] Cynthia Talbot provides a nuanced and gendered analysis of female rule during the Kakatiya dynasty further to the south in Andhra. Lacking a son, her father appointed Rudrama-devi as his heir and for several years ruled jointly with her. Surviving challenges to her authority upon her father's death in 1261, Rudrama-devi, like Razia, led troops into battle until her death in 1289. She constructed a public male persona, assuming a male name and wearing masculine clothes, and fulfilled both the warrior role of the male ruler and the cultural patronage activities of a female consort.[22] Other women rulers appeared during these centuries in Orissa and Kashmir, regions on the geographic fringes of larger political units and possibly more open to variants of the male-dominated empires situated in the Indo-Gangetic Plain of northern India.

During the 1990s, scholars have delineated the significant informal political influence and religious patronage of imperial Mughal women during the Mughal dynasty (1526–ca. 1750) and begun to explore the construction of elite masculinity.[23] Research on the domestic world of the first three Mughal rulers—Babur, Humayan, and Akbar—demonstrates how some sources such as the memoir of Gulbadan (b. 1523), sister of Humayan and aunt of Akbar, have been accorded a lesser status than memoirs produced by men at the imperial court. Yet Gulbadan illuminated both the tensions and sense of community that prevailed among imperial women at the heart of the Mughal court and instances when women functioned as critical political intermediaries. One example occurred when Khanzadeh Begam, an aunt of Humayan, interceded with his rebellious brothers in Qandahar to effect a rapprochment.[24] This work is a welcome contrast to the memoirs and reports of European merchants, officials, and missionaries who probably never met Nur Jahan (1577–1645), the Persian wife of Jahangir, the fourth Mughal emperor, but demonized her as exerting an improper ascendancy over her husband.[25]

Imperial Mughal women who operated more discreetly to preserve power for their sons and brothers enjoyed more positive images. They include Mumtaz Mahal (ca. 1593–1631), the wife of Shah Jahan, who built the Taj Mahal as their joint tomb, who was the trusted keeper of the imperial seal that validated imperial decrees. After Mumtaz's death during the birth of her fourteenth child, her eldest daughter, Jahanara (ca. 1613–ca. 1683), took charge of the imperial siblings, supervised the imperial household, and gave candid advice to her brother, the emperor Aurangzeb.

The lavish patronage of imperial Mughal women from diverse ethnic backgrounds indicates their control of substantial financial resources and how private piety could serve public agendas.[26] These women funded mosques in major urban areas such as Agra and Delhi and endowments to support religious scholars. Their largess extended to the building of tombs for emperors who were increasingly venerated both politically and religiously and for caravansaries, which frequently included a mosque, thus fostering trade that contributed to their personal income and the prosperity of the empire. Their activities enhanced the reputation of the imperial establishment for religious piety, thereby amplifying its political hegemony.[27]

THE COLONIAL PERIOD, 1750–1945

While Babur was extending Mughal control from Kabul to Delhi at the heart of the Indo-Gangetic Plain during the early sixteenth century, the Portuguese established a European trading presence on the western periphery at Goa on the Malabar Coast. Dutch and British trading companies followed a century later, but British political power became palpable only with the acquisition in 1765 of the right to collect revenues in the rich province of Bengal.

Recent historiography has dramatically revised the image of the eighteenth century in India from being an era of political chaos, economic stagnation, and cultural decadence to one where powerful regional states were created out of the remnants of a declining empire, and expanding trade networks, specialized production of textiles, and agricultural products supported economic growth and new forms of cultural activity. Only recently has gender become a category of analysis. On the one hand, in the expanding Maratha state the Brahman Peshwa, ostensibly the prime minister but the de facto ruler, enforced strict control over the sexuality of Brahman women, enjoining prepubertal marriages and ascetic widowhood in order to maintain the ritual purity and status of Brahmans, which legitimated their social and political powers.[28] On the other hand, a study of the pension funds of the English East India Company for widows and policies toward orphans reveals that racist attitudes toward the Indian wives and children of British civil and military officers and European fears of miscegenation existed long before the generally accepted date of the 1850s.[29] Scholarly attention to sati, as mentioned earlier, continues to flourish.

In the early 1500s European observers described the spectacle of sati (frequently transliterated as "suttee") but did not compare widow burning in India to the contemporaneous witch burning in Europe. These men made Hindu widows into fetishes of Indian barbarity or associated them with European wives who poisoned their husbands and thus considered Hindu widows somehow being punished for the deaths of their husbands.[30]

For much of the eighteenth century, European men and the English East India Company were ambivalent about sati. Based on an analysis of texts by officials, reformist and orthodox Indians, and missionaries, Lata Mani has produced a foundational study of why British officials first tolerated the practice, then legalized it if it were voluntary, and in 1829 prohibited sati. Her work traces the origins of the trajectory of white and brown men contending for political hegemony on the bodies of Indian, especially Hindu, women.[31] In part a response to highly publicized British policies relating to Indian women and partly to the linkages between Indian nationalism and women issues, there is more research on Indian women and gender issues in the context of the nineteenth and early twentieth centuries.

In 1817 James Mill, an official of the English Company in London and the father of John Stuart Mill, wrote that one could judge the level of a civilization by the status of its women and concluded that India was at the bottom of the scale because of the position of women in India.[32] Consequently, the British cited their moral obligation to "improve" the status of women in India as one source of legitimation for political and economic domination/ exploitation of their Indian colony. The principal targets were the early age of marriage for Indian women and the prohibition on the remarriage of Hindu widows, two practices seen as related to the incidence of sati and female infanticide. Simultaneously, early Indian social reformers felt compelled to explain these customs as aberrations from an earlier golden age for Hindu women during the Vedic period.

British and Indian men employed diverse means, including legislation, education, propaganda, and associations, to recast Indian women into desired roles.[33] Geraldine Forbes's seminal overview analyzes these male efforts at reform and also the multiple ways in which Indian women shaped their own destinies.[34] Initially, the British colonial government and some Indian reformers, particularly Ram Mohan Roy in Bengal and Behramji Malabari in Bombay, advocated legal reforms. These measures included prohibitions, notably Lord Bentinck's minute suppressing sati in 1829; the Female Infanticide Act of 1870; the Age of Consent Act of 1891 that raised the age for consent to sexual relationships for girls from ten to twelve; and the Child Marriage Restraint Act (referred to as the "Sarda Act" after its sponsor) of 1929 that set the ages of fourteen for girls and eighteen for boys as the minimum ones for marriage.[35]

Since the 1980s, scholarship has challenged British and Indian claims of benevolence.[36] British officials and Indian nationalists, both reformers and revivalists, used the bodies and minds of Indian women to legitimate their claims to power and to buttress their masculinity. British officials were challenged at home by British feminists and new sexual identities, and Indian nationalists were impugned by British rhetoric about Indian (especially Bengali) effeminacy and the tentative efforts of some Indian reformers to reduce patriarchal control of female sexuality.[37]

The British often initiated conditions that tended to stimulate or at least condone situations that legislation sought to correct. Thus in 1813 the British first made sati legal if it were voluntary, but then they outlawed it in 1829. Moreover, when gathering evidence for their intended prohibition of sati, British officials consulted and reinforced the authority of Brahman pandits and the Laws of Manu at the expense of customary law that tended to accord women more economic and social rights. Similarly, British revisions of property law in Punjab and Haryana took away certain women's rights under customary law, thereby undercutting women's economic resources, particularly the economic and sexual options for Hindu widows,[38] and fostered an increase in demands for dowry.[39] The legislation that prohibited female infanticide created "infanticidal" women as a criminal category when the colonial state was concerned about challenges to its authority and colonized men were unconcerned about the economic circumstances such as extreme poverty and social censure of sexual relations out of wedlock that motivated women to commit infanticide.[40]

The controversy over the Age of Consent Act of 1891 reveals not only the continuing efforts of white and brown men to use Indian women and their bodies as means to achieve their own agendas but also the growing agency of Indian women to speak for themselves. Tanika Sarkar has traced how "revivalist" Hindu male nationalists arguing for early marriage projected Hindu women as the symbol of the Indian nation and the embodiment of the spiritual superiority of Indian culture with respect to Western culture and British political dominance.[41] For Indian opponents of the bill, Indian women in the home were a sphere that was to be sheltered from British intrusion and domination. In Maharashtra, however, some women challenged Indian male attacks on the 1891 Act by first criticizing early, arranged marriages as producing unhappy women and tension-filled relationships and then advocating adult marriages and choice of partners.[42]

More experienced, more highly organized women would be active campaigners for the Child Marriage Restraint Act.[43] Although the legislation applied to all religious groups including Muslims, its immediate impact was negative, as was that of the 1891 Act. Many parents rushed to marry off their daughters during the gap between the passage of the act in October 1929 and when it went into effect in April 1930. Other legislation that extended legal rights to Indian women, such as the Hindu Widows Remarriage Act of 1856, were equally ineffective because neither British officials nor Indian male social reformers did much to encourage widow remarriage in the face of family opposition.

Indian and a few British reformers attempted to establish institutions and programs to improve the legal rights and social status of women. In Bengal the Brahmo Samaj promoted education for women, encouraged some women to become teachers and physicians in order to serve their sisters, and sought to make women into emblems of modernity as companionate wives. Publicists edited magazines and wrote books that prescribed reformed, modern behavior for Hindu and Muslim women as daughters, wives, and mothers.[44] Many of these efforts sought to mold women into companionate wives, combining Victorian virtues such as punctuality, cleanliness, and literacy with Hindu ones, especially self-sacrificing devotion to husbands that was based on love, not coercion.

Women's voices in folk tales, published works, and public actions disputed male constructions of Hindu conjugal life. Two examples are illustrative. Rashsundari Debi (ca. 1809–ca. 1900), an upper-caste Bengali, justified her learning in secret to read and write as necessary to read Bengali bhakti texts about Lord Krishna. In her autobiography, which is both a spiritual journal and reflection on her life and times, she recounts the emotional trauma and hard work of her conjugal life as trials she was able to bear only with divine assistance. As Tanika Sarkar observes, Rashsundari "had it both ways. She proclaimed her predicament to the whole world through the print-medium and she reserved the image of the self-effacing Hindu wife who suffers her deprivations with smiling forbearance."[45] Writing in Marathi in western India, Tarabai Shinde (ca. 1850–ca. 1910) rebuked Indian male reformers who urged Indian women to follow ideals to which they themselves did not conform and then ascribed faults to Indian women that the men exhibited in greater intensity. Rosalind O'Hanlon has suggested that "as caste groupings search for new ways of expressing identity and social distinction . . . the public conduct of their women became paramount, and was judged according to standards increasingly brahmanical in character."[46] The same phenomenon was occurring in Punjab, as high-caste Hindu and Sikh men subordinated women relatives to reconfigured patriarchy and distinctive communal identities in order to achieve dominance within Indian society as an emerging middle class that mediated between the British and lower classes.[47]

Pandita Ramabai (1858–1922) is an extraordinary example of Indian women who promoted female education and publicized the needs of non-elite women. Educated sufficiently by her father in Sanskrit texts so she gained the title of pandita, widowed after a few years of marriage, and a questioning convert to Christianity, Pandita Ramabai campaigned for education for women. She also established shelters and educational institutions for Hindu widows and their children. To support these ventures Ramabai undertook extensive fundraising campaigns in the United States and wrote books on Indian women that countered the representations of British and American women of Indian women, mainly as victims.[48]

In an influential essay, Partha Chatterjee argues that by the end of the nineteenth century Indian men had resolved the issue of Indian women by confining them to the private sphere, where women would preserve a superior Hindu culture from colonial contamination.[49] At the same time, Indian men shifted their rhetoric to call for Indian women to be good mothers of sons who would fight to protect Mother India from foreign transgressors. In the shift, women's sexuality, even within the confines of marriage, was downplayed, as was their role as wives.

While some Indian men were restricting women's roles and retreating from legal reforms, more elite Indian women were articulating their needs and critiquing male prescriptions for women. Hindu women began to write for male-edited journals such as the Bengali *Bamabodhini Patrika,* and north Indian Muslim women contributed to the Urdu *Tahzib-un-Niswan* and *Khatun.* By the early 1900s, women had established their own journals, such as *Antahpur* in Bengali, *Stree Darpan* in Hindi, and the *Indian Ladies Magazine* and *Stri Dharma* in English. Although their early articles were prescriptive, some au-

dacious Indian women challenged restrictive practices. In "Ladyland," a utopian story, Rokeya Hossain (1880–1932), a Bengali Muslim, attacked male
authority by portraying men confined to purdah quarters because of their
uncontrolled sexual desires and women governing and addressing the needs
of all citizens.[50]

By the 1910s, elite Indian women formed associations that advocated for
women's education, lobbied for legal rights that included the franchise, and
discussed controversial issues such as birth control. These groups included the
All India Muslim Ladies Conference (AIMLC), founded at Aligarh in 1914;
the Women's India Association (WIA), established in Madras in 1917; the
National Council of Women in India (NCWI), formed in 1925; and the All-
India Women's Conference (AIWC), which first met in Poona in 1927. Initially, some British women collaborated in these efforts, notably Margaret
Cousins (1878–1954), an Anglo-Irish theosophist, and Dorothy Jinarajadasa,
an English woman married to a Sinhalese theosophist. Their intervention
reveals the tensions between the feminist goals of education, companionate
marriage, and women's franchise and an orientalist assumption of a golden
age for Indian women in the distant past.[51]

Geraldine Forbes has pioneered in recovering the memoirs, private papers, and photographs of remarkable Indian women leaders and the ephemeral publications of their organizations.[52] She clearly demonstrates that such
women exercised considerable agency by raising consciousness among wom-
en, propagandizing in public for their causes, lobbying British and Indian
politicians and officials in India and in London, and establishing institutions
to provide opportunities for non-elite women.[53]

Some gains for women came quickly. Desiring to distance themselves from
potential controversy, the British allowed provincial legislatures where Indians
were in a majority (after the Indian Councils Act of 1919) to decide whether
Indian women should have the right to vote. From 1923 to 1930 all the provincial legislatures extended the franchise to women, as well as the right to
stand as candidates for legislatures with the usual restrictive qualifications such
as literacy and the payment of taxes.[54] In a reversal of patterns in the United
States, the councils of municipal corporations such as the one of Madras were
more reluctant to allow women to be elected members, although some wom-
en were appointed to the Council in Madras City by 1926. Other goals, such
as effective legislation to raise the age of marriage and achieve a uniform civil
law code, were less successful. Moreover, by the late 1930s Muslim women,
lower-class women in urban areas, and peasant women began to challenge the
right of women's organizations to establish agendas for them.

During the 1920s Indian women became more visible in the nationalist
movement to secure first swaraj, or self-rule, and later independence from the

114

British. Their activities ranged from the constitutional to terrorist. Indian women had long attended opening sessions of the Indian National Congress, the most extensive nationalist organization. Mahatma Gandhi (1869–1948), however, was the most active Congress leader in mobilizing women, especially those of the middle and peasant classes, into the political process.

Because of their reputed capacity for sacrifice and nonviolence, Gandhi claimed that Indian women had a special aptitude for practicing satyagraha—nonviolent resistance to British rule. Initially, he recruited women for political campaigns that could be waged within the domestic sphere. Because women controlled consumption, they could practice *swadeshi*, buying Indian-made products and boycotting British ones. Swadeshi promoted the Indian economy and would bring economic pressure on the British parliament to reduce its political dominance in India.

In order to create a new Indian society, Gandhi called upon women to avoid discriminatory practices toward untouchables, whom he called "harijans" or children of God; to spin yarn for Indian hand-loom weavers; and to picket toddy shops. The last action would diminish consumption of alcohol and thereby both reduce British taxes and the abuse of women and children by alcoholic husbands and fathers. Some feminist scholars have criticized Gandhi for reinforcing the socialization of women to be self-sacrificing and maintaining boundaries between the private and public spheres for middle-class women. Others, however, have pointed out that Gandhi's strategy enabled women of many different social classes to participate in politics from the domestic spheres in ways that conservative male relatives would permit.[55]

Rejecting Gandhi's call for nonviolent resistance, educated young women in Bengal joined their brothers in elitist terrorism with the goal of political freedom when changes in Indian society would encompass reforms for women. Santi Ghose (b. 1916) and Suniti Choudhury (b. 1917), who successfully assassinated the district magistrate in Comilla in 1931, and Pritilata Waddedar (d. 1932), who led a raid by fifteen men on the Chittagong Club, became nationalist heroines, especially in Bengal. Although she was not an active participant, Kalpana Dutt's account of that raid provides a gendered account that reveals women's commitment to their vision of a nation.[56]

Some of the most lively recent scholarship has examined several issues of sexuality during the twentieth century. Debates within the AIWC and between foreign advocates of birth control such as Margaret Sanger and Marie Stopes and Mahatma Gandhi over the need for and provision of contraception are revealing.[57] They disclose how middle-class women used eugenic rhetoric to promote birth control programs that not only sought to lower maternal and infant mortality rates but also might restrict the sexual autonomy of lower-class women. Within reform groups such as the Arya Samaj in the United Provinces, Hindu men sought to police women's sexual expressions, ostensibly to control obscenity, while encouraging Hindu men to remarry Hindu widows to prevent them from marrying Muslims and contain their sexuality within marriage.[58] As the Laws of Manu had validated male domination of women's sexuality to preserve caste purity, Hindu men during the twentieth century would constrain women's sexuality to preserve the purity of the religious community.

Concerns over women's modesty were one reason for the relatively few women who worked in the industrial sector. Hired for unskilled work in the jute, textile, and match-making industries, women lost that small foothold with the introduction of more sophisticated machinery in textile and jute mills.[59] Industrialists also preferred male employees because they were more mobile than women and considered to be cheaper whenever legislation was passed calling for brief maternity leaves and crèches or rudimentary facilities for workers' children. The irony is that such legislation was rarely implemented.

The overwhelming majority of women in India were peasants who carried the double burden of household labor—reproducing and caring for children, preparing food, and cleaning clothes and houses—and work related to the production of crops. Most peasant women worked at tasks such as cleaning and grinding grain within the zenana that escaped statistical surveys. Among some groups such as Jats in northern India and low castes in southern India, women did seasonal work in the fields. When mechanization occurred, such as the introduction of rice-husking machines in Bengal, women lost what little income they had previously earned from husking rice by hand within their homes.

As independence approached after World War II, peasant women joined militant struggles to gain economic rights from landlords and governments and changes in customs that oppressed women. From 1945 to 1947, Warli tribal women in western India revolted with men to alleviate the degrading conditions of forced labor. After achieving some improvements, including restrictions on sexual exploitation by landlords, Warli women who still confronted sexually oppressive practices within their community were excluded from public politics and relegated to their homes and fields.[60] Similar fates awaited peasant women in Bengal during the *tebhaga* movement of 1946 that demanded an increase from one-half to two-thirds of the crops for the sharecroppers who produced them.[61] During the Telengana revolt of the early 1950s in Andhra, further to the south, peasant women shared in armed struggles to reduce harsh revenue demands and obtain titles to the land they cultivated. The oral histories of these women record their excitement at their active participation and their disappointment at being confined to more restrictive roles in the domestic sphere after the revolt was suppressed.[62]

These three groups of peasant women—the Warli and those in Bengal and Andhra—reflect that Indian nationalist leaders and Indian women's organizations that claimed to represent them and promised to improve their lives were too removed from the daily concerns of marginalized and non-elite women.

THE ERA OF INDEPENDENCE, 1947 TO PRESENT

Although the Indian constitution of 1950 guaranteed significant legal rights for women, the vague promises of nationalist leaders that political freedom would enable sweeping improvements in women's situations were not fulfilled. Moreover, postcolonial politicians continued to invoke women—and by extension their bodies—as symbols of the nation and its honor, with tragic consequences for women.

As a consequence of the partition of the British Indian empire into the independent states of a secular India and a Muslim-majority Pakistan in August 1947, many Hindu, Muslim, and Sikh women suffered horrific terror and death. Estimates of the numbers of refugees exchanged between India and Pakistan are around ten million; between five hundred thousand and two million people died. Those numbers, because of the chaotic conditions that prevailed from 1946 to 1948, will never be beyond dispute. Except for a few eyewitness accounts by Britons and other Europeans, decades passed before most Indian and Pakistani survivors of partition were willing to talk about their experiences or record them for public consumption. Early accounts of the event were confined to fiction; *Garm Hawa,* the first Indian film depicting partition, appeared in 1975.

It was not until the late 1980s that historians in India attempted to recapture what happened to Indian women during the partition of Punjab. Using primarily oral histories and the few available categories of government documents, their work reveals that some women suffered death at the hands of male relatives to preserve family and national honor. They also endured rape, abduction, and/or death by men of other religions or even their own. The programs that the governments of India and Pakistan established to recover abducted women in Punjab were motivated more by the imperative to rehabilitate national honor by retrieving the women and less from concern for the women's physical welfare, economic future, or personal desires. If they returned to India, Hindu women had to leave any children conceived with Muslim fathers in Pakistan, both because of the fathers' claims and the stain such children produced on their mothers' chastity. Muslim women were to leave their children behind in India, although later the children might be ostracized as symbols of the violation of India. Natal Hindu families in India frequently did not welcome recovered daughters and wives, whose sexual relations with Muslim men were deemed to pollute and denigrate family honor and status. Even so, some recovered women carved out fulfilling careers in education and government service that would have been impossible within the patriarchy of their natal or marital families.[63]

During the late 1940s and the 1950s, many upper- and middle-class women gained substantial positions within the political and professional structures of independent India and Pakistan. Vijayalakshmi Pandit, the sister of Jawaharlal Nehru, was ambassador to the United States, the Soviet Union, and Great Britain as well as both delegate and later president of the General Assembly of the United Nations; Rajkumari Amrit Kaur, a close follower of Gandhi (and as a woman and a Christian fulfilling two categories) became India's health minister; and in 1966 Indira Gandhi, the daughter of Jawaharlal Nehru, became the prime minister of India. By 1991 Indian women held 7.1 percent of seats in Parliament, whereas women held only 6.4 percent of the seats in the U.S. Congress. Middle-class women increasingly entered the teaching and medical professions in India and gained prominent bureaucratic roles in social work. For the most visible, a secular independent India fulfilled some nationalist promises, but publication of *Towards Equality* in 1974 was a rude awakening.

In preparation for the International Year of Women in 1975, the Indian government appointed a committee of nine women and one man to assess the impact of the independent Indian government on the condition of the women. The results indicate several areas in which women suffered declining health and fewer economic opportunities. Perhaps the most startling statistic was the declining ratio of women to men between 1901 (when it was 972 to 1000) and 1971 (when it was 930 to 1000).[64] The authors of *Towards Equality* noted "that attitudes toward women's equality vary sharply." When the constitutional debate was on abstract principles, there was no dissent. When the principle of women's equality was applied "to established preserves of traditional male privileges, such as the right to property and the unchallenged dominance of the husband in family life," there were sharp differences, with the most radical claiming that the principle of women's equality was "totally inapplicable and undesirable for Indian society."[65] The elite women who spent almost two years preparing this report were radicalized by their findings and joined with many other groups in a renewed feminist movement.

Because of an alleged threat to national security, Indira Gandhi proclaimed a state of emergency in 1975. She also arrested many political opponents and restricted the exercise of some civil rights. During the mid-1970s there were popular protests against rising food prices, the rape of non-elite women in police stations, the rising incidence of bride-burning when dowries of young wives were deemed inadequate, and the campaigns of forced sterilization that Sanjay Gandhi, the younger son of the prime minister, spearheaded.

Women involved in these protests coalesced into a feminist movement that had many aspects. Although, as earlier, legislation such as the Dowry Prohibition Act of 1986 was used to achieve social change, courageous women also created institutions themselves. In 1972 Ela Bhatt formed the Self-Employed Women's Association (SEWA), a self-help group for the most marginal of women in Ahmadabad, the ragpickers and sidewalk vegetable vendors. Moving from an initial focus on securing low-cost credit and literacy training, SEWA undertook the organization of women employed in the informal sectors, such as those who made *bedis* (cheap cigarettes) in their homes; the creation of a women's bank; and support groups for women experiencing domestic violence. Other groups sponsored shelters for victims of domestic abuse, provided assistance for women in negotiating the legal system, and increasingly confronted resistance from right-wing groups.

During the 1990s, the Sangh Parivar intensified efforts to capture political power and cultural dominance in the name of Hindutva, or "Hinduness." A "family" of Hindu nationalist groups, the Sangh Parivar was led by a triad consisting of the Bharatiya Janata Party (BJP), an electoral political party; the Rashtriya Swayamsevak Sangh (RSS), a militant Hindu nationalist organization; and the Vishwa Hindu Parishad (VHP), a Hindu cultural association with particular appeal to the Indian diaspora. Their goal is to transform India from a secular into an avowedly Hindu nation. Hindutva organizations focus on Hindu women as symbols and servants of a renewed and purified Hindu community.[66]

The Rashtriya Sevika Samiti, the women's wing of the RSS founded in 1936, has been successful in organizing high-caste, middle-class urban women and inculcating an ideology that emphasizes their role as mothers who are to produce sons committed to the ideology of India as a Hindu nation stretching from Afghanistan to Burma.[67] Hindutva ideology displaces any frustrations with patriarchy within their families onto alleged threats from Muslim men. Samiti camps ostensibly train young women in self-defense techniques and project Muslim men as the source of violence. They also provide intensive indoctrination in the need to obey family injunctions and maintain the honor of the larger family of the Hindu community. Again, the focus is on Hindu women's reproductive functions as mothers of sons (daughters are rarely mentioned) and the socializers of children into Hindu culture.

Women in Pakistan and Bangladesh have had experiences similar to those of women in India. First, elite women related to powerful male political leaders have gained high office. In Pakistan, Benazir Bhutto, the daughter of a prime minister, was twice prime minister during intermittent periods of civilian rule. In Bangladesh, Khaleda Zia, the widow of an assassinated military dictator, was prime minister in the early 1990s. In 1996 Sheikh Hasina Wajed, the daughter of Sheikh Mujib, the father and first prime minister of Bangladesh, was elected and was still prime minister in early 2004. Like Indira Gandhi, these women indicate the possibility of women achieving the highest political positions, but none of them are known for policies particularly crafted to promote the equality of women.

In both Pakistan and Bangladesh, Islam has been used to define national identity and legitimate political power, but with different results for women. In 1961 Pakistan, which proclaimed itself an Islamic state from its first constitution, enacted the Muslim Family Laws Ordinance, which extended significant legal safeguards to Muslim women in contrast to India, where Muslim women remained under Qur'anic personal law and did not gain such state-legislated protection. Provisions in Pakistan ranged from compulsory registration of marriages and divorces and greater rights for women to initiate divorce to ensuring that children of a predeceased son would inherit from their grandfather.[68]

Although the 1961 Ordinance was considered a model during the 1960s, subsequent military dictators in Pakistan have passed discriminatory laws that restrict the sexuality and civil rights of women. One example is the Hudood ordinances that punish *zina*, unlawful sexual relations outside of marriage, in ways that disastrously affect women. If a woman is pregnant after sexual relations out of wedlock, for example, she is assumed to have consented and therefore subject to punishment. Other restrictions on dress and participation in the public sphere, where women would interact with men in sports, television, and the professions, seek state-legislated modesty in conformity with Islamist interpretations of Muslim law.

As had occurred in 1947 with the birth of India and Pakistan as nation-states, women were subjected to rape during the struggle for Bangladeshi independence in 1971. The rapes were coded as violations of Bangladeshi territory and honor and signs of the new state's inability to protect either its territory or its women. The perpetrators were largely Pakistani troops, and the new government acclaimed the raped women as *birangona* (war heroines), but they were not enthusiastically welcomed home.

Sheikh Mujib declared that Bangladesh was a secular, democratic, socialist republic, but two consecutive military leaders, Ziaur Rahman and H. M. Ershad, pursued policies influenced by Islamization as means of legitimation and to appeal to Middle Eastern Muslim aid-donors. Once again, women's bodies became symbols of communal and national identities. Government policies denigrated customs associated with Hindu elements of Bengali culture, such as wearing the bindi, the mark on the forehead indicating a married woman, and sarees and encouraged the *hijab* (headscarf) and modest behavior among women.

Perhaps more influential for women were development projects target-
ing women that would attract foreign aid and promote an export-oriented
economy. The first objective produced hundreds of nongovernmental organizations (NGOs) in rural and urban areas that usually sought to alleviate
poverty with no major changes in patriarchal familial or hierarchal political
structures. The most successful NGO, which now has some government support, is the Grameen Bank, a micro credit project that extends credit to poor
village women in order to promote their empowerment and income-earning
activities. Many NGO workers with funds to distribute, however, function as
new patrons who rival old patrons for control of lower-class workers, including women. The second objective stimulated the rise of a garment export
industry that became the largest earner of foreign exchange by the late 1990s
and an employer of more than six hundred thousand women. These women
wage-earners have not only gained some autonomy but also have attracted
criticism for being visible in the public sphere and challenging patriarchal
authority in the private sphere.[69]

After three decades of historical scholarship on women and gender in
modern South Asia, a more complex understanding of the interpenetration
of the public and private spheres in the construction of nationalist movements
and in the creation of new nation-states has emerged. Most easily recovered
are the public roles played by women in nationalist organizations, political
parties, and state structures. Less visible and requiring more historical imagination and innovative research are the ways in which women's bodies and
sexualities become nationalist symbols in freedom struggles against foreign
or indigenous governments and then national symbols of territory, honor, and
culture. As a consequence, the creation of new nation-states brings physical
and mental violence, even death, to women and rejection by families and
communities if they survive the trauma of rape and mutilation. Independence
and new nation-states can extend new legal rights for women but then not
provide the infrastructure which women need to exercise their rights and
contest those who deny them these rights. And now women confront new
challenges as their nations grapple with the tentacles of globalization.

Women and Gender in Southeast Asia

Most world history textbooks devote fewer than twenty pages to the history
of Southeast Asia because historians lament the lack of archival sources for
the centuries before European colonial intervention. Moreover, surveys had
the ill-defined assumption that the culture and politics of much of premodern Southeast Asia was somehow derivative of Indian and Chinese patterns
because the world religions of Buddhism, Hinduism, and Islam, the South

Asian epics of the Ramayana and the Mahabharata (to a lesser extent), and Indian and Chinese political ideologies and structures were assimilated in various regions of that area.

During the 1990s, resourceful and imaginative historians began to question new categories of sources—poetry, prose, chronicles,[70] and Dutch mercantile and governmental records—not only to add women to the historical narrative but also to highlight how gender roles for men and women were constructed and the political, economic, and social implications of particular definitions of masculinity and femininity. The studies reveal the diversity of cultural and political patterns within Southeast Asia as well as between South and Southeast Asia.

BEFORE 1500

The names of very few women appear in histories of Southeast Asia before the early modern period. One striking exception is three women in Vietnam who were honored as heroines challenging Chinese control of their homeland. The two Trung sisters are lauded for leading an army that included women officers and won independence in 40 C.E. But when the Chinese were victorious three years later, the Trung sisters committed suicide. In 247 C.E., Trieu Thi Trinh, a nineteen-year-old peasant girl, similarly led resistance to the Chinese and chose suicide when defeated.[71] Centuries later these women had symbolic value to recruit Vietnamese women to resist French colonialism and American military intervention.

The activities of Buddhist women are also mentioned. In a two-pronged movement: Theravada Buddhism moved from Sri Lanka into Burma and Thailand in the thirteenth century while Mahayana Buddhism traveled from China into Vietnam and Java. When merchants and monks began to carry Theravada Buddhism from Sri Lanka to Burma and Thailand, the ordination of women as nuns had lapsed. Buddhist women could acquire merit through *dana* (giving gifts to Buddhist monks and charitable institutions), and some gifts by elite Buddhist patrons were recorded. During the classical age of Burmese history, Queen Phwa Jaw (Pwazaw) in the state of Pagan announced:

> [W]henever I am born, I wish to be fully equipped with *dana* [gift-giving], precepts, faith, wisdom, nobility, which are virtues, and not know a bit of misery. At the end, having enjoyed bliss as man [*sic*] and *nat* [spirit], I wish the state of arahantship which is noble, having internalized the doctrine of release and the tranquil and serene peace of *nibbana*. Thus I donate these lands, gardens, *kywan* [bondsmen], cows, and properties. All of these endowed properties are bona fide, none will have cause for argument later.[72]

This royal woman accepted that personal Buddhahood was achieved through a hierarchy of rebirths from woman to man to spirit, but she made a forthright statement that royal women controlled movable and immovable property and could transfer such property.

As in the South Asian and American contexts, there are questions about how women could be attracted to a religious tradition in which the founder only reluctantly agreed to the establishment of a monastic order for women and where women were not viewed as capable of directly attaining nibbana. More recent research has emphasized the valorization of the role of women as mothers who gave birth to and nurtured sons who joined the *sangha* (monastic orders critical for the institutional continuity of Buddhism). Furthermore, women of many social classes provided food, clothing, and money for monks. Thus Buddhism could be naturalized in Southeast Asia where the respect accorded to mothers crossed class and ethnic boundaries.[73]

The advent and assimilation of other world religions—Hinduism, Islam, and Christianity—in Southeast Asia had mixed effects on conceptions of divinity as female, on the role of women in religious rituals, and on women's social status and sexuality. Women's functions in indigenous spirit possession rituals in the Malay-Indonesian sphere and later in the Philippines were increasingly denigrated. But compared to the provocative literature on the persistence of worship of female deities in South Asia either as a generalized Mother Goddess, specific manifestations such as Durga and Kali, or new incarnations such Santosh Ma, we know relatively little about the continued veneration of indigenous female deities in Southeast Asia.

EARLY MODERN, 1500–1800

Many ancient and early modern travelers to Southeast Asia remarked on the relatively high social status of women in the diverse cultures they encountered. Such agency has been related to their economic activities as craftspeople and traders, the veneration of fertility in indigenous religions, and bilateral kinship systems in which descent and property may pass through both female and male lines. Women's kinship and sexual relationships, however, must be situated temporally and geographically. *Adat* (local customary law and practices) mitigated the constraints of the three dependencies of South Asian women as the Laws of Manu spread to areas such as Cambodia, the three obediences or followings of Confucian ideology in northern Vietnam, and Muslim shari'a or law in much of Malaysia and Indonesia. After the advent of Islam around 1600, for example, the Minangkabau in western Sumatra evolved an accommodation of their custom of matrilinity with Qur'anic law.[74] More generally, daughters in much of Southeast Asia were not devalued, divorce was possible for women and did not lower their economic or social status, premarital sexual relations were accepted, and pregnancy usually led to marriage so illegitimacy was precluded.

Using indigenous literary, court chronicles, inscriptions, and folk sources along with European records, scholars have started to specify these broad generalizations about female autonomy in early modern Southeast Asia. In the economic sphere, women were active in both local and export trading networks. Moreover, between 1400 and 1600 there was "a remarkable tendency for just those states participating most fully in the expanding commerce of the regions to be governed by women."[75] Early Dutch merchants encountered a formidable trader in pepper in Cochin-China, a tin merchant in Aceh, and royal women such as the wife of the Sultan Hasanuddi of Makassar on Sulawesi and the women who occupied the thrones of Aceh, Jambi, and Indragiri on Sumatra who participated in the international trade. In Aceh at the northern tip of Sumatra, four queens (1641–99) ensured its dominance as the leading port in insular Southeast Asia, although a fatwa, or decree (supposedly from Mecca), enjoined that their rule was against the laws of Islam.

Even more exotic to European visitors was the existence of female bodyguard corps that the rulers of Aceh and Mataram on Java maintained. Reporting on the sultan of Mataram on Java in the mid-seventeenth century, Rijklop van Goens claimed that his corps

> Contained about 150 young women altogether, of whom thirty escorted the ruler when he appeared in audience. Ten of them carried the ruler's impedimenta—his water vessel, sirih [items for making betel digestives] set, tobacco pipe, mat, sun-shade, box of perfumes, and items of clothing for presentation to favored subjects—while the other twenty, armed with bare pikes and blow-pipes, guarded him on all side . . . although they were chosen from the most beautiful girls in the kingdom, the ruler seldom took any of them as a concubine, though they were frequently presented to the great nobles of the land as wives.[76]

In the eighteenth century another Dutch commentator added "that the young women proved 'not a little high-spirited and proud' when given as wives knowing as they did that their husbands would not dare to wrong them for fear of the ruler's wrath."[77] A diary by an anonymous member of such a corps in Java from 1781 to 1791 confirms that the women were literate and had a shrewd grasp of court politics.[78] These sources projected an exotic image of Amazon warriors and also document the physical mobility and intellectual achievements of some elite women and an alternative to marriage as a path to political influence.

At the same time, inter- and intra-state political relationships could be established, affirmed, and strengthened through kinship ties; daughters were political capital to be deployed in marriage alliances. One example is Tun Kudu, the daughter of a chief minister in mid-fifteenth-century Malacca. Sultan Muzaffar Syah divorced her without seeking her consent, a critical aspect of Muslim divorce protocol, in order to marry her to his treasurer. Through this maneuver the sultan sought to suture a rupture between two court factions, one of which the brother of Tun Kudu led.[79] Early European merchants and officials adapted indigenous practices to their needs.

EUROPEAN COLONIALISM AND SOUTHEAST ASIAN SOCIETIES

Although Europeans did not significantly penetrate most local societies in Southeast Asia until the nineteenth century, following the pattern in South Asia they established urban trading centers—most notably the Portuguese at Malacca (1511), the Spanish at Manila (1571), and the Dutch at Batavia (1619). The European economic and political presence along with the spread of Islam and Christianity constricted the sexual and economic autonomy of women in Southeast Asia. Before the arrival of Europeans, societies from Burma to the Philippines had permitted local women to cohabit with foreign traders in "temporary" marriages. The women provided entry to local economies, knowledge of indigenous conditions, family support groups, and sexual relations. The men reciprocated with gifts and contacts with wider trading networks. Upon their departure, the trader-spouses granted appropriate gifts and support for any children who would remain with the mothers. The women were then free to enter other such marriages or sexual relationships without loss of social status.

Osoet Pegua, an entrepreneurial Mon (Burmese and consequently on the margins of Siamese society) woman who had been raised in the Dutch settlement at Ayutthaya, a major entrepôt and the capital of Siam (Thailand), epitomizes the opportunities available to some women in temporary marriages. From around 1630 to 1651 Osoet had liaisons with three Dutch trader-officials, unions that produced one son and three daughters. Facilitating Dutch access to local products, Osoet obtained lucrative contracts for her commercial services, even obtaining a monopoly on supplying provisions for the Dutch establishment in Ayutthaya. She accumulated sufficient wealth to send lavish gifts to the Dutch governor-general in Batavia to prevent her Dutch partners from repatriating their Mon-Dutch children until after her death in 1658.[80]

As more European and Chinese traders gravitated to colonial ports during the seventeenth century, temporary marriages degenerated into commercial exchanges of sexual services for cash. Wives metamorphosed into concubines and then prostitutes, with fewer rights and degraded social status. Gradually, European and Chinese men appropriated sexual services from female slaves who lacked family support networks. Some of these men controlled slave-concubines who earned money for their owners through their sexual services or who could be sold for cash.[81] Contemporary prostitution in Southeast Asia, especially sexual tourism, might have antecedents in these deviations in the practice of temporary marriages.

The growth of a European-dominated export trade in conjunction with new prescriptions of appropriate female modesty and chastity reduced the economic autonomy of women. One example occurred in the pepper trade in Sumatra. When pepper was first brought from India to Southeast Asia, women cultivated it in family gardens. As European demands led to large-scale plantations, men displaced women, for whom plantation labor was incompatible with domestic duties and contrary to religious injunctions about female modesty. Because coastal centers were notorious sites of prostitution, the same proscriptions also restricted women from taking their pepper crops to the cities for sale to Europeans. Consequently, economic options were limited for women in Sumatra when they could not compete in the production or marketing of pepper.[82]

The impact of Christianization on women in the Philippines has not been as intensively examined as in other areas of the Spanish Empire. Colonial policies initially encouraged the lower levels of the small Spanish official hierarchy and later Chinese traders to intermarry with local women, but the resulting mestizo community was much smaller than the one in Latin America. As in the Indonesian archipelago, concubinage and prostitution gradually became more prevalent in urban centers. The introduction of Roman law in the Philippines formally reduced the customary rights of indigenous women, especially in regard to their children, to property, and to divorce. Christian proscriptions regarding premarital and marital sexual morality eroded the sexual autonomy of Filipino women. Parents were enjoined to guard the chastity of their daughters while at home, and elite girls were socialized at school to protect their virtue.

The impact of Spanish Christianization was most profound on indigenous animist shamans or priestesses (*baylan* in Visayan or *catalonan* in Tagalog). These women communicated with the world of spirits through drama, song, and dance and performed rituals at birth, during illnesses, and at death. Spanish missionaries, categorizing these women as idolaters and witches, urged young male converts to desecrate and destroy their images, or "idols," and ritual instruments. As alternatives, the missionaries promoted Christian sacraments, especially baptism, images, and institutions such as hospitals in order to usurp the shamans' roles as midwives, healers, and ritualists dealing with death.[83]

As in Latin America, first lay organizations and then convents emerged as alternative religious institutions for women. From the late 1500s confraternities and the Third Order of St. Francis, or tertiaries, included women's groups that socialized Filipino women to be self-sacrificing, modest, and ac-

cepting of gender roles submissive to male authority. In 1621 Mother Jerón-
ima de la Asuncion, a sixty-five-year-old Spanish Poor Clare, arrived in Manila
and founded a cloistered community. Because of the sharp contrast in its
practices (such as silent prayer, the cutting of members' hair, and abstention
from sexual relations) from those of shamans, the community had meager
local appeal. A century later, Ignacia del Espiritu Santo established an order
later known as the Religious of the Virgin Mary, specifically to accommodate
indigenous women.

Although the Portuguese and Spanish encouraged some intermarriage
of their officials with indigenous women, the Dutch in Indonesia fostered the
most substantial mestizo community in Southeast Asia. This Dutch policy is
in sharp contrast to the British disparagement of intermarriage by its officials
with women in South Asia and its reticence to acknowledge legally the children of any informal sexual relationships. The Dutch permitted marriages
between Dutch men and Javanese women if the latter had converted to Christianity. Other officials could form unofficial unions with local women. If Dutch
men recognized the children of these liaisons, they were deemed legitimate
and accorded legal status as Europeans.

During their mid-teens the Eurasian daughters married senior Dutch
officials two or more decades older than themselves. Creators of a mestizo
culture in which they wore Indonesian sarongs and blouses, chewed betel, and
lived in semiseclusion, these women—known as *njai*—served as intermediaries between the two cultures and as guardians of the social order in a frontier
society. They produced sons for employment and daughters for marriage
within the Dutch establishment. They also possibly influenced their husbands
in officially sanctioned masculine qualities such as sobriety, moral rectitude,
and financial moderation and away from such undesirable relationships as
homosexuality.[84]

Thus in Indonesia, the category *European* included Eurasian children, in
sharp contrast to British India where such children were never officially cate-
gorized as British or European. This official Dutch support for concubinage
"revealed how deeply the conduct of private life, and the sexual proclivities
which individuals expressed were tied to corporate profits and to the security
of the colonial states."[85]

By the 1920s, Dutch colonial policy sought to replace concubinage and
marriage between Dutch officials and Eurasian and Indonesian women with
marriage among "full-blooded" Europeans or even sexual relations with prostitutes to maintain cultural boundaries with respect to nationalist challenges.
The attempt only partly succeeded because 27.5 percent of the Europeans in
Indonesia continued to marry either indigenous or "mixed-blood" women in
1927, and 20 percent still chose such women as late as 1940.[86] Still, a new

category of *njonjas* (colonial matrons) emerged, similar to memsahibs in British India. As occurred in other colonial contexts such as India, Fiji, and Africa, white men entrusted their white female partners with responsibility for helping maintain colonial authority, viewed any sexual attraction and relations between white women and indigenous men as threatening to that authority and their own masculinity, restricted their female relatives to domestic space, and then condemned these women as being racist for their lack of empathy for indigenous culture. Many white Dutch women benefited from their complicity with the imperial enterprise, but their position was ambiguous because they were clearly subordinate associates.[87]

WOMEN IN COLONIAL SOUTHEAST ASIA, 1880–1950

Because of the availability of her extensive letters and publicity by colonial mentors, Indonesians and many foreigners eulogize Raden Ajeng Kartini (1879–1904) as the quintessential female Indonesian advocate of women's rights and national liberation. The daughter of a *priyayi* (an aristocratic Javanese who served as a Dutch civil servant) and his secondary wife, Kartini attended a European primary school where she became proficient in Dutch and socialized with Dutch girls. When secluded from 1891 to 1895 in preparation for marriage, Kartini read the works of Pandita Ramabai and some Dutch feminists and became a friend of the Dutch wife of a local official. In 1899 Kartini began to write to Dutch and Indonesian friends and championed education as a means of self-improvement, escape from arranged marriage and polygyny, and preparation for motherhood.[88] These themes echoed those that elite women in India had begun to advocate in autobiographies, letters, and journals a few decades earlier. For some feminists the great paradox in Kartini's life was that after declining a scholarship in the Netherlands she agreed in 1903 to an arranged marriage with an elderly man who had three secondary wives. Their marriage lasted ten months because Kartini died on September 17, 1904, four days after the birth of a son.

Scholars, both abroad and in Indonesia, have analyzed the persona and legacy of Kartini. This Indonesian woman is now seen as symptomatic of the priyayi's desire to enhance their social position by educating their daughters in order that they might develop congenial social relations with the Dutch wives of colonial officials. Nonetheless, Kartini challenged priyayi values in her call for personal freedom for unmarried girls and in her early desire for a career.

The ambiguities in Kartini's life and writings permit contemporary Indonesian authors and political leaders to shape the legacy of Kartini for their own goals. Pramoedya Ananta Toer—Indonesia's greatest living novelist, whose works were banned in his own country—portrayed Kartini as able to challenge traditional values and transcend differences between classes.[89] After 1965 the New Order Indonesian Government promoted Hari Ibu (Mother) Kartini or Mother Kartini Day. For that occasion, young girls were to wear tight, fitted jackets, batik shirts, elaborate hairstyles, and ornate jewelry to school, supposedly replicating Kartini's attire but in reality wearing an invented and more constricting ensemble than she ever did.[90]

Thus Kartini validates the New Order policy of State Ibuism, "which defines women as appendages and companions to their husbands, as procreators of the nation, as mothers and educators of children, as housekeepers, and as members of Indonesian society—in that order."[91] In neither colonial nor independent Indonesia is there room for the Kartini who proclaimed "I long to be free, to be allowed, to be able to make myself independent, to be dependent on no-on else, . . . to never have to marry."[92]

Compared to the extensive scholarship on Kartini, other Indonesian women activists remain in historiographical purdah, as do most other women during the colonial period in Southeast Asia. One significant exception is women in Vietnam. "By the 1920s, 'women and society' had become something of a focal point around which other issues revolved [in Vietnam]. . . . Women became conscious of themselves as a social group with particular interests, grievances, and demands."[93] Social radicals concerned about women working on plantations, in mines and factories, and as concubines and prostitutes joined traditionalist and modern feminists. By 1925 Ho Chi Minh recognized the oppression of women by men, and five years later the newly formed Indochinese Communist Party included the fight for equality between the sexes among its ten principal tasks. In the late 1930s, the party advocated reforms appropriate to various classes of women, such as equal pay for equal work for employed women, equal inheritance rights for middle-class women, the elimination of polygyny, and the right to free choice in marriage and divorce.

Scholarship on women's economic activity during the colonial period has just begun. Women during the nineteenth century in Manila worked in new occupations, whether making cigars in state-run tobacco factories or teaching in colonial government schools. They also worked in traditional jobs as vendors, shopkeepers, seamstresses, embroiderers, prostitutes, and midwives. Reversing the pattern in India, a school for midwives was established first in 1879, and the Superior Normal School for Women followed in 1892. In the early twentieth century the arrival of Americans brought coeducation, which produced a literacy rate among women of 82 percent by 1970.[94] The education, however, was in English. By the 1930s women composed nearly 50 percent of the laborers on rubber plantations in Malaya and Vietnam and were a major presence on the tea, coffee, rubber, tobacco, and sugar plantations of Indonesia.[95] They also worked under exploitative conditions in the textile mills of Vietnam.

As in South Asia, elite women created women's organizations during the 1920s throughout Southeast Asia, but their agendas differed in relation to regional religious cultures and political situations. Once again, scholarship on Indonesia is the most extensive. Initially, Indonesian women were more attracted to sections of Indonesian nationalist and religious organizations such as the Aisjijah, the female section of the Muhammaddijah formed in 1912. The group sought to privilege Qur'anic law over *adat* (customary law) and prescribed a head-dress for members that left the face bare but covered the head and neck. This partial veiling occurred in the twentieth century in a culture where most Muslim women earlier had not worn any head-covering. At the same time, the Aisjijah called for more opportunities for education and greater participation in religious activities for Muslim women.

After the first Indonesian Women's Congress in 1928, two major women's coalitions were formed—the elite Perikatan Perempuan Indonesia (PII) and the more radical Isteri Sedar, which was committed to political freedom and improving the situation of proletarian women. Dutch women did not involve themselves in the groups as British women did in India. Moreover, religious affiliations influenced their goals, as the debates over marriage laws illuminate. The PII and the Aisjijah opposed efforts to secure a minimum age of marriage law. Consequently, such legislation was not enacted until 1974, when the New Order program of family planning provided impetus for later marriage.[96] The same groups protested any governmental efforts that promoted monogamy because they supported polygyny as religiously sanctioned.[97]

The Dutch colonial government was much less receptive to granting the franchise to any women, whether Dutch or Indonesian, than were the British in India. Moreover, between the world wars the government and Dutch and Indonesian feminists "agreed on conservative notions of motherhood, on harmony and cooperation with men, on the restrictions of the vote to a specific class, and on the silently acknowledged fact that women's suffrage would have to be earned as a prize for the struggle by women themselves."[98] Only in 1935 did the Dutch government nominate C. H. (Cor) Razoux Schultz-Metzer, a Eurasian and political loyalist, as the first women member of the People's Council that had been established in 1918. Their action precipitated increased pressure from Indonesian women's groups that Indonesian women who had better educational qualifications and were the majority should be given the franchise. Despite pressure from the metropole, the colonial government delayed granting limited suffrage to literate women until 1941. The threat and subsequent reality of Japanese invasion, however, rendered this advance void.

All citizens in Indonesia only gained the right to vote in 1955, and they exercised it for the second time in 1999.[99]

Historians have outlined the development of women's organizations and highlighted a few women prominent in nationalist movements in other Southeast Asian countries during the twentieth century, but there is not the same level of analysis as is available on Indonesia and India. In Vietnam, women's organizations emerged during the 1920s. Despite its name, the Women's Labor-Study Association, formed in 1926, was an elite group. Its founder, Madame Ngu-yen Koa Tung, campaigned for more education for women and a "buy-Vietnamese" program similar to swadeshi work by Indian women, which reinforced women's role as consumers and controllers of household expenditures. By the 1930s, women went in two directions: a retreat to the private world of the family or an espousal of Marxism and a fundamental restructuring of Vietnamese society. In 1946, around 25 percent of the adult female Vietnamese population belonged to the Vietnam Women's Union of the Viet Minh. Women were willing to pay with their lives to expel first the French and then American political control and remake Vietnamese society.[100]

In the Philippines, women's organizations emerged during the early years of the American occupation. Broader groups were formed in the 1920s but had to lobby a Filipino male legislature for the franchise, and they were less supportive than their counterparts in India. Despite the support of President Manuel Luis Quezon, Filipino women did not achieve the franchise until 1937. There are only snippets of scholarship in English on legal and social reforms regarding women's rights and autonomy; women's organizations; women as workers; and women's participation in nationalist movements for women in Burma, Malay, Cambodia, and Laos.

Paralleling the situation in South Asia, historians of Southeast Asia are only beginning to delineate changes and continuities in the lives of women across the great divide between the colonial and postcolonial periods. Social scientists have produced innovative and imaginative scholarship that illuminates the lives of lower-class women in both rural and urban areas. They are particularly sensitive to the questionable economic and legal effects of globalization on the lives of women in Southeast Asia. Attention is also beginning to be paid to the relationships between religion and gender in state formation.[101]

Notes

1. Barbara N. Ramusack and Sharon Sievers, *Women in Asia: Restoring Women to History* (Bloomington: Indiana University Press, 1999); Marysa Navarro and Virginia Sánchez Korrol, with Kecia Ali, *Women in Latin America and the Caribbean: Restoring Women to History*

(Bloomington: Indiana Unversity Press, 1999); Guity Nashat and Judith E. Tucker, *Women in the Middle East and North Africa: Restoring Women to History* (Bloomington: Indiana University Press, 1999); Iris Berger and E. Frances White, *Women in Sub-Saharan Africa: Restoring Women to History* (Bloomington: Indiana University Press, 1999).

2. Sally J. M. Sunderland, "Sita and Draupadi: Aggressive Behavior and Female Role-Models in the Sanskrit Epics," *Journal of the American Oriental Society* 109, no. 1 (1989): 63–79.

3. *The Laws of Manu,* trans. Wendy Doniger with Brian K. Smith (London: Penguin, 1991), 115, ch. 5, verse 148.

4. *Laws of Manu,* trans. Doniger, 198, ch. 9, verse 17.

5. Anand A. Yang, "Whose Sati? Widow Burning in Early Nineteenth Century India," *Journal of Women's History* 1, no. 2 (1989): 8–33.

6. Catherine Weinberger-Thomas, *Ashes of Immortality: Widow-Burning in India,* trans. Jeffrey Mehlman and David Gordon White (New Delhi: Oxford University Press, 2000).

7. Wendy Doniger, "Why Did They Burn?" *Times Literary Supplement,* Sept. 14, 2001, 4.

8. John Stratton Hawley, ed., *The Blessing and the Curse: The Burning of Wives in India* (New York: Oxford University Press, 1994); Mala Sen, *Death by Fire: Sati, Dowry Death and Female Infanticide in Modern India* (London: Weidenfeld and Nicolson, 2001).

9. Judith Tucker, *Gender and Islamic History* (Washington: American Historical Association, 1994), 5.

10. Sylvia Vatuk, "Purdah Revisited: A Comparison of Hindu and Muslim Interpretations of the Cultural Meaning of Purdah in South Asia," in *Separate Worlds: Studies of Purdah in South Asia,* ed. Hanna Papanek and Gail Minault (Columbia, Mo.: South Asian Books, 1982), 54–78.

11. Stephanie Jamison, *Sacrificed Wife, Sacrificer's Wife: Women, Ritual and Hospitality in Ancient India* (New York: Oxford University Press, 1996).

12. Kumkum Roy, *The Emergence of Monarchy in North India Eighth–Fourth Centuries B.C.: As Reflected in the Brahmanical Tradition* (Delhi: Oxford University Press, 1994), 156 and ch. 8.

13. Uma Chakravarti, "Conceptualising Brahmanical Patriarchy in Early India: Gender, Caste, Class and State," *Economic and Political Weekly,* April 3, 1993, 579–85.

14. Giti Thadani, *Sakhiyani: Lesbian Desire in Ancient and Modern India* (London: Cassell, 1996).

15. Roy, *The Emergence of Monarchy,* ch. 8.

16. *The Arthasastra,* ed., rearr., trans., and intro. by L. N. Rangarajan (New Delhi: Penguin, 1992), 66–70, 351–53, 393–412.

17. Vidya Dehejia, *Antal and Her Path of Love: Poems of a Woman Saint from South India* (Albany: State University of New York Press, 1990).

18. Kumkum Sangari, "Mirabai and the Spiritual Economy of *Bhakti,"Economic and Political Weekly,* July 7 and 14, 1990, 1464–75, 1537–52.

19. Parita Mukta, *Upholding the Common Life: The Community of Mirabai* (Delhi: Oxford University Press, 1994).

20. Richard Maxwell Eaton, "Sufi Folk Literature and the Expansion of Indian Islam," *History of Religions* 14 (Nov. 1974): 117–27.

21. Peter Jackson, "Sultan Ridiyya Bint Iltutmish," in *Women in the Medieval Islamic World: Power, Patronage, and Piety,* ed. Gavin R. G. Hambly (New York: St. Martin's Press, 1998), 181–97.

22. Cynthia Talbot, "Rudrama-devi, the Female King: Gender and Political Authority

in Medieval India," in *Syllables of Sky: Studies in South Indian Civilization in Honour of Velcheru Narayana Rao*, ed. David Shulman (Delhi: Oxford University Press, 1995), 391–430.

23. Rosalind O'Hanlon, "Issues of Masculinity in North Indian History: The Bangash Nawabs of Farrukhabad," *Indian Journal of Gender Studies* 4, no. 1 (1997): 1–19; Rosalind O'Hanlon, "Manliness and Imperial Service in Mughal North India," *Journal of the Economic and Social History of the Orient* 42, no. 1 (1999): 47–93.

24. Ruby Lal, "Rethinking Mughal India: Challenge of a Princess' Memoir," *Economic and Political Weekly*, Jan. 4–10, 2003, 53–65.

25. Ellison Banks Findly, *Nur Jahan: Empress of Mughal India* (New York: Oxford University Press, 1993).

26. Stephen P. Blake, "Contributors to the Urban Landscape: Women Builders in Safavid Isfahan and Mughal Shahjahanabad," in *Women in the Medieval Islamic World*, ed. Hambly, 407–28.

27. Gregory C. Kozlowski, "Private Lives and Public Piety: Women and the Practice of Islam in Mughal India," in *Women in the Medieval Islamic World*, ed. Hambly, 469–88.

28. Uma Chakravarti, *Rewriting History: The Life and Times of Pandita Ramabai* (New Delhi: Kali for Women, 1998), 1–31, esp. 31.

29. Durba Ghosh, "Making and Un-making Loyal Subjects: Pensioning Widows and Educating Orphans in Early Colonial India," *Journal of Imperial and Commonwealth History* 31, no. 1 (2003): 1–28.

30. Pompa Banerjee, *Burning Women: Widows, Witches, and Early Modern European Travelers in India* (New York: Palgrave Macmillan, 2003).

31. Lata Mani, *Contentious Traditions: The Debate on Sati in Colonial India* (Berkeley: University of California Press, 1998).

32. James Mills, *The History of British India*, 2 vols. (New York: Chelsea House, 1968), 309–10.

33. Three foundational works are Neera Desai, *Women in Modern India* (Bombay: Vora, 1957); Meredith Borthwick, *The Changing Role of Women in Bengal, 1849–1905* (Princeton: Princeton University Press, 1984); and *Recasting Women: Essays in Indian Colonial History*, ed. Kumkum Sangari and Sudesh Vaid (New Brunswick: Rutgers University Press, 1990).

34. Geraldine Forbes, *Women in Modern India*, New Cambridge History of India, ser. 4, vol. 2 (New York: Cambridge University Press, 1996) is the most comprehensive and insightful overview of the period from 1800 to the present and includes an extensive bibliographical essay.

35. Janaki Nair, *Women and Law in Colonial India: A Social History* (New Delhi: Kali for Women, 1996).

36. Sangari and Vaid, eds., *Recasting Women;* Tanika Sarkar, *Hindu Wife, Hindu Nation: Community, Religion and Cultural Nationalism* (Bloomington: Indiana University Press, 2001).

37. Dagmar Engels, "The Age of Consent Act of 1891: Colonial Ideology in Bengal," *South Asia Research* 3 (Nov. 1983): 107–34; Mrinalini Sinha, *Colonial Masculinity: The "Manly Englishman" and the "Effeminate Bengali" in the Late Nineteenth Century* (Manchester, U.K.: Manchester University Press, 1995); Mrinalini Sinha, "Giving Masculinity a History: Some Contributions from the Historiography of Colonial India," *Gender and History* 11 (Nov. 1999): 445–60.

38. Prem Chowdhry, *The Veiled Women: Shifting Gender Equations in Rural Haryana, 1880–1990* (Delhi: Oxford University Press, 1994).

39. Veena Talwar Oldenburg, *Dowry Murder: The Imperial Origins of a Cultural Crime* (New York: Oxford University Press, 2002).

40. Padma Anagol, "The Emergence of the Female Criminal in India: Infanticide and Survival under the Raj," *History Workshop Journal* 53 (Spring 2002): 73–93.

41. Sarkar, *Hindu Wife, Hindu Nation,* 191–225.

42. Padma Anagol-McGinn, "The Age of Consent Act (1891) Reconsidered," *South Asia Research* 12, no. 2 (1992): 100–118.

43. Geraldine Forbes, "Women and Modernity: The Issue of Child Marriage in India," *Women's Studies International Quarterly* 2, no. 4 (1979): 407–19; Mrinalini Sinha, "The Lineage of the 'Indian' Modern: Rhetoric, Agency and the Sarda Act in Late Colonial India," in *Gender, Sexuality and Colonial Modernities,* ed. Antoinette Burton (New York: Routledge, 1999), 207–21.

44. For Hindu Bengali women, see Borthwick, *The Changing Role of Women.* On Muslim women, see Sonia Amin, *The World of Muslim Women in Colonial Bengal, 1876–1939* (Leiden: E. J. Brill, 1996) and Gail Minault, *Secluded Scholars: Women's Education and Muslim Social Reform in Colonial India* (Delhi: Oxford University Press, 1998).

45. Sarkar, *Hindu Wife, Hindu Nation,* 112.

46. Rosalind O'Hanlon, *A Comparison between Women and Men: Tarabai Shinde and the Critique of Gender Relations in Colonial India* (Madras: Oxford University Press, 1994), 12.

47. Anshu Malhotra, *Gender, Caste, and Religious Identities: Restructuring Class in Colonial Punjab* (New Delhi: Oxford University Press, 2002); Doris R. Jakobsh, *Relocating Gender in Sikh History: Tranformation, Meaning and Identity* (New Delhi: Oxford University Press, 2003).

48. Pandita Ramabai Sarasvati, *The High-Caste Hindu Woman* (1887, repr. Westport: Hyperion Press, 1976); Meera Kosambi, "Women, Emancipation and Equality: Pandita Ramabai's Contribution to the Women's Cause," *Economic and Political Weekly,* Oct. 29, 1988, WS38–WS49; Antoinette Burton, *At the Heart of Empire: Indians and the Colonial Encounter in Late-Victorian Britain* (Berkeley: University of California Press, 1997), ch. 2; Chakravarti, *Rewriting History.*

49. Partha Chatterjee, "The Nationalist Resolution of the Women's Question," in *Recasting Women,* ed. Sangari and Vaid, 233–53.

50. Rokeya Sakhawat Hossain, *Sultana's Dream and Selections from the Secluded Ones,* trans. and intro. Roushan Jahan, afterword by Hanna Papanek (New York: Feminist Press, 1988).

51. Purnima Bose, *Organizing Empire: Individualism, Collective Agency and India* (Durham: Duke University Press, 2003), ch. 2; Catherine Candy, "Relating Feminisms, Nationalisms and Imperialisms: Ireland, India and Margaret Cousins's Sexual Politics," *Women's History Review* 3, no. 4 (1994): 581–94; Barbara N. Ramusack, "Catalysts or Helpers? British Feminists, Indian Women's Rights, and Indian Independence," in *The Extended Family: Women and Political Participation in India and Pakistan,* ed. Gail Minault (Columbia, Mo.: South Asia Books, 1981), 109–50; Barbara N. Ramusack, "Cultural Missionaries, Maternal Imperialists, Feminist Allies: British Women Activists in India, 1865–1945," *Women's Studies International Forum* 13, no. 4 (1990): 295–308.

52. Shudha Mazumdar, *Memoirs of an Indian Women,* ed. with intro. by Geraldine Forbes (1977, repr. Armonk: M. E. Sharpe, 1989). Forbes is the editor of the series entitled Foremothers, which has published several other memoirs of women from India, Africa, and the Middle East.

53. Forbes, *Women in Modern India.*

54. Ibid., 93–112.

55. Madhu Kishwar, "Women and Gandhi," *Economic and Political Weekly*, Oct. 5–12, 1985, 1691–702, 1753–58; Sujata Patel, "Construction and Reconstruction of Woman in Gandhi," *Economic and Political Weekly*, Feb. 20, 1988, 377–87.

56. Bose, *Organizing Empire*, ch. 3.

57. Sanjam Ahluwalia, "Histories of Oppression: Birth Control and Sexual Politics in Colonial India," in *Confronting the Body: The Politics of Physicality in Colonial and Post-Colonial India*, ed. James H. Mills and Satadru Sen (London: Anthem Press, 2004), 183–202; Barbara N. Ramusack, "Embattled Advocates: The Debate over Birth Control in India, 1920–40," *Journal of Women's History* 1, no. 2 (1989): 34–64.

58. Charu Gupta, *Sexuality, Obscenity, Community: Women, Muslims, and the Hindu Public in Colonial India* (New York: Palgrave Macmillan, 2002).

59. Samita Sen, *Women and Labour in Late Colonial India: The Bengal Jute Industry* (New York: Cambridge University Press, 1999).

60. Indra Munshi Saldanha, "Tribal Women in the Warli Revolt, 1945–47: 'Class' and 'Gender' in the Left Perspective," *Economic and Political Weekly*, April 26, 1986, WS41–WS52.

61. Peter Custers, *Women in the Tebhaga Uprising* (Calcutta: Naya Prokash, 1987).

62. Stree Shakti Sanghatana, *"We Were Making History": Life Stories of Women in the Telangana People's Struggle* (London: Zed Books, 1989).

63. Urvashi Butalia, *The Other Side of Silence: Voices from the Partition of India* (1998, repr. Durham: Duke University Press, 2000); Ritu Menon and Kamla Bhasin, *Borders and Boundaries: Women in India's Partition* (New Brunswick: Rutgers University Press, 1996).

64. *Towards Equality: Report of the Committee on the Status of Women in India* (New Delhi: Government of India, Ministry of Education and Social Welfare, Department of Social Welfare, December 1974), 10 (statistical table), more generally, see 9–36.

65. *Towards Equality*, 8.

66. Tanika Sarkar and Urvashi Butalia, eds., *Women and the Hindu Right: A Collection of Essays* (New Delhi: Kali for Women, 1995).

67. Paola Bacchetta, "Hindu Nationalist Women as Ideologues: The Sangh, the Samiti and Differential Concepts of the Hindu Nation," in *Embodied Violence: Communalising Women's Sexuality in South Asia*, ed. Kumari Jayawardena and Malathi de Alwis (London: Zed Books, 1996), 126–67.

68. Lucy Carroll, "The Muslim Family Laws Ordinance, 1961: Provisions and Procedures—A Reference Paper for Current Research," *Contributions to Indian Sociology* 13, no. 1 (1979): 117–43.

69. Dina M. Siddiqi, "Taslima Nasreen and Others: The Contest over Gender in Bangladesh," in *Women in Muslim Societies: Diversity within Unity*, ed. Herbert L. Bodman and Nayereh Tohidi, (Boulder: Lynne Rienner, 1998), 205–27; Naila Kabeer, *The Power to Choose: Bangladeshi Women and Labour Market Decisions in London and Dhaka* (London: Verso, 2000).

70. Helen Creese, *Women of the Kakawin World: Marriage and Sexuality in the Indic Courts of Java and Bali* (Armonk: M. E. Sharpe, 2004) is a pioneering example of this scholarship.

71. David G. Marr, *Vietnamese Tradition on Trial, 1920–1945* (Berkeley: University of California Press, 1981).

72. Michael Aung-Thwin, *Pagan: The Origins of Modern Burma* (Honolulu: University of Hawaii Press, 1985), 41.

73. Barbara Watson Andaya, "Localising the Universal: Women, Motherhood and

the Appeal of Early Theravada Buddhism," *Journal of Southeast Asian Studies* 30 (2002): 1–30.

74. Lucy Whalley, "Urban Minangkabau Muslim Women: Modern Choices, Traditional Concerns in Indonesia," in *Women in Muslim Societies,* ed. Bodman and Tohidi, 229–49.

75. Anthony Reid, "Female Roles in Pre-colonial Southeast Asia," *Modern Asian Studies* 22 (1988): 640.

76. Ann Kumar, "Javanese Court Society and Politics in the Late Eighteenth Century: The Record of a Lady Soldier," pt. 1: "The Religious, Social and Economic Life of the Court," *Indonesia* 29 (April 1980): 5.

77. Kumar, "Javanese Court Society," 5.

78. Ann Kumar, "Javanese Court Society," pt. 2: "Political Developments: The Courts and the Company, 1784–1791," *Indonesia* 30 (Oct. 1980): 100–101.

79. Ruzy Hashim, "Bringing Tun Kudu Out of the Shadows: Interdisciplinary Approaches to Understanding the Female Presence in the *Sejarah Melayu,"* in *Other Pasts: Women, Gender and History in Early Modern Southeast Asia,* ed. Barbara Watson Andaya (Honolulu: Center for Southeast Asian Studies, University of Hawai'i at Mânoa, 2000), 105–204.

80. Dhiravat na Pombejra, "VOC Employees and their Relationships with Mon and Siamese Women," in *Other Pasts,* ed. Andaya, 195–214.

81. Barbara Watson Andaya, "From Temporary Wife to Prostitute: Sexuality and Economic Change in Early Modern Southeast Asia," *Journal of Women's History* 9, no. 4 (1998): 11–34.

82. Barbara Watson Andaya, "Women and Economic Change: The Pepper Trade in Pre-Modern Southeast Asia," *Journal of the Economic and Social History of the Orient* 38, no. 2 (1995): 165–90.

83. Carolyn Brewer, *Shamanism, Catholicism and Gender Relations in Colonial Philippines, 1521–1685* (Aldershot, U.K.: Ashgate, 2004).

84. Jean Gelman Taylor, *The Social World of Batavia: European and Eurasian in Dutch Asia* (Madison: University of Wisconsin Press, 1983).

85. Ann Stoler, "Making Empire Respectable: The Politics of Race and Sexual Morality in Twentieth-Century Colonial Cultures," *American Ethnologist* 14, no. 4 (1989): 638.

86. Frances Gouda, *Dutch Culture Overseas: Colonial Practice in the Netherlands Indies, 1900–1942* (Amsterdam: Amsterdam University Press, 1995), 165.

87. Gouda, *Dutch Culture Overseas,* ch. 5.

88. Joost Coté, *On Feminism and Nationalism: Kartini's Letters to Stella Zeehandelaar, 1899–1903* (Clayton, Australia: Monash Asian Institute, Monash University, 1995).

89. Danilyn Rutherford, "Unpacking a National Heroine: Two Kartinis and Their People," *Indonesia* 55 (April 1993): 23–40.

90. Laurie J. Sears, introduction to *Fantasizing the Feminine in Indonesia,* ed. Laurie J. Sears (Durham: Duke University Press, 1996), 37–38.

91. Julia I. Suryakusuma, "The State and Sexuality in New Order Indonesia," in *Fantasizing the Feminine,* ed. Sears, 101.

92. As quoted in Sylvia Tiwon, "Models and Maniacs: Articulating the Female in Indonesia," in *Fantasizing the Feminine,* ed. Sears, 55, ellipsis is Kartini's.

93. Marr, *Vietnamese Tradition,* 191.

94. Kumari Jayawardena, *Feminism and Nationalism in the Third World* (London: Zed Books, 1986).

95. Lenore Manderson, "Right and Responsibility, Power and Privilege: Women's Roles in Contemporary Indonesia," in *Kartini Centenary: Indonesian Women Then and Now,* ed. Ailsa Thomson Zainu'ddin (Clayton, Australia: Center of Southeast Asian Studies, Monash University, 1980).

96. Susan Blackburn and Sharon Bessell, "Marriageable Age: Political Debates on Early Marriage in Twentieth-Century Indonesia," *Indonesia* 63 (April 1997): 107–41.

97. Elsbeth Locher-Scholten, *Women and the Colonial State: Essays on Gender and Modernity in the Netherlands India 1900–1942* (Amsterdam: Amsterdam University Press, 2000), ch. 6.

98. Locher-Scholten, *Women and the Colonial State,* 178.

99. Susan Blackburn, "Western Feminists Observe Asian Women: An Example from the Dutch East Indies," in *Women Creating Indonesia: The First Fifty Years,* ed. Jean Gelman Taylor (Clayton, Australia: Monash Asia Institute, Monash University, 1997); Locher-Scholten, *Women and the Colonial State,* ch. 5.

100. Jayawardena, *Feminism and Nationalism;* Marr, *Vietnamese Tradition.*

101. Jaqueline Aquino Siapno, *Gender, Islam, Nationalism and the State in Aceh: The Paradox of Power, Co-optation and Resistance* (London: Taylor and Francis, 2002).

BIBLIOGRAPHY OF ADDITIONAL SOURCES

Anagol, Padma. *Feminism, the Politics of Gender and Social Reform in India, 1850–1920.* Aldershot, U.K.: Ashgate, 2005.

Andaya, Barbara Watson. "The Changing Religious Role of Women in Pre-Modern South East Asia." *South East Asia Research* 2 (Sept. 1994): 99–116.

Bagchi, Jasodhara. "Representing Nationalism: Ideology of Motherhood in Colonial Bengal." *Economic and Political Weekly,* Oct. 20–27, 1990, WS66–WS71.

Barry, Kathleen, ed. *Vietnam's Women in Transition.* London: Macmillan, 1996.

Burton, Antoinette. *Dwelling in the Archive: Women Writing House, Home, and History in Late Colonial India.* New York: Oxford University Press, 2003.

Camagay, Ma. Luisa. *Working Women of Manila in the Nineteenth Century.* Manila: University of Philippines Press and University Center for Women's Studies, 1995.

Chatterjee, Indrani, ed. *Unfamiliar Relations: Family and History in South Asia.* New Brunswick: Rutgers University Press, 2004.

Clancy-Smith, Julia, and Frances Gouda, eds. *Domesticating the Empire: Race, Gender and Family Life in French and Dutch Colonialism.* Charlottesville: University Press of Virginia, 1998.

Coté, Joost, trans. and intro. *Letters from Kartini: An Indonesian Feminist, 1900–1904.* Clayton, Australia: Monash Asian Institute, Monash University, 1992.

Engels, Dagmar. *Beyond Purdah? Women in Bengal 1890–1939.* Delhi: Oxford University Press, 1996.

Grever, Maria, and Berteke Waaldijk. *Transforming the Public Sphere: The Dutch National Exhibition of Women's Labor in 1898.* Translated by Mischa F. C. Hoyinck and Robert E. Chesal. Introduction by Antoinette Burton. Durham: Duke University Press, 2004.

Jayawardena, Kumari. *The White Woman's Other Burden: Western Women and South Asia during British Rule.* New York: Routledge, 1995.

Lambert-Hurley, Siobhan. "Fostering Sisterhood: Muslim Women and the All-India Ladies' Association." *Journal of Women's History* 16, no. 2 (2004): 40–65.

Locher-Scholten, Elsbeth. "Morals, Harmony, and National Identity: 'Companionate

Feminism' in Colonial Indonesia in the 1930s." *Journal of Women's History* 14, no. 4 (2003): 38–58.

Rouse, Shahnaz. *Shifting Body Politics: Gender, Nation, State in Pakistan.* New Delhi: Women Unlimited, 2004.

Sarkar, Tanika. *Words to Win: The Making of Amar Jiban: A Modern Autobiography.* New Delhi: Kali for Women, 1999.

Sreenivas, Mytheli. "Emotion, Identity, and the Female Subject: Tamil Women's Magazines in Colonial India, 1890–1940." *Journal of Women's History* 14, no. 4 (2003): 59–82.

Uberoi, Patricia, ed. 1996. *Social Reform, Sexuality and the State.* New Delhi: Sage Publications.

Van Bemmelen, Sita et al., eds. 1992. *Women and Mediation in Indonesia.* Leiden: KITLV Press, 1992.

Zainu'ddin, Ailsa Thomson. "Kartini: Her Life, Work and Influence." In *Kartini Centenary: Indonesian Women Then and Now,* edited by Ailsa Thomson Zainu'ddin. Clayton, Australia: Center of Southeast Asian Studies, Monash University, 1980.

4

Medieval Women in
Modern Perspective

JUDITH M. BENNETT

Medieval Europe often seems a childlike time. As publishers and toy manufacturers know well, modern children can pass many happy hours imagining medieval worlds of brave ladies, bold knights, saintly maids, and wily monks. As
they grow up, some children simply clothe medievalism in the futuristic robes
of science fiction (the most playful of adult literary genres), but most abandon
the Middle Ages for more practical pursuits. Feudal kings, saintly nuns, and
hardworking serfs are well and good, but they are not very modern, and their
study can seem indulgent or even whimsical—antiquarianism rather than history. This might seem especially true in the case of medieval women. What
possible relevance can the Middle Ages—often imagined (wrongly) as a time
when one faith reigned supreme, all people knew their place, and nothing ever
changed—offer to modern feminist scholars? Most modern people seem to
waver between seeing medieval women as hopelessly oppressed or wonderful-
ly free. In either case they usually assume that the experiences of medieval
women are distant, arcane, and irrelevant to the challenges of the present.

Yet the Middle Ages have been and remain highly significant to modern
times. When feminists first began to organize in late-nineteenth-century Europe, they quickly turned to the Middle Ages for information about the issues that concerned them: women's work, women's education, women's status under the law, and women's participation in political life. Today, the
feminist study of the Middle Ages has again become a flourishing field that
enriches literary, philological, musical, philosophical, and religious studies

as well as history. Feminist medievalists—many *hundreds* of them—have an association, a journal, bibliographic projects, and even long-standing research collaborations.[1]

In some ways feminist medievalists participate in the most elitist traditions of the academy. Expensively trained in long-dead languages, feminist medievalists study a region with an exceptionally troubled history of racism and colonialism, and they even tend to focus, within Europe, on a tiny minority of rich, literate, and powerful people.[2] In some ways feminist medievalists are also peculiarly handicapped, approaching a distant past through incomplete and intransigent sources that were, with few exceptions, created and preserved by men.[3]

Yet despite these obstacles, and in part because of them, investigations of the Middle Ages are critical to feminist scholarship, especially to women's history. If students are attentive to matters of difference among modern women, they will be intrigued by the new differences—for example, religion, region, and marital status—that medievalists have added to the feminist canon of race, class, and gender. If students are curious about feminist spirituality or the place of religion in women's lives, they will take many insights from richly investigated histories of female mysticism, monasticism, and heresy in medieval Europe. If students assume that women's status has steadily improved over the centuries—and that they now live in the "best of all worlds" for women—they will be surprised by ongoing debates about whether, when, and how the status of women changed during the medieval millennium. In these cases and many others, feminist medievalists are not only *adding* medieval information to the databanks of history but also *shaping* history itself, developing new questions, new concepts, and new interpretations of the past.

For teachers, the history of medieval women offers unusual pedagogical opportunities. First, because the field has a long history it can illustrate the evolution of history-writing. Each generation of feminist medievalists has brought its own concerns to the study of medieval women. Is it an accident, for example, that Annie Abram wrote one of the first studies of medieval women's work when many of her fellow Englishwomen were entering the workforce during World War I or that she then reached the encouraging conclusion that medieval women were "persons of strong character and undeniable business activity"?[4] Second, the distance between the Middle Ages and the present allows a long view on critical feminist issues. How important are differences among women in understanding women's history? In what ways has women's status varied across time, by region, according to class status, or by other criteria? How might we best conceptualize the periodization of women's history? Because the Middle Ages span so many centuries—the Early Middle Ages (ca. 500–1000), the Central Middle Ages (ca. 1000–1300), and the Later Middle Ages (ca. 1300–1500)—these questions can be studied both within the medieval millennium itself and in terms of the relationship between the Middle Ages and more modern centuries. They also can lead to fruitful comparisons of gender relations in the medieval West and other contemporary societies. Third, because medieval Europe is so far removed from our own time it can offer an effective example—both clear and unthreatening in its distance—of the profound powers and troubling inconsistencies of gender ideologies. Medieval misogyny can strike modern students with horrific force, but by subjecting it to study students can trace both the medieval meanings of misogyny *and* their modern analogs. They can also grapple with the powerful ways in which gender has been ideologically implicated in how we imagine the past, as particularly illustrated by hackneyed myths about chastity belts, female popes, and a lord's "right of the first night." Fourth, medieval Europe offers many subjects of considerable interest to students today: virginity, women and war, rape, women and spirituality, women and food, and, of course, such extraordinary characters as Queen Radegund (ca. 525–87), Eleanor of Aquitaine (ca. 1122–1203), Hildegard of Bingen (1098–1179), and Joan of Arc (ca. 1412–31).[5]

An Early and Still Influential Conceptualization of Medieval Women's History

In 1926 Eileen Power, medieval historian at the London School of Economics, wrote an essay about women for a general volume on *The Legacy of the Middle Ages*.[6] Even at that early date she was able to draw on extensive research into the lives of medieval women—research about women's status before the law, about nuns and queens, and about the working lives of women in medieval cities. Indeed, that the editors felt their volume would be incomplete without a discussion of women speaks to the distinguished work already then completed by feminist medievalists who had worked in the late nineteenth and early twentieth centuries.[7] Yet the editors also wanted a particular sort of essay, and they rejected an earlier effort by Power because it was, in her words, "not sufficiently respectful to (a) women (b) the Church (c) the Proprieties." At their insistence, she produced an essay so inoffensive that it could be read aloud, as she wryly wrote to a friend, "by the kindergarten mistress during needlework."[8]

This mild essay was not one of Power's personal favorites, but it is now one of the most influential of her many publications. Although modified in many details, it still offers a compelling conceptualization of the history of medieval women. Writing especially about the Central and Later Middle Ages, Power focused her essay on the relative position of women with respect to men, raising a question—how might we best assess the status of medieval women?—that teachers and students still ponder.

In her answer, Power stressed three points that still resonate today. First, she balanced theory against practice, arguing not only that medieval ideas about women were distinct from the everyday experiences of women but also that these ideas were so confused and self-contradictory that they could have had little direct effect on everyday life. Second, Power favorably judged the overall status of medieval women. She recognized that medieval women faced some serious problems—a culture rife with misogyny, a legal system based on assumptions of female inferiority, and a social structure that invested men with considerable power over women's lives. But, arguing that the true position of medieval women "was one neither of inferiority nor of superiority, but of a certain rough-and-ready equality," Power constructed a positive assessment of medieval gender roles, an image of the Middle Ages as a time that was, if not golden for women, then nevertheless very good indeed. Third, Power focused on class as *the* critical marker of differences among medieval women. Ignoring matters of religious difference and devoting only a few paragraphs to singlewomen, widows, and nuns, Power's essay implicitly equated "medieval women" with "Christian wives." The bulk of her essay was devoted to studying these Christian wives within three discrete social classes: feudal ladies, townswomen, and countrywomen.[9]

Today, you can pick up almost any textbook on medieval women and observe the enduring force of Eileen Power's historical imagination. Most modern descriptions begin, as her essay did, with medieval theories about woman and female nature. Whether called "the heritage of ideas," "the mold for women," or "the origins of medieval attitudes," these introductions seek, as Power did long ago, to understand both the internal ambiguities of medieval gender ideologies and their social meanings. Similarly, most studies of medieval women echo Power's upbeat assessment of women's lot in the Middle Ages. As Margaret Wade Labarge recently put it, medieval women might have been viewed "as subordinate and inferior by medieval men . . . but they were neither invisible, inaudible, nor unimportant." Finally, most textbooks categorize the subject of medieval women, as Power did, primarily according to class and, to a lesser degree, marital status or religious faith: feudal ladies compared to townswomen and peasant wives; all these compared to those who took holy vows; and perhaps some brief comparisons of these various Christian women with Jewish and, more rarely, Islamic women. In the textbooks and classrooms in which medieval women are now studied, they can still be seen, as Power saw them in 1926, as living in a Christian world fraught with ideological ambivalence about the female sex, filled with practical opportunity for female action, and fractured by profound divisions of class.[10]

Power's vision endures because it is commonsensical, politically useful, and eminently teachable. But it is also now incomplete. From the 1930s through the early 1960s, in the doldrums of modern feminism, little new research on medieval women was undertaken. But since the late 1960s the field has blossomed again, and this research has recast Power's conclusions about medieval ideologies of gender, her arguments about the status of women, and her attempts to categorize medieval women by class alone. The second wave has also identified new subjects, questions, and interpretive possibilities. In ways that are sometimes untidy but always stimulating, our understandings of medieval women now extend far beyond the neat confines of Power's formidable summation in 1926.

Difference and Medieval Women

To many scholars of the modern world, the categories of "race, class, and gender" seem to encompass all critical differences among women. Feminist medievalists, not so easily satisfied, have creatively explored the many meanings of difference for medieval women. If we understand "race" in the pseudo-biologic sense that now inheres to the term, medieval concepts of race applied not only to the "monstrous races" imagined to live outside of Europe but also to ethnic distinctions (for example, Scots versus Irish versus English); socioeconomic distinctions (some claimed, for example, that peasants were descended from Ham); and religious distinctions (Jews and Muslims were often thought to be racially distinct from Christians).[11] If we understand "class" in a sense that incorporates status and role as well as economic relation, then feudal, urban, and peasant women were profoundly marked by class differences. If we understand "gender" to encompass the ways in which human societies seek to elaborate distinctions of male and female sex, then the medieval world was rich in both gender distinctions and gender blurrings. Yet the modern trinity of "race, class, and gender" only begins to describe the many differences that fractured medieval society and created many different sorts of "medieval women."

First, marital status critically shaped the lives of medieval women. Some passed their entire lives as singlewomen, others married so young that they spent their adulthood as wives, and still others lost husbands so early that their lives were mostly shaped by widowhood. Of course, some women passed slowly through all three stages, living as singlewomen, then wives, and finally widows and experiencing different circumstances at each juncture. Second, religious status cut along many lines: Christians, Muslims, and Jews, to be sure, and also laywomen, professed nuns, or pious mystics and orthodox Christians as opposed to heretics. Third, legal status similarly cut deep divides among women, differentiating free from serf and serf from slave. Fourth, ethnicity was important because the various people who settled Europe brought with them varied customs and laws. (Although the status of women on the peripheries of Europe has long been the subject of mythic valorization, neither the Irish nor the Norse can now lay claim to medieval pasts of gender equality.)[12] Fifth, sexual status also mattered—so much so that medieval municipalities sought to segregate prostitutes from other women by prescribing special dress, special accommodations, and special behaviors. And, sixth, region shaped women's lives. By the Later Middle Ages, if not before, Europe divided into two distinct marriage regimes. In the south and east, women married young to husbands often twice their age, and, except for those who took holy vows, marriage was virtually universal. In the north and west, non-elite women married later to husbands roughly their own age, and a considerable number of women neither married nor entered monastic life. In 1400 an eighteen-year-old woman in Florence was likely to be the mother of a child or two; her counterpart in England was probably a servant who would not marry for several years or perhaps not at all.[13]

In some cases, historians are just beginning to identify and understand the meanings of these differences. Regional distinctions are not yet fully recognized by historians of family, marriage, and women; their origins are as yet obscure, and, most important, their meanings for women are uncertain.[14] Christiane Klapisch-Zuber has harshly judged the circumstances of women in late medieval Italy. Married young and without choice to husbands much older than themselves, they spent their married years in subjection to husbands and their lineages, and, once widowed, they often faced impossible circumstances. But Stanley Chojnacki, Elaine Rosenberg, Thomas Kuehn, and others have reached much more favorable conclusions about women's lot in late medieval Italy. Stressing women's ability to maneuver within patriarchal structures, they see wives as influential partners to husbands. Similar disagreements mark discussions of women's circumstances under the northwestern marriage pattern, as shown, for example, by the contrast between Maryanne Kowaleski's bleak assessment of women's lot in late medieval English towns and the more upbeat evaluations of such scholars as Jeremy Goldberg.[15]

In other cases, historians have more successfully incorporated difference into their studies of medieval women. For example, widows once served as archetypal women, so that historians, observing *widows* in tax registers, rentals, and guild lists, argued that *women* were taxpayers, landholders, and members of guilds. This confusion of "widow" with "woman" resulted in an overestimation of the opportunities open to medieval women. Although few women were enriched by widowhood (most received just half or a third of conjugal property), widows controlled more resources than did most other women. As a result, insofar as noblewomen held manors, offices, and fiefs, they were usually widows; insofar as townswomen were members of guilds or heads of businesses, they were usually widows; and insofar as countrywomen held acreage in the fields of their villages, they were usually widows.

But widows were not "typical" medieval women, and recognition of differences among women has now modified this earlier interpretation in two respects. Recognizing that the life of any woman varied according to marital status, scholars have now begun to address each life-stage on its own terms.[16] Scholars are also more aware of how the widowed state could involve pathetic poverty as well as unprecedented power. Writing in Paris in the early fifteenth century, Christine de Pizan (1364–1429) spoke from bitter experience about how often elite widows were denied properties rightfully theirs; urban officers witnessed sufficient poverty among widows to provide special almshouses for their relief; and, in most rural areas, widows and orphans were the particular concern, at least in theory, of parochial beneficence. Moreover, as Klapisch-Zuber has particularly noted, widows could be torn in many directions, facing the impossible task of balancing the competing interests of their marital and natal families.[17]

In still other cases, historians have, through examining difference, realized that medieval women sometimes shared more common experiences than did medieval men. There were, for example, striking cross-class similarities—political, legal, social, and economic—in the lives of medieval women. First, formal political structures were usually closed to women: feudal ladies did not sit in parliament, townswomen were not elected mayors, and peasant women were never reeves or bailiffs. Second, legal systems—whether feudal, royal, urban, or manorial—invariably restricted the proprietary and contractual options of married women, offered more opportunity to widows and singlewomen, and privileged men over women. Third, social customs dictated that wives of all classes were to be helpmeets of their husbands, always ready to assist or even replace them if need be. This involved different things for women of different classes—plowing or assisting at harvest for a peasant wife, as opposed to defending a castle or cultivating connections at court for a noblewoman— but all wives were expected to be their husbands' assistants and, indeed, understudies. Fourth, the economic arrangements of all classes stressed women's domestic labors. The administration of an aristocratic establishment required skills not much used by women who managed urban or rural households, but women of all classes shared the fundamental work of housewifery. A feudal lord could not guide a plow and a plowman could not fight from horseback, but feudal ladies, urban goodwives, and poor countrywomen all could spin, wield a needle, care for children, and prepare a meal. Peasant woman spun from need and noble ladies for leisure, but each regarded the distaff and spindle with a familiarity that would have eluded a knight confronted with a plow or a plowman with a warhorse.

In these varied ways, difference has proven to be a productive and important part of the history of medieval women. Yet its study is haunted by old ideological practices that combine "difference" with "women's status" to produce a sort of litmus test of civilization. During the nineteenth century, for example, Europeans claimed cultural supremacy over colonized people by, among other things, imagining that European women enjoyed higher status than did women in India, Africa, the Americas, or, indeed, any place other than Europe. Some discussions of difference in the Middle Ages similarly seek, almost as a matter of course, to identify some women as better off than other women and in the process to valorize some groups over others. Were peasant women to be envied compared to noble women? Did Jewish women enjoy higher status than Christian women? Was the life of a widow better than that of a wife? These sorts of comparisons can provoke creative analyses among historians and energetic debates among students. They can also lead to facile conclusions that support myths of a past gender equality rooted in primitivism or poverty, that simplify quite complex differences, and that provide yet more arenas in which the "status of women" is used to validate one group in opposition to another.

Consider, for example, how the study of heretical women has been long dominated by the false assumption that women flocked to heresies because they supposedly offered more woman-friendly theologies and practices. As Peter Biller, Richard Abel, and Ellen Harrison have shown for Catharism and Shannon McSheffrey for Lollardy, there is little historical basis for these rosy assessments. Women were no more numerous among heretics than among the general population; heretical practices tended, not surprisingly, to reproduce mainstream gender hierarchies; and heretical theologies did not offer women liberation from traditional Christian teachings. By positing a higher status for women among heretical sects, the older interpretation gave clear meaning to clear differences (and perhaps also implicitly buttressed modern Protestant critiques of medieval Catholicism), but it accorded poorly with the facts.[18]

Consider as well the rich and as yet understudied subject of Jewish women in medieval Christendom. Just a few years after Eileen Power ignored Jewish women in her 1926 overview, Michael Adler and Israel Epstein published separate essays arguing that, as Epstein put it, the medieval Jewish woman "enjoyed a larger measure of freedom, influence, authority, and respect than was the case with her Gentile sister." More recently, Renée Levine Melammed has favorably assessed the lot of Jewish women in Christendom compared to their sisters in Islamic regions. As she put it, "The world in which Sephardi women lived was powerfully influenced by Islamic culture, with all its negative implications for female autonomy." In ways familiar as well as troubling, these conclusions both subtly valorize the Jewish minority of the Middle Ages and assess Christianity as preferable to Islam. To be sure, historians of medieval Jews would be hard-pressed to ignore the Christian and Muslim majorities among whom medieval Jews lived, but there is more to comparison than constructing some women as better off than other women. Fortunately, some scholars have begun to compare in more subtle ways, looking, among other things, at how Christian majorities and Jewish minorities did and did not influence each other. In her study of German-Jewish pietists of the Central Middle Ages, for example, Judith Baskin has reached the measured conclusion that their ambivalence toward women was "in part, a consequence of their situation in a Christian milieu which preached the evils of carnality and the virtues of celibacy."[19]

As a final example, consider how class-based assessments of "better off/ worse off" have worked to contradictory ends. Drawing loose conclusions based on diverse sources and incomparable factors, some historians have argued for the comparatively higher status of feudal women; others have argued the same for townswomen; and still others have asserted that peasant women were, in fact, the most advantaged of all medieval women. The argument for women of royal or noble birth rests on their ability to command lesser men. A woman like Eleanor of Aquitaine could expect both respect and obedience from all men whose social status fell beneath her own—administrators, vassals, burgesses, free peasants, and serfs. The argument for townswomen cites privileges associated with mercantile law and urban life. In towns more than elsewhere, daughters might expect to inherit equally with sons; married women could sometimes obtain some measure of legal independence from husbands (by attaining a special dispensation to trade as *femmes soles*); and widows could be formally accommodated in public positions vacated by their dead husbands (by becoming, for example, freewomen of cities or members of guilds). The argument for peasant women is the oldest, for it dates back to the fifteenth century, when Christine de Pizan, writing from the comfort of the French court, imagined that the lives of peasant women "were more secure and more abundant than the lives of some who are placed very high."[20] Eileen Power and many other historians have since agreed, arguing that because the rural economy required the dual contributions of men and women, peasant wives especially benefited from a respectful partnership with their husbands.

A competition in which any category can claim top place is not, to say the least, a very definitive competition. Nor is it a very useful exercise in comparative history, for each of these judgments presents a partial picture. Queens, countesses, and baronial ladies could be imperious and powerful, but throughout the Middle Ages men of their own rank found it hard to stomach the authority of women. The illegitimacy of female rule provided one rationale for the coronation of Charlemagne in 800 (the imperial title was considered vacant because it was held by a woman, the Empress Irene in Constantinople); it encouraged the resistance of some Anglo-Norman nobles to the rule of Matilda in mid-twelfth-century England (a revolt eventually resolved by accepting the claims of Matilda's son, the eventual Henry II); and it also provoked the roughly contemporaneous troubles of Queen Melisende of Jerusalem, whose inherited right to rule was challenged by both her husband and her son. The power of feudal ladies was accepted by custom, reinforced by office, and sometimes even sanctified by coronation, but it was easily undermined.[21] Similarly, urban workshops were not a woman's paradise. Apprenticeships were more often arranged for sons than for daughters; household work was centered around the occupations of husbands, not wives; and widows were more temporary substitutes for their dead husbands than independent business-women.[22] Finally, in my own work I have argued that the happy notion of egalitarian peasant households not only romanticizes poverty but also misrepresents the facts. The legal, political, economic, and social structures of medieval villages promoted male privilege not sexual egalitarianism.[23]

Differences among "medieval women" can be cut in many ways: Christian, Jewish, or Islamic; feudal, bourgeois, or peasant; free, serf, or slave; orthodox Christians or heretics; nuns or laywomen; singlewomen, wives, or widows; Celts, Norse, Franks, Saxons, or Latins; northern European or southern European; and young, middle-aged, or old. The divisions were real and important in medieval life, but they can be overvalued, especially if women's lives are divided along one axis alone. After all, a peasant woman was not just a peasant—she was also young or old; married or not; Christian, heretic, or Jew; and northern or southern European. Rather than focusing on one category and then seeking to rank which women among its divisions enjoyed the best (or least horrible) lot, difference is better approached in the classroom in at least two alternative ways—in terms of the choices women made, given the available resources, and in terms of how ideas about women and gender participated in medieval constructions of difference.

First, students can usefully approach diversity by studying medieval women on their own terms, weighing the choices they made, assessing the ways in which women could be simultaneously "victims" and "agents," and examining how women in diverse circumstances struck "patriarchal bargains." Deniz Kandiyoti has coined this last term to explain the ways in which women accommodate to, cope with, and, indeed, benefit from patriarchal rules. The patriarchal bargain consists of "set rules and scripts regulating gender relations." Although men and women can redefine and contest these rules a bit, they also have good reasons to acquiesce to them in most respects. In somewhat mitigating women's plight, patriarchal bargains offer women some opportunity within general constraint, but they also help sustain the survival of the patriarchal status quo. Hence, in Kandiyoti's studies of sub-Saharan Africa and the Middle East she has shown how women in these societies have gained certain opportunities that partly ameliorate their general disempowerment.[24] And hence, in a medieval village, a young woman might have forfeited important legal rights when she married—thereafter, her husband could speak for her in court and control her lands or earnings—but she gained a great deal in return: greater economic security (because husbands earned higher wages and held more land); enhanced social status (because marriage was normative); a more secure venue for sexual expression (because only sex within marriage was sanctioned by the Church); and, if she was lucky, the pleasures of a loving husband and loving children.

In a course on medieval women, the concept of patriarchal bargains can help students see that difference was often just different, not necessarily "better" or "worse." Feudal women maneuvered within a set of restrictions and opportunities, and bourgeois and peasant women did much the same. In terms of class and status, feudal women were certainly privileged. In terms of gender, however, they did not necessarily win out over other women. In other words, feudal women enjoyed certain benefits of their class—more secure housing, better clothing, a richer diet, and, of course, deference from lesser men and women. But *within their own social group,* feudal women worked within a set of restrictions and opportunities that were specific to their gender as well as their class. So, too, did bourgeois and peasant women. Moreover, by examining the opportunities, choices, and decisions that feudal women, townswomen, and peasant women made, students can approach these women in historical context. Why were arranged marriages tolerable to feudal women? Why did young townswomen not protest when their brothers were apprenticed in trades while they were kept at home? Why would a laboring women accept wages half those paid to the man who worked alongside her? In seeking answers to these and similar questions, modern students can come to understand not only the restrictions that medieval women faced, but also the opportunities, choices, and joys of their lives—in short, their patriarchal bargains.

Second, students can also approach medieval diversity by examining the complex ways in which ideas about women and gender participated in articulating and maintaining boundaries between different groups of medieval people. The tenth through thirteenth centuries witnessed not only many of the glories of medieval civilization—the development of canon law, the growth of universities, and the building of cathedrals—but also the institutionalization of new forms of violence, as used in both colonization and persecution. Christian Europeans began to expand their territorial influence (as, for example, in the Iberian *Reconquista*) and began to fear many of their neighbors, especially Jews, prostitutes, male homosexuals, heretics, and lepers. Recent studies of the growth of persecutions in the Central Middle Ages recognize that prostitutes were harassed alongside other minorities and stress how often majority groups imagined rampant sexual deviance among reviled "others," but they generally ignore or downplay gender. Few scholars have yet linked the increasing virulence of misogynous ideas among Christians with expanding discourses against other groups. Even as magisterial a book as Robert Bartlett's study of medieval colonization is much weakened by inattention to gender.[25] Nevertheless, students can begin to examine how gender ideologies informed constructions of "otherness" in medieval Europe from at least three perspectives: sexual relations between Christians and Jews or Muslims, French epics that tell of Saracen princesses who convert to Christianity, and the persistence of *female* slavery in some regions of medieval Europe.

As David Nirenberg has explored in his study of Christians, Jews, and Muslims in medieval Spain, boundaries between these three groups were especially maintained by prohibitions against intergroup sexual relations. Evoking memories of U.S. laws against miscegenation, these medieval regulations might sound familiar to students, and there are certainly parallels between modern and medieval anxieties. Medieval complaints about intergroup sexuality, for example, tended to coincide with famines, plagues, or other crises, and accusations of such deeds were often based more in personal enmity or political design than actual fact. But Nirenberg argues that medieval prohibitions operated on a different register from modern anxieties. All medieval groups—Jewish and Muslim minorities as well as the Christian majority—attempted to prevent intergroup sexual contact; medieval prohibitions exhibited few anxieties about any "racial impurity" that might result from children born of such unions; and intergroup sexual unions accomplished through prostitution were a particular focus of medieval concern. In Nirenberg's view, the idea that all Christian women were "brides of Christ" made any intergroup sexual contact a sort of "cuckolding of Christ," feared because it was likely to bring God's wrath onto all. And the status of Christian prostitutes as "public women" transformed them into bodies through which Christian men "united to each other by a common sexual bond," a bond profoundly polluted if a prostitute offered her services to a Jewish or Muslim client. In other words, whether attached to a Christian wife or a Christian prostitute, the sign "woman" marked the boundaries of acceptable interaction between Christian, Muslim, and Jew.[26]

The famous medieval tale of *The Song of Roland* ends with the christening of Bramimonde, widow of Charlemagne's Muslim arch-enemy, Marsile, the king of Spain. Active in the planning of the campaign against the French, she suffers loss, grief, terror, and captivity before accepting Christian ways. With her conversion, this epic tale of battle between Christian and Muslim reaches its final resolution. Bramimonde, renamed Juliana at her baptism, is just one of nearly two dozen Saracen princesses found in medieval French epic. In most of these stories the princess falls in love with a Christian knight, abandons her people, converts to Christianity, and eventually marries her lover, thereby saving her soul and, in many cases, also enriching her new husband. These stories evoke modern parallels with the sexual exoticization and commodification of minority women found in so many contemporary contexts. But they have special medieval twists: most epics "whiten" Saracen women, depicting them as epitomes of Frankish standards of beauty, not as women made desirable by physical otherness; they create Saracen heroines who threaten established norms of female behavior by rejecting their families, mocking men, and committing adultery; and although they speak to male fantasies, they also reflect male anxieties. Most important, the stories work to legitimate the profits of military victory. When the Old French epic *The Capture of Orange* ends with the marriage of the Frankish lord Guillaume Fierebrace to Orable, queen of the city he has conquered, reconciliation happens on many levels. Christianity is recognized as superior to Islam; an extraordinarily assertive woman is returned to wifely submissiveness; and a territorial authority won by war is legitimized by marriage. In this story as in many others, it is only through a woman that full conquest is achieved.[27]

In prohibitions against intergroup sexual contact as well as tales of Saracen princesses, women's intermediary roles placed them at critical points in the negotiation of difference in the Middle Ages. In a third arena of such negotiation—medieval practices of slavery—women were not so much intermediaries as essential. Compared to both ancient and modern Europeans, medieval people relied relatively little on slavery. Discouraged by the Church and rendered uneconomic by manorialism, slavery slowly disappeared from many regions of medieval Europe and survived elsewhere in only attenuated forms. Yet as Susan Mosher Stuard has shown, this "medieval traffic in slaves was overwhelmingly a traffic in women." This was especially true on the frontiers of Europe, where women were easily obtained from ethnic or religious groups different from those of the slave-owners. In Scandinavia, the Balkans, and Spain, the long persistence of slavery was tied to both frontier conditions and the supply of women. In the north, Vikings often killed men but enslaved women and children, and when they settled Iceland and later Greenland they especially relied on slave women for both sexual and reproductive work. In the south, the great urban households of late medieval Italy created a market for young, pliant women from the Balkans who could be trained in domestic work and be made sexually available to the men of the household. These female slaves were also intermediaries—Dalmatian girls in Italian households, Celts among the Norse who settled Iceland, and Muslims among the Christians of Spain—but their liminality worked more to disempower them than to promote or represent intercultural contact.[28]

Forthright discussion in the classroom can usually undercut the subtle allure of ranking some women as better off than others, and the study of medieval Europe—with its various judgments that noble ladies were more respected than peasant women, or that Christian women were better off than Muslim women, or that heretical women enjoyed more spiritual satisfaction than Christian women—provides fertile ground for informed critiques. Once students recognize the pernicious values that can be attached to such rankings they will be prepared to criticize this practice in others and avoid it themselves. They can then attend to difference in more productive ways. In the process they might come to appreciate not only the trials, pleasures, and choices of actual women but also the ideological uses of gender—today as well as in the Middle Ages—in constructing ideas of the "other."

Chronology: Women's Status during the Middle Ages and Beyond

The study of medieval women also provides useful examples of historical debate about changes in women's status over time. This is a fraught and difficult topic. The "status of women" is a slippery concept for any society, much less one as remote as the European Middle Ages; the concept of a unitary status of women tends toward an over-generalization of which feminists are justly skeptical; and, just as in studies of other sorts of differences, hidden ideological burdens often lie behind the judgment that one era offered greater opportunity to women than another. Yet despite these liabilities, the desire to trace advances and declines in the status of women over time persists among both students and teachers. Given this lingering appeal, the issue of change and continuity in women's status is better confronted than ignored, especially in circumstances, such as the study of medieval women, in which it can provide useful examples of historical interpretation and controversy.

Interestingly enough, this issue often pits students against teachers (especially if teachers are medievalists). For some students, the Middle Ages are a void about which they have no preconceived notions; for some others, the period evokes pleasant thoughts of chivalry and the gentle treatment of women; but for most (in my classrooms, at least), medieval Europe was a time when women were horribly and grossly oppressed. At the outset of the semester, students tend to assume that the Middle Ages epitomize woman-hating: jealous husbands who clasped chastity belts on their wives before heading off on crusade; brutal knights who, like the lord in the movie *Braveheart*, claimed the virginity of all young brides on their estates; and young women who were driven, like Pope Joan, to cross-dress in order to attend school. No medieval chastity belts survive, and those found in European museums are modern creations attributed to a medieval past. The myth of the "right of the first night" is a similar concoction of heated postmedieval imaginations. And the story of Pope Joan, who supposedly ruled in the ninth century, arose as an antifeminist legend of the thirteenth century.[29] It might be disappointing to students that these are myths rather than history, but, as fabrications, these stories show the importance of gender in modern constructions of the medieval past. For many modern people, nothing better illustrates the barbarity of medieval society than its brutal treatment of women. Once again, if the status of women is used as a litmus text of civilized society, then this is a test that a medieval Europe characterized by chastity belts, "right of the first night," and female popes certainly fails.

Many medievalists embrace an opposite interpretation. Ideas of a medieval golden age for women circulated long before Eileen Power invoked the rough-and-ready equality of medieval women in 1926, and they have persisted long since.[30] No one argues that things were terrific for women during the Middle Ages, but many argue that medieval women were better off than their descendants in more modern centuries. This professional interpretation is at odds with popular images of the subjugation of women in the Middle Ages, but it serves many purposes. Because high status in the past implies the possibility of high status in the present, a medieval golden age appeals to many feminist scholars. Because a high status for medieval women valorizes the Middle Ages as a superior civilization, a past golden age appeals to many medievalists. And because the business of history is so much the business of finding change and assessing it, a past golden age works well in both history-writing and history-teaching.

I have proposed a third alternative of "patriarchal equilibrium," arguing that stasis rather than change might best describe women's status across the centuries. In my studies of working women in the Later Middle Ages I have found much change in the specifics of women's work. For example, women left some occupations and took up others; their wages rose a bit in some decades and fell in others; and they worked more in the home at some times than at others. But I have also found considerable continuity, despite such changes, in the basic structures of women's work. In 1300, 1500, and 1700, women's work varied in time-specific ways, but it remained (as it remains today) characteristically low skilled, low status, and poorly remunerated. This has led me to argue that much of women's history overemphasizes change, overemphasizes the difference between some eras as "barbaric" and others as "golden." If so, it might be best to understand the dynamic of medieval women's history as operating within an ever-fluid but self-adjusting system of male dominance, a system in which the many changes in medieval women's experiences were seldom accompanied by transformations—either for better or worse—in women's status.

In their treatment of women during the long medieval millennium, teachers might choose among these three perspectives—emphasizing "change for the better," "change for the worse," or "change without transformation." But students also respond well to the challenge of assessing all three interpretations.

"Change for the better" is the most common interpretation of my students, and it is also sometimes expressed, in an unexamined way, by historians of modern Europe. In this view, the Middle Ages, because it was a less developed civilization than that of modern Europe, *must* have oppressed women in especially egregious ways. Therefore, the improving status of women joins such factors as secularism, individualism, and scientism as one of the defining characteristics of modernity. Most medievalists reject the assumptions behind such depictions of the medieval-modern divide, but "change for the better" has also been traced within the Middle Ages itself. Looking at English towns, Jeremy Goldberg and Caroline Barron have separately concluded that the century after the Great Plague of 1347–49 offered unusual opportunities for women. In their view, the labor crisis that followed the demographic devastation of the plague allowed women to demand higher wages than before, to enter better trades than before, and even to avoid marriage if they chose. Goldberg and Barron base their arguments on sparse evidence drawn particularly from the cities of London and York, and, in any case, the changes they trace were ephemeral, at best. As the labor market tightened in the later fifteenth century, they argue, economic opportunities for women contracted, rates of marriage increased, and fertility shot up.[31]

"Change for the worse" is so common in history writing today that a teacher can stand at almost any historical marker and find a negative trend. The centralizing reforms of Charlemagne: bad for women. The Norman invasion of 1066: bad for women. The new monastic orders of the twelfth century: bad for women. The growth of humanism in the fourteenth century: bad for women. The rapid development of capitalism in the fifteenth century: bad for women. Although "change for the worse" has been found in almost every century in the medieval millennium, it has been most fully elaborated for the Central—or "High"—Middle Ages. As developed particularly in studies by Jo Ann McNamara and Susan Mosher Stuard, the eleventh and twelfth centuries have been figured as a time of "gender crisis," when an old ideology of gender similarity was usurped by a new ideology of gender difference. In

McNamara's view, an early twelfth-century *Herrenfrage* (masculine identity crisis) emerged from both the relative pacification of European society (which meant that masculinity could no longer be asserted by military prowess alone) and the strict imposition of clerical celibacy (which fostered male fears of women). The most critical shift centered on a new need to separate the sexes. In 1120 or thereabouts, women and men had still mingled together in both religious and lay settings, but thereafter an "incessant, hysterical criticism" destroyed the cooperative possibilities created by joint male-female celibacy and with it the ability of aristocratic women to work with men in public governance and administration. In Stuard's view, a new polarity of gender roles emerged from such factors as the Gregorian reform, the development of new customs of marriage, and the recovery of once-lost classical texts. As a result, "Women were more likely to find themselves being directed, rather than directing . . . as they had done in the past."[32]

Changing ideologies of gender, working through such factors as the imposition of clerical celibacy and the resurgence of ancient authorities, contributed to this "change for the worse," but so too did more material causes. In an article published in 1962, David Herlihy first argued that many social factors promoted the particular prominence of aristocratic women in the Early Middle Ages: a family system that valued kinship over lineage, a division of labor in which women performed extensive and critical tasks, a legal structure that offered women considerable rights of inheritance, and even a military situation in which men spent considerable time away from their estates. Building on Herlihy's groundwork, many historians have since pointed to various ways in which the shifting boundaries of public and private worked, during the Central Middle Ages, to the disadvantage of women. For example, early feudalism, with its reliance on private power and household-based administration, offered considerable scope to elite women who could, in their capacity as wives, participate in the day-to-day affairs of feudal governance. But the power of feudal women waned during the Central Middle Ages, as monarchs began to assert control over localities, as bureaucrats began to replace ad hoc administrators, and as formal institutions began to supplant the informal arrangements of the household. For another example, early monasticism, with its emphasis on family foundations controlled at the local level, easily accommodated female autonomy and authority. But as the Church began to control monasteries more closely from the tenth century on, female houses lost much wealth, power, and independence.[33]

These arguments about "change for the worse" work well in the classroom. First, they conform to certain expectations, providing the sort of chronological change students expect from history and offering useful examples of how shifting definitions of "public" and "private" can shape the experiences of women. Second, they upset expected patterns in pedagogically useful ways. They suggest that the history of women is not a history of steady improvement; they suggest that a good period for men can be a bad period for women (the twelfth century is conventionally seen, after all, as the apogee of medieval civilization); and they confound students' assumptions about the utter subjection of medieval women.

Yet despite their pedagogical usefulness, these arguments are not definitive. First, it is not at all clear that ideas of gender separation and polarity were strikingly new in the eleventh and twelfth centuries. After all, early Christian theologians scarcely saw women as equal to men or welcomed their company, and early medieval theologians followed suit. Hence, for example, in the late sixth century Pope Gregory I advised men to love women as if they were sisters but flee from them as if they were enemies.[34] Gender ideologies certainly can change, but they may not have changed as quickly and as thoroughly as these arguments suggest. Second, the pronouncements of intellectuals have not yet been clearly linked with the practices of people. Perhaps, as Stuard has argued, people "sought answers from authorities" in a time of considerable hardship and change, but perhaps not.[35] Perhaps women's power contracted with the centralization of feudal governments and the medieval Church, but perhaps women's power, always limited, merely waned in some arenas as it waxed in others.[36]

"Change without transformation" suggests that the developments traced by such scholars as Barron and Goldberg, on the one hand, and McNamara and Stuard, on the other, altered the experiences of women without transforming their status. First, despite changes, perhaps the status of women always remained low. Yes, women might have garnered better wages in the late fourteenth century than before (or after), but they remained at the bottom of the wage ladder. Yes, feudal women seem to have exercised less power in the thirteenth century than earlier, but the power of such women had always been indirect and dependent on men. Second, perhaps changes in one sector were offset by changes elsewhere. Is it an accident, for example, that women who earned good money in the Later Middle Ages were often the special subject of public ridicule and gossip? Is it an accident that the same century associated with the declining public influence of feudal women also saw their expanding cultural influence in courtly literatures? In other words, perhaps changes so counterbalanced each other that a rough but steady equilibrium of male authority over women was maintained.

Arguments about a patriarchal equilibrium across the medieval millennium promote a healthy skepticism about the too-ready enthusiasm of historians for tracing change, whether for the worse or the better. They also problematically create abstractions out of the lived experiences of actual women.

If women's wages improved in the late fourteenth century, some women were actually able to live better than they had before, even if they still earned lower wages than did male workers. Women's lives changed, however briefly and modestly. If male bureaucrats took over functions once trusted to wives, some twelfth-century women actually lost powers they had once enjoyed. Maybe aristocratic women developed more influence in new areas—such as courtly love or patronage—but they still were less publicly visible than before. And if Church reform in the eleventh century resulted in fewer monastic opportunities for women, then pious women had to seek out new venues for expressing devotion. That women successfully found such venues—beguinages instead of nunneries, sainthood through mysticism rather than learning—might not really balance out the record. Moreover, an emphasis on transformation might set too high a bar, obfuscating or downplaying alterations in women's status that are, by the standards of this interpretation, wrongly deemed too limited in extent, too slight, or too short term.[37]

Some teachers might find that other measurements work better in their classrooms. Instead of assessing whether the status of women improved, deteriorated, or did not change much at all across the medieval millennium, students can also productively examine any particular group of medieval women in terms of "agency" (to what extent were these women active shapers of their own lives, what coping strategies did they adopt, and did they seek to improve their position?) and "victimization" (to what extent were these women oppressed and were they complicit in their oppression?). Both sets of questions can be directed at a wide variety of medieval circumstances, not only at discrete groups of women but also in comparative studies of different groups or times. For classroom use, the case of female spirituality among medieval Christians works exceptionally well. As Caroline Walker Bynum has explored so carefully, pious Christian women in the Central and Later Middle Ages often expressed faith through extreme acts of bodily self-denial, especially fasting. In Bynum's view, these acts, horrifying as they might be to modern readers, speak to the creative and positive ways in which female Christian mystics then approached their God. Yet other historians take a less sanguine view, considering that the extreme self-abnegation of these women illustrates the active misogyny of the medieval Church or even mental illness. Students are fascinated by stories of these women and eager to debate whether their extreme asceticism should be seen as positive expressions of female medieval piety, sad proof of female oppression, or merely evidence of individual pathology (especially anorexia nervosa). As part of this debate, students struggle to interpret the writings of thirteenth- and fourteenth-century mystics, but they also place these women within the broader history of women in the medieval Church.[38] Pious nuns, powerful within ecclesiastical structures, seem to dom-

inate the Early Middle Ages; pious laywomen, powerful for their mystical vir-
tuosity, seem to dominate the Later Middle Ages. Seen in this long view, did
religious opportunities for Christian women improve, decline, or change in
shape but not extent? What changed (or did not change) between the powers wielded by Hild (d. 680), who presided over monks as well as nuns in her
capacity as abbess of the great Anglo-Saxon monastery at Whitby, and those
enjoyed by Catherine of Siena, a pious laywomen and revered mystic who
essentially starved herself to an early death in 1380?

Medieval Ideologies of Gender

To Eileen Power, medieval thought about women was "an inconsistent and
contradictory thing," and since Power's time, historians have richly elaborated the complex meanings of medieval representations of women. In the view
of Penny Schine Gold, for example, it was ambivalence per se that created a
"unity between image and experience" in the Middle Ages. Hence, conflicting
images in literature (e.g., the central yet marginal roles of women in the chan-
sons de geste) were paralleled by conflicting practical experiences (e.g., wom-
en's critical yet peripheral participation in the transfer of feudal properties).[39]

What Gold found in twelfth-century France has been found in many other
contexts. In life as in literature and art, medieval women were simultaneously central and marginal, and medieval gender ideologies were similarly marked
by internal contradictions, ambiguities, and profound ambivalence. The Middle Ages are not, of course, unique in this regard, and many medieval ideas
about gender grew from ancient traditions, especially as articulated, altered,
and transmitted by Christian theologians in the third through fifth centuries.
To these early "Fathers" of the Church, women seemed both terrifying tempt-
resses and admirable virgins.[40] Defamed and defended, attacked and praised,
caricatured as Eve and venerated as the Virgin, medieval women were both
fully human and profoundly other. It is no wonder that the ideologies that
sought to account for them were deeply inconsistent and contradictory.[41]

Even the Virgin Mary was a shifting and ambivalent object of veneration.
Although early Christians acknowledged Mary's virginity, her veneration was
largely a product of medieval piety. Neither New Testament authors nor the
early Church paid much attention to the mother of Jesus, but from the twelfth
century she became a special subject of Christian devotion. Ordinary people
embraced the Virgin with passionate enthusiasm, dedicating shrines, churches,
and lady chapels to her; adopting rosary beads to guide them in Marian devotion; and attributing miracles to her benevolence. Ecstatic mystics, especially
Bernard of Clairvaux in his sermons on the Song of Songs, found in the Virgin a vessel for their ineffable experiences. And learned theologians also con-

tributed to medieval Mariology, debating such issues as whether the Virgin was born with or without original sin. (Thomas Aquinas vigorously agreed with Bernard of Clairvaux that the Virgin must have been so tainted, but their position never held full sway, and it was finally superseded by papal affirmation of the Immaculate Conception in 1854.) Venerated in many different aspects, the Virgin was the bride of Christ as well as his mother; she was a young mother with child as well as a grieving mother of a crucified son; and she was the embodied throne for a child Christ held in her lap as well as a regal consort, enthroned alongside her adult son.[42]

For ordinary women the Virgin offered a model fraught with ambivalence. Virginity was perhaps the most fully articulated sexual identity in the Middle Ages, but its meanings for women were not wholly positive. Insofar as virginity made women admirable, it almost made them not-women. A virgin nun was seen as a virago, as a woman who had triumphed over the base sexual urges characteristic of her sex. Yet although a holy virgin could be thus admired for her masculine self-control, she never lost her femaleness. The history of female monasticism—of women who sought to commit themselves to lives of virginity or, if widows, chastity—is riddled with stories of the ways in which assumptions about female inferiority and anxieties about female sexuality limited ecclesiastical opportunities for women. This was especially true from the eleventh century on, when a better-organized Church insisted more firmly on male celibacy. In the Central and Later Middle Ages many monks saw nuns less as holy sisters and more as burdensome temptations. St. Francis himself opposed the affiliation of nunneries to his Franciscan order, commenting, "God has taken our wives from us, and now Satan has given us sisters." Nuns might have been pure, but they were never free from sexual innuendo, scandal, and misogyny.[43]

Moreover, the meanings of virginity changed over the course of the Middle Ages. In the Early Middle Ages, virginity was understood in physical terms, and fear of its loss was so great that a few nuns even mutilated themselves to avoid sexual assault and rape. Virginity without purity of thought was not good, but neither was spiritual purity without its physical integrity. For women who committed themselves to a life of pious virginity, mutilation or death was sometimes preferable to its loss.[44] By the Later Middle Ages, ideals about holy purity began to merge with ideals of married life. Saints' lives depicted female martyrs less as cloistered ascetics and more as prosperous, worldly goodwives, and pious practices accommodated the asceticism of wives as well as the self-denial of virgins. Virginity remained important, but other ascetic practices—chastity within marriage, denial of food and comfort, and pilgrimages—enabled married women to achieve holiness, too. Elizabeth of Hungary and Birgitta of Sweden signaled a relatively new phenomenon in the Later Middle Ages: married female saints. Virginity remained important—it was essential to the mission of Joan of Arc and critical to such other saints as Catherine of Siena—but it was no longer an exclusive route to sanctity.[45]

The Virgin offered another sort of ambivalent model to ordinary women: that of wielding power indirectly through men. In her role as an intercessor between sinners and God, the Virgin simultaneously held power and lacked it. As a kindly, concerned, and ever-submissive mother, the Virgin petitioned her son on behalf of others and thereby gently helped the needy, the sinful, and even the damned. But she helped them through her influence over her son, not through her own direct powers. Strict monotheism required, of course, an intercessory role for all saints, the Virgin included: omnipotent power rested with God, unchallenged by any saintly autonomy. Yet intercession remained the special forte of the Virgin, and insofar as it extended to other saints it remained a predominantly female trait. For example, the Virgin's mother, St. Anne, also came to be an object of considerable intercessory prayer during the fourteenth and fifteenth centuries.[46]

These representations of the intercessory acts of the Virgin and other female saints spoke to the prescribed behaviors of actual wives and mothers, emphasizing that women's place was to influence men to action, urging women to remain submissive even when their influence was unsuccessful, and reflecting expectations that actual women—say, a mother in a peasant family in Saxony or a wife in an artisanal household in Ghent—should rely more on indirect influence than direct authority. This role could be empowering as well as confining. In courtly literatures, veneration of women reflected, in part, their function as intermediaries between lovers and husbands. Poems praised husbands by praising their wives, and poets sought the favor of wives in order to secure favors from husbands. In clerical advice, wives were sometimes seen as critical agents in the governance of husbands. To Thomas of Chobham, for example, wives were to use their "persuasive voices" to guide husbands toward pious generosity and pious behavior. And in royal and noble courts, intercessory influence could even translate into practical power. When Blanche of Castile (1188–1252) commissioned a moralized Bible around 1235, she had her relationship with her son, Louis IX, represented in an illustration that directly replicated sculptures of the Virgin and Christ found on the cathedrals of her day. Like the Virgin, Blanche appeared crowned, enthroned, seated to her son's right hand, in direct eye contact with him, and gesturing toward him in supplication. The intercessory powers of the Virgin legitimated Blanche's own powers as the mother of a reigning king. Whether Virgin Mother, queen, or humble wife, women ideally exercised power in the Middle Ages by influencing men.[47]

The ambivalence of medieval gender ideologies extended to the misogyny for which medieval Europe is justly famous. Even without chastity belts, "right of the first night," and Pope Joan, students often easily assume that medieval ideas about women were peculiarly awful. The arranged marriages so common among the propertied classes are readily imagined as always forced on women and always bitterly unhappy. The legal practice of coverture—whereby a married woman's rights to property were largely ceded to her husband—might seem horrifyingly anti-woman. The custom of sending adolescents away from their families—to serve as attendants in courts, apprentices in cities, or servants in villages—can suggest that medieval parents were heartless and unloving. And the absence of women from the ordained clergy, the legal profession, and, indeed, the university-educated might lead students to conclude that medieval women exercised little choice—either the marriage bed or the nunnery, but no other alternatives.

After students examine the histories of medieval women, they can appreciate the advantages as well as disadvantages that customs such as these offered to medieval women. But at the outset, many students expect that medieval culture was awash with a particularly virulent and unmitigated misogyny. These expectations are both right and wrong. Medieval culture was certainly misogynous, but it was an ambivalent sort of woman-hating, cloaked in misogamy (hatred of marriage) as well as misogyny and strongly inflected by humor, genre, and tradition. Students react with justified horror to misogynous texts, but they also respond well to debates about their meanings, particularly debates about whether misogyny was or was not a mere literary pastime.

As Alcuin Blamires has shown, the literary expression of medieval misogyny grew from ancient origins, and it was nurtured by clerical celibacy and misogamy (especially as manifested in the ideal of an ascetic philosophic life). It drew on a remarkably small number of texts and authors—some biblical (especially Ecclesiastes), some ancient (especially Ovid and Juvenal), some patristic (especially Jerome), and some medieval (especially Walter Map and Andreas Capellanus). And it followed quite predictable forms, listing examples of evil women, relying on satirical caricatures, polemicizing against marriage, and creating first-person complaints. To Blamires, misogyny is best seen as a literary game, a forum in which authors could "show off their literary paces." Yet misogyny was more than just a literary game, more than, as Howard Bloch has put it, merely "a way of speaking about women as distinct from doing something to women."[48] As has been particularly examined in cases of medieval brewsters (that is, female brewers) and prostitutes, actual women suffered from misogynous ideas. Because women were perceived as naturally greedy, oversexed, and untrustworthy, male brewers came to be preferred to supposedly unruly brewsters, and eventually commercial brewing became a trade of men. And because all women were thought to use sex in order to gain money, position, and advantage, the prostitute was seen, as Ruth Karras has put it, as "simply the market-oriented version of a more general phenomenon."[49]

Despite the ideological power of misogyny, medieval literatures were not devoid of contemporaneous defenses—and even praise—of women. Court-ly love—a term coined in the nineteenth century to describe twelfth-centu-ry literary conventions that emphasized male ennoblement through adora-tion of women—epitomizes medieval praise of women, but it has proven remarkably difficult to grasp. To Bloch, courtly discourses were as misogy-nous as anti-woman attacks because any speech that essentialized women— "in which woman is the subject of the sentence and the predicate a more general term"—refused to perceive women as individuals. In Bloch's view, therefore, there was nothing positive for women in the development of ro-mantic love in twelfth- and thirteenth-century courts. Instead, courtly ideal-ization of women was merely an inverted form of misogyny; a troubadour's worship of his lady was as antifeminist as the characterization of women as the "devil's gateway." Yet Diane Bornstein has read these same courtly texts in different ways, suggesting that courtly love was a "new feminism" that coun-teracted the misogyny of the Church. Bloch's bleak assessment so universal-izes misogyny as to render it insignificant. Bornstein's positive assessment minimizes the troubling ways in which courtly literatures create women as mirrors of male desires, as impossibly perfect beings, as passive decorations, and as sites for male self-aggrandizement and competition.[50] The meanings of courtly love can be fruitfully debated in the classroom, but they cannot be fully understood as either a new misogyny or a new feminism.

Tracts in defense of women were equally ambivalent. The Middle Ages boasted not only a tradition of misogyny but also a long-standing defense-of-women tradition. These defenses followed predictable strategies. They at-tacked the motives of misogynists, they denounced negative generalizations, they declared God's special concern for women, they rejected the culpability of Eve, they listed exemplary women from the past, and they asserted wom-en's moral superiority over men. Most authors in this tradition were men, and modern readers cannot help but be struck by the "unfeminist quality of me-dieval profeminine discourse." Working within the traditions of their time, these defenders of women took for granted that women should be guided by men, that gender differences were natural, and that the justification of God's will could trump any other argument. Christine de Pizan, who published sev-eral tracts in defense of women during the early fifteenth century, did much the same, but she also brought a greater clarity and intensity to the discussion. No one could claim, as some have said of male defenders of women, that Christine de Pizan's passionate arguments reek of "facetious devil's advoca-cy." Christine de Pizan was not, as she is too often seen, a lone feminist voice crying out in a misogynous wilderness, but she certainly reinvigorated an old and somewhat ambivalent defense-of-women tradition.[51]

In less direct ways, other medieval women also spoke about their world and their places within it. To Eileen Power in 1926, it had seemed that "we hardly ever hear what women thought about themselves," but scholars have since accumulated substantial evidence of women's active participation in the creation, propagation, and consumption of medieval culture and, hence, medieval gender ideologies.[52] Although little is yet known about the cultural activities of ordinary women in villages and towns, there is now no doubt that elite women were active as artists and writers, as patrons, and as readers. In these varied roles, women both participated in masculinist ideologies and created distinctly female viewpoints.

Christine de Pizan praised the artist Anataise who illustrated some of her works, but few other female artists of the Middle Ages are known to us by name. Most seem to have worked in small scale, either illustrating manuscripts (if nuns) or fashioning embroideries (if laywomen). The most remarkable textual images produced by medieval women exist today only in copy. In the late twelfth century, Herrad, abbess of Hohenbourg (d. 1195), created *Garden of Delights*, a pictorial encyclopedia that guided her nuns, by word and image, through Christian history. She might have completed some of the preliminary drawings herself, and she certainly supervised the others, which were probably executed by her nuns. Destroyed by fire in 1870, the manuscript (of which we have a nineteenth-century tracing) included an extraordinary drawing that carefully identified by name forty-six nuns and lay sisters of the abbey. The most remarkable fabric images produced by medieval women—and possibly some men as well—can still be seen today in Bayeux, the city from which the tapestry now takes its name. Vividly illustrating William of Normandy's conquest of England in 1066, it shows, in its main sections, only three women among its countless knights and horses: Queen Edith (1025–75); one Aelfgyva, whose story is unknown to us; and an unnamed victim of war, fleeing with her child from a burning house. Today, nothing certain is known about the production of this tapestry. It might have been produced in Canterbury or Bayeux; it might reflect the imagination of one designer or several; and it might have been stitched in a workshop that included men as well as women. But given the prominence of women as embroiderers throughout the Middle Ages, the tapestry memorializes women's art as well as Norman conquest.[53]

Identified female authors are more numerous than female artists, and this might be no accident, for in the Middle Ages most female authors were privileged by vocation as well as class. In the ninth century, the noblewoman Dhuoda (ca. 803–45) wrote a manual to guide her young son's conduct in the court of Charles the Bald, but her lay status was unusual. Until the last medieval

MEDIEVAL WOMEN IN MODERN PERSPECTIVE

centuries, most female authors—at least those whose texts survive today—were nuns or mystics.[54] In the tenth century, Hroswitha of Gandersheim (ca. 935–99) wrote legends, histories, and comedies, the last modeled on those of the classical author Terence. In the twelfth century, Hildegard of Bingen wrote extensively in almost every genre, including letters, theological tracts, mystical revelations, and plays; Heloise of the Paraclete (1101–64) exchanged letters with Peter Abelard and Peter the Venerable; Marie de France (fl. 1150s-80s) composed *lais* that demonstrate such "mastery of plot, characterization, and diction" that some consider her to be the best of all medieval female authors; and *trobairitz* (female troubadours) wrote of love in frank and direct poems. From the twelfth to the fifteenth centuries, many female mystics— among them Hadewijch of Antwerp (fl. 1230s), Mechthild of Magdeburg (1212–83), Marguerite Porete (d. 1310), and Julian of Norwich (ca. 1343–1420s)—described in words committed to parchment their extraordinary experiences as well as their theological insights. In the late fourteenth century, Christine de Pizan, the first woman in European history to support herself by the pen, began to produce poems, essays, advice manuals, and books. And a few decades later, Margery Kempe (1373–1438)—proud daughter of a mayor, an aspiring mystic, and an illiterate woman—dictated her life story to scribes. Her book, lost for centuries until rediscovered by Hope Emily Allen in 1934, is today considered to be the first English-language autobiography.[55]

Working in images and texts, did these women create in ways that were distinctively female? Only Christine de Pizan might be called a feminist, for she criticized the misogyny of her day and also advised women about how they might best live in a male-dominated world. Yet as Beatrice Gottlieb has argued, the word *feminist* can obscure more about de Pizan than it reveals. De Pizan certainly did argue that women deserved a better lot in life, but she also accepted gender and class hierarchies as natural, enthusiastically embraced ideals of courtly love, and advised wives of abusive husbands to seek comfort not in resistance but instead in God. Students readily debate the nature of de Pizan's "feminism," and they usually find it quite fitting that her last known work celebrates another woman well known to feminists today but quite traditional in her views about gender roles: Joan of Arc. In this final poem Christine de Pizan thanked God for sending Joan, she rejoiced in Joan's victories over the English, and she saw all women as vindicated by Joan's accomplishments.

> What honor this for womankind,
> Well-beloved of God, it would appear,
> When that sad crowd to loss resigned
> Fled from the kingdom in great fear,
> Now by a woman rescued here. . . .[56]

Other female artists and authors were even less inclined than Christine de Pizan to address the fate of women in critical terms. Yet women's works might contain distinctive female elements, or, as Matilda Bruckner has suggested, a distinctive "double voice" in which women spoke simultaneously from within formalized conventions and from outside them. In her view, we may never hear "the direct, spontaneous expression of a 'real' woman's voice," but we can hear "something different." Jeffrey Hamburger has concluded that medieval nuns "champion[ed] art as a vehicle for devotional experience," creating a visual culture that, although profoundly shaped by male advisers, was distinctly their own. William Paden has suggested that the trobaritz wrote more personal verse than did the troubadours; the women's poems are direct and concrete while the men's are more abstract and removed. Peter Dronke has found in a wide range of female-authored texts an "immediacy" less apparent in works written by men. Joanna E. Ziegler has argued that beguines in the Low Countries developed a particularly tactile and material spirituality that manifested itself especially in the *Pietà,* a sculpted representation of the Virgin grieving over the body of her crucified son. Joan Ferrante has observed that female authors particularly addressed matters of interest to women. The voices of medieval women were, it seems, distinct in their emphasis on sight and touch, their directness and immediacy, and their attention to female concerns. Yet the voices of women writers were also affected by conventions about what "the female voice" should be. This conventional "female voice" not only shaped the creativity of medieval women but also provided a female perspective that could be appropriated by male artists and authors.[57]

If female artists and authors left their distinctive mark on medieval culture, so, too, did female patrons. In 1982 Susan Groag Bell laid out medieval women's "special relationship to books." Eager for spiritual consolation and responsible for the early education of their children, elite women particularly fostered, Bell argued, the production of vernacular translations and texts. Wealthy women also served, when they married and moved from one court to another, as agents of cultural exchange. Anne of Bohemia (1366–94), for example, transported books, Bohemian illustrators, and vernacular translations of the Gospels to England when she married Richard II in 1382. She also brought her own ideas, inspiring Chaucer to write *The Legend of Good Women,* which he dedicated to her. For a privileged woman like Anne of Bohemia, cultural patronage was an acceptable way to exercise public power. Through patronage, elite laywomen—particularly widows (who had independence as well as means)—advanced political agendas, satisfied personal interests, expressed religious piety, educated their children, and entertained their courts.[58] In more humble ways and at more modest levels, ordinary laywomen often did much the same. As Katherine French has shown for late medieval England, women's groups were very active at the parish level, raising funds for parochial uses, organizing social activities, and encouraging certain forms of worship. With somewhat less success and autonomy, laywomen were also active in the organizations for lay piety—especially in groups focused on charity rather than flagellation—that proliferated in fourteenth- and fifteenth-century Italian cities.[59]

Abbesses, nuns, and other saintly women were also enthusiastic patrons. Some dispensed their own wealth in support of projects. After Queen Radegund left her husband Clothar, for example, she used her extensive fortune not only to found the monastery to which she retired but also to foster the career of Venantius Fortunatus (who eventually became bishop of Poitiers). Some offered more encouragement than money. When Hild, abbess of Whitby, discovered that the humble herdsman Caedmon had a talent for composing vernacular verse, she took him into her monastery and so encouraged him that his work became widely known for its scriptural learning and sweet melodies. Whether lay or religious, female patrons seem to have inclined toward certain agendas. They often dedicated their churches and chapels to the Virgin, they particularly favored female hagiography, and they promoted female monasteries with special enthusiasm. Throughout the Middle Ages, female patrons seem to have worked "to the glory of their sex," but by the fourteenth century that trend so intensified that perhaps, as June Hall McCash has suggested, "for the first time in European literature women, through their patronage, were seeking to clarify that which was unique to them."[60]

As writers and patrons, then, medieval women acted in distinctive ways, choosing voices, subjects, and projects that reflected their sex as well as their class, their piety, and their personalities. Yet despite women's importance as patrons and writers, most medieval texts were composed by men, and women's most common cultural role was as an audience for male-created artifacts. This simple fact has raised some thorny questions. Did women see images, hear stories, and read books in the same ways as men? Did women passively accept the misogynous diatribes and stories in medieval literature? Were women complicit in ideologies that constructed them as inferior, as objects of exchange, and as oversexed sexual objects? In the late fourteenth century, Geoffrey Chaucer created, in the character of the Wife of Bath, a fictional woman who complained about her husband's "book of wicked wives." And a few years later, a real woman, Christine de Pizan, reacted so strongly against negative depictions of women that she precipitated a literary quarrel centered on the virtues and vices of the *Romance of the Rose*.[61] But aside from these two cases most medieval women—actual or fictional—seem to have been silent about the misogyny of their day. What did they think of the songs, sermons, tales, and images that surrounded them?

Two scholars of Old French literature have ventured provocative and productive answers. Roberta Krueger has argued that verse romances facilitated debate about relations between men and women. The cross-dressed heroine of the *Romance of Silence*, for example, was presented by its author as an unnatural woman, but her characterization also urged audiences to question gender norms. In a similar way, courtesy manuals encouraged proper gender roles at the same time that they spoke to profound anxieties about what those roles should be. In other words, to Krueger, many Old French texts simultaneously encouraged conformity in women and invited their resistance. Jane Burns has found in the artifacts of medieval culture even more evidence of female resistance. Focusing on female characters in male-authored texts, Burns has argued that they often spoke in disruptive ways, talking back against the ideologies of their texts and the men who wrote them. In Burns's reading—and perhaps, indeed, in the readings of medieval women—female characters in Old French texts rewrote the very stories that sought to define them.[62]

Medieval gender ideologies, then, were created, consumed, and performed by women as well as men, and although women perhaps participated in some distinctively female ways, these ideologies remained profoundly, albeit ambivalently, misogynous in their assessments of the nature and potential of women. Women were necessary but inferior. They needed to act but never freely. Women could be saved but were evil. At every turn, medieval culture struggled with the simultaneous humanity and otherness of women, and its gender ideologies were deeply inconsistent and contradictory. As students come to understand the rich complexities of medieval gender ideologies they can approach both the past and the present with greater sophistication. They might explore the complex traditions and readings to be found in specific medieval texts. They might raise questions about the cultural activities of women today, and, with insights gained from a long-distance critique of medieval culture, they might look anew at modern movies, music, and magazines. They might also investigate how their own ideas about the Middle Ages have been shaped by the trick of obfuscating modern misogyny by displacing it onto the medieval past.

Real People and Abstract Topics in the Classroom

Medievalists have recently explored many topics that can intrigue and startle students: the culture of rape among the feudal aristocracy;[63] the somatic piety of female mystics, especially as manifested by such extreme fasting that some historians compare it to modern anorexia;[64] the ways in which medieval women might have sought to practice contraception and induce abortions;[65] the working lives of women in both town and country;[66] the rule of early medieval abbesses over monasteries that contained monks as well as nuns; the veneration of virginity in the Middle Ages;[67] the proscriptions, perceptions, and practices of lesbian sexuality;[68] the nature of motherhood in a world where many children died young and many others left home at young ages;[69] female education and literacy;[70] the construction of masculinity in medieval cultures;[71] the place of prostitution in medieval towns and canon law;[72] and the gender transgressions of women who cross-dressed as men.[73] All of these subjects can fascinate students, but all also present pedagogical challenges. The pious practices of St. Catherine of Siena, for example, will certainly command attention in classes, but students might be inclined more to dismiss her piety as weird than to understand it in the context of female roles and Christian traditions in fourteenth-century Italy.

Many strategies—attention to debates among historians, in-depth analysis of selected phenomena, exploration of patriarchal bargains, and studies of the ideological power of representations—can work against such dismissals. So, too, can biographical study. Women's history has properly moved beyond the problems of elitism and the improper generalization associated with the study of "women worthies." But the lives of individual medieval women— ordinary women as well as extraordinary ones—offer concrete opportunities for students to delve into issues that initially seem foreign, abstract, and even downright odd. In the process, students can come to understand that what might seem peculiar to us was practical, possible, or perhaps even pleasurable to medieval women. In other words, biographical approaches allow students to investigate different patriarchal bargains, to understand medieval women in their own terms, and to explore the down-to-earth realities behind abstract historical generalizations.

For the Early Middle Ages, the life of Radegund provides an excellent opportunity for students to assess the constraints and opportunities of wellborn women.[74] Radegund, a princess of Thuringia, was abducted by the son of the first Christian king of the Franks and forcibly married to him. After enduring an unhappy marriage, she left him to take refuge in religion. Thereafter, as the founder and patron of the Abbey of Ste-Croix, she nurtured a center of piety and learning that eventually housed more than two hundred nuns. Through her life, students can trace the effects on women of the flexible marriage system then in place among the Frankish aristocracy; the public power that aristocratic women wielded in a time of informal and household-based governance; the critical importance of women's reproductive capacities; and the power, refuge, and comfort that religious life could offer women.[75]

Many more biographical possibilities exist for the Central Middle Ages. Heloise of the Paraclete, whose life is forever joined to that of Peter Abelard in a gripping story of seduction, premarital pregnancy, secret marriage, castration, and enduring love, is a fascinating figure to modern students. Her life effectively illustrates the educational constraints of women; their acceptance of misogyny, misogamy, and female inferiority; and the struggles of female monasteries after the Gregorian reform. Moreover, Barbara Newman's skillfully told story of how scholars have treated Heloise's letters provides a striking example of sexism at work in history-writing.[76]

Eleanor of Aquitaine was an extraordinary woman in almost every respect—married to one king at fifteen and another at thirty, governing Aquitaine in her own right, going on crusade, giving birth to ten children, organizing revolts against her husband, suffering imprisonment at his command, and finally retiring to the abbey at Fontevrault. Yet her life offers a quite ordinary example of the possibilities and limitations that feudal women faced in an age of centralizing monarchy. Eleanor of Aquitaine was an heiress in her own right, and therein lay both power and danger. Her life also illustrates the familial dynamics of the medieval aristocracy, allowing students to understand how marriage could combine diplomacy and love just as motherhood could be simultaneously selfless and self-interested. Moreover, because Eleanor of Aquitaine has been considered a central character in the history of women in the twelfth century—both the eroding power of French queens, as argued by Marion Facinger, and the developing influence of courtly love, as argued by Amy Kelly and others—her life is a useful pivot for students trying to assess whether the Central Middle Ages witnessed change for the better, change for the worse, or merely a rebalancing of the patriarchal equilibrium.[77] Finally, Katharine Hepburn's striking depiction of Eleanor of Aquitaine in the film *The Lion in Winter* offers rich possibilities for exploring how medieval women have been imagined—or indeed, recreated—in modern times.

Hildegard of Bingen led a much more sedate life than either Heloise of the Paraclete or Eleanor of Aquitaine, but thanks to recent productions of her plays and music she is well known to some students. Her accomplishments as a mystic, theologian, musician, artist, dramatist, and correspondent illustrate well how much women could achieve through monastic vocation.[78] Her life can also lead to explorations of female mysticism in the Middle Ages. To what extent was there a special female form of Christian mysticism in the Middle Ages? Can female mysticism be disentangled from extreme asceticism? In terms of women's relationship to the ecclesiastical Church, did mysticism empower women or exemplify their disempowerment? How can we best understand mystical writings that use sexual images and confound gender in ways that we today might find disconcerting or confusing? How did medieval people distinguish between authentic mystics and mad demoniacs?[79]

Because Hildegard of Bingen wrote extensively on natural philosophy, her life also raises a variety of medical topics that invariably fascinate students. Exploring the medieval complexities that Thomas Laqueur overlooked in tracing the "one-sex body" from the Greeks to Freud, Joan Cadden has illustrated how medieval science complemented medieval gender roles; how Galenic and Aristotelian teaching on reproduction fostered different conceptions of the sexes; and how Hildegard of Bingen sought to find, within the traditions of medieval science, woman-positive interpretations. Monica Green has studied the medical care and practice of women—the place of female practitioners, the medical treatment of women, the texts of gynecological knowledge, and the formulation of ideas about female sexuality. And John Riddle has suggested that various herbs and plants might have aided both contraception and abortion in the Middle Ages.[80]

Hildegard of Bingen was not the last of her kind, but in the thirteenth century and after, accomplished nuns, of whom Clare of Assisi (1193–1253) is the most prominent example, were often overshadowed by other forms of female piety: recluses and anchoresses, women in tertiary orders, beguines, and independents who pursued their own pious agendas under the guidance of local clergy. Christina of St. Trond (ca. 1150–1224), popularly known as Christina the Astonishing, provides an example that most students will never forget. Her life of extraordinary self-denial will help students explore the unique characteristics—affective, theological, and institutional—of female piety in the Later Middle Ages. Through her life, they can examine the asceticism of female mystics; they can consider how the Church attempted to cope with the *mulieres sanctae* of the time; and they can better understand the growth of beguinages, anchorholds, and the other extra-ecclesiastical institutions for the accommodation of pious women. Margery Kempe, whose early fifteenth-century autobiography has been reproduced in many forms, provides another startling example of female piety. She convinced her husband to accept a celibate marriage; she traveled to Rome, Jerusalem, and elsewhere on pilgrimage; she relied on some clerics who supported her piety while others vigorously opposed her; and she endured neighborly gossip as well as neighborly support.[81] And Joan of Arc, a peasant girl from the borderlands of France, who dressed as a man, led the forces of the French against English armies, and suffered a martyr's death at Rouen in 1431, provides yet another example of the powers and limitations of female mysticism in the Later Middle Ages.[82] Her life, like that of Eleanor of Aquitaine, can also lead students into investigations of the military roles of women.[83]

As is so often the case with biographical approaches, it is easier to focus on the wellborn than the humble, but even the lives of quite ordinary medieval women are available to students. Christina of St. Trond and Margery Kempe were born into merchant families, and their lives can facilitate not only discussions of female piety but also explorations of women's work in towns, bourgeois marriage, prostitution, and other such issues.[84] The short but startling story of John, a.k.a. Eleanor Rykener, who cross-dressed as a woman and worked as a prostitute, can generate discussions about sexuality, gender roles, and women's work in medieval towns.[85] The correspondence of the Paston family of fifteenth-century England offers glimpses into middling life, although in this case gentle rather than urban. Through the Paston letters, students can analyze how Margaret Paston (1423–84), the matriarch of this minor landowning family, supported her husband, disciplined her children, worked with servants, argued with tenants, and managed the family estates.[86]

Although Joan of Arc's humble origins do not feature large in her brief life of militant mysticism, students can approach the lives of peasant women through her story. My attempt to reconstruct the life of Cecilia Penifader (ca. 1297–1344), a peasant who lived in the English midlands just before the Great Plague, might also be useful. Unlike Joan of Arc, Cecilia Penifader lived a profoundly ordinary life unmarked by mysticism, patriotism, or sanctity, but her story offers students an on-the-ground picture of rural society and the place of women within it.[87]

Conclusion

Feminist investigations of the European Middle Ages have enormous intellectual importance to both medievalists and feminists. Medieval studies still has stodgy moments to be sure, but feminists have reinvigorated the field by introducing new theoretical approaches, forcing historical reinterpretations, and creating a fuller understanding of the centuries that lay between Roman hegemony and modernity. At the same time, feminist medievalists have been challenging women's studies to resist modernist self-absorption. Presentism haunts women's studies, but medievalists have pushed feminist colleagues in many disciplines to critique modern categories and methodologies, to see feminist issues in a longer view, and to acknowledge the power of the histories and literatures of people long dead.

In the classroom, the history of medieval women can both provoke the historical imaginations of students and turn their thoughts toward the present relevance of past times. Just as the Middle Ages have enlivened the play of many children, so now can the history of medieval women enliven classrooms. Students respond well to the histories of such strong women as Eleanor of

Aquitaine, such pious women as Hildegard of Bingen, and such peculiar women as Margery Kempe. Students are interested in the religious faiths of medieval women, in women's relationships with husbands and children, and in the ways in which women coped with misogynous ideas and patriarchal customs. And students are curious about the sexual practices of the medieval past; about medieval contraception, abortion, and medical care; and about the hard work of medieval women in villages and towns. These subjects and many others can add much-needed vigor to the "dry as dust" history of the Middle Ages.

And they do more than that. At the same time as this vigorous history captures students' attentions it can also turn their minds toward tough intellectual issues. Medieval women's history teaches students about history-writing and its sources, traditions, and controversies. Medieval women's history addresses hard questions—about relations between women and men, about differences among people, and about the possibility of human equality—that are of pressing interest to all modern people. And medieval women's history asks students to think critically about the complex workings of ideology and religion. For those privileged to teach it, the subject creates classrooms filled with energetic curiosity and timely debate.

Notes

This essay is a corrected but unrevised version of a pamphlet published in 2000. For sharing syllabi, suggesting bibliography, and offering critiques, I thank Sandy Bardsley, Stanley Chojnacki, Katherine French, Monica Green, Paul Halsall, Cynthia Herrup, Ruth Karras, Maryanne Kowaleski, Catherine Peyroux, and my colleagues in the North Carolina Research Group on Medieval and Early Modern Women. I also thank the graduate students with whom I worked in a course on medieval women in fall 1999: Jill Aitoro, Beth Barr, Kate Crassons, Evan Gatti, Paul Graeve, Cara Hersch, Joanna Kucinski, Amanda McMillan, Susan Pearson, and Liz Rothenberg. Thanks also to Blain Roberts for her cheerful help as a research assistant.

1. The Society for Medieval Feminist Scholarship produces the *Medieval Feminist Newsletter* (subscription available by writing mff@oregon.uoregon.edu); a listserv (subscription available from medfem-l@u.washington.edu); and the two bibliographic projects listed in the bibliography. Because all research on medieval women seeks to advance a previously ignored and undervalued subject, it has a feminist impulse, but some studies are, of course, more feminist than others. I adopt an ecumenical definition here, equating scholarship on women with feminist scholarship, a term that also embraces the feminist study of such topics as masculinity and sexuality. Feminist research in medieval studies is particularly active in English-speaking countries. For brief summaries of similar scholarship in Germany, Spain, France, and Italy, see Miri Rubin, "A Decade of Studying Medieval Women, 1987–1997," *History Workshop Journal* 46 (1998): 213–39; see also Susan Mosher Stuard, ed., *Women in Medieval History and Historiography* (Philadelphia: University of Pennsylvania Press, 1987). In conformity with

the pedagogical dictates of this volume and the other two in the series, I cite only studies available in English.

2. This essay focuses on women in western Europe during the medieval millennium. For research on women in Islamic societies, see especially Gavin R. G. Hambly, ed., *Women in the Medieval Islamic World* (New York: St. Martin's Press, 1998), and Jonathan Berkey, "Women in Medieval Islamic Society," in *Women in Medieval Western European Culture*, ed. Linda E. Mitchell (New York: Garland, 1999), 95–111. For Byzantine women, see especially Lynda Garland, *Byzantine Empresses: Women and Power in Byzantium, AD 527–1204* (New York: Routledge, 1999); Alice-Mary Talbot, "Women," in *The Byzantines*, ed. Guglielmo Cavallo (Chicago: University of Chicago Press, 1997), 117–43; Angeliki E. Laiou, "Women in Byzantine Society," in *Women in Medieval Western European Culture*, ed. Mitchell, 81–94; and Alice-Mary Talbot, ed., *Holy Women of Byzantium: Ten Saints' Lives in English Translation* (Washington: Dumbarton Oaks, 1996).

3. In dealing with the remains of medieval culture, feminist scholars have both uncovered new sources and reinterpreted old ones in new ways. Fascinating in themselves, the new sources and methods are beyond the scope of this essay, but for an introduction see Joel Rosenthal, ed., *Medieval Women and the Sources of Medieval History* (Athens: University of Georgia Press, 1990).

4. A. Abram, "Women Traders in Medieval London," *Economic Journal* 26 (1916): 276–85, quotation from 285.

5. At the first mention of each individual woman I will indicate estimated dates of birth and death, or, in some obscure cases, provide a general indication of when she lived.

6. Eileen Power, "The Position of Women," in *The Legacy of the Middle Ages*, ed. C. G. Crump and E. F. Jacob (Oxford: Clarendon Press, 1926), 401–33 (in 1943 edition). Because the essay is peppered with brief citations in Old French, Middle English, and Latin, it might be more useful for teachers than for students.

7. For the early history of feminist work on the Middle Ages, see Judith M. Bennett, "Medievalism and Feminism," *Speculum* 68 (1993): 309–31, reprinted in *Studying Medieval Women: Sex, Gender, Feminism*, ed. Nancy F. Partner (Cambridge: Medieval Academy of America, 1993), 7–29, 171–75. See also Stuard, ed., *Women in Medieval History and Historiography*.

8. Maxine Berg, *A Woman in History: Eileen Power, 1889–1940* (New York: Cambridge University Press, 1996), 125–26.

9. Power, "The Position of Women," 410.

10. For surveys on medieval women, see the bibliography. Margaret Wade Labarge, *A Small Sound of the Trumpet: Women in Medieval Life* (Boston: Beacon Press, 1986), 238.

11. As Robert Bartlett has put it, "While the language of race . . . is biological, its medieval reality was almost entirely cultural." *The Making of Europe: Conquest, Colonization and Cultural Change 950–1350* (Princeton: Princeton University Press, 1993), 197. Some students might be fascinated by medieval ideas about exotic people—such as giants, one-legged folk, or people with faces on their chests—thought to live in regions outside Europe. See John Block Friedman, *The Monstrous Races in Medieval Art and Thought* (Cambridge: Harvard University Press, 1981).

12. Lisa M. Bitel, *Land of Women: Tales of Sex and Gender from Early Ireland* (Ithaca: Cornell University Press, 1996); Jenny Jochens, *Women in Old Norse Society* (Ithaca: Cornell University Press, 1995).

13. The research on regional differences is nicely summarized in Maryanne Kowaleski, "Singlewomen in Medieval and Early Modern Europe: The Demographic Perspec-

tive," in *Singlewomen in the European Past, 1250–1800*, ed. Judith M. Bennett and Amy M. Froide (Philadelphia: University of Pennsylvania Press, 1998), 38–81.

14. Contrast, for example, how the first of these works explores regional differences and the second obscures them. Richard M. Smith, "The People of Tuscany and Their Families in the Fifteenth Century: Medieval or Mediterranean?" *Journal of Family History* 6 (1981): 107–28; David Herlihy, *Medieval Households* (Cambridge: Harvard University Press, 1985).

15. Christiane Klapisch-Zuber, *Women, Family and Ritual in Renaissance Italy*, trans. Lydia G. Cochrane (Chicago: University of Chicago Press, 1985); Stanley Chojnacki, *Women and Men in Renaissance Venice* (Baltimore: Johns Hopkins University Press, 2000); Elaine G. Rosenberg, "The Position of Women in Renaissance Florence: Neither Autonomy nor Subjection," in *Florence and Italy*, ed. Peter Denley and Caroline Elam, Westfield Publications in Medieval Studies, 2 (1988): 369–81; Thomas Kuehn, *Law, Family, and Women: Toward a Legal Anthropology of Renaissance Italy* (Chicago: University of Chicago Press, 1991); Maryanne Kowaleski, "Women's Work in a Market Town: Exeter in the Late Fourteenth Century," in *Women and Work in Preindustrial Europe*, ed. Barbara A. Hanawalt (Bloomington: Indiana University Press, 1986), 145–64; P. J. P. Goldberg, "Women in Fifteenth-Century Town Life," in *Towns and Townspeople in the Fifteenth Century*, ed. J. A. F. Thomson (Gloucester: Sutton, 1988), 107–28.

16. Sue Sheridan Walker, ed., *Wife and Widow in Medieval England* (Ann Arbor: University of Michigan Press, 1993); Louise Mirrer, ed., *Upon My Husband's Death: Widows in the Literatures and Histories of Medieval Europe* (Ann Arbor: University of Michigan Press, 1992); Caroline M. Barron and Anne F. Sutton, eds., *Medieval London Widows 1300–1500* (London: Hambledon Press, 1994); Sandra Cavallo and Lyndan Warner, eds., *Widowhood in Medieval and Early Modern Europe* (New York: Longman, 1999); Bennett and Froide, eds., *Singlewomen in the European Past;* Katherine J. Lewis et al., eds., *Young Medieval Women* (New York: St. Martin's Press, 1999); Michael M. Sheehan, *Marriage, Family and Law in Medieval Europe: Collected Studies*, ed. James K. Farge (Toronto: University of Toronto Press, 1996); Dyan Elliott, *Spiritual Marriage: Sexual Abstinence in Medieval Wedlock* (Princeton: Princeton University Press, 1993).

17. Christine de Pizan, *The Treasure of the City of Ladies*, trans. Sarah Lawson (Harmondsworth: Penguin, 1985), 156–60; Christiane Klapisch-Zuber, "The 'Cruel Mother': Maternity, Widowhood, and Dowry in Florence in the Fourteenth and Fifteenth Centuries," in Klapisch-Zuber, *Women, Family, and Ritual*, 117–31.

18. Richard Abels and Ellen Harrison, "The Participation of Women in Languedocian Catharism," *Mediaeval Studies* 41 (1979): 215–51; Peter Biller, "The Common Woman in the Western Church in the Thirteenth and Early Fourteenth Centuries," in *Women in the Church*, ed. W. J. Sheils and Diana Wood (Oxford: Basil Blackwell, 1990), 127–57; Peter Biller, "Cathars and Material Women," in *Medieval Theology and the Natural Body*, ed. Peter Biller and Alastair J. Minnis, York Studies in Theology and the Natural Body 1 (1997): 61–107; Shannon McSheffrey, *Gender and Heresy: Women and Men in Lollard Communities, 1420–1530* (Philadelphia: University of Pennsylvania Press, 1995). For a brief summary of McSheffrey's argument that works well with students, see her "Women and Lollardy: A Reassessment," *Canadian Journal of History* 26 (1991): 199–223.

19. Michael Adler, "The Jewish Woman in Medieval England," in Adler, *The Jews in Medieval England* (London: Jewish Historical Society of England, 1939), 17–42; Israel Epstein, "The Jewish Woman in the Responsa 900–1500 C.E.," in *The Jewish Library 3: Woman*, ed. Leo Jung (New York: Jewish Library, 1934), 123–52; Renée Levine

Melammed, "Sephardi Women in the Medieval and Early Modern Periods," in *Jewish Women in Historical Perspective*, 2d ed., ed. Judith R. Baskin (Detroit: Wayne State University Press, 1998), 128–49, quotation from 141; Judith R. Baskin, "From Separation to Displacement: The Problem of Women in *Sefer Hasidim,*" *Association of Jewish Studies Review* 19 (1994): 1–18, quotation from 18. For additional studies on medieval Jewish women see Barrie Dobson, "The Role of Jewish Women in Medieval England," in *Christianity and Judaism*, ed. Diana Wood (Oxford: Basil Blackwell, 1992), 145–68 (Dobson notes [146] that "one of the hazards facing the historian of the medieval Jewess may be the temptation to idealize her just because she is a Jewess"); Judith R. Baskin, "Jewish Women in the Middle Ages," in Baskin, *Jewish Women in Historical Perspective*, 94–114; Kenneth R. Stow, "The Jewish Family in the Rhineland in the High Middle Ages: Form and Function," *American Historical Review* 92 (1987): 1085–110; Emily Taitz, "Women's Voices, Women's Prayers: Women in the European Synagogues of the Middle Ages," in *Daughters of the King: Women and the Synagogue*, ed. Susan Grossman and Rivka Haut (Philadelphia: Jewish Publication Society, 1992), 59–71; Diane Owen Hughes, "Distinguishing Signs: Ear-rings, Jews, and Franciscan Rhetoric in the Italian Renaissance City," *Past and Present* 112 (1986): 3–59; Louise Mirrer, *Women, Jews and Muslims in the Texts of Reconquest Castile* (Ann Arbor: University of Michigan Press, 1996).

20. de Pizan, *The Treasure*, 176.

21. There is a large and growing literature on aristocratic women and queens, including John Parsons, ed., *Medieval Queenship* (New York: St. Martin's Press, 1993); Marion F. Facinger, "A Study of Medieval Queenship: Capetian France, 987–1237," *Studies in Medieval and Renaissance History* 5 (1968): 3–47; Louise Olga Fradenburg, ed., *Women and Sovereignty* (Edinburgh: Edinburgh University Press, 1992); Theresa M. Vann, ed., *Queens, Regents and Potentates* (Dallas: Academia, 1993); Pauline Stafford, *Queen Emma and Queen Edith: Queenship and Women's Power in Eleventh-Century England* (Oxford: Basil Blackwell, 1997); Marjorie Chibnall, *The Empress Matilda: Queen Consort, Queen Mother, and Lady of the English* (Oxford: Basil Blackwell, 1992); Margaret Howell, *Eleanor of Provence: Queenship in Thirteenth-Century England* (Oxford: Basil Blackwell, 1998); Jennifer C. Ward, *English Noblewomen in the Later Middle Ages* (London: Longman, 1992); Michael K. Jones and Malcolm G. Underwood, *The King's Mother: Lady Margaret Beaufort, Countess of Richmond and Derby* (New York: Cambridge University Press, 1992); and Peggy K. Liss, *Isabel the Queen: Life and Times* (New York: Oxford University Press, 1992). See also the sources collected by Jennifer Ward in *Women of the English Nobility and Gentry, 1066–1500* (Manchester: Manchester University Press, 1995).

22. For women in towns, see especially Hanawalt, ed., *Women and Work;* Lindsey Charles and Lorna Duffin, eds., *Women and Work in Pre-Industrial England* (London: Croom Helm, 1985); Martha C. Howell, *Women, Production and Patriarchy in Late Medieval Cities* (Chicago: University of Chicago Press, 1986); P. J. P. Goldberg, *Women, Work, and Life Cycle in a Medieval Economy: Women in York and Yorkshire, c. 1300–1520* (New York: Oxford University Press, 1992); Judith M. Bennett, *Ale, Beer, and Brewsters in England: Women's Work in a Changing World* (New York: Oxford University Press, 1996); Martha C. Howell, *The Marriage Exchange: Property, Social Place, and Gender in Cities of the Low Countries, 1300–1550* (Chicago: University of Chicago Press, 1998); and Maryanne Kowaleski and Judith M. Bennett, "Crafts, Guilds, and Women in the Middle Ages: Fifty Years after Marian K. Dale," in *Sisters and Workers in the Middle Ages*, ed. Judith M. Bennett et al. (Chicago: University of Chicago Press, 1998), 11–25, also in *Signs* 14 (1989): 474–501. For an overview that places women's work in the Middle Ages in a broad

historical context, see Judith M. Bennett, "Medieval Women, Modern Women: Across the Great Divide," in *Culture and History, 1350–1600: Essays on English Communities, Identities, and Writing*, ed. David Aers (London: Harvester Wheatsheaf, 1992), 147–75, revised version in *Feminists Revision History*, ed. Ann-Louise Shapiro (New Brunswick: Rutgers University Press, 1994), 47–72. David Herlihy, *Opera Muliebria: Women and Work in Medieval Europe* (New York: McGraw-Hill, 1990) is designed for classroom use but not up to date.

23. For peasant women, see especially Judith M. Bennett, *Women in the Medieval English Countryside: Gender and Household in Brigstock before the Plague* (New York: Oxford University Press, 1987), and Judith M. Bennett, *A Medieval Life: Cecilia Penifader of Brigstock, c. 1297–1344* (Boston: McGraw-Hill, 1998). For more positive assessments, see Barbara Hanawalt, "Peasant Women's Contribution to the Home Economy in Late Medieval England," in Hanawalt, *Women and Work*, 3–19, and Helen Jewell, "Women at the Courts of the Manor of Wakefield, 1348–1350," *Northern History* 26 (1990): 59–81.

24. Deniz Kandiyoti, "Bargaining with Patriarchy," *Gender and Society* 2 (1988): 274–90. The "bargain" in "patriarchal bargain" can throw students off track, for it is not meant to suggest that women arranged particularly good deals, or that gender arrangements were constantly negotiated anew, or that these negotiations occurred between equally empowered women and men. Yet the term *bargain* does indicate what Kandiyoti sees as the mechanisms through which women could (and can) somewhat mitigate their patriarchal oppression.

25. R. I. Moore, *The Formation of a Persecuting Society: Power and Deviance in Western Europe, 950–1250* (New York: Oxford University Press, 1987); Jeffrey Richards, *Sex, Dissidence and Damnation: Minority Groups in the Middle Ages* (London: Routledge, 1991); Bartlett, *The Making of Europe*. For studies that have begun to address issues of gender, see Mirrer, *Women, Jews and Muslims in the Tests of Reconquest Castile;* Joan Young Gregg, ed., *Devils, Women, and Jews: Reflections of the Other in Medieval Sermon Stories* (Albany: State University of New York Press, 1997), which is more useful for its texts than for its analysis, and David Nirenberg, *Communities of Violence: Persecution of Minorities in the Middle Ages* (Princeton: Princeton University Press, 1996).

26. Nirenberg, *Communities of Violence*, esp. 129–65, quotations from 151 and 155. For a useful study of women in Castilian society, see Heath Dillard, *Daughters of the Reconquest: Women in Castilian Town Society, 1100–1300* (New York: Cambridge University Press, 1984); see also Mirrer, *Women, Jews and Muslims in the Texts of Reconquest Castile*.

27. Sharon Kinoshita, "The Politics of Courtly Love: *La Prise D'Orange* and the Conversion of the Saracen Queen," *Romanic Review* 86 (1995): 265–87; Sarah Kay, "Contesting 'Romance Influence': The Poetics of the Gift," *Comparative Literature Studies* 32 (1995): 320–41; Jacqueline de Weever, *Sheba's Daughters: Whitening and Demonizing the Saracen Woman in Medieval French Literature* (New York: Garland, 1998); Louise Mirrer, *Women, Jews and Muslims in the Texts of Reconquest Castile*, 17–30 (Mirrer also discusses Christian representations of Jewish women, 31–44).

28. Susan Mosher Stuard, "Ancillary Evidence for the Decline of Medieval Slavery," *Past and Present* 149 (1995): 3–28; see also Ruth Mazo Karras, "Desire, Descendants, and Dominance: Slavery, The Exchange of Women, and Masculine Power," in *The Work of Work: Servitude, Slavery, and Labor in Medieval England*, ed. Allen J. Frantzen and Douglas Moffat (Glasgow: Cruithne Press, 1994), 16–29.

29. Alain Boureau, *The Lord's First Night: The Myth of the Droit de Cuissage*, trans. Lydia G. Cochrane (Chicago: University of Chicago Press, 1998). Donna Woolfolk Cross's novel *Pope Joan* (New York: Crown, 1996) includes a historical postscript that purports

to prove that the story has a basis in truth, as does Peter Stanford's *The She-Pope* (London: William Heineman, 1998). For a discussion of the story, see Valerie R. Hotchkiss, *Clothes Make the Man: Female Cross-Dressing in Medieval Europe* (New York: Garland Publishing, 1991), 69–82. I know of no modern account that discusses the myth of chastity belts, but I also know of no chastity belts that can be dated earlier than the sixteenth century.

30. Susan Mosher Stuard, "The Dominion of Gender; or, How Women Fared in the High Middle Ages," in *Becoming Visible: Women in European History*, 3d ed., ed. Renate Bridenthal et al. (Boston: Houghton Mifflin, 1998), 129–50.

31. For a summary of debates on this issue, see Mavis Mate, *Women in English Society* (New York: Cambridge University Press, 1999), esp. 27–95; Goldberg, *Women, Work, and Life Cycle;* Caroline Barron, "The 'Golden Age' of Women in Medieval London," in *Medieval Women in Southern England,* Reading Medieval Studies 15 (1989): 35–58. For a critique of Goldberg and Barron, see Bennett, "Medieval Women, Modern Women," 147–75. Sandy Bardsley argues that one lynchpin on the "change for the better" model—equal wages for women and men—is not borne out in the documentary evidence. Bardsley, "Women's Work Reconsidered: Gender and Wage Differentiation in Late Medieval England," *Past and Present* 165 (1999): 3–29.

32. Jo Ann McNamara, "The *Herrenfrage:* The Restructuring of the Gender System, 1050–1150," in *Medieval Masculinities*, ed. Clare A. Lees (Minneapolis: University of Minnesota Press, 1994), 3–29, quotation from 15; Stuard, "The Dominion of Gender," 145.

33. David Herlihy, "Land, Family and Women in Continental Europe, 701–1200," *Traditio* 18 (1962): 89–120; Facinger, "A Study of Medieval Queenship"; Jo Ann McNamara and Suzanne Wemple, "The Power of Women through the Family in Medieval Europe, 500–1100," in *Women and Power in the Middle Ages*, ed. Mary Erler and Maryanne Kowaleski (Athens: University of Georgia Press, 1988), 83–101, also in *Feminist Studies* 1 (1973): 126–41, and in *Clio's Consciousness Raised: New Perspectives on the History of Women*, ed. Lois Banner (New York: Harper and Row, 1974), 103–18; Jane Tibbetts Schulenburg, "Female Sanctity: Public and Private Roles, ca. 500–1100," in *Women and Power in the Middle Ages*, ed. Erler and Kowaleski, 102–25.

34. James A. Brundage, *Law, Sex, and Christian Society in Medieval Europe* (Chicago: University of Chicago Press, 1987), 428.

35. Stuard, "The Dominion of Gender," 147.

36. For a critique of one particularly long-standing tradition of "change for the worse," see Pauline Stafford, "Women and the Norman Conquest," *Transactions of the Royal Historical Society* 4, 6th ser. (1996): 221–50.

37. For further critiques, see responses by Sandra Greene, Karen Offen, and Gerda Lerner to my "Confronting Continuity," *Journal of Women's History* 9 (1997): 73–94, found on 95–118 of the same issue.

38. Caroline Walker Bynum, *Holy Feast and Holy Fast: The Religious Significance of Food to Medieval Women* (Berkeley: University of California Press, 1987). For a brief summary that works well in the classroom, see Caroline Bynum, "Fast, Feast, and Flesh: The Religious Significance of Food to Medieval Women," *Representations* 11 (1985): 1–16. See also Rudolph M. Bell, *Holy Anorexia* (Chicago: University of Chicago Press, 1985). For primary sources, see especially *Medieval Women's Visionary Literature*, ed. Elizabeth A. Petroff (New York: Oxford University Press, 1986), and *Women Mystics in Medieval Europe,* ed. Emilie Zum Brunn and Georgette Epiney-Burgard (New York: Paragon House, 1989).

39. Power, "The Position of Women," quotation from 407; Penny Schine Gold, *The Lady and the Virgin: Image, Attitude and Experience in Twelfth-Century France* (Chicago: University of Chicago Press, 1985), quotation from 145.

40. An excellent summary of early Christian attitudes is Elizabeth A. Clark, "Devil's Gateway and Brides of Christ: Women in the Early Christian World," in *Ascetic Piety and Women's Faith* (Lewiston, N.Y.: E. Mellen, 1986), 23–60.

41. For a recent and fascinating exploration of medieval ideology as it pertained to women and gender, see Dyan Elliott, *Fallen Bodies: Pollution, Sexuality, and Demonology in the Middle Ages* (Philadelphia: University of Pennsylvania Press, 1998). For a study that links certain representations of gender to specific literary genres, see Simon Gaunt, *Gender and Genre in Medieval French Literature* (New York: Cambridge University Press, 1995).

42. Marina Warner, *Alone of All Her Sex: The Myth and the Cult of the Virgin Mary* (New York: Knopf, 1976); Jaroslav Pelikan, *Mary through the Centuries: Her Place in the History of Culture* (New Haven: Yale University Press, 1996).

43. There is a vast literature on medieval nuns, but see especially Jane Tibbetts Schulenburg, *Forgetful of Their Sex: Female Sanctity and Society, ca. 500–1100* (Chicago: University of Chicago Press, 1998); Bruce L. Venarde, *Women's Monasticism and Medieval Society: Nunneries in France and England, 890–1215* (Ithaca: Cornell University Press, 1997); Jo Ann Kay McNamara, *Sisters in Arms: Catholic Nuns through Two Millennia* (Cambridge: Harvard University Press, 1996); Penelope D. Johnson, *Equal in Monastic Profession: Religious Women in Medieval France* (Chicago: University of Chicago Press, 1991); Marilyn Oliva, *The Convent and the Community in Late Medieval England: Female Monasteries in the Diocese of Norwich, 1350–1540* (Woodbridge, Suffolk: Boydell Press, 1998); Gertrud Jaron Lewis, *By Women, for Women, about Women: The Sister-Books of Fourteenth-Century Germany* (Toronto: Pontifical Institute of Mediaeval Studies, 1996); Roberta Gilchrist, *Gender and Material Culture: The Archaeology of Religious Women* (London: Routledge, 1994); and John A. Nichols and Lillian Thomas Shank, eds., *Medieval Religious Women*, vol. 1: *Distant Echoes*, Cistercian Publications 71 (1984). For the quotation of St. Francis, see Shulamith Shahar, *The Fourth Estate: A History of Women in the Middle Ages* (London: Methuen, 1983), 36.

44. Jane Tibbetts Schulenburg, "The Heroics of Virginity: Brides of Christ and Sacrificial Mutilation," in *Women in the Middle Ages and the Renaissance*, ed. Mary Beth Rose (Syracuse: Syracuse University Press, 1986), 29–72, also found as chapter 3 in Schulenburg, *Forgetful of Their Sex*.

45. Clarissa Atkinson, "'Precious Balsam in a Fragile Glass': The Ideology of Virginity in the Later Middle Ages," *Journal of Family History* 8 (1983): 131–43.

46. Kathleen Ashley and Pamela Sheingorn, eds., *Interpreting Cultural Symbols: Saint Anne in Late Medieval Society* (Athens: University of Georgia Press, 1990).

47. Sharon Farmer, "Persuasive Voices: Clerical Images of Medieval Wives," *Speculum* 61 (1986): 517–43. For the image of Blanche and Louis IX, see Warner, *Alone of All Her Sex*, figure 15; for a contemporary image of the Virgin from Chartres Cathedral, see Gold, *Lady and Virgin*, plate 6. For discussion about the nature of women's power in the Middle Ages, see *Women and Power in the Middle Ages*, ed. Erler and Kowaleski.

48. Alcuin Blamires, ed., *Woman Defamed and Defended: An Anthology of Edited Texts* (New York: Oxford University Press, 1992), quotation from 12; R. Howard Bloch, "Medieval Misogyny," *Representations* 20 (1987): 1–24, quotation from 22n15. Bloch's argument in this essay generated heated debate. See responses by eight feminist scholars

in the *Medieval Feminist Newsletter* 6 (Dec. 1988): 2–15, and Bloch's response in the *Medieval Feminist Newsletter* 7 (Spring 1989): 8–12. Bloch's opinions are somewhat moderated in his *Medieval Misogyny and the Invention of Western Romantic Love* (Chicago: University of Chicago Press, 1991). For misogamy, see especially Katharina M. Wilson and Elizabeth M. Makowski, *Wykked Wyves and the Woes of Marriage: Misogamous Literature from Juvenal to Chaucer* (Albany: State University of New York Press, 1990).

49. For brewsters, see Bennett, *Ale, Beer, and Brewsters*, 124–44; for prostitutes, see Ruth Mazo Karras, *Common Women: Prostitution and Sexuality in Medieval England* (New York: Oxford University Press, 1996), quotation from 141.

50. Bloch's argument is developed in his *Medieval Misogyny*, the quotation is from page 5. Diane Bornstein, "Courtly Love," in *Dictionary of the Middle Ages*, vol. 3, ed. Joseph Strayer (New York: Scribner, 1983), 667–74 (a clear and brief introduction to courtly love). For the social context of courtly love, see Constance Brittain Bouchard, *Strong of Body, Brave and Noble: Chivalry and Society in Medieval France* (Ithaca: Cornell University Press, 1998). For the emotional context, see C. Stephen Jaeger, *Ennobling Love* (Philadelphia: University of Pennsylvania Press, 1999).

51. Alcuin Blamires, *The Case for Women in Medieval Culture* (New York: Oxford University Press, 1997), quotations from 12 and 5. For the question of Christine de Pizan's feminism, see Beatrice Gottlieb, "The Problem of Feminism in the Fifteenth Century," in *Women of the Medieval World*, ed. Julius Kirshner and Suzanne F. Wemple (Oxford: Basil Blackwell, 1985), 337–64. For a fascinating analysis of the complexities of reading the defenses offered by both fictive and historical women, see Helen Solterer, *The Master and Minerva: Disputing Women in French Medieval Culture* (Berkeley: University of California Press, 1995).

52. Power, "The Position of Women," 408. Particularly interesting in this regard is the argument of Elisabeth van Houts that medieval women actively contributed to creation of historical memory. Van Houts, *Memory and Gender in Medieval Europe, 900–1200* (London: Macmillan, 1999).

53. Annemarie Weyl Carr, "Women as Artists in the Middle Ages: 'The Dark Is Light Enough,'" in *Dictionary of Women Artists*, ed. Delia Gaze (London: Fitzroy Dearborn, 1997), 3: 3–21; Carr also wrote the pathbreaking "Women Artists in the Middle Ages," *Feminist Art Journal* 5 (1976): 5–9, 26. Lila Yawn-Bonghi, "Medieval Women Artists and Modern Historians," *Medieval Feminist Newsletter* 12 (1991): 10–19; Herrad of Hohenbourg, *Hortus Deliciarum*, ed. R. Green et al., Studies of the Warburg Institute 36, 2 vols. (London: Warburg Institute, University of London, 1979); Wolfgang Grape, *The Bayeux Tapestry: Monument to a Norman Triumph* (Munich: Prestel, 1994); Kay Stanisland, *Medieval Craftsmen: Embroiders* (Toronto: University of Toronto Press, 1991); Jeffrey F. Hamburger, *Nuns as Artists: The Visual Culture of a Medieval Convent* (Berkeley: University of California Press, 1997); Christa Grössinger, *Picturing Women in Late Medieval and Renaissance Art* (Manchester: Manchester University Press, 1997).

54. Of course, many secular women might have written texts that have either not survived or not been properly attributed, and that might particularly be the case for the Early Middle Ages. In *Carolingians and the Written Word* (New York: Cambridge University Press, 1989), esp. 223–27, Rosamund McKitterick argues that aristocratic women then were often literate. Janet Nelson has even suggested that women might have written anonymous histories from the Early Middle Ages that display three characteristics: a relatively free style incorporating oral sources; interest in the dynamics of power within families; and attention to the roles of women. Janet L. Nelson, "Gender

and Genre in Women Historians of the Early Middle Ages," *L'historiographie médiévale en Europe* (Paris: CNRS, 1991), 149–63. Because they were not ordained, nuns were also technically laity, but I have adopted in this essay the now-common convention of differentiating between nuns, on the one hand, and laywomen, on the other.

55. For some texts produced by women writers in the Middle Ages, see Peter Dronke, *Women Writers of the Middle Ages: A Critical Study of Texts from Perpetua (†203) to Marguerite Porete (†1310)* (New York: Cambridge University Press, 1984); Katharina Wilson, ed., *Medieval Women Writers* (Athens: University of Georgia Press, 1984); de Pizan, *The Treasure;* Christine de Pizan, *The Book of the City of Ladies,* trans. Earl Jeffrey Richards (New York: Persea Books, 1982); Christine de Pizan, *The Selected Writings of Christine de Pizan,* trans. Renate Blumenfeld-Kosinski and Kevin Brownlee (New York: W. W. Norton, 1997); Brunn and Epiney-Burgard, eds., *Women Mystics in Medieval Europe;* Petroff, ed., *Medieval Women's Visionary Literature;* Robert Hanning and Joan Ferrante, eds., *The Lais of Marie de France* (Durham: Labyrinth Press, 1978), 1; Julian of Norwich, *Revelations of Divine Love,* trans. Clifton Wolters (Harmondsworth: Penguin, 1966); Margery Kempe, *The Book of Margery Kempe,* trans. B. A. Windeatt (Harmondsworth: Penguin 1985); and Matilda Tomaryn Bruckner et al., eds., *Songs of the Women Troubadours* (New York: Garland, 1995). Further sources are in the bibliography. See also the general study of medieval Englishwomen's writings by Laurie A. Finke, *Women's Writing in English: Medieval England* (London: Longman, 1999).

56. Charity Cannon Willard, *Christine de Pizan: Her Life and Works* (New York: Persea Books, 1984), 206. This is the best biography of Christine de Pizan. For the issue of her feminism, see Gottlieb, "The Problem of Feminism."

57. Matilda Tomaryn Bruckner, "Fictions of the Female Voice: The Women Troubadours," *Speculum* 67 (1992): 865–91, quotations from 890; Hamburger, *Nuns as Artists,* 222; William D. Paden, "Introduction," in *The Voice of the Trobairitz: Perspectives on the Women Troubadours,* ed. William D. Paden (Philadelphia: University of Pennsylvania Press, 1989), 1–28; Dronke, *Women Writers,* x; Joanna E. Ziegler, *Sculpture of Compassion: The Pietà and the Beguines in the Southern Low Countries, c. 1300–c. 1600* (Brussels: Institut Historique Belge de Rome, 1992); Joan M. Ferrante, *To the Glory of Her Sex: Women's Roles in the Composition of Medieval Texts* (Bloomington: Indiana University Press, 1997). On a related topic, Roberta Gilchrist (*Gender and Material Culture*) has traced how ideas about femaleness shaped monastic architecture. Nuns lived in monasteries different—in terms of locations, ground plans, buildings, and iconography—from those inhabited by most monks. For students, an article by Gilchrist is more accessible than her book: "'Blessed Art Thou among Women': The Archaeology of Female Piety," in *Woman Is a Worthy Wight: Women in English Society c. 1200–1500,* ed. P. J. P. Goldberg (Stroud: Sutton, 1992), 212–26.

58. Susan Groag Bell, "Medieval Women Book Owners: Arbiters of Lay Piety and Ambassadors of Culture," in *Women and Power in Medieval Europe,* ed. Erler and Kowaleski, 149–87, quotation from 150, also found in *Signs* 7 (1982): 742–68, and in *Sisters and Workers,* ed. Bennett et al., 135–61.

59. Katherine L. French, "'To Free Them from Binding': Women in the Late Medieval English Parish," *Journal of Interdisciplinary History* 27 (1997): 387–412; Katherine L. French, "Maidens' Lights and Wives' Store: Women's Parish Guilds in Late Medieval England," *Sixteenth Century Journal* 29 (1998): 399–426; Nicholas Terpstra, "Women in the Brotherhood: Gender, Class, and Politics in Renaissance Bolognese Confraternities," *Renaissance and Reformation,* new series 14, no. 3 (1990): 193–212.

60. For women and patronage during the Middle Ages, see especially June Hall McCash, "The Cultural Patronage of Medieval Women: An Overview," in *The Cultural Patronage of Medieval Women*, ed. June Hall McCash (Athens: University of Georgia Press, 1996), 1–49, quotations from 29; Ferrante, *To the Glory of Her Sex;* and Clare A. Lees and Gillian R. Overing, "Birthing Bishops and Fathering Poets: Bede, Hild, and the Relations of Cultural Production," *Exemplaria* 6 (1994): 35–66.

61. For a general introduction to this debate see John Kelly, "Early Feminist Theory and the *Querelles des Femmes*, 1400–1789," in *Women, History and Theory* (Chicago: University of Chicago Press, 1984), 65–109; see also Solterer, *The Master and Minerva*.

62. Roberta L. Krueger, *Women Readers and the Ideology of Gender in Old French Verse Romance* (New York: Cambridge University Press, 1993); E. Jane Burns, *Bodytalk: When Women Speak in Old French Literature* (Philadelphia: University of Pennsylvania Press, 1993); see also Anne Clark Bartlett, *Male Authors, Female Readers: Representation and Subjectivity in Middle English Devotional Literature* (Ithaca: Cornell University Press, 1995), and Jocelyn Wogan-Browne, "Saints' Lives and the Female Reader," *Forum for Modern Language Studies* 27 (1991): 314–32.

63. Kathryn Gravdal, *Ravishing Maidens: Writing Rape in Medieval French Literature and Law* (Philadelphia: University of Pennsylvania Press, 1991). For students, this article might be more accessible: Kathryn Gravdal, "Chrétien de Troyes, Gratian, and the Medieval Romance of Sexual Violence," *Signs* 17 (1992): 558–85; see also Anna Roberts, ed., *Violence against Women in Medieval Texts* (Gainesville: University of Florida Press, 1998).

64. Bynum, *Holy Feast and Holy Fast;* Bynum, "Fast, Feast, and Flesh"; Bell, *Holy Anorexia*.

65. John M. Riddle, *Contraception and Abortion from the Ancient World to the Renaissance* (Cambridge: Harvard University Press, 1992). This brief article might work better for classroom use: John M. Riddle, "Contraception and Abortion in the Middle Ages," in *Handbook of Medieval Sexuality*, ed. Vern L. Bullough and James A. Brundage (New York: Garland, 1996), 261–78.

66. See especially the essays in *Women and Work in Preindustrial Europe*, ed. Hanawalt, and *Women and Work in Pre-Industrial England*, ed. Charles and Duffin; see also Bennett, "Medieval Women, Modern Women."

67. Sources are cited in note 43.

68. Jacqueline Murray, "Twice Marginal and Twice Invisible: Lesbians in the Middle Ages," in *Handbook of Medieval Sexuality*, ed. Bullough and Brundage, 191–223. This article generates vigorous classroom discussion. For an introduction to church efforts to regulate sexual behavior, see James A. Brundage, *Law, Sex, and Christian Society*.

69. Clarissa W. Atkinson, *The Oldest Vocation: Christian Motherhood in the Middle Ages* (Ithaca: Cornell University Press, 1991); Ann Marie Rasmussen, *Mothers and Daughters in Medieval German Literature* (Syracuse: Syracuse University Press, 1997); John Carmi Parsons and Bonnie Wheeler, eds., *Medieval Mothering* (New York: Garland Publishing, 1996). Lois Huneycutt's article in *Medieval Mothering* works particularly well with students: "Public Lives, Private Ties: Royal Mothers in England and Scotland, 1070–1204" (295–311).

70. Many useful essays on female literacy and education can be found in the three-volume proceedings of a 1993 conference, all edited by Lesley Smith and Jane H. M. Taylor: *Women, The Book and the Godly* (Woodbridge: D. S. Brewer, 1995); *Women, The Book and the Worldly* (Woodbridge: D. S. Brewer, 1995); and *Women and the Book: Assessing the Visual Evidence* (London: British Library, 1997).

71. Lees, ed., *Medieval Masculinities;* Jeffrey Jerome Cohen and Bonnie Wheeler, eds., *Becoming Male in the Middle Ages* (New York: Garland, 1997); D. M. Hadley, ed., *Masculinity in Medieval Europe* (London: Longman, 1999); Jacqueline Murray, ed., *Conflicted Identities and Multiple Masculinities: Men in the Medieval West* (New York: Garland, 1999).

72. Karras, *Common Women;* Leah Lydia Otis, *Prostitution in Medieval Society: The History of an Urban Institution in Languedoc* (Chicago: University of Chicago Press, 1985). Few things are as gripping for students as the case of a transvestite prostitute who worked in London and Oxford, see Ruth Mazo Karras and David Lorenzo Boyd, "'Ut Cum Muliere': A Male Transvestite Prostitute in Fourteenth-Century London," in *Premodern Sexualities,* ed. Louise Fradenburg and Carla Freccero (London: Routledge, 1996), 101–16.

73. Hotchkiss, *Clothes Make the Man;* Vern L. Bullough, "Cross Dressing and Gender Role Change in the Middle Ages," in *Handbook of Medieval Sexuality,* ed. Bullough and Brundage, 223–42. In addition to the case of the transvestite prostitute, an excellent example for use in the classroom can be found in Michael H. Shank, "A Female University Student in Late Medieval Krakow," in *Sisters and Workers,* ed. Bennett et al., 190–97, and also in *Signs* 12 (1987): 373–80. See also Rudolf M. Dekker and Lotte C. van de Pol, *The Tradition of Female Transvestism in Early Modern Europe* (London: Macmillan, 1989).

74. Jo Ann McNamara and John E. Halborg, ed. and trans., *Sainted Women of the Dark Ages* (Durham: Duke University Press, 1992), 60–105. To place Radegund's life in context, see McNamara and Wemple, "The Power of Women," and Suzanne Fonay Wemple, *Women in Frankish Society: Marriage and the Cloister, 500 to 900* (Philadelphia: University of Pennsylvania Press, 1981).

75. Another good option for the Early Middle Ages is Hild of Whitby. See Christine E. Fell, "Hild, Abbess of Streonaeshalch," in *Hagiography and Medieval Literature: A Symposium,* ed. Hans Bekker-Nielson et al. (Odense, Denmark: Odense University Press, 1981), 76–99; Lees and Overing, "Birthing Bishops"; Anne Warin, *Hilda: The Chronicle of a Saint* (London: Lamp Press, 1989) (a historical novel). Hroswitha and her plays (especially *Dulcetius,* which tells of three virgins who successfully resist the ludicrous advances of a Roman) can both amuse students and help them imagine the esprit de corps of early medieval virgins. Students also react strongly to "The Heroics of Virginity," Jane Schulenburg's exploration of how early medieval nuns might have preferred self-mutilation to rape.

76. Betty Radice, ed., *The Letters of Abelard and Heloise* (Harmondsworth: Penguin, 1974); Barbara Newman, "Authority, Authenticity, and the Repression of Heloise," *Journal of Medieval and Renaissance Studies* 22 (1992): 121–57; see also Constant J. Mews, *The Lost Love Letters of Heloise and Abelard: Perceptions of Dialogue in Twelfth-Century France* (New York: St. Martin's Press, 1999).

77. For a brief overview see Elizabeth A. R. Brown, "Eleanor of Aquitaine: Parent, Queen, and Duchess," in *Eleanor of Aquitaine: Patron and Politician,* ed. William W. Kibler (Austin: University of Texas Press, 1976), 9–34. There are many book-length studies, of which the best is probably Douglas D. R. Owen, *Eleanor of Aquitaine: Queen and Legend* (Oxford: Basil Blackwell, 1993). For students, the liveliest biography is Marion Meade, *Eleanor of Aquitaine: A Biography* (New York: Penguin, 1977), but it interprets Eleanor in somewhat anachronistic ways. Amy Kelly, *Eleanor of Aquitaine and the Four Kings* (Cambridge: Harvard University Press, 1950), is now old, but responsible for the argument that places Eleanor at the center of the development of courtly love.

78. Sabina Flanagan, *Hildegard of Bingen: A Visionary Life,* 2d ed. (London: Routledge, 1998); Barbara Newman, *Voice of the Living Light: Hildegard of Bingen and Her World*

(Berkeley: University of California Press, 1998). Among the many editions of the many writings of Hildegard of Bingen, her edited letters might be most accessible: *The Letters of Hildegard of Bingen*, vols. 1 and 2, trans. Joseph L. Baird and Radd K. Ehrmann (1994, repr. New York: Oxford University Press, 1998).

79. On mysticism, see Bynum, *Holy Feast and Holy Fast*, as well as Carolyn Walker Bynum, *Jesus as Mother: Studies in the Spirituality of the High Middle Ages* (Berkeley: University of California Press, 1982); Amy Hollywood, *The Soul as Virgin Wife: Mechthild of Magdeburg, Marguerite Porete, and Meister Eckhart* (Notre Dame: University of Notre Dame Press, 1995); Ulrike Wiethaus, ed., *Maps of Flesh and Light: The Religious Experience of Medieval Women Mystics* (Syracuse: Syracuse University Press, 1993); Brunn and Epiney-Burgard, eds., *Women Mystics in Medieval Europe;* Petroff, *Medieval Women's Visionary Literature;* Elizabeth Petroff, *Body and Soul: Essays on Medieval Women and Mysticism* (New York: Oxford University Press, 1994); and Ronald E. Surtz, *Writing Women in Late Medieval and Early Modern Spain: The Mothers of Saint Teresa of Avila* (Philadelphia: University of Pennsylvania Press, 1995). Barbara Newman's "Possessed by the Spirit: Devout Women, Demoniacs, and the Apostolic Life in the Thirteenth Century," *Speculum* 73 (1998): 733–70, works well in the classroom.

80. Joan Cadden, *Meanings of Sex Difference in the Middle Ages: Medicine, Science, and Culture* (New York: Cambridge University Press, 1993); Thomas Laqueur, *Making Sex: Body and Gender from the Greeks to Freud* (Cambridge: Harvard University Press, 1990); Monica H. Green, "Women's Medical Practice and Health Care in Medieval Europe," in *Sisters and Workers*, ed. Bennett et al., 39–78, also in *Signs* 14 (1989): 434–73; Monica H. Green, "Female Sexuality in the Medieval West," *Trends in History* 4 (1990): 127–58, and Monica H. Green, "Documenting Medieval Women's Medical Practice," in *Practical Medicine from Salerno to the Black Death*, ed. Luis García-Ballester et al. (New York: Cambridge University Press, 1994), 322–52 (all appropriate for classroom use). Riddle's "Contraception and Abortion in the Middle Ages" works well with students.

81. Among the extensive studies of these forms of female piety, see especially Sharon Elkins, *Holy Women of Twelfth-Century England* (Chapel Hill: University of North Carolina Press, 1988); Brenda M. Bolton, "Mulieres Sanctae," in *Women in Medieval Society*, ed. Susan Mosher Stuard (Philadelphia: University of Pennsylvania Press 1976), 141–58; numerous essays in *Medieval Women*, ed. Derek Baker (Oxford: Basil Blackwell, 1978); Diane Watt, ed., *Medieval Women in their Communities* (Toronto: University of Toronto Press, 1997); Ziegler, *Sculpture of Compassion;* E. McDonnell, *The Beguines and Beghards in Medieval Culture* (New Brunswick: Rutgers University Press, 1954); and Ann K. Warren, *Anchorites and their Patrons in Medieval England* (Berkeley: University of California Press, 1985). For Christina of St. Trond specifically, see Thomas de Cantimpré, *The Life of Christina of St. Trond*, trans. Margot H. King (Saskatoon, Can.: Peregrina, 1985). For Margery Kempe, the most straightforward historical study is Clarissa W. Atkinson, *Mystic and Pilgrim: The Book and the World of Margery Kempe* (Ithaca: Cornell University Press, 1983); the most accessible edition of her biography is *The Book of Margery Kempe*, trans. B. A. Windeatt (Harmondsworth: Penguin, 1985). Some students enjoy a popular biography by Louise Collis, *Memoirs of a Medieval Woman: The Life and Times of Margery Kempe* (New York: Harper Colophon, 1964). For additional primary sources, see *Ancrene Wisse: Guide for Anchoresses*, trans. Hugh White (Harmondsworth: Penguin, 1993); *The Life of Christina of Markyate*, ed. and trans. C. H. Talbot (New York: Oxford University Press, 1959); and Julian of Norwich, *Revelations of Divine Love*.

82. For Joan of Arc, see especially Marina Warner, *Joan of Arc: The Image of Female*

Heroism (New York: Vintage, 1981), and Régine Pernoud, *Joan of Arc: By Herself and Her Witnesses* (New York: Stein and Day, 1982). Set into a narrative format, this latter text provides documents from the many trials of Joan of Arc.

83. For women warriors, see Megan McLaughlin, "The Woman Warrior: Gender, Warfare and Society in Medieval Europe," *Women's Studies* 17 (1990): 193–209 (students respond well to this article), and Helen Nicholson, "Women on the Third Crusade," *Journal of Medieval History* 23 (1997): 335–49. See also brief comments in Jonathan Riley-Smith, *The First Crusaders, 1095–1131* (New York: Cambridge University Press, 1997).

84. For a primary source on urban housewifery, see Tania Bayard, trans. and ed., *A Medieval Home Companion: Housekeeping in the Fourteenth Century* (New York: HarperCollins, 1991).

85. Karras and Boyd, "Ut Cum Muliere."

86. Richard Barber, ed., *The Pastons: A Family in the Wars of the Roses* (Harmondsworth: Penguin, 1984). For teaching purposes, one of the best introductions to these letters remains Henry Stanley Bennett, *The Pastons and Their England: Studies in an Age of Transition* (New York: Cambridge University Press, 1968). A book by Frances and Joseph Gies might also work well, *A Medieval Family: The Pastons of Fifteenth-Century England* (New York: HarperCollins, 1998). For one of many studies by feminist scholars, see Philippa Maddern, "Honour among the Pastons: Gender and Integrity in Fifteenth-Century English Provincial Society," *Journal of Medieval History* 14 (1988): 357–71.

87. Bennett, *A Medieval Life.*

BIBLIOGRAPHY OF ADDITIONAL SOURCES

Bibliographies, Bibliographic Essays, and Web Sites

Echols, Anne, and Marty Williams. *An Annotated Index of Medieval Women.* New York: Markus Wiener, 1992. An ambitious but flawed biographical listing.

"Feminae: Medieval Women and Gender Index." http://www.haverford.edu/library/reference/mschaus/mfi/mfi.html. An invaluable resource for up-to-date bibliography on women and gender. Users can search by subject as well as author and title, and many entries are annotated.

"The Labyrinth: Resources for Medieval Studies." http://www.labyrinth.georgetown.edu. This excellent site will lead to other useful resources on the Web.

Nelson, Janet. "Family, Gender, and Sexuality in the Middle Ages." In *Companion to Historiography*, edited by Michael Bentley, 153–76. London: Routledge, 1997.

Partner, Nancy, ed. *Studying Medieval Women: Sex, Gender, Feminism.* Cambridge: Medieval Academy of America, 1993. Accompanied in this edition by bibliographies, these essays first appeared in *Speculum* 68 (1993).

Rosenthal, Joel T., ed. *Medieval Women and the Sources of Medieval History.* Athens: University of Georgia Press, 1990.

Rubin, Miri. "A Decade of Studying Medieval Women, 1987–97." *History Workshop Journal* 46 (1998): 213–39.

Schaus, Margaret, and Susan Mosher Stuard. "Citizens of No Mean City: Medieval Women's History." *Journal of Women's History* 6 (1994): 170–98.

Sheehan, Michael M., and Jacqueline Murray. *Domestic Society in Medieval Europe: A Select Bibliography.* Toronto: Pontifical Institute of Mediaeval Studies, 1990.

Stuard, Susan Mosher, ed. *Women in Medieval History and Historiography.* Philadelphia: University of Pennsylvania Press, 1987.

General Surveys

Bitel, Lisa. *Women in Early Medieval Europe, 400–1000*. New York: Cambridge University Press, 2002.

Ennen, Edith. *The Medieval Woman*. Translated by Edmund Jephcott. Oxford: Basil Blackwell, 1989. Despite its title, this text focuses on German towns and is unsuitable for classroom use.

Gies, Frances, and Joseph Gies. *Women in the Middle Ages*. New York: Barnes and Noble, 1978. Because each chapter focuses on a representative woman, this book is accessible for students but not up to date.

Jewell, Helen. *Women in Medieval England*. Manchester: Manchester University Press, 1996. Not as useful as the equivalent book by Leyser.

Klapisch-Zuber, Christiane, ed. *A History of Women in the West. II: Silences of the Middle Ages*. Cambridge: Harvard University Press, 1992. Interesting articles but not recommended as a textbook.

Labarge, Margaret Wade. *A Small Sound of the Trumpet: Women in Medieval Life*. Boston: Beacon Press, 1986. Dated but reliable and readable.

Leyser, Henrietta. *Medieval Women: A Social History of Women in England 450–1500*. New York: St. Martin's Press, 1995. Readable and reliable but focused on England alone.

Lucas, Angela M. *Women in the Middle Ages: Religion, Marriage and Letters*. New York: St. Martin's Press, 1983. Not recommended.

Mitchell, Linda E., ed. *Women in Medieval Western European Culture*. New York: Garland, 1999. The essays in this collection range widely in quality; some are useful, others not. If you use this book, use it with care.

Shahar, Shulamith. *The Fourth Estate: A History of Women in the Middle Ages*. New York: Methuen, 1983. Packed with information but too dense for many students and dated.

Uitz, Erika. *The Legend of Good Women: Medieval Women in Towns and Cities*. Mount Kisco: Moyer Bell, 1988. Not recommended.

Williams, Marty, and Anne Echols. *Women in the Middle Ages: Between Pit and Pedestal*. Princeton: Markus Wiener, 1994. Not recommended.

Collections of Sources

Amt, Emilie, ed. *Women's Lives in Medieval Europe: A Sourcebook*. New York: Routledge, 1993. The best general collection, suitable for classroom use.

Blamires, Alcuin, ed. *Woman Defamed and Defended: An Anthology of Medieval Texts*. Oxford: Clarendon Press, 1992.

Blumenfeld-Kosinski, Renate, and Kevin Brownlee, trans. and eds. *The Selected Writings of Christine de Pizan: New Translations, Criticism*. New York: W. W. Norton, 1997.

Bruckner, Matilda T. et al., eds. *Songs of the Women Troubadours*. New York: Garland, 1995.

Brunn, Emilie Zum, and Georgette Epiney-Burgard, eds. *Women Mystics in Medieval Europe*. New York: Paragon House, 1989.

Cazelles, Brigitte, ed. *The Lady as Saint: A Collection of French Hagiographic Romances of the Thirteenth Century*. Philadelphia: University of Pennsylvania Press, 1991.

Crawford, Anne, ed. *The Letters of the Queens of England, 1066–1547*. Stroud: Sutton, 1994.

Dronke, Peter, ed. *Women Writers of the Middle Ages: A Critical Study of Texts from Perpetua (†203) to Marguerite Porete (†1310)*. New York: Cambridge University Press, 1984.

Fiero, Gloria K. et al., eds. *Three Medieval Views of Women*. New Haven: Yale University Press, 1989.

Goldberg, P. J. P., ed. *Women in England, c. 1275–1525*. Manchester: Manchester University Press, 1995. An excellent general collection, but very restricted in terms of time and place.

Gregg, Joan Young, ed. *Devils, Women, and Jews: Reflections of the Other in Medieval Sermon Stories*. Albany: State University of New York Press, 1997. An edition of exempla (stock stories used in sermons).

Internet Medieval Sourcebook. http://www.fordham.edu/halsall/sbook.html. This invaluable resource provides many out-of-copyright sources for teaching medieval history. It directs readers to materials specifically on "sex and gender" as well as to the Internet Women's History Sourcebook.

Larrington, Carolyne, ed. *Women and Writing in Medieval Europe: A Sourcebook*. London: Routledge, 1995. Despite its title, this is an excellent general collection, suitable for classroom use.

McSheffrey, Shannon, ed. *Love and Marriage in Late Medieval London*. Kalamazoo: Medieval Institute Publications, 1995. A collection of testimonies given in marriage cases brought before church courts.

Millett, Bella, and Jocelyn Wogan-Browne, eds. *Medieval English Prose for Women: The "Katherine Group" and Ancrene Wisse*. New York: Oxford University Press, 1990.

Petroff, Elizabeth A., ed. *Medieval Women's Visionary Literature*. New York: Oxford University Press, 1986.

Terry, Patricia, ed. *The Honeysuckle and the Hazel Tree: Medieval Stories of Men and Women*. Berkeley: University of California Press, 1995.

Ward, Jennifer, ed. *Women of the English Nobility and Gentry 1066–1500*. Manchester: Manchester University Press, 1995.

Wilson, Katharina M., ed. *Medieval Women Writers*. Athens: University of Georgia Press, 1984.

In addition to these collections, two publishers are sponsoring series of texts for the classroom. Peregrina Publishing produces inexpensive editions of saint's lives that are accompanied by useful introductions and notes. Boydell and Brewer, under the "Library of Medieval Women" series edited by Jane Chance, offers texts accompanied by interpretative essays as well as introductions and notes.

5

Women and Gender
in Colonial Latin America

ANN TWINAM

Current understanding of the history of the women and men of colonial Latin America resembles the unfinished warp and weft of a complicated tapestry. Some threads are clearly delineated, and some patterns emerge; many
strands and much of the design remain to be worked out. Even those sections
that appear finished, when examined in detail, need further labor. Consideration of this incomplete product brings certain advantages, for such an unfinished nature necessarily bares internal structure. Any evaluation of what
has been done, what has not been done, and what needs redoing inevitably
reminds that the process of historical inquiry can be as illuminating as any
ultimate product.

Research concerning women and gender in colonial Latin America has
followed the normal paths of historical inquiry. Pioneers laid the first threads,
using readily available sources such as legal codes, chronicles, and travel accounts; they also asked the obvious first questions, concentrating on prominent
personages and notable events. Their conclusions created the first designs, even
if sometimes oversimplified and stereotypical.[1] These patterns have now been
overwoven by successive waves of practitioners using indigenous-language and
colonial sources from imperial, national, and regional archives and alternative—
ethnographic, demographic, and comparative—methodologies. Such research
has altered and embellished the design and illuminated bare spots. The result
is an ongoing creative process: confirmation of conclusions, challenges to others, and continuous exploration of new pathways.

Research into the history of women and gender remains a comparatively new field for Latin Americanists. It was but a generation ago, in 1978, when Asunción Lavrin published one of the pathbreaking collections that established the field that she concluded that the "historical literature on Latin women is rather limited." Just a few years later Joan Scott delivered a call for the use of gender as a tool with as powerful a cutting edge as that of race or class.[2]

For Latin Americanists, research into the history of women has made substantial progress; understanding the history of men is hardly underway. The usual proportionality of the field also pertains given there is not only more published, but also more published in English, on Spanish than on Portuguese America. Yet withal, Lavrin and Scott raised the core challenge: Research into women and gender must not be relegated to historical sideways but must be embedded to inform the most traditional aspects of historical inquiry.

For colonial Latin Americanists, three such "traditional" venues emerged, all consequences of the momentous encounter between the European world and the American continent since 1492. One traced the precontact worlds of indigenous women and men as the prologue to understanding how gender relations altered with conquest and colonization. Another explored corresponding issues from the European perspective, particularly themes emerging from early, postconquest decades. A final design emerged as researchers gendered the worlds of the complex colonial society of castes and classes that developed from the late sixteenth through the early nineteenth centuries. The following provides but an overview of some of the richness and the bareness of a tapestry still being woven.

Pre- and Postcontact Themes

Any evaluation of the impact of conquest on indigenous women and men must credit the interpretive transformation wrought by the scholarship of the last decades. A cohort of researchers has used previously unexplored pre- and postcontact sources (codices, mythologies, chronicles, genealogies, histories, and archival documents) in a variety of indigenous languages, including Nahua-Aztec, Mayan, and Quechua-Inca. Inquisition documents, legal cases, and testamentary dispositions have led historians, ethnohistorians, and anthropologists to reconsider how the worlds of indigenous women and men might, and might not, have changed after the European conquest.

Such an undertaking has spanned a precontact world peopled with more than eighty million inhabitants in 1492.[3] Most research has focused on the sedentary native civilizations conquered by the Spanish, ranging from the

Pueblo in New Mexico, through the Maya in Yucatan, the dominant Aztecs in the Mexican center, the Mixtec and Zapotec in the south, and the Inca of South America. Perhaps inevitably, analysis of such disparate and complex civilizations occasioned a quest for comparability. Much research focused on gender parallelism or gender complementarity, concepts detailing the equivalent—although rarely the equal—cultural, ideological, and material positions of native women and of men in a particular society. Understanding precontact gender status provided a platform to compare the dislocations wrought by conquest as well as three ensuing centuries of colonial rule.

Gender parallelism/complementarity proved to be a methodological correction, a political agenda, a stimulus, and ultimately something of an intellectual straitjacket. Early in the 1980s, in their introduction to *Women and Colonization*, editors Mona Etienne and Eleanor Leacock criticized an "ethnocentric and male-center bias" that had led anthropologists automatically to assume that women were subordinated in every indigenous context. The case studies in their collection challenged this assumption through analysis of male and female roles in native societies throughout the globe—including the Aztecs (June Nash) and the Incas (Irene Silverblatt). The editors summarized the contributions of Nash and Silverblatt with the challenging assertion that "Aztec and Inca women were . . . more respected and had more rights than did women in the Spanish kingdom that conquered them."[4] The obvious conclusion was that the complementarity of relationships between native men and women had been eroded by the imposition of Spanish colonial hierarchy and cultural patriarchy.

While the sweeping generalizations of Etienne and Leacock might not have received universal endorsement, gender parallelism proved a common methodological focus, suggesting a range of topics to be compared in precontact civilizations from New Mexico to Peru. A first wave of researchers explored potential arenas where the status of men and women was complementary, including descent and marriage patterns, access to land, inheritance, legal standing, and religious practices. Some authors pointed out contradictory trends, particularly the hierarchical and patriarchal implications inherent in the typical reservation of the political and military realms to men. Such topics provided the logical base to analyze how European conquest and colonialism altered gender balances, and particularly where women's status deteriorated. A second wave of researchers then revisited gender parallelism, emphasizing less the destruction and more the endurance of precontact customs and the flexibility of local responses, including "counterhegemonic" activities ranging from lawsuits, to economic activities, witchcraft, and outright rebellion. Finally, some have challenged the utility of the gender parallelism construct. The only way to explore such a diversity of currents is to take the plunge—from the Pueblos in New Mexico to the Incas in Peru—and consider some variations on these themes.

A classic exploration of gender parallelism occurred in Irene Silverblatt's *Moon, Sun, and Witches*, which analyzed how "gender could be a metaphor for both complementarity and hierarchy in the Andes."[5] She explored two conquests, that of the Incas as they imposed unified rule over local kingdoms to forge an empire that stretched from Ecuador to Chile (1450–1532) and then their subsequent conquest by the Spanish conquistador Francisco Pizarro (1532–35). Relying primarily on postcontact sources, given that the Incas had no written language, Silverblatt portrayed the Andean cosmovision as governed by a reciprocity that included gender complementarity. Even before Inca conquests, for example, Andean people established parallel religious cults for women and for men. Equivalent descent practices meant that women took their status from their mothers and men from their fathers; access to community land and resources traditionally flowed from mother to daughter and from father to son.

As the Inca conquered beyond the Cuzco Valley, eventually extending their influence throughout the Andes, they did not challenge such gendered reciprocities. Rather, they overlay a conquest hierarchy on top of existing customs and practices, particularly in the realm of religion and politics. The *sapay Inca* (Inca ruler) and the *coya* (his female consort) legitimized their religious headship by claiming direct descent from the sun (male) and the moon (female) deities whose imperial cults were superimposed over existing local male and female religious practices. Not coincidentally, such religious descent also validated a gendered political hierarchy headed by the Inca and coya who established domination over conquered people. Yet as the Incas expanded beyond their Cuzco Valley base, the ensuing conquests and bureaucracy necessary to maintain control, collect taxes, and redistribute resources inevitably skewed gender complementarities, for those who fought and ruled were male.

Silverblatt's exploration of gender complementarity in Inca civilization was pathbreaking. The paucity of precontact sources, however, combined with the smaller number of researchers ultimately to leave Andean civilizations less intensely studied than Mesoamerican counterparts. Looking first at the Mexican center—the Aztecs, dominant at the time of Spanish arrival in 1519—and then the periphery (Maya, Mixtec, Zapotec, and Pueblo) suggests similarities and differences from Andean themes.

Rising from the Mexican Central Valley, the Aztec capital of Tenochtitlán (the current Mexico City) presided with allied kingdoms over a tribute empire that stretched from the Caribbean to the Pacific and was founded in war and based on human sacrifice. Aztec gender parallelism was embedded from birth, reinforcing the corresponding roles of men and women in the expansion and maintenance of the kingdom. At birth, baby boys received a shield and arrows; baby girls received weaving implements and a broom. The umbilical cords of boys were buried in battlefields, that of girls in houses. Aztec religion assigned the most favorable afterlife to warriors, either men who died in battle or were captured and sacrificed or women whose death in childbirth was considered death in battle. Aztec religious cults were gendered, with male and female deities and priests and priestesses. Aztec men and women held complementary offices in markets, neighborhoods, or as teachers. Women inherited equally with men and played "significant public roles." Although the higher political and military offices were reserved to men, "These separate but equivalent aspects of gender roles . . . outweighed hierarchy."[6]

Researching Aztec homes provided subtle insight into the parallel worlds of men and women. Pre- and postcontact codices reveal that "domesticated central places and dangerous peripheral zones were complementary opposites, their gender signs reversed, which together constituted a whole." In effect, an Aztec home was literally the central female focus, a gendered home front that complimented the male zone of a battlefield. Aztecs did not consider women's domestic activities such as cleaning, cooking, and weaving to be subordinate and marginal to the male world. Rather, they were "imbued with symbolic means" and governed by their own "rules and omens." Sweeping the floor was a "ritual act," purifying the home as the temple. Cooking nourished, and specially prepared foods supported the war effort. Textile production was economically critical to a household and as integrally linked to female identity and sexuality as warfare was for men. Although their worlds were distinct, "house and battlefield" were a "duality" that the Aztec mentality "ultimately joined into one."[7]

Analysis of weaving and cooking in precontact Mexico revealed how a conquest hierarchy might differentiate female indigenous worlds.[8] Just as in the Andean world of the Inca, some native women lived in Mexican kingdoms that were conquerors and others in places that had been conquered. Archeological excavations reflect this power disparity, and the resulting differences in female work, by the uneven distribution of spindle whorls, the ceramic disks that provide weight during weaving. These are sparser in the victorious Aztec central valley than on the vanquished peripheries, suggesting that urban women were not only more oriented to a market economy where they might purchase textiles rather than weave but also not as pressured as female counterparts in conquered zones to weave to meet tribute demands. Food preparation techniques also differed from the conquering center to the conquered periphery. More griddles—evidence of the intensive labor associated with the tortilla—appeared in the central valley, whereas the periphery preserved ceramics, which are typically associated with timesaving, one-pot meals. Such explorations into material culture nuance changes and continuities in indigenous women's work before and after conquests.

While essentially agreeing that Aztecs assigned gender complementarity to home and battlefield, a tale from Aztec mythohistory suggests that any ultimate balance could be more ambiguous. The telling legend related how a ruler of Tlateloco, a city-state facing defeat at the hands of the Aztec capital of Tenochtitlán, sent women into battle to fight "with their femininity." The myth recounts how the women exposed their genitalia, squeezed milk from their breasts, slapped their bellies, and attacked with the traditional domestic weapons of brooms and weaving batons. The ultimate effect of this myth proved an "inversion" that highlighted the good-bad aspects of women inasmuch as these female Amazons, lacking modesty and manifesting aggression, appeared as strong negative models. That characterization locates the Aztecs among the large majority of civilizations that separate war along a male-female axis, viewing "the opposition of war to peace, aggression to resistance, and victory to defeat, in terms of gender."[9] Because women seem to be perpetually on the losing side, such linkage to "peace," "resistance," and, most tellingly, "defeat" seems a significant imbalance to gender parallelism.

Studies of dynastic ties among the Aztec and nearby Chalco nobility reveal gender complementarities in the use of women as strategic conduits of political power. Long before the Spanish arrived the native elite arranged strategic sexual-marital alliances that mitigated the oppression of internal conquests through mutual heirship of succeeding generations. Sometimes the lord of highest rank united with a woman of lower rank, and their son, through his mother, became the next ruler in his mother's city. Or, rulers might give daughters in marriage to rulers of lower rank so their offspring would govern. Or, perhaps princes from Tenochtitlán would marry women of high rank from conquered city-states, and their sons would succeed. Analysis of the seventeenth-century Nahua historian Chimalpán's chronicles of alliances of the noblewomen of Chalco from 987 to the sixteenth century showed that "women were critical to the integrity of the altepetl (kingdom) and they were key agents in the preservation of the rulerships."[10] No doubt polygyny facilitated such strategies, given that rulers might cement a variety of political relationships with multiple wives. Yet a question naturally arises: To what extent should these dynastic alliances be considered evidence of gender complementarity? Unfortunately, genealogies provide mostly names and rank. The women who appear emerge as hardly more than mates and wombs, lacking agency or personality.

Analyses of precontact sexual-marital alliance customs, however, provide fundamental insight into indigenous strategies during the Spanish conquest.

By Cortés's arrival in 1519, although the Aztecs had conquered much of Mexico, typical Mesoamerican marriage alliance patterns persisted. Indigenous rulers implicitly recognized that the conqueror of one day might become the conquered the next. The role of female relatives was to mate and/or marry, thus muting domination through mutual heirship. When the Spanish appeared as conquerors, native rulers naturally continued their own conquest strategies. Some gave conquistadors female relatives of high rank to be their first "wife" or even their second or third. They also maintained traditional patterns of offering lesser-ranked women as bearers, food producers, and sexual objects. Such strategies would not have been that alien to Europeans, who evolved their own patterns of sexual/marital liaisons in the early conquest years.

To what extent did the conquest and colonization of the Americas alter precontact ways? Clearly, Europeans had no interest in indigenous gender complementarities. They arrived with very different aims: to reorient indigenous economies from reciprocal or internal exchange to the creation of surplus for the conquerors; to abolish native religion, replacing it with Catholicism; and eventually to impose peninsular (Spanish, Portuguese) culture. The consequences of this transformation affected native women and men in different ways, altering precontact gendered balances already stressed by the greatest demographic disaster known in human history. Successive waves of epidemics—smallpox, measles, influenza, and typhus—returned again and again to strike native populations deprived of immunities due to thousands of years of isolation from the European-Asian-African landmass. Cumulative mortality rates ranged from 60 to 100 percent. For every hundred natives in the Americas in 1492 there were ten or twenty by 1650.[11]

Some effects of the meeting of the Old World with the New are unambiguous. In the economic sphere, the overall thrust was the erosion of preconquest communal property holdings and descent structures that awarded women independent access to resources through their mothers. Spanish tribute burdens fell particularly heavily on women because they might be illegally taxed as individuals rather than members of family units and, if they married outside their kin grouping, taxed doubly.[12] One way to escape Spanish levies was to flee. This proved a more likely remedy for men than for women given that the latter were left to tend the old and the children.

In religion, the conquistadors and their successors strove mightily to extinguish all native beliefs, whether special to men or to women, and replace them with a Catholicism that denied native men priestly roles and designated women as sinful and inferior. An early conquest society (1492–1570s), composed of a small number of white Europeans and an overwhelming indigenous population, was altered radically through the next centuries as successive epidemics decimated the native population and further Spanish arrivals combined with the importation of millions of African slaves to create a complex society of castes and classes.[13]

Yet within these dominant patterns emerges a contrasting thread: Nowhere were native populations passive receptors of change. Instead, indigenous groups developed a variety of responses, including accommodation, resistance, and rebellion. It is within this context of conquest and colonization that researchers have worked to detail both change and continuities in pre- and postcontact indigenous gender relations.

The lack of gendered analysis of the process and consequences of native depopulation has left an immense hole in the interpretative tapestry. This is understandable given that much data on demographic decline derives from computer-based simulations of mortality rates that cannot inform how epidemics variably affected male and female populations. Some hints emerge, however. One reason that famines customarily followed epidemics was that sick or dying women were unavailable for food preparation. The course of modern disease suggests that pregnant women might have proven more susceptible to epidemics, native women who nursed their sick families further increased their vulnerability, and female survivors of epidemics may have precariously existed without supporting male kin.

Insight into differentials of native depopulation remains murky, but scholars have explored fundamental postcontact shifts in gender balances in the economic sphere. Some research suggests that the precontact pattern, where Mesoamerican communal ownership of lands passed from male to male and from female to female, shifted after the conquest because Spanish legal codes denigrated the status of native women from legal adult to legal minor.[14] Aztec testaments show that sixteenth-century indigenous women were active litigators, participating in the legal process as vigorous defenders of their property rights. Yet as Spanish customs began to prevail by the seventeenth century, the independent legal status of some women was no longer as manifest. Husbands dealt with legal issues that affected women; if a woman made an appearance, it was with her spouse's permission. The situation continued to deteriorate even further for some women in nineteenth-century Mexico, given the "erosion of a protective [colonial] judiciary."[15]

Although some native women lost traditional access to communal properties, evidence exists of continuity as well as adaptation. Andean women in sixteenth-century Ecuador wrote testaments that both maintained precontact practices, leaving valuable textiles and property to daughters, and blended "many European options into the futures of their survivors."[16] Maya women also continued many daily routines, maintaining their material possessions and status essentially unchanged from the sixteenth through the eighteenth centuries. Exploration of Maya hieroglyphic texts, particularly of wills, reveals continuities in the gendered division of material possessions and work. Women were more likely to leave land associated with *solar* (household) activities such as bee-keeping, orchards, or weavings to female descendants; men customarily bequeathed *kax* (forests), *milpa* (cultivated fields), or tools. Scholars conclude that the "division of labor by gender provided women with a role no less important or dignified than that of their male kin."[17]

Even where continuity exists, a telling example from the late colonial era epitomizes the difficulties in maintaining female property not only in the Maya world but also throughout the Spanish Empire. A late colonial (1804) petition in the Maya language listed eight men and ten women of one family as owners of a particular piece of land.[18] Provocatively, the translation of the same document in Spanish totally eliminated the names of the women, listing only the men. It was through such innumerable transactions that native women became lost as historical agents as Spanish legal and cultural assumptions assuming masculine priority became dominant.

Postcontact transformation of gender roles was not solely in the economic sphere but struck at the most intimate issues: sin, sex, housework, and lifecourse. Spanish friars, through confessionals or sermons, peered into the bedroom, attempting to redefine native parameters of sex and sin according to European Catholic rules.[19] Churchmen demanded that natives incorporate Catholic definitions of sexual sinning, insisted on European rather than native kinship rules as to who might marry whom, and prohibited precontact practices of arranged marriages and multiple wives. The latter, which proved particularly controversial, led to rebellion in the case of the Tarahuma. Yet from Mexico through Chile, historians have noted that even after conversion and baptism some natives continued to live in polygyny.[20]

European transforming efforts also extended to housework as friars unsuccessfully tried to teach Aztec women proper female Spanish ways, no doubt including the curricula that sweeping, cooking, and weaving were secular rather than treasured religious rituals. In spite of the friars, women continued to sweep long into the colonial period—and not only to eliminate dirt. Eighteenth-century Nahua-language testaments still contained clauses in which indigenous women demanded that their heirs continue ritual sweeping, only now before the home altars of Catholic saints rather than native deities.[21]

Understanding how the conquest altered material culture, including women's and men's work, remains a challenge. Some aspects of contact positively changed the lives of Maya women.[22] They now had access to new food sources such as pigs and chickens, and their lives were improved by easier access to water through the introduction of Spanish wells. Just as in any situation of cultural encounter, Maya women both accepted and repudiated Spanish offerings. They abandoned precontact fashions such as tattooing and tooth filing, rejected Spanish cosmetics, and clung to their native dress.

The typical lifecourse progression, as manifested in the generational authority of older native men and women, was also distorted after the European arrival. The New Mexican Pueblo, located on the northern frontier of the Spanish colonial empire, found that friars attempted to undermine precontact gender balances not only by discrediting the legitimacy of elder generations but also by favoring males.[23]

Lifecourses established a system of fundamental reciprocity in the Pueblo world because female and male seniors, or elders, held the required knowledge of adult skills and doled it out to juniors in exchange for presents and goods. Such gender differentiation between sexes began at birth. Older women taught girls to make religious fetishes and pottery and to weave baskets; older men trained boys to conjure, hunt, and wage warfare. The Spanish arrival unbalanced such mutual indebtedness between seniors and juniors. Friars dispensed new knowledge and new gifts (such as pigs and chickens) to younger males, consciously attempting to wean them from the influence of male elders. It was through such actions in the Pueblo world and elsewhere that the Spanish altered precontact generational and gendered reciprocities.

Precontact sexual and marital alliance patterns were another arena inevitably altered by the European arrival. A few elite indigenous women married conquistadors, were incorporated into the early conquest society, and sometimes retained or even improved access to land and material resources.[24] They and their mestizo children became intermediaries between disparate worlds. With the exception of the *caciques* or *kurakas* (leaders) who cooperated with Europeans, the vast majority of native men lost out because the conquerors claimed first access to native women. The provocative comment that the Spanish arrival proved to be an "emasculating experience" for indigenous males awaits detailed exploration.[25]

More recently, researchers have explored how indigenous resistance to conquest produced modifications and alterations in gender roles. Ironically, it was precisely because they had been rendered anonymous—and were less feared and less watched than men—that indigenous women often functioned as preservers of precontact religious traditions. If, in the plaza, native men might slaughter llamas to provide meat for a Catholic feast day, it was Andean women who surreptitiously collected the llama blood and carried it as before to nourish *huacas* (religious spirits) in their hidden places.[26] Yet there was always variation. In the Maya world it was the men who maintained precontact traditions precisely because they considered doing so too dangerous for women.

When women resisted they risked the ire of Catholic clerics who branded them with the European construct of witch and saw the devil at work when they guarded huacas in the Andes or continued ritual sweeping in Mexico. At times some women became believers themselves, either continuing native traditions or adopting European variants of sexual witchcraft as desperate situations encouraged them to ensorcell recalcitrant lovers or quell the passion or brutality of husbands.[27] Sometimes female resistance was not so subtle, as in the 1781 rebellion of Tupac Amaru, where Inca traditions endured. Micaela Bastidas, the wife of the leader, was hailed as the female Inca, La Coya, hearkening back to precontact gender parallelism. In the Tupac Amaru revolt, Andean women "played crucially important roles" as "adherents, military advisors, commanders, logicians and even combatants," evidencing a "higher degree of personal freedom and autonomy than that enjoyed by their Spanish and creole counterparts."[28] Nor was such female activism rare given that a traditional space for native women in Mexico was on the front line, where they taunted authorities during local disturbances.

Lately, historians have explored even more subtle forms of resistance. Yucatec Maya men proved geniuses at using "sexual humor" to attack and shame colonial authorities.[29] They exploited the insecurities of church officials, "using the legal system to their advantage" when they complained to the Inquisition that local priests said mass with "stiff penises" and that all the priests thought of was "intercourse with their mistresses." In a similar vein, highland Maya women became the "vanguard of cultural resistance" during a 1795 typhus epidemic, when they took the initiative and forcibly seized authorities who attempted to curtail traditional postdeath vigils and church burials.[30] Through such tactics, indigenous men and women turned the tables, nullifying enforcement of colonial legislation and playing "their own game of adaptation and accommodation."[31]

More recent research has stressed not only resistance but also resilience. Consistently recurring patterns of gender parallelism emerge in postconquest Mixtec society in southern Mexico. Even after the Spanish arrival, Mixtec female cacicas (chiefs) held equal rank and titles with men and enjoyed wealth, property, and status. In contrast to studies of Aztec women suggesting that the Spanish legal system deprived them of juridical status rending them legal minors, Mixtec and Zapotec women remained active, independently suing husbands, local leaders, and even Spaniards from the early to the late colonial period. Farther north, women appeared as witnesses and litigants in native-language court cases in late colonial Tepotzlán, testifying in boundary disputes, suing for their rights, complaining against friars, and defending themselves against spousal abuse. Even in the Mexican hinterland, native women, especially widows, mothers, or older women from San Esteban de Nueva Tlaxcala, were not loathe to defy the system, whether in suits against abusive husbands, to prevent offspring from unequal marriages, or to prevent intrusions from Spaniards. The women proved to be "central actors in the drama of cultural contact and struggle for community integrity that played itself out not only in the more heavily indigenous heartland but on the distant frontier as well."[32]

Although gender parallelism has proven useful as a construct to make pre- and postcontact comparisons across the Americas, the price has been to flatten the uniqueness of discrete cultures and experiences as well as raise unanswered questions. Ranges of historical variables—the differences between native civilizations, classes, races, regions, and timeframes—necessarily produce different outcomes. Without doubt, "The experience of an Inca princess married to a Spanish conquistador was totally unlike that of a Guaraní woman living in a Jesuit mission or a Chichimec woman enslaved and sold to the highest bidder."[33]

Contradictions also abound. What of the fascinating disparity in interpretations of lawsuits? Are these evidences of strength as indigenous women steadfastly defended property rights or litigated against oppressive husbands or lovers? Or, are they manifestations of weakness as women lost access to material resources and found their status so demeaned within their homes that they were forced to seek outside help? Were women in some native civilizations—perhaps the Maya, Mixtec, or Zapotec—more likely to maintain the precontact status quo than others—possibly the Aztec or Inca—or more able to use Spanish institutions for their benefit? To what extent did women actively shape the colonial environment or become victims of patriarchy and colonialism? What of native men?

Researchers have begun to challenge aspects of the gender parallel/balance paradigm, concluding it is too "simplistic" because it fails to "convey the complex reality" where women were "flexible, adaptive, and dynamic elements in a dynamic system."[34] Others question reliance on a Native American "rhetoric about gender" that "did not always match the reality." Still other patterns, only beginning to emerge, are pre- to postcontact transformations in the nonheterosexual world, either of coerced or of consensual same-sex relationships.[35] There is yet another knotty issue: As the colonial centuries pass, when do "indigenous men" or "native women" metamorphose into alternative identities and become mestizos, or castas, or creoles, or peasants, or citizens? Who decides who fits where—and when? Researchers have located some fascinating threads, but placement of patterns within the larger historical tapestry remains a work in progress, and few threads are tightly in place.

Exploration of another indigenous society provides a final, thought-provoking comparison. How should one evaluate gender parallelism in a society where women held high-status political positions? Some even served in the military. Others inherited equally with men, passed property independently to daughters, were active petitioners for their rights, and engaged in trade. Some of the most revered religious icons of this society were female. In short, if these are the criteria, a case could be made that gender complementarity was as viable for sixteenth- through eighteenth-century Spain or Portugal as it might have been in the Americas. What is clear is that any understanding of the clash between Europe and indigenous America must consider the effect from both perspectives.

The Conquest Society

One of the intriguing ironies of research on colonial Latin America is that there are as many gaps in historical understanding of the conquerors as of the conquered. Assumptions concerning peninsular patriarchy, gender roles, or female agency customarily derive from prescriptive sources such as laws, or literary products such as novels and plays, rather than from analysis of the lifecourses of men and women.[36] Historians know surprisingly little about how women and men negotiated gender roles in daily discourse on the peninsula; nor are they certain of the impact of the discovery and colonization of America on both those who left and those who remained behind. No doubt the overarching stereotype for Iberian women would be that of the cloister because women were either enclosed at home under the patriarchal domination of fathers or husbands, or they were sheltered in convents under the control of church fathers. Yet even a superficial glance at Spanish and Portuguese history, laws, and customs reveals alternative patterns modifying even more during the conquest and colonization of the Americas.

It was, after all, a Spanish queen, Isabella, who in 1492 not only accompanied her armies to defeat the Moors at Granada but also authorized the original patent of exploration to Columbus. Spanish noblewomen were customarily influential at court as marriage partners and political advisers as well. Even a cursory examination of the archives reveals that their humbler sisters were not divorced from politics—at least they were never shy in requesting favors and pensions from the monarchy. A rare few Spanish women even crossdressed as men and served with the military in the Americas; the famous nun Catalina de Erauso, for example, recounted her adventures in a memoir.[37]

No doubt there were significant restrictions for peninsular women. Spanish and Portuguese law restricted the freedom of married women to make contracts, and single women remained under the control of their fathers into their mid-twenties. Yet embedded within prescriptive norms were wide latitudes for negotiation. The Catholic church sided with women and insisted on freedom of marital choice. Peninsular laws permitted women substantial access to material resources, for with the infrequent exception of *mayorazgo* or *morgado* (entail), inheritance divided property equally between brothers and sisters. Women regained their dowries after their husbands died and enjoyed half of the community property accumulated during marriage.[38]

Laws or customs that discouraged women's ability to manage wealth, make contracts, or engage in business had loopholes; for the poor, the dictates of survival always trumped the law. Even in religion, where the ideology and priesthood of the Catholic church restricted official power to men, in the popular religion of the masses a woman triumphed, given the ceremonial rituals and extreme reverence attached to the cult of the Virgin Mary. Ironically, some of the more interesting future insights on colonial gender roles may derive from a better understanding of Spanish and Portuguese contributions to the American mix.

One issue is clear: In Spanish America the early decades of conquest and colonization (1490s–1570s) marked a unique era characterized by historians as a society of conquest distinguished by particular institutions and sexual-social relationships. As conquistadors engaged in extraordinarily dangerous expeditions they conquered through urban foundation, establishing *cabildos* (city councils) literally on top of such indigenous cities as Tenochtitlán–Mexico City or founding new towns like Veracruz in Mexico or Lima in Peru. Conquistadors and later settlers governed locally and distributed unoccupied property within their jurisdictions through cabildos, although these were rapidly overlaid by a complex—and equally male—bureaucratic hierarchy controlled by the crown.

Another fixture of early postconquest society was the *encomienda*, an institution legitimized by both Spanish and indigenous traditions that mandated that the conquered had to support the conqueror. Throughout the Americas the crown ratified awards to conquistadors of grants of tribute from natives from designated locations. Some male and female members of the indigenous nobility also received encomiendas. The demographic disaster eventually eroded the viability of the encomienda, however, because millions of dying or dead natives could not meet designated tribute quotas. Thus alternative mechanisms such as *repartimiento* (labor levies) or debt peonage emerged to exploit native production.

Distinctive patterns of sixteenth-century "gender dynamics" characterized this conquest society and were, much as described for a later phase of European expansion, "fundamental to the securing and maintenance of the imperial enterprise."[39] Both Spaniards and natives negotiated sexual-kinship alliances either to gain or maintain control over populations and territory. The forcible expropriation and rape of women figured as a leitmotif of conquest and warfare. Almost immediately, Spanish women also arrived in the Americas as potential brides and transmitters of peninsular culture. Conquest, civil war, colonization, and epidemics created a skewed demographic where a comparatively small cohort of conquistadors, elite native women, first-generation mestizos, and Spanish women assumed special roles and achieved significant postcontact mobility. Not only high native but also high conquistador mortality led to multiple sexual liaisons and marriages during the era. Some of these threads are clear, but the pattern mostly unfolds through anecdotal histories of prominent personages, and much research is undone.

The dearth of knowledge concerning Spanish gender roles, particularly masculine norms, leaves little known concerning the conquistadors beyond capsule biographies of their ages, social backgrounds, and literacy.[40] The original stereotype, that conquistadors were from the minor nobility—*segundones* (second sons deprived of inheritance and forced to seek their fortunes in the New World)—has been supplanted by appreciation of their varied social origins and regional backgrounds. Peruvian conquerors were "modest hidalgos, with one of two fairly near the courtly nobility, followed by notaries, artisans, seamen and lower plebeians."[41] Also somewhat discounted is conquistador professional military background, given that the conquerors might more accurately be styled as Indian fighters.

Just as indigenous rulers followed traditional practices by presenting women to cement alliances with victors, so arriving Europeans received women as natural and legitimate spoils of conquest. Throughout the Americas, native women fed, bedded with, and guided Spanish and Portuguese men. In Brazil, native women prepared and cooked manioc. In Mesoamerica, the home of the tortilla, where hours of corn grinding necessarily accompanied food preparation, indigenous women proved to be fundamental provisioners. Every army from the Spanish conquest through the Mexican revolution necessarily traveled with a cohort of women lugging *metates* (grinding stones) to prepare tortillas. Without such women, the conquistadors soon learned, expeditions starved.[42]

Indigenous women engaged in consensual and nonconsensual sexual relations with conquistadors. In coastal Brazil, early traders, *bandierantes* (trailblazers), and later settlers formed marital/sexual alliances with Tupi-Guarani women, cementing control through their *mameluco* (mixed-blood) children. The process of racial mixing occurred in equal strength throughout Spanish America. Although traditions "of legal polygyny may at first have made concubinage with . . . conquerors appear less degrading to indigenous women than it was later to prove," it would not take long for the Roman Catholic church to establish that any woman after the first wife fell to the level of mistress.[43]

Without one native woman the Cortés expedition would almost certainly have been defeated and the conquest of Mexico left to later arrivals.[44] Malinche, baptized as Doña Marina, figured among a cohort of native women given as gifts to Cortés on the coast. She originally passed as gift-cum-slave from the Nahua-speaking center of Mexico to the Maya-speaking coast, where, once acquired by Cortés, she became a bilingual pivot of the early Spanish translation team. In conjunction with Jerónimo de Aguilar, a Spaniard who had been shipwrecked on an early expedition and learned Mayan, she helped Cortés solve two of the immediate problems of any alien encounter: communication and intelligence. Cortés spoke Spanish to Aguilar, who translated in Mayan dialect to Doña Marina, who translated in Nahua to Montezuma, the Aztec ruler. As time passed Doña Marina learned Spanish and translated directly to Cortés. Without her translations, knowledge of customs, and warning against surprise attack, the Cortés expedition might well have met defeat. Doña Marina has been the object of contradictory interpretations characterized both as the "Mexican Eve" and, more recently and sympathetically, as a "gifted women in impossible circumstances carving out survival one day at a time."[45]

Although her translation skills made Doña Marina unique, in other respects her fate—sexual imposition and motherhood to a first generation of mestizos—resembled that of a select cohort of native women in close and sustained contact with the conquistadors. Once Cortés recognized Doña Marina's language skills, he appropriated her for his own, and she eventually bore an illegitimate son, Don Martin, who was recognized in Cortés's will. Like many of the first generation of mestizos acknowledged by their fathers, Don Martin moved in elite Spanish society. An equally usual part of the pattern was Cortés's subsequent shedding of Doña Marina as he married her off to conquistador Juan de Jaramillo, who was reportedly drunk at the wedding. Doña Marina eventually gave birth to a daughter and died soon after.

While Doña Marina received encomiendas because of her invaluable contributions to the Cortés expedition, another cohort of native women— close kin of indigenous male rulers—also held rights to tribute and figured as desirable brides for conquistadors. Such was the later history of Techich-potzin, a daughter of Montezuma.[46] Baptized as Doña Isabel, she received an encomienda and married conquistador Alonso de Grado in 1525. When he died the next year, Doña Isabel then went to live with widower Cortés and from their liaison emerged a daughter, Doña Leonor, another of Cortés's illegitimate mestizo offspring recognized in his will. Even before she gave birth to this mestiza daughter, Doña Isabel was married to another conquistador. When he died a few years later, she married yet again.

A similar process occurred in Peru. Conquistador Francisco Pizarro appropriated the native princess Doña Inés Yupanqui Huaylas, who gave birth to two of his mestizo children.[47] He then married her off after he found another mistress. The replacement, Doña Angelina Yupanqui, another member of Inca nobility, met a similar fate. She and Pizarro produced two mestizo children, and she then married Spaniard Juan de Betanzos. The pattern repeated over and over. Spaniards married every daughter of the Inca ruler Huayna Capac.[48]

The children of Doña Marina, Doña Isabel, Doña Inés, and Doña Angelina shared one of the two possibilities open to the first generations of mestizos. If they were legitimate or illegitimates recognized by their conquistador fathers they were usually accepted in Spanish society; if not, they merged into the native population. In Peru, fathers placed mestiza daughters in Santa Clara Convent as a "holding ground" so they might assimilate the paternal Spanish rather than the maternal, Inca, cultural tradition.[49] The subsequent marriage of these convent-trained mestizas supported colonial hegemony by permitting both Spanish fathers and bridegrooms to "reproduce . . . their lineages" and establish social hierarchy in Peru. In Mexico, native men rejected Aztec women who had been so trained, reflecting a larger "cultural conflict over the importance of controlling the education of women so as to preserve the indigenous identity of the community."[50]

More than sometimes credited, conquistadors proved to be loving fathers who recognized their mestizo offspring in testaments and petitioned for their legitimation from the crown. The Spanish code of the *Siete Partidas* (1256–65) mandated that responsible fatherhood was a mark of manhood. For many men their mestizo offspring would be the only children they might father. Unknown, of course, is the fate of a far larger and anonymous cohort of illegitimate mixed-blood offspring that resulted from rape or from temporary or abandoned liaisons with indigenous women. In conquest society these tended to be absorbed into the native population, although in the later colony "mestizo" would become a significant demographic cohort in its own right, eventually composing majorities of some colonial populations.

A contrasting thread in the postconquest tapestry emerged with the early arrival of peninsular women to the Americas. Elite indigenous women became less valued as consorts when victors had the option of a liaison or marriage with a culturally familiar female. Analysis of passenger lists of Spanish ships sailing to the Indies reveals that—contrary to any sheltered stereotype—women either participated in conquests or arrived during or soon after them.[51] Isabel Rodrígues (La Conquistadora) marched with Pizarro's army in Peru, and Inés Suarez fought the Araucanian Indians as well as lived with Pedro de Valdivia in Chile.

More commonly, arriving female cohorts included married women reuniting with conquistador husbands. Those women brought along unmarried relatives who were also eager to acquire rich spouses. Almost half the women who landed in the Americas sought husbands, although some were not enamored of their choices. At least one prospective bride, surveying members of the Alvarado expedition in Guatemala, was so shocked by their condition she supposedly exclaimed, "Are we going to marry those broken down old creatures? You can marry who you like, but I certainly don't intend to marry any of them. They . . . are in such a state that they look as if they had escaped from hell: some are lame and some have arms missing, and some ears, and some an eye, and some half their faces, and the best-looking of them has got one or two or three scars across his face."[52]

A Spanish bride might not have to endure an ugly conquistador husband for long. High male mortality resulting from further conquests, civil war, or premature death from physical stress and disease led to multiple husbands during a woman's lifecourse. Such transitions characterized the marital history of many female arrivals, including Leonor de Bobadilla, the illegitimate daughter of a Spanish noble who sailed with the Hernando de Soto fleet. She quickly married, but her first husband died on an expedition to Florida. She then traveled to Peru, where she married again but became a widow when her husband died in the Peruvian civil wars. By the time Leonor was thirty she had been married and widowed three times; survived the death of brothers and a son; and been to Cuba, Panama, and Peru.

Spanish women provided the glue that bound the first generations of conquistadors and encomenderos together, a process furthered by the crown's insistence that encomiendas only be passed to legitimate heirs. Of almost five hundred encomenderos in Peru in 1563, only thirty-two were unmarried.[53] In early conquest society the sisters, daughters, and female kin of conquistadors intermarried to consolidate the encomendero class. In Mexico, Leonel de Cervantes was but one who passed his encomienda to his son and cemented his position with colleagues by marrying his five daughters to fellow encomenderos.[54] Several of his daughters married multiple times given the high husband mortality—a pattern replicated in Peru, where civil wars over conquest spoils contributed to even greater male mortality. While originally the military obligations attached to encomiendas led historians to forward that Spanish officials forced widowed women to remarry to maintain their dead husband's encomiendas, more recent research suggests that women in Mexico had greater agency. There, only one of every three widows holding encomiendas remarried, and those most likely for personal reasons. The remaining two-thirds either held encomienda titles in their own right or passed them to offspring. One of the most upwardly mobile cohorts in the Americas was early Spanish female arrivals who outlived husbands, fathers, or other male relatives and thus inherited the spoils of their conquests.

Spanish women who were early arrivals not only benefited but also contributed significantly to the formation of colonial society. They proved to be fundamental transmitters of peninsular culture, teaching Spanish to natives and introducing familiar foods, furniture, and customs. Collections of early letters written by Spanish men in the Americas to prospective or actual wives reveal the essential role of women as cultural buttresses in the alien American world.[55] They arrived with shared knowledge of family, kin, friends, and community. They established the comforting familiarities of Spanish home life. The influence of Portuguese women was important, but their numbers were substantially fewer and their influence correspondingly muted. Both native women in the hinterland and a huge influx of African women brought to be urban and rural slaves contributed more substantially to the Brazilian mix. As several generations passed, arriving women from Spain or Portugal no longer had enhanced value, going from "scarcity to parity . . . to oversupply."[56] The unique patterns of conquest society gave way to greater complexities and additional patterns in the historical tapestry.

Colonial Patterns

A treasure trove of censuses, notary records, and civil and ecclesiastical judicial cases located in archives in Spain and throughout Latin America have revealed the customary as well as atypical roles of colonial women and men as they bought, sold, accumulated, and passed on property; entered the religious world; negotiated private and public worlds; and defended their honor in the process of loving, courting, having sex, marrying, cheating, beating on each other, and having same-sex sex. As the colonial centuries drew to a close, the Bourbon State (1763–1808) intervened with social reforms affecting sexual politics and gender relations. Overall, historians have challenged a number of prevailing stereotypes for women and underlined yet again that insight into the masculine world remains in its infancy. Research has distinguished between the normative and the lived experience to understand not only laws and stereotypes but also the day-to-day processes through which men and women constructed gender roles and negotiated across the gender divide.

One of the fascinating contradictions in gendering economic history is that analysis of the occupational histories of men remains terra incognita even though Latin American historians have customarily studied colonial productivity as a masculine activity. Colonial elite males were landowners, agriculturists, ranchers, miners, merchants, bureaucrats, and churchmen. Plebeian men labored as peones, muledrivers, blacksmiths, gauchos, carpenters, farmers, storeowners, and day laborers. Absent is much understanding about how colonial males viewed or experienced their occupational choices; the extent they exercised agency; or the degree to which convention, family pressure, dire necessity, or lifecourse changes forced them into varying occupational paths.

Some broad outlines appear. Family histories reveal the difficulty elite men experienced maintaining rank over generations given the tradeoff between high status and financially remunerative occupations. Landowning may have been more prestigious, but commerce might be more profitable. A masterful study of the priesthood in Mexico has complicated portraits of male religious, outlining the diversity of ecclesiastical roles that vary from priests with mistresses and families, to part-time, poverty-stricken clerics, to those living poorly or lavishly from *capellanías* (chantries), or to the fabulously wealthy hierarchy.[57] The degree that men entered the priesthood because of vocation or the extent that families channeled them to the church, as to any other occupation, remains unexplored. The life experiences of plebeian males remain even more uncharted.

An understanding of how gender differentiated the worlds of African men and their descendants forced into slavery in Spanish and Portuguese America has also just begun. The traditional caveat remains that the working conditions and lifecourses of slaves in the Americas varied dramatically, depending whether they lived in the Caribbean, Brazil, or throughout Spanish America; whether they worked in agriculture—and then whether in sugar, or cotton, or coffee; whether they were servants, skilled artisans, miners, or hired out; whether the local economy was expanding or contracting; whether they lived in the city or in the country; and whether the male-female demographic ratio was skewed.

Unlike Anglo-America, slaves in Spanish and Portuguese America might buy liberty if they could accumulate their purchase price. For slave men, such liberation was likely the result of capital accumulated through working skills. Even so, an expert miner in Mexico or Colombia or Peru was far more likely to be successful than a sugarcane fieldhand isolated in the Cuban or Brazilian countryside. European custom and status considerations could trump physical capacity determining male slave occupations. A male slave, for example, might be tapped for a less arduous but higher status job as an artisan or coachman, whereas a female slave might be sent to perform heavy labor in the Caribbean fields.[58]

Evidence of the economic activities of men appears everywhere in colonial documents, but the daily, productive, and substantive ways that elite, plebeian, and slave women added economic resources to their own lives as well as that of their families are more difficult to discover. The exception is research on the laboriousness of food production in the tortilla-eating zone of Mexico and Central America, where tortillas necessitated an average of five female preparation hours a day.[59] Beyond that, historians know little of the material culture of colonial homes and the fundamental contributions of women within the domestic space, where even the simplest of activities—providing water, warmth, cleanliness, and food—were laborious and time-consuming.

Spanish and Portuguese law provided contradictory messages concerning the accumulation of wealth by colonial women. Some restrictions were "so formidable as to prevent any resounding feminine impact."[60] Unmarried women remained minors until they were twenty-five, and married women were forbidden to make contracts without their husbands' permission. Yet women who were single, widowed, or religious faced no such legal restrictions, and in day-to-day transactions most women seem to have experienced few limitations. Throughout Spanish America and Brazil there were stark contrasts between the "patriarchal values of the culture" and the incredible generosity of the legal system when women became "heirs and wives."[61] Researchers have explored these contrasting paths to wealth acquisition—how, in the public sphere, colonial women might acquire substantial or pitiful resources through personal economic activities, or how women, as members of families, received wealth throughout their lifecourses through inheritance, dowry, and communal property.

Just as indigenous women might appear as property owners in Mayan-language documents but disappear in the Spanish translations, so the economic activities of colonial women receive similar eclectic mention. Consider, for example, the 1798 census of Celaya, Mexico, that listed widows Maria Manzales and Gertrudis Pacheo as tavernkeepers and widow Rita Camacho as manager of a store.[62] Subsequent censuses noted that these women lived in the same houses, although their occupations were never listed again. Does it seem likely that Maria, Gertrudis, and Rita worked only in 1798, or were their later economic activities simply ignored?

A number of demographers suggest one answer, pointing to striking evidence of skewed male-female sex ratios in eighteenth-century colonial cities. Female-headed households composed a provocative percentage of urban establishments, ranging from 20 to 40 percent in some Mexican cities (including Celaya) to 45 percent in Vila Rica, Brazil, to a stunning 59 percent in late colonial Bogotá.[63] Unattached women typically migrated to cities for personal security.[64] If women such as Maria, Gertrudis, and Rita headed or lived in same-sex households, they had, by necessity, to have been active participants in their local economy. There, they no doubt were joined by a cohort of married women who worked in family businesses or whose personal activities buttressed family income.

How did women sustain themselves? They administered property and engaged in commerce; occupied positions in institutions such as hospitals, convents, and orphanages; headed or worked in small stores, taverns, bakeries, and boarding houses; provided domestic services, including as wet or dry nurses; sewed, starched, and washed clothes; and peddled items ranging from fish to candies. Women took responsibility for chickens, goats, and guinea pigs; on the frontier they sheared sheep, carded, spun, and wove wool.[65] In both cities and countryside, women planted gardens and then harvested, processed, stored, and prepared food. Some remained in a "position of tutelage," experiencing "systematic exclusion" from economic life or "significant control over resources."[66] No doubt many colonial women, whether white, mestizo, mulatto, black, or native, managed "pathetically small operations" that were "often in serious financial trouble." For many, such economic activities were not empowering, but rather the "result of dire . . . necessity."[67]

The occupational experiences of slave women, just as those of slave men, varied according to a range of variables. Compared to their free mulatto and black counterparts, slave women may have experienced more androgynous workloads given that they were forced to perform heavy physical labors, particularly in agriculture. Slave women also specialized in female tasks, serving as wet or dry nurses, cooks, and housemaids. Gender differentiated some female paths toward the purchase of freedom. Because slave women tended to concentrate in urban locales, peddling and truck gardening proved a ready source of capital that promoted emancipation. Unlike slave men, the horrors of rape and sexual imposition typically imposed on women may also have accelerated their manumission. In Lima, slave women proved to be more successful purchasers of freedom than male counterparts because they used forced or consensual cohabitation as "emotional and social blackmail" to create "margins for negotiation" among their masters, themselves, and their joint offspring.[68]

Without question, the richest women in colonial Spanish and Portuguese America were the daughters, wives, and widows of the wealthiest men. Four generations of letters of eight female members of the noble Mexican Regla family demonstrate that some women were extremely involved in the family's business dealings whereas others chose to remain aloof. The Countess of Miravalle dramatically increased family resources as she managed haciendas, endlessly litigated, bought slaves, remitted goods and silver, purchased public offices for male relations, and arranged advantageous marriage alliances for offspring. Elite women engaged in a "complexity" of roles that "belie stereotypes of subservience and lack of control over the economic aspects of their family," proving to be "pivotal in the fate of their families as marriageable pawns, child bearers, heiresses, advisers, and administrators."[69] Although the most obvious entrepreneurial freedom and material resources accrued to widows, it seems likely that many women chose to exercise substantial influence privately, within the family, throughout their lifecourses.

When colonial women had resources to bestow they expended them somewhat differently than men. The liberation of slaves proved a gendered activity, for when men emancipated they often freed their female lovers or their own blood kin. When women bestowed freedom, they were more likely to be widows freeing nonrelated, elderly servitors.[70] If charitable money was to be expended, both men and women tended first to choose dowry funds that facilitated the marriage of single women. In Mexico, the next choice for men was to will resources to *recogimientos* (institutions that sheltered single, abandoned, or divorced women, sometimes even prostitutes or criminals). In contrast, the second choice of women was to found or maintain convents. The distinction is significant. Recogimientos were compatible with the traditional "masculine role" of protecting women, and men ran these institutions. Convents were female organizations, internally governed by women although ultimately subject to the male church hierarchy.[71]

Images of convents, the most obvious institutions where women clustered in colonial Hispanic America, have ranged from the horrible to the bizarre. Extremes extend from nineteenth-century traveler Fanny Calderon de la Barca's idea that they were tombs for unhappy girls lured into their depths, to historian Charles Boxer's comment in the 1970s that some convents' condominiumlike apartment dwellings, luxurious lifestyles, and lavish entertainments meant they more resembled a "Bunny Club."[72] More distorting is the mistaken notion that within convent walls Latin American women remained isolated from the outside world, carrying on timeless and unchanging ritual. Over the last decades, a series of pathbreaking articles has opened the worlds of nuns and nunneries from Mexico to Peru.[73]

Convents, sometimes multiple convents, dotted colonial cities; by the late eighteenth century there were fifty-seven such establishments solely in Mexico.[74] The comparative scarcity of women in Brazil delayed the establishment of convents there because the crown discouraged their foundation in the sixteenth century, instead promoting marriage and the establishment of creole families. Elite families, however, bypassed the state and continued to designate "excess" daughters, whose dowries were not sufficient for a peer marriage, to convents, shipping the young women to Portugal until the requisite institutions appeared in Brazil.

Convents proved to be dynamic institutions, microcosms reflecting their patriarchal, hierarchical, colonial, local, familial, and religious milieu. Their establishment and continuance rested on men because foundation necessitated approval by imperial bureaucrats, with nuns owing continued obedience to the bishop, archbishop, metropolitan, or male superior of their order. A female social hierarchy replicated the outside. The properly dowered white, elite women at the top of the conventual social order wore the most prestigious garments, such as black veils, and sometimes lived in individual apartments tended by servants and slaves. These were followed by lesser-status religious who wore white veils and then, farther down the scale, by their mestiza, mulata, native, and slave servants.

Convents reflected colonial tensions and colonial mandates. Nuns from the peninsula often disparaged the religiosity and discipline of their creole

(American-born) counterparts, and internal politics often divided between the peninsular and the American-born. Royal authorities limited conventual foundation and profession to peninsular and creole women; Indian women, given their "weak intellectual and spiritual capacity," were excluded.[75] Centuries of hagiographic literature on the "piety and faith" of Indian women eventually resulted in the establishment in 1724 of the first indigenous convent of Corpus Christi in Mexico. Even then, the white religious overseeing the early years of the institution attempted to maintain control by delaying the profession of indigenous novices as well as the exercise of their voting rights.

Convents were local and urban institutions, often located at the heart of a city and occupying several blocks surrounded by walls that enclosed the nuns' houses and apartments and the church. Many—such as Santa Catalina in Arequipa, Peru—were veritable mazes with their own streets, patios, and gardens. Convents were tightly linked to their surrounding economy, functioning somewhat as banks as they promoted capital flow. Nuns formed ambitious alliances with outside kin, business partners, and indigenous leaders, lending them money accumulated from the dowries of entering postulates and from charitable bequests. These *censos* (financial instruments) provided an annual income for the convent and capital for borrowers, who paid fixed-percentage annuities until they repaid the principal. The *locutorio* (conventual window grill to the outside) became an exchange point where such deals were transacted. The fortunes of convents mirrored the local economy, with depression following revolts such as Tupac Amaru in Peru. Conventual wealth began to decline even further with imperial Bourbon tax reforms and the Wars for Independence.

Convents were familial, familylike, and even reproductive institutions. Elite families not only entered daughters with predetermined vocations but also, in some instances, may have encouraged the entrance of essentially "surplus" daughters who could not be properly dowered for marriage with social equals. By absorbing such women, convents helped maintain endogamous marriages and the colonial social hierarchy. Yet many women may have welcomed the protection and alternative freedoms of convent life, deeming it superior to spinsterhood, marriage to an unequal or incompatible spouse, or the possibility of premature death in childbirth. Convents became extensions of family life because entering postulates might be greeted at the door by their aunts, sisters, and cousins. Those institutions that took in the abandoned and educated the young often resembled "complex, colonial households, with infants and toddlers, adolescents, maids and slaves."[76] Within their "capacious cells" nuns became "matriarchs" of "alternative families." Reproduction occurred when women religious recruited relatives from their families as well as from the abandoned and the orphaned to beget the next conventual generation.

At their heart, convents remained religious establishments where women prayed in cycles of observance ranging from the austere disciplines of the "barefoot" or discalced communities such as the Capuchines, to the modest or even somewhat extravagant lifestyles of the calced, or "shod," orders. The autobiographies and letters that ordinary nuns wrote for their confessors reveal a continual search for spiritual perfection and provide insight into the daily experiences of women religious in colonial Latin America. Yet even here female religious writings might escape convent walls. A confessor or a bishop might edit and rescript the writings of an extraordinarily pious nun to submit as evidence in the hopes she might meet Vatican standards for canonization. Meanwhile, the local populace might hope that one of their own would become a saint.[77]

The lives of female religious contextualize the biographies of the two most famous women of colonial Spanish America: the brilliant Sor Juana Inés de la Cruz (1648–95) and the New World's first saint, Rose of Lima (1586–1617, canonized in 1671). Their stories remind of the different ways that societies value exceptionality. If Sor Juana and St. Rose lived today, the first would likely hold a distinguished professorship, and the second might well be on medication for a psychiatric disorder.[78] In Sor Juana's seventeenth-century Mexico and St. Rose's sixteenth-century Peru, the life of a genius intellectual ended in crisis, and a pain-seeking ascetic was canonized. Yet both Sor Juana and St. Rose found that religious vows provided shelter to express their individuality; both also had to negotiate the consequences of celebrity with the masculine ecclesiastical establishment.

The uncontested genius of the future Sor Juana distinguished her in early childhood as a Baroque prodigy, leading to her arrival at age sixteen at the viceregal court in Mexico City, where her literary genius flourished as she composed poetry, epigrams, and plays.[79] Yet a young single woman could not live alone at court. Her out-of-wedlock birth, her family's modest resources, and her own disinclination for matrimony led an ecclesiastical patron to dower her entry into the Convent of San Jeronimo at age twenty-one. There she remained one of Mexico City's colonial celebrities, conversing brilliantly at the locutorio, continuing her literary production and publication, collecting one of the largest libraries in colonial Mexico, and garnering fame throughout Europe.

Powerful patronage by the wives of the viceroys and church officials such as the Bishop of Puebla gave Sor Juana a certain immunity during her most prolific years of literary production. After her female patrons left Mexico, however, an essay critiquing a Jesuit sermon launched her in the discussion of theology. That led to severe critique and chastisement. A female genius might write poetry but not explicate the pronouncements of priests. The result was capitulation. Scholars debate whether she experienced a psychological breakdown due to pressure to conform. Perhaps, as Octavio Paz suggests, it was because of the loss of male patronage, or possibly, as Asunción Lavrin forwards, she experienced a religious crisis and decided that her literary activities were unworthy.[80] In 1692 Sor Juana sold most of her library and scientific instruments at the archbishop's order. Although she continued to write, she died two years later while ministering to her religious sisters during an epidemic. Her *Respuesta* (Reply), written as a defense against clerical attack, provides insight into a complex woman of genius, a "Mexican Phoenix" who negotiated some leeway but ultimately remained trapped by the constraints of her day.[81]

Although Sor Juana's intellectual and literary achievement might resonate more comfortably with contemporary mores, Isabel de Flores y de Oliva became America's first saint. According to her biographers, the young Isabel exhibited a classic pattern of sainthood. She hid in dank and dark places in her Limeño garden, where she refused to play but instead prayed constantly, undertook severe fasts, blistered her face with peppers, whipped herself, and generally manifested a "thirst for suffering."[82] She rejected her family's attempts to arrange a marriage, and instead became a *beata*, an alternative form of female religious life common throughout the colonies. Beatas were usually widows or unmarried; some lived together in groups, others with families or alone. Although they remained uncloistered, beatas often took religious vows; the future St. Rose belonged to the Third Order of St. Dominic. Like many beatas, she begged alms for charity and cared for the sick, Indians, and slaves.

Unlike most beatas, however, the future saint engaged in extreme physical suffering. Isabel undertook severe fasts, wore a hair shirt studded with iron nails, and, under her veil, a crown of ninety silver thorns that she constantly moved and pressed into her skull to produce maximum suffering. She also slept on a bed of broken glass, potsherds, and thorns. As some other nuns and beatas, she confessed to mystical religious experiences that became the subject of inquiry by church authorities. Such investigations—particularly by the Inquisition—could be dangerous because church officials were more likely to condemn than to authenticate lay female spiritual visions.[83] Before her not surprisingly premature death at age thirty-one, however, both the authorities and the public recognized St. Rose as a heroine and credited her intercessionary prayers with holding off an attacking Dutch fleet and preventing an earthquake. Although their worlds and lives differed dramatically, both Sor Juana and St. Rose created spaces for their intellectual and ascetic efforts; both became celebrities during and after their lifetimes.

The large majority of women and men in colonial Latin America were neither famous nor celibate. Since the 1990s, historians have explored contradictions between stereotypical portraits, suggesting rigid gender norms aimed at the control of female sexuality, and demographic data that demonstrate high illegitimacy rates resulting from nonmarital sexual relationships. Exploration of church and civil guidelines, issues of mentality (public-private or honor), and popular customs have provided qualitative insights about how colonial men and women of different classes and castes negotiated gendered issues.

Because men could never be absolutely certain to the last positive shred of doubt that they had ever fathered a particular child, patriarchal norms stereotypically exalted female virginity before matrimony and demanded sexual faithfulness within it, with substantial penalties for deviance. For colonial Latin American women, especially those of the elite, such sexual control was linked to maintenance of public reputation or "honor." Early historiography portraying honor replied on prescriptive sources such as medieval Spanish law or literature that promoted exaggerated images of swashbuckling, boasting Don Juans who seduced women who were thereby reduced to a "total collapse of social esteem and personal pride" as they lost honor.[84] Anthropological studies of Mediterranean honor abounded with extreme images of male sexual aggressiveness or female shame.

Historians have questioned such ahistoric approaches, noting that the "honor complex draws too much from the playhouse and too little from the public house" and that a too casual borrowing "from the Mediterranean context" has not "done justice to the complexities."[85] The goal has been to listen to the voices of colonial men and women and try to understand the nuanced customs surrounding the loss of virginity, courtship, betrothal, marriage, and concubinage and to gauge the prices paid for violation of norms.

Certainly, many transgressions occurred as demographers have documented high illegitimacy rates for Spanish America and Brazil. The most extensive work has been on Mexico, where, demographers estimate, average illegitimacy rates ranged from 7 to almost 50 percent during the seventeenth century, varying from cities to towns and among whites, natives, and castas. Rates declined a bit, from 7 to 35 percent averages, during the eighteenth century. Such illegitimacy percentages are striking when contrasted to those in the American English colonies, where rates remained under 5 percent, or Europe, where they ran under 10 percent with the exception of large cities such as Frankfort or Paris.[86]

Seen from a grand perspective, illegitimacy was the natural consequence of a colonial population experiencing drastic change. First was the decimation of the native population by epidemics, followed by a recovery from the lowest numbers after the 1650s. Next was the arrival of untold numbers of Spaniards and Portuguese and the proliferation of their creole descendants. Added to the mix were five or more millions of Africans who arrived as slaves, were scattered throughout the Americas, and contributed generations of slave and free offspring. Spaniards, Portuguese, natives, and Africans mingled not only within their own groupings but also with each other, creating populations of mixed bloods or castas.

Sexual encounters that spanned class and racial boundaries typically occurred outside of matrimony. In Mexico, the highest illegitimacy rates were among castas (roughly in the 30 to 40 percent range), trending somewhat lower among the indigenous population (20 to 30 percent). Even among the white population, which included Spanish and creole elites, illegitimacy rates averaged above 10 percent, trending even higher to 20 to 30 percent in Mexico City. The obvious challenge for historians is to explore the interstice between massive evidence of nonmarital liaisons and the norms of a society that so valued virginity and the control of female sexuality.

The first place to start is with those setting the ecclesiastical and civil ground rules: the Catholic church and the Spanish and Portuguese states. Throughout the Catholic world the reforms of the Council of Trent (1545–63) proved a watershed that divided sexually active men and women into the married, whose liaisons were sanctified and whose offspring were legitimate, and the rest, who sinned when they coupled and whose children were illegitimate. When a marriage occurred, it had to be freely contracted by both bride and groom and formalized by a priest.[87] Even though the church might reform, there were limits to the rapidity that popular beliefs and practices altered. Before Trent, marriage had been a longer process, as reflected in the medieval Spanish *Siete Partidas* (1256–65), which recognized that couples might begin a relationship, including sexual intimacy, not only with the *esponsales de presente* (exchange of vows) but also with the *esponsales de futuro* (promise to marry in the future).

Such customs persisted in colonial Spanish and Portuguese America, providing more latitude for negotiations over sexual activity than usually recognized. Men might use the *palabra de casamiento* (promise of matrimony) as a particularly potent weapon of seduction, promising an eventual ceremony in exchange for immediate sexual intimacy. Couples might engage in sexual relationships for months, years, or even decades before any ceremony occurred. Both Spanish and Portuguese law maintained the pre-Trent recognition of the special nature of such arrangements. The illegitimate offspring of single lovers belonged to a favored category (*hijo natural*) that could be automatically and fully legitimated when parents married, even if the ceremony took place decades after the birth.[88] As a result, a woman's reputation might be in limbo during an extended engagement that put her "between" spinsterhood and matrimony for years, although marriage could transform her at any time into a respectable matron with legitimate children. Men paid few prices if they promised matrimony and reneged. The church might refuse permission for a man who rejected a fiancee to wed someone else. Civil officials might pressure men by threats of jail or exile to fulfill their marriage promises. State propensity to intervene lessened by the late colony, making women even more vulnerable to loss of reputation.[89]

Not only civil and ecclesiastical laws but also popular practices, particularly the construction of private and public spheres, created spaces for sexual latitude. Colonial elites marked the private-public divide by recognizing a private world peopled by family, kin, and intimate friends and a public world composed of everyone else, although social peers mattered most. Such bifurcation created opportunities for the private circle to cooperate and even conspire to project superior persona in the public sphere when deviance from norms might tarnish reputation or honor.[90]

Such duality could be particularly important for the public reputation of elite women and men. If a woman engaged in a sexual relationship before marriage, her partner was expected to remain mute so she continued to enjoy a public reputation as a virgin. If pregnancy ensued and marriage was unlikely or impossible, the circle of lover, family, and friends might cooperate to arrange a "private pregnancy," concealing knowledge of the conception and maintaining the woman's honor. The duality between private and public could be extreme. Even though Doña Magdalena de la Vega of Mexico tragically perished in childbirth, witnesses also agreed that she "died with the reputation of a virgin."[91] Men also appropriated the spaces between the private and public. They might be loving fathers among friends and relatives but refuse to recognize illegitimate children in public.

The Catholic church in Brazil and Spanish America supported the private-public duality. Priests agreed not to list the names of mothers and fathers on the baptismal certificates of their illegitimate children if knowledge of sexual activity might damage standing. Such protection saved the reputation of sexually active single women, or priests, or adulterers of both sexes. In contrast, single men whose sexual activities did not damage their reputation commonly appeared as fathers on such documents.

The private-public dichotomy also sheltered men who engaged in same-sex acts. Altough religions and civil codes damned sodomy, the case of Bolivian prelate Dr. Don Gaspar Gonzales de Sosa exemplifies a certain popular tolerance for private deeds—as long as they were not made evident. Witness after witness originally conspired to protect the cleric's public reputation. It was only when Don Gaspar insisted on some particularly ostentatious flaunting of his sexual preference that penalties ensured. It was "not so much what the doctor . . . did behind closed doors that was of central concern; rather it was [his] public behavior and . . . lack of discretion."[92]

Similar tolerance for males who kept same-sex acts fairly private has been chronicled throughout Spanish America and Brazil. If, however, such sexual preference became public and notorious it could be fatal. In 1658 fourteen sodomites burned in Mexico.[93] Such draconian penalties were not the norm, however. For the majority of Hispanic society the private-public division permitted substantial latitude concerning private sexual conduct in spite of official and rigid gender norms.

For colonial elites, the private-public bifurcation proved integrally linked to maintenance of honor, the essential component of public reputation. Honor legitimized the colonial hierarchy's sanction of discrimination by those who had it against everyone who did not. Essential characteristics were *limpiesa de sangre* (literally, "clean blood" free of Jewish, Moorish, or racial mixture) as well as generations of legitimate descent. Honor was gendered but not absolute. Unlike stereotypical portrayals, it could be in negotiation at many points along a continuum.[94]

Elite women had to maintain public reputations as persons of honor in order to marry well and pass honor to the next generation. Women put honor in danger when they engaged in intercourse with their lovers; they risked reputation if pregnancy ensued, although the cost varied, depending on whether the pregnancy remained private or became public. Unwed mothers bargained honor with unwilling fiances, social peers, and communities as they waited for extended engagements to end in marriage or abandonment. Women might reconstruct a challenged reputation with years of proper conduct or fully restore it with marriage. Even those who engaged in sexual relationships with priests or married men might ease their own loss of honor with the purchase of a *gracias al sacar* (civil legitimation) providing honor for their offspring.

For men, honor was essential for access to political office, to elite occupations and social power. Both patriarchy and biology gave men much more latitude when certain issues of honor were at stake because public knowledge of sexual relationships or broken promises to wed did not, ultimately, damage male honor. Negotiations might still occur as men struggled with their consciences when they reneged on promises to marry or failed to provide support for lovers and offspring. Some fathers came to realize that certain issues of honor could not be negotiated; their refusal to wed precluded passage of honor to beloved but illegitimate sons and daughters, who consequently suffered discrimination.

More recently, historians have moved beyond elite constructions to explore whether the honor mentality extended to the rest of society, finding "unambiguous references" to honor values and behaviors in plebeians. By the late eighteenth century, honor culture in Buenos Aires "had penetrated every level of masculine society and informed nearly every male action."[95] In Arequipa (Peru), masculine plebeian honor rested on attributes such as good reputation, occupational skills, evidence of hospitality, generosity, and control and defense of the women of the family. For plebeian women, virginity before marriage was not as critical as faithfulness within it. Marriage was preferable, but long-term relationships also carried a certain respectability.[96] In contrast to elites, who protected honor through concealment or lawsuits, plebeians commonly defended their honor by verbal or physical violence, whether by swearing, fighting, or drinking for men or, for women, all of these in addition to shaming a rival by cutting her hair.

Enhancing such qualitative explorations of mentality are demographic studies revealing tantalizing quantitative data on how gender intersected with scarcity, birth, and race to have impact on sexual and marital liaisons. Just as in the conquest society, where uneven male-female ratios provided early female Spanish arrivals with marital advantage, so imbalanced proportions continued to influence the "matrimonial fair."[97] In regions where the ratio favored women, such as Florida, California, Sonora, or Vera Cruz, widows were more likely to remarry because scarcity gave them competitive leverage to move potential lovers to the altar.

Race, birth, and gender also interacted when a woman married because she typically assumed the class and racial status of her husband. Patriarchy might have impact on upward or downward mobility because an illegitimate or racially mixed woman might find it easier to "pass" upward to assume the legitimate or white status of her spouse. In contrast, when a white woman married downward to an Indian, mestizo, or mulatto she might literally find herself denigrated to the lower racial category at the next census, assuming the status of her husband.[98]

Evidence also suggests that reputation might trump race, making a woman more likely to "marry down" than a man. That is, a woman engaging in a sexual liaison with a racial inferior, particularly a mestizo, might find downward racial mobility less damaging than the countervailing stigma attached to female sexual intimacy outside matrimony. In a similar vein, Cuban couples manipulated the issue of reputation by "eloping," thereby leveraging the damage caused by public knowledge of the woman's loss of virginity against parental disapproval of the class or race of the potential bridegroom.[99] The goal was to pressure parents to agree to the marriage.

In contrast, men were far more likely to live in concubinage with racial inferiors because society tolerated—even expected—sexual promiscuity in bachelors. The inability of Brazilian elite men to accumulate sufficient resources to marry peers was a significant contributor to the high levels of concubinage and illegitimacy among that group.[100] Racially mixed women, the partners of such men, may also have strategized, choosing concubinage over marriage and in the process whitening, and thus advancing, their children's move up the racial spectrum. A saying from Cuba expressed it best: "Rather the mistress of a white man than the wife of a Negro."[101] Because men were more geographically mobile than women, they were also more likely to contract bigamous relationships. Internal networks of friends, kin, and neighbors proved amazingly effective in identifying and punishing such multiple-marriers.[102]

Those who had the least maneuverability in forming marital relationships were slaves, at the bottom of every pyramid. The solitary male was a "pervasive feature" of Brazilian slavery, given the inability of most slave men to maintain long-term relationships with slave women.[103] Both the sexual exploitation of women by masters and the constant testamentary redivision of slaves to heirs when their masters and mistresses died were particularly isolating for men. Because slave women were less likely to be separated from their young children, the effect was to create matrifocal slave families, isolating masculine slave lovers and fathers.

Conditions no doubt varied throughout Spanish and Portuguese America. Birth intervals among Puerto Rican slaves suggest that longer-term, stable consensual unions were more common than usually credited; slave men in Guatemala experienced modest success in marrying upward.[104] In Lima, slave women negotiated between their masters and husbands, and "their combined options showed success, yet they opted to play by the rules set in place by the system, their owners, and their husbands."[105]

In a colonial society where private and public, honor, and even race and birth were negotiable, the potentials for maneuvering proved endless. As the eighteenth century drew to a close, the Spanish state intervened in a vain attempt to curtail upward mobility and maintain the exclusivity of elite families. The Pragmatic Sanction of 1778 challenged the principle of freedom of marital choice traditionally supported by the church. This measure permitted elite fathers to petition to forbid the marriages of sons and daughters with those of inferior birth or race, a phenomenon increasingly common and obviously threatening to the social and racial status quo.[106]

Of the many gender stereotypes challenged by historians, one resists revisionism: When married women engaged in extramarital affairs they endangered more than reputation—they risked their lives. Absent husbands were common in a colonial setting where men who were merchants, miners, bureaucrats, or muledrivers might be away for months or even for years and where word might even trickle back that they were dead. Doña Teresa Medina, a Tucumán matron, was just one who lived a nightmare no doubt feared by many women. This Argentine wife had mourned the death of her absent merchant husband for two years. She then had a child with someone else and was nursing the baby when word arrived that her husband had returned. Even a male observer critical of her affair was struck by her subsequent "suffering" due to the husband's physical abuse, and Doña Teresa's female neighbors were even more sympathetic. Ultimately, such "ill-treatment and pain" proved fatal for it "caused a fever from which she died."[107] Doña Theresa's suffering may have been common. In Brazil, the ecclesiastical legal code expressed explicit concern for the physical safety of women who committed adultery.[108] Both Spanish and Portuguese American archives abound with cases of wives "caught in the act" suffering death at the hands of husbands who were subsequently exonerated.[109]

Violence was a common experience of domestic life, pervasive in all classes and castes although perhaps worse at the bottom than at the top. Such mistreatment included haircutting, which marked a woman as "morally loose," and slapping and beating that escalated to rape, physical mutilation, and murder. Women who failed to perform expected tasks or did not act with decorum outside the home could be subjected to a "high degree of physical abuse."[110] There was little recourse because neighbors were usually reluctant to intervene. Plebeian women in Mexico might use town elders to act as mediators in family disputes, and women in colonial Brazil might take the initiative in separation proceedings, citing abuse as a primary cause.[111] The politics of what colonials referred to as *la mala vida* (the bad life) was a phenomenon unhappily common enough to develop its own discourse.[112]

Since the 1990s historians have translated illuminating documents and constructed vivid microbiographies portraying the good and the bad, the heroic and the stupid, and the happy and the tragic experiences of women and men of colonial Latin America. A number of document collections—including those by Richard Boyer and Geoffrey Spurling, David Sweet and Gary Nash, and Kenneth Mills and William B. Taylor—provide wonderful, accessible vignettes that illustrate many trends noted in this essay.[113]

Conclusion

The warp and weft of the colonial tapestry forms the underlying support on which the weaving and reweaving of historical researchers have uncovered both pattern and revealed bareness. Certain underlying themes appear and reappear. The first is the imperative for historians to explore the worlds of colonial men and women and privilege their perspective as much as any contemporary agenda. Blending the "hard" statistics of demographers with "soft," qualitative narrative adds value, making each more than the sum of its parts. Differentiating between the stereotype and the lived experience reveals the ingenious ways that men and women negotiated the boundaries between expectation and reality. Attention to process—identifying the myriad of variables affecting and distinguishing outcome—provides the fundamental historical context.

Notes

Special thanks to Asunción Lavrin and Linda Lewin for comments that added and clarified and to Virginia Sánchez Korrol and Bonnie Smith for polishings. Although the bibliography has been mostly limited to English works to facilitate consultation by U.S. readers, it is also necessary to mention a number of first-rate scholars who publish in Spanish and Portuguese on similar topics. These include, for Argentina, Richard Cicerchia, Daisy Rípodas Ardanaz, and Eduardo R. Saguier; for Brazil, Lana Lage da Gama e Lima, Mary Del Priore, Luz R. B. Mott, Ilana W. Novinsky, Renato Pinto Venacio, and Ronaldo Vainfas; for Colombia, Beatriz Patiño Millán and Pablo Rodrígues Jiménez; for Mexico, Tomas Calvo, Carmen Castaneda, Pilar Gonzalbo Aizpuru, Elsa M. Malvido Josefina Muriel, Juan Javier Pescador, C. Noemi Quezada, and Cecilia Andrea Rabell; and, for Peru, María Emma Mannarelli.

1. William Lyle Schurz, *This New World: The Civilization of Latin America* (New York: Dutton, 1954), 276–338; Luis Martin, *Daughters of the Conquistadores: Women of the Viceroyalty of Peru* (Dallas: Southern Methodist University Press, 1983).

2. Asunción Lavrin, ed., *Latin American Women: Historical Perspectives* (Westport: Greenwood Press, 1978), 302; Joan W. Scott, "Gender: A Useful Category of Historical Analysis," *American Historical Review* 91 (Dec. 1986): 1053–75.

3. See Noble David Cook, *Born to Die: Disease and New World Conquest, 1492–1650* (Cambridge: Cambridge University Press, 1998), for discussion and historiography on demographic decline.

4. Mona Etienne and Eleonore Leacock, eds., *Women and Colonization: Anthropological Perspectives* (New York: Praeger, 1980), 4, 7; Irene Silverblatt, "'The Universe Has Turned Inside Out. . . . There Is No Justice for Us Now': Andean Women under Spanish Rule," in *Women and Colonization*, ed. Etienne and Leacock, 140–85; June Nash, "Aztec Women: The Transition from Status to Class to Empire and Colony," in *Women and Colonization*, ed. Etienne and Leacock, 134–85.

5. Irene Silverblatt, *Moon, Sun and Witches: Gender Ideologies and Class in Inca and Colonial Peru* (Princeton: Princeton University Press, 1987), xxxviii.

6. Susan Kellogg, "The Woman's Room: Some Aspects of Gender Relations in Tenochtitlán in the Late Prehispanic Period," *Ethnohistory* 42, no. 4 (1995): 563–76; Susan Kellogg, *Law and the Transformation of Aztec Culture, 1500–1700* (Norman: University of Oklahoma Press, 1995), 92.

7. Louise M. Burkhart, *The Slippery Earth: Nahua-Christian Moral Dialogue in Sixteenth-Century Mexico* (Tucson: University of Arizona Press, 1989), 26, 52.

8. Elizabeth Brumfiel, "Weaving and Cooking: Women's Production in Aztec Mexico," in *Engendering Archaeology: Women and Prehistory*, ed. Joan M. Gero and Margaret W. Conkey (Oxford: Basil Blackwell, 1991), 224–51.

9. Cecelia F. Klein, "Fighting with Femininity: Gender and War in Aztec Mexico," in *Gender Rhetorics: Postures of Dominance and Submission in History*, ed. Richard Trexler (Binghamton: Medieval and Renaissance Texts and Studies, 1994), 219, 240.

10. Susan Schroeder, "The Noblewomen of Chalco," *Estudios de Cultura. Náhuatl* 22 (1992): 50; Susan D. Gillespie, *The Aztec Kings: The Construction of Rulership in Mexico History* (Tucson: University of Arizona Press, 1989).

11. Cook, *Born to Die*, 5.

12. For example, on women and *mita* (Andean forced labor), see Bianca Premo, "From the Pockets of Women: The Gendering of the Mita, Migration and Tribute in Colonial Chucuito, Peru," *The Americas* 57 (July 2000): 63–94.

13. Phillip Curtain, *The African Slave Trade* (Madison: University of Wisconsin Press, 1969), 288. Numbers on the slave trade are still in flux. Curtain's estimate of 3.6 million for Brazil and 1.5 million for Spanish America are at the conservative end of the scale of 9.4 million for all the Americas.

14. Susan Kellogg, "From Parallel and Equivalent to Separate but Unequal: Tenochca Mexica Women, 1500–1700," in *Indian Women of Early Mexico*, ed. Susan Schroeder, Stephanie Wood, and Robert Haskett (Norman: University of Oklahoma Press, 1997), 123–44.

15. Deborah E. Kanter, "Native Female Land Tenure and Its Decline in Mexico, 1750–1900," *Ethnohistory* 42 (Fall 1995): 613.

16. For Ecuador, see Frank Salomon, "Indian Women of Early Colonial Quito as Seen Through Their Testaments," *The Americas* 44 (Jan. 1988): 340; for Chile, see Della M. Flusche and Eugene H. Korth, *Forgotten Females: Women of African and Indian Descent in Colonial Chile 1535–1800* (Detroit: Blame Ethridge, 1983), 51; for Mexico, see Susan Kellogg, "Indigenous Testaments of Early-Colonial Mexico City: Testifying to Gender Differences," in *Dead Giveaways: Indigenous Testaments of Colonial Mesoamerica and the Andes*, ed. Susan Kellogg and Matthew Restall (Salt Lake City: University of Utah Press, 1998), 37–58.

17. Marta Espejo-Ponce Hunt and Matthew Restall, "Work, Marriage, and Status: Maya Women of Colonial Yucatan," in *Indian Women of Early Mexico*, ed. Schroeder, Wood, and Haskett, 247, 238.

18. Espejo-Ponce Hunt and Restall, "Work, Marriage, and Status," 233.

19. Asunción Lavrin, "Sexuality in Colonial Mexico: A Church Dilemma," in *Sexuality and Marriage in Colonial Latin America*, ed. Asunción Lavrin (Lincoln: University of Nebraska Press, 1989), 47–95; Burkhart, *The Slippery Earth;* Serge Gruzinski, "Individualization and Acculturation: Confession among the Nahua of Mexico from the Sixteenth to the Eighteenth Century," in *Sexuality and Marriage*, ed. Lavrin, 96–117; for rebellion, see Susan M. Deeds, "Double Jeopardy: Indian Women in Jesuit Missions of Nueva Vizcaya," in *Indian Women of Early Mexico*, ed. Schroeder, Wood, and Haskett, 255–72.

20. Sarah Cline, "The Spiritual Conquest Reexamined: Baptism and Christian Marriage in Early Sixteenth-Century Mexico," *Hispanic American Historical Review* 73, no. 3 (1993): 476; Flusche and Korth, *Forgotten Females*, 38; Ward Stavig, *The World of Tupac Amaru* (Lincoln: University of Nebraska Press, 1999), 24–57.

21. Stephanie Wood, "Adopted Saints: Christian Images in Nahua Testaments of Late Colonial Toluca," *The Americas* 47 (Jan. 1991): 259–93.

22. Inga Clendinnen, "Yucatec Maya Women and the Spanish Conquest: Role and Ritual in Historical Reconstruction," *Journal of Social History* 15 (Spring 1982): 427–42.

23. Ramón A. Gutierrez, *When Jesus Came the Corn Mothers Went Away: Marriage Sexuality and Power in New Mexico, 1500–1846* (Stanford: Stanford University Press, 1991).

24. Pedro Carrasco, "Indian-Spanish Marriages in the First Century of the Colony," in *Indian Women of Early Mexico*, ed. Schroeder, Wood, and Haskett, 87–104. For classic views see Magnus Morner, *Race Mixture in the History of Latin America* (New York: Little, Brown, 1967); James Lockhart, *Spanish Peru, 1532–1560: A Social History* (Madison: University of Wisconsin Press, 1968); Elinor Burkett, "Indian Women and White Society: The Case of Sixteenth-Century Peru," in *Latin American Women*, ed. Lavrin, 101–28; and Ann M. Wightman, *Indigenous Migration and Social Change: The Forasteros of Cuzco, 1570–1720* (Durham: Duke University Press, 1990).

25. Burkett, "Indian Women and White Society," 119; Richard C. Trexler, *Sex and Conquest: Gendered Violence, Political Order, and the European Conquest of the Americas* (Ithaca: Cornell University Press, 1995).

26. For Inca, see Silverblatt, *Moon, Sun and Witches*, 201; for Maya, see Clendinnen, "Yucatec Maya Women," 436.

27. For Peru, see Silverblatt, *Moon, Sun and Witches;* Louise M. Burkhart, "Mexica Women on the Home Front: Housework and Religion in Aztec Mexico," in *Indian Women of Early Mexico*, ed. Schroeder, Wood, and Haskett, 25–54; for Mexico, see Ruth Behar, "Sexual Witchcraft, Colonialism, and Women's Power: Views from the Mexican Inquisition," in *Sexuality and Marriage*, ed. Lavrin, 178–208; for Guatemala, see Martha Few, *Women Who Live Evil Lives: Gender, Religion, and the Politics of Power in Colonial Guatemala* (Austin: University of Texas Press, 2002).

28. Leon Campbell, "Women and the Great Rebellion in Peru, 1780–1783," *The Americas* 42, no. 2 (1985): 190–91 (for Tupac Amaru); for places of women, see William Taylor, *Drinking, Homicide and Rebellion in Colonial Mexican Villages* (Stanford: Stanford University Press, 1979), 116, and Kevin Gosner, "Women, Rebellion, and the Moral Economy of Maya Peasants in Colonial Mexico," in *Indian Women of Early Mexico*, ed. Schroeder, Wood, and Haskett, 217–30.

29. Matthew Restall and Pete Sigal, "'May They Not Be Fornicators Equal to These Priests': Postconquest Yucatec Maya Sexual Attitudes," *UCLA Historical Journal* 12 (1992): 92, 98.

30. Alvis E. Dunn, "A Cry at Daybreak: Death, Disease, and Defense of Community in a Highland Ixil-Mayan Village," *Ethnohistory* 42 (Fall 1995): 602; Matthew Restall, "'He Wished It in Vain': Subordination and Resistance in Post-Conquest Yucatán," *Ethnohistory* 42 (Fall 1995): 577–94.

31. Ronald Spores, "Mixteca *Cacicas:* Status, Wealth, and the Political Accommodation of Native Elite Women in Early Colonial Oaxaca," in *Indian Women of Early Mexico*, ed. Schroeder, Wood, and Haskett, 195.

32. For Nueva Tlaxcala, see Leslie S. Offutt, "Women's Voices from the Frontier: San Esteban de Nueva Tlaxcala in the Late Eighteenth Century," in *Indian Women of Early Mexico*, ed. Schroeder, Wood, and Haskett, 289; for Mixtec and Zapotec, see Spores, "Mixteca *Cacicas,*" and Lisa Mary Sousa, "Women and Crime in Colonial Oaxaca: Evidence of Complementary Gender Roles in Mixtec and Zapotec Societies," in *Indian Women of Early Mexico*, ed. Schroeder, Wood, and Haskett, 199–216; for Tepotzlán, see

Robert Haskett, "Activist or Adulteress? The Life and Struggle of Doña Josefa María of Tepoztlan," in *Indian Women of Early Mexico*, ed. Schroeder, Wood, and Haskett, 145–64.
    33. Susan M. Socolow, *The Women of Colonial Latin America* (New York: Cambridge University Press, 2000), 50.
    34. Brumfiel, "Weaving and Cooking," 246; for rhetoric, see Ann Zulawski, *"They Eat from Their Labor": Work and Social Change in Colonial Bolivia* (Pittsburgh: University of Pittsburgh Press, 1995), 154; for additional comments, see Irene Silverblatt, "Lessons of Gender and Ethnohistory in MesoAmerica," *Ethnohistory* 42 (Fall 1995): 3399–650.
    35. Pete Sigal, "Gendered Power, the Hybrid Self, and Homosexual Desire in Late Colonial Yucatan," in *Infamous Desire: Male Homosexuality in Colonial Latin America*, ed. Pete Sigal (Chicago: University of Chicago Press, 2003), 102–33; Richard C. Trexler, "Gender Subordination and Political Hierarchy in Pre-Hispanic America," in *Infamous Desire*, ed. Sigal, 70–101; Ward Stavig, "Political 'Abomination' and Private Reservation: The Nefarious Sin, Homosexuality, and Cultural Values in Colonial Peru," in *Infamous Desire*, ed. Sigal, 134–51; Pete Sigal, *From Moon Goddesses to Virgins: The Colonization of Yucatacan Maya Sexual Desire* (Austin: University of Texas Press), 2000.
    36. Exceptions are Heath Dillard, *Daughters of the Reconquest: Women in Castilian Town Society, 1100–1300* (New York: Cambridge University Press, 1984); Mary Elizabeth Perry, *Gender and Disorder in Early Modern Seville* (Princeton: Princeton University Press, 1990), also her "From Convent to Battlefield: Cross-Dressing and Gendering the Self in the New World of Imperial Spain," in *Queer Iberia: Sexualities, Cultures, and Crossing from the Middle Ages to the Renaissance*, ed. Josiah Blackmore and Gregory S. Hutcheson (Durham: Duke University Press, 1999), 394–419; and Ida Altman, *Emigrants and Society: Extremadura and Spanish America in the Sixteenth Century* (Berkeley: University of California Press, 1989), also her *Transatlantic Ties in the Spanish Empire: Brihuega, Spain, and Puebla, Mexico, 1560–1620* (Stanford: Stanford University Press, 2000). Federico Garza Carvajal, *Butterflies Will Burn: Prosecuting Sodomites in Early Modern Spain and Mexico* (Austin: University of Texas Press, 2003) has problematic analysis concerning sodomy but presents revealing peninsular cases.
    37. For women at court, see Magdalena S. Sanchez, *The Empress, the Queen and the Nun: Women and Power at the Court of Philip III of Spain* (Baltimore: Johns Hopkins University Press, 1998); for the runaway nun, see Catalina de Erauso, *Lieutenant Nun: Memoir of a Basque Transvestite in the New World* (Boston: Beacon, 1996).
    38. Asunción Lavrin and Edith Couturier, "Dowries and Wills: A View of Women's Socioeconomic Role in Colonial Guadalajara and Puebla, 1640–1790," *Hispanic American Historical Review* 59 (May 1979): 280–304; Asunción Lavrin, "Women in Colonial Mexico," in *The Oxford History of Mexico*, ed. Michael C. Meyer and William H. Beezley (New York: Oxford University Press, 2000), 49–75; Asunción Lavrin, "Women in Spanish American Colonial Society," in *The Cambridge History of Latin America*, ed. Leslie Bethell (New York: Cambridge University Press, 1984), 321–56; Muriel Nazzari, *Disappearance of the Dowry: Women, Families, and Social Change in Sao Paulo, Brazil, 1600–1900* (Stanford: Stanford University Press, 1991).
    39. Anne McClintock, *Imperial Leather: Race, Gender, and Sexuality in the Colonial Contest* (New York: Routledge, 1995), 7.
    40. For Mexico, see Bernard Grunberg, "The Origins of the Conquistadors of Mexico City," *Hispanic American Historical Review* 74 (1994): 260–73, and Robert Himmerich y Valencia, *The Encomenderos of New Spain, 1521–1555* (Austin: University of Texas

Press, 1991); for Peru, see James Lockhart, *The Men of Cajamarca: A Social and Bibliographical Study of the First Conquerors of Peru* (Austin: University of Texas Press, 1972); for black conquistadors, see Matthew Restall, "Black Conquistadors: Armed Africans in Early Spanish America," *The Americas* 57 (Oct. 2000): 171–206.

41. Lockhart, *The Men of Cajamarca*, 111.

42. Burkett, "Indian Women and White Society," 107; Arnold J. Bauer, "Millers and Grinders: Technology and Household Economy in Meso-America," *Agricultural History* 64 (Winter 1990): 1–17.

43. Salomon, "Indian Women of Early Colonial Quito," 327.

44. The best primary source account of Doña Marina is the few pages in Bernal Diaz de Castillo, *The Conquest of New Spain* (New York: Penguin 1986); see also Octavio Paz, *The Labyrinth of Solitude* (New York: Grove Press, 1985), 65–88, and Frances Karttunen, "Rethinking Malinche," in *Indian Women of Early Mexico*, ed. Schroeder, Wood, and Haskett.

45. Karttunen, "Rethinking Malinche," 312; Sandra Messinger Cypress, *La Malinche in Mexican Literature from History to Myth* (Austin: University of Texas Press, 1991).

46. Socolow, *The Women of Colonial Latin America*, 35–36.

47. Lockhart, *The Men of Cajamarca*, 154.

48. Burkett, "Indian Women and White Society," 106.

49. Kathryn Burns, *Colonial Habits: Convents and the Spiritual Economy of Cuzco, Peru* (Durham: Duke University Press, 1999), 17.

50. Asunción Lavrin, "Indian Brides of Christ: Creating New Spaces for Indigenous Women in New Spain," *Mexican Studies* 15 (Summer 1999): 228.

51. For passenger lists, see Peter Boyd-Bowman, *Patterns of Spanish Emigration to the New World (1493–1580)* (Buffalo: Council on International Studies, State University of New York at Buffalo, 1973); for female conquistadors, see Martin, *Daughters of the Conquistadores*, 13–14, 22–24.

52. Garcilaso de la Vega, *Royal Commentaries of the Incas and General History of Peru* (Austin: University of Texas Press, 1966), vol. 2, bk. 2, ch. 1, 733–34.

53. Lockhart, *Spanish Peru*, 172.

54. Himmerich y Valencia, *The Encomenderos of New Spain*, 3–68, 98–99, 103.

55. James Lockhart and Enrique Otte, eds., *Letters and People of the Spanish Indies: The Sixteenth Century* (New York: Cambridge University Press, 1976).

56. Socolow, *The Women of Colonial Latin America*, 59.

57. William Taylor, *Magistrates of the Sacred: Priests and Parishioners in Eighteenth-Century Mexico* (Stanford: Stanford University Press, 1996).

58. Claire Robertson, "Africa into the Americas? Slavery and Women, the Family, and the Gender Division of Labor," in *More Than Chattel: Black Women and Slavery in the Americas*, ed. David Barry Gaspar and Darlene Clark Hine (Bloomington: University of Indiana Press, 1996), 22.

59. Bauer, "Millers and Grinders." Also see Arnold J. Bauer, *Goods, Power, History: Latin America's Material Culture* (New York: Cambridge University Press, 2001).

60. Eugene H. Kordi and Della M. Flusche, "Dowry and Inheritance in Colonial Spanish America: Peninsular Law and Chilean Practice," *The Americas* 43 (April 1987): 397.

61. Alida C. Metcalf, "Women and Means: Women and Family Property in Colonial Brazil," *Journal of Social History* 24 (Winter 1990): 277.

62. Catherine Doenges, "Sources and Speculations Concerning Women's Activity in Provincial Colonial Mexico," *Urban History Workshop Review* 2 (Spring 1994): 18.

ANN TWINAM

63. Javier Pescador, "Vanishing Woman: Female Migration and Ethnic Identity in Late-Colonial Mexico City," *Ethnohistory* 42 (Fall 1995): 617–26; Robert McCaa, "Gustos de los padres, inclinaciones de los novios y reglas de una feria nupcial colonial: Parral, 1770–1814," *Historia Mexicana* 40, no. 4 (1991): 579–614; for Mexico, see Doenges, "Sources and Speculations"; for Brazil, see A. J. R. Russell-Wood, "Female and Family in the Economy and Society of Colonial Brazil," in *Latin American Women*, ed. Lavrin, 60–100; for Colombia, see Guiomar Dueñas-Vargas, "Gender, Race, and Class: Illegitimacy and Family Life in Santafé Nuevo Reino de Granada, 1770–1810," Ph.D. diss., University of Texas at Austin, 1995; for Bolivia, see Ann Zulawski, "Social Differentiation, Gender, and Ethnicity: Urban Indian Women in Colonial Bolivia, 1640–1725," *Latin American Research Review* 25, no. 2 (1990): 93–114.

64. Anore Horton, "Constraint, Coercion, and Creation: Women's Migration and Mestizaje in Colonial Spanish America," in *New Perspectives on Women and Migration in Colonial Latin America*, ed. Anore Horton (Princeton: Princeton University Press, 2001), 47–57; Socolow, *The Women of Colonial Latin America*, 73–74, 77; Susan M. Socolow, "Women and Migration in Colonial Latin America," in *New Perspectives on Women and Migration*, ed. Horton, 1–20; Susan M. Socolow, "Women of the Buenos Aires Frontier, 1740–1810 (or, the Gaucho Turned Upside Down)," in *Contested Ground: Comparative Frontiers on the Northern and Southern Edges of the Spanish Empire*, ed. Donna Guy and Thomas E. Sheridan (Tucson: University of Arizona Press, 1998), 67–82; Susan M. Socolow, "Women and Crime: Buenos Aires, 1757–97," *Journal of Latin American Studies* 12 (May 1980): 39–54.

65. Elizabeth Kuznesof, "A History of Domestic Service in Spanish America, 1492–1980," in *Muchachas No More: Household Workers in Latin America and the Caribbean*, ed. Elsa M. Chaney and Mary Garcia Castro (Philadelphia: Temple University Press, 1989), 19, 20; Socolow, *The Women of Colonial Latin America*, 76; Kordi and Flusche, "Dowry and Inheritance," 30; Kimberly Gauderman, *Women's Lives in Colonial Quito: Gender, Law, and Economy in Spanish America* (Austin: University of Texas Press, 2003).

66. Kuznesof, "History of Domestic Service," 18.

67. Zulawski, *"They Eat from Their Labor,"* 161–62.

68. Christine Hunefeld, *Paying the Price of Freedom: Family and Labor among Lima's Slaves, 1800–1854* (Berkeley: University of California Press, 1994), 129.

69. Edith Couturier, "Women in a Noble Family: The Mexican Counts of Regla, 1750–1830," in *Latin American Women*, ed. Lavrin, 130–32, 145.

70. Kathleen J. Higgins, *"Licentious Liberty" in a Brazilian Gold-Mining Region: Slavery, Gender, and Social Control in Eighteenth-Century Sabará, Minas Gerais* (University Park: Pennsylvania State University Press, 1999), 149, 172.

71. Edith Couturier, "'For the greater service of God': Opulent Foundations and Women's Philanthropy in Colonial Mexico," in *Lady Bountiful Revisited: Women, Philanthropy, and Power*, ed. Kathleen D. McCarthy (New Brunswick: Rutgers University Press, 1990); 130; see also Nancy E. Van Deusen, "Determining the Boundaries of Virtue: The Discourse of Recogimiento among Women in Seventeenth-Century Lima," *Journal of Family History* 22 (Oct. 1997): 373–89, and Nancy E. Van Deusen, *Between the Sacred and the Wordly: The Institutional and Cultural Practice of Recogimiento in Colonial Lima* (Stanford: Stanford University Press, 2002).

72. Frances Calderón de la Barca, *Life in Mexico* (New York: Dutton, 1970), 199; C. R. Boxer, *Women in Iberian Expansion Overseas, 1415–1815: Some Facts, Fancies, and Personalities* (New York: Oxford University Press, 1975), 57; for Brazil, see Susan A. Soeiro,

"The Feminine Order in Colonial Bahia, Brazil: Economic, Social, and Demographic Implications, 1677–1800," in *Latin American Women*, ed. Lavrin, 173–97, and Russell-Wood, "Female and Family."

73. See Lavrin's numerous articles as well as Burns, *Colonial Habits*, and John James Clune, "A Cuban Convent in the Age of Enlightened Reform: The Observant Franciscan Community of Santa Clara of Havana, 1768–1808," *The Americas* 57 (Jan. 2001): 309–28.

74. Soeiro, "The Feminine Order," 174.

75. Lavrin, "Indian Brides of Christ," 229–30; Ann Miriam Gallagher, "The Indian Nuns of Mexico City's Monasterio of Corpus Christi, 1724–1821," in *Latin American Women*, ed. Lavrin, 150–72.

76. Burns, *Colonial Habits*, 116.

77. Asunción Lavrin, "Vida Conventual: Rasgos Históricos," in *Sor Juana y su Mundo: Una Mirada Actual*, ed. Sara Poot Herrera (Mexico: Universidad del Claustro de Sor Juana, 1995), 33–91; Asunción Lavrin, "Female Religious," in *Cities and Society in Colonial Latin America*, ed. Louisa S. Hoberman and Susan M. Socolow (Albuquerque: University of New Mexico Press, 1986), 165–95. For rescripting see Kathleen Ann Myers, *Neither Saints nor Sinners: Writing the Lives of Women in Spanish America* (New York: Oxford University Press, 2003). Also see Kathleen Myers and Amanda Powell, *A Wild Country Out in the Garden: The Spiritual Journals of a Colonial Mexican Nun* (Bloomington: Indiana University Press, 1999); Kathryn Joy McKnight, *The Mystic of Tunja: The Writings of Madre Castillo, 1671–1742* (Amherst: University of Massachusetts Press, 1997); Loreta Loreto López, "The Devil, Women, and the Body in Seventeenth-Century Puebla Convents," *The Americas* 59 (Oct. 2002): 221–34; Kristine Ibsen, *Women's Spiritual Autobiography in Colonial Spanish America* (Gainesville: University Press of Florida, 1999).

78. Even hagiographic biographers like Donald Attwater acknowledged that St. Rose's life posed "delicate questions of religion and psychology." Attwater, *The Avenel Dictionary of Saints* (New York: Penguin, 1965), 300.

79. Electa Arenal and Amanda Powell, *Sor Juana Inés de la Cruz: The Answer/La Respuesta* (New York: Feminist Press at the City University of New York, 1994), xiv–xvii; Lavrin, "Female Religious."

80. Octavio Paz, *Sor Juana; or, The Traps of Faith* (Cambridge: Harvard University Press, 1988), 459–62; Lavrin, "Female Religious," 187.

81. "La Respuesta" is available in a number of English editions; for example, see Arenal and Powell, *Sor Juana Inés de la Cruz*.

82. John Gilmary Shea, *Little Pictorial Lives of the Saints* (New York: Benzinger, 1878), 453–55; Carlos Miró-Quesda Laos, *De Santa Rosa a la Perrichola* (Lima: Talleres Gráficos, 1958), 11–38. A provacative exploration is Frank Graziano, *Wounds of Love: The Mystical Marriage of Saint Rose of Lima* (New York: Oxford University Press, 2004).

83. Jacqueline Holler, "The Spiritual and Physical Ecstasies of a Sixteenth-Century Beata," in *Colonial Lives: Documents on Latin American History, 1550–1850*, ed. Richard Boyer and Geoffrey Spurling (New York: Oxford University Press, 2000), 77–100.

84. Lucy A. Sponsler, "Women in Spain: Medieval Law versus Epic Literature," *Revista de Estudios Hispánicos* 7 (Oct. 1973): 433; for review, see Ann Twinam, *Public Lives, Private Secrets: Gender, Honor, Sexuality and Illegitimacy in Colonial Spanish America* (Stanford: Stanford University Press, 1999), 31–34.

85. Richard Boyer, "Honor among Plebeians: Mala Sangre and Social Reputation," in *The Faces of Honor: Sex, Shame and Violence in Colonial Latin America*, ed. Lyman John-

son and Sonya Lipsett-Rivera (Albuquerque: New Mexico University Press, 1998), 153; Van Deusen, "Determining the Boundaries," 374.

86. Twinam, *Public Lives,* 7–12, explores illegitimacy statistics.

87. See Nancy E. Van Duesen, "Wife of My Soul and Heart and All My Solace," in *Colonial Lives,* ed. Boyer and Spurling, for a case study where a Native women in Peru insisted on her freedom of choice in matrimony. For church practices, see Twinam, *Public Lives,* 36–41.

88. Twinam, *Public Lives,* 75–82; for Brazil, see Linda Lewin, *Surprise Heirs,* vol. 1: *Illegitimacy, Patrimonial Rights, and Legal Nationalism in Luso Brazilian Inheritance, 1750–1821* (Stanford: Stanford University Press, 2003); also see Linda Lewin, "Natural and Spurious Children in Brazilian Inheritance Law from Colony to Empire: A Methodological Essay," *The Americas* 11 (Jan. 1992): 351–96.

89. Twinam, *Public Lives,* 371; for controversy over timing, see Patricia Seed, *To Love, Honor, and Obey in Colonial Mexico: Conflicts over Marriage Choice, 1574–1821* (Stanford: Stanford University Press, 1988).

90. For examples throughout colonial Latin America, see Twinam, *Public Lives,* 26–30.

91. Ibid., 66; on private pregnancy, 66–73; on fathers and illegitimate offspring, 130–57; for the Brazilian variant, see Muriel Nazarri, "An Urgent Need to Conceal," in *The Faces of Honor,* ed. Johnson and Lipsett-Rivera, 103–26.

92. Geoffrey Spurling, "Honor, Sexuality, and the Colonial Church," in *The Faces of Honor,* ed. Johnson and Lipsett-Rivera, 63. See also Spurling's translation of another sodomy case in "Under Investigation for the Abominable Sin: Damian de Morales Stands Accused of Attempting to Seduce Anton de Tierra de Congo," in *Colonial Lives,* ed. Boyer and Spurling, 112–29.

93. For a thoughtful analysis of the Mexican example, see Serge Gruzinski, "The Ashes of Desire: Homosexuality in Mid-Seventeenth-Century New Spain," in *Infamous Desire,* ed. Sigal, 211; for Peru, see Stavig, "Political 'Abomination,'" 134–51; for Brazil, see David Higgs, "Tales of Two Carmelites: Inquisitorial Narratives from Portugal and Brazil," in *Infamous Desire,* ed. Sigal, 152–67, and Luiz Mott, "Crypo-Sodomites in Colonial Brazil," in *Infamous Desire,* ed. Sigal, 168–96.

94. Twinam, *Public Lives,* 25, 30–33, 41–50, 91–94; Ann Twinam, "Honor, Sexuality and Illegitimacy in Colonial Spanish America," in *Sexuality and Marriage,* ed. Lavrin, 118–55; Ann Twinam, "The Negotiation of Honor," in *The Faces of Honor,* ed. Johnson and Lipsett-Rivera, 103–26.

95. Johnson and Lipsett-Rivera, eds., *The Faces of Honor,* 11; Lyman L. Johnson, "Dangerous Words, Provocative Gestures, and Violent Acts," in *The Faces of Honor,* ed. Johnson and Lipsett-Rivera, 129.

96. Sarah Chambers, *From Subjects to Citizens: Honor, Gender and Politics in Arequipa, Peru, 1780–1854* (University Park: Pennsylvania State University Press, 1999), 173–79.

97. McCaa, "Gustos de los padres."

98. For Parral, see McCaa, "Gustos de los padres," 607; for Argentina, see Susan M. Socolow, "Acceptable Partners: Marriage Choice in Colonial Argentina, 1778–1810," in *Sexuality and Marriage,* ed. Lavrin, 231.

99. Verena (Stolcke) Martinez Alier, *Marriage, Class and Colour in Nineteenth-Century Cuba: A Study of Racial Attitudes and Sexual Values in a Slave Society* (New York: Cambridge University Press, 1974).

100. Muriel Nazzari, "Concubinage in Colonial Brazil: The Inequalities of Race, Class, and Gender," *Journal of Family History* 21 (April 1996): 107–24.

101. Alier, *Marriage, Class and Colour,* 129.

102. Richard Boyer, *Lives of the Bigamists: Marriage, Family, and Community in Colonial Mexico* (Albuquerque: University of New Mexico Press, 1995); Alexandra Cook and Noble David Cook, *Good Faith and Truthful Ignorance: A Case of Transatlantic Bigamy* (Durham: Duke University Press, 1991).

103. Alida C. Metcalf, "Searching for the Slave Family in Colonial Brazil: A Reconstruction from Sao Paulo," *Journal of Family History* 16, no. 3 (1991): 290.

104. For Puerto Rico, see David M. Stark, "Discovering the Invisible Puerto Rican Slave Family: Demographic Evidence from the Eighteenth Century," *Journal of Family History* 21 (Oct. 1996): 395–418; for Guatemala, see Paul Lokken, "Marriage as Slave Emancipation in Seventeenth-Century Guatemala," *The Americas* 58 (Oct. 2001): 175–200.

105. Hunefeld, *Paying the Price,* 206.

106. Twinam, *Public Lives,* 307–13; Socolow, "Acceptable Partners."

107. Twinam, *Public Lives,* 85–86.

108. Nazarri, "Urgent Need," 4.

109. Thomas A. Abercrombie, "Affairs of the Courtroom: Fernando de Medina Confesses to Killing His Wife," in *Colonial Lives,* ed. Boyer and Spurling, 54–76.

110. Socolow, *The Women of Colonial Latin America,* 79, 81; see also Sonya Lipsett-Rivera, "A Slap in the Face of Honor," in *The Faces of Honor,* ed. Johnson and Lipsett-Rivera, 179–200.

111. For Mexico, see Steve J. Stern, *The Secret History of Gender* (Chapel Hill: University of North Carolina Press, 1995); for Brazil, see Maria Beatriz Nizza da Silva, "Divorce in Colonial Brazil: The Case of Sao Paulo," in *Sexuality and Marriage,* ed. Lavrin, 313–40.

112. Richard Boyer, "Women, *La Mala Vida,* and the Politics of Marriage," in *Sexuality and Marriage,* ed. Lavrin; Sonya Lipsett-Rivera, "The Intersection of Rape and Marriage in Late-Colonial and Early National Mexico," *Colonial Latin American Historical Review* 6 (Fall 1997): 559–90.

113. Boyer and Spurling, eds., *Colonial Lives;* see also David G. Sweet and Gary B. Nash, eds., *Struggle and Survival in Colonial America* (Berkeley: University of California Press, 1981); Kenneth Mills and William B. Taylor, eds., *Colonial Spanish America: A Documentary History* (Wilmington: Scholarly Resources Press, 1998); and Sueann Caulfield, "The History of Gender in the Historiography of Latin America," *Hispanic American Historical Review* 81 (Aug.–Nov. 2001): 451–92.

WORKS CITED

Abercrombie, Thomas A. "Affairs of the Courtroom: Fernando de Medina Confesses to Killing His Wife." In *Colonial Lives: Documents on Latin American History 1550–1850,* edited by Richard Boyer and Geoffrey Spurling. New York: Oxford University Press, 2000.

Altman, Ida. *Emigrants and Society: Extremadura and Spanish America in the Sixteenth Century.* Berkeley: University of California Press, 1989.

———. *Transatlantic Ties in the Spanish Empire: Brihuega, Spain, and Puebla, Mexico, 1560–1620.* Stanford: Stanford University Press, 2000.

Arenal, Electa, and Amanda Powell. *Sor Juana Inés de la Cruz: The Answer/La Respuesta.* New York: Feminist Press at the City University of New York, 1994.

Attwater, Donald. *The Avenel Dictionary of Saints.* New York: Penguin, 1965.

Bauer, Arnold J. *Goods, Power, History: Latin America's Material Culture.* New York: Cambridge University Press, 2001.

———. "Millers and Grinders: Technology and Household Economy in Meso-America." *Agricultural History* 64 (Winter 1990): 1–17.

Behar, Ruth. "Sexual Witchcraft, Colonialism, and Women's Power: Views from the Mexican Inquisition." In *Sexuality and Marriage in Colonial Latin America,* edited by Asunción Lavrin, 178–208. Lincoln: University of Nebraska Press, 1989.

Boxer, C. R. *Women in Iberian Expansion Overseas, 1415–1815: Some Facts, Fancies, and Personalities.* New York: Oxford University Press, 1975.

Boyd-Bowman, Peter. *Patterns of Spanish Emigration to the New World (1493–1580).* Buffalo: Council on International Studies, State University of New York at Buffalo, 1973.

Boyer, Richard. "Honor among Plebeians: Mala Sangre and Social Reputation." In *The Faces of Honor: Sex, Shame and Violence in Colonial Latin America,* edited by Lyman Johnson and Sonya Lipsett-Rivera. Albuquerque: New Mexico University Press, 1998.

———. *Lives of the Bigamists: Marriage, Family, and Community in Colonial Mexico.* Albuquerque: University of New Mexico Press, 1995.

———. "Women, *La Mala Vida,* and the Politics of Marriage." In *Sexuality and Marriage in Colonial Latin America,* edited by Asunción Lavrin. Lincoln: University of Nebraska Press, 1989.

———, and Geoffrey Spurling, eds. *Colonial Lives: Documents on Latin American History, 1550–1850.* New York: Oxford University Press, 2000.

Brumfiel, Elizabeth. "Weaving and Cooking: Women's Production in Aztec Mexico." In *Engendering Archaeology: Women and Prehistory,* edited by Joan M. Gero and Margaret W. Conkey, 224–51. Oxford: Basil Blackwell, 1991.

Burkett, Elinor. "Indian Women and White Society: The Case of Sixteenth-Century Peru." In *Latin American Women: Historical Perspectives,* edited by Asunción Lavrin, 101–28. Westport: Greenwood Press, 1978.

Burkhart, Louise M. "Mexican Women on the Home Front: Housework and Religion in Aztec Mexico." In *Indian Women of Early Mexico,* edited by Susan Schroeder, Stephanie Wood, and Robert Haskett, 25–54. Norman: University of Oklahoma Press, 1997.

———. *The Slippery Earth: Nahua-Christian Moral Dialogue in Sixteenth-Century Mexico.* Tucson: University of Arizona Press, 1989.

Burns, Kathryn. *Colonial Habits: Convents and the Spiritual Economy of Cuzco, Peru.* Durham: Duke University Press, 1999

Calderon de la Barca, Frances. *Life in Mexico.* New York: Dutton, 1970.

Campbell, Leon. "Women and the Great Rebellion in Peru, 1780–1783." *The Americas* 42, no. 2 (1985): 163–96.

Carrasco, Pedro. "Indian-Spanish Marriages in the First Century of the Colony." In *Indian Women of Early Mexico,* edited by Susan Schroeder, Stephanie Wood, and Robert Haskett, 87–104. Norman: University of Oklahoma Press, 1997.

Caulfield, Sueann. "The History of Gender in the Historiography of Latin America." *Hispanic American Historical Review* 81 (Aug.–Nov. 2001): 451–92.

Chambers, Sarah. *From Subjects to Citizens: Honor, Gender and Politics in Arequipa, Peru, 1780–1854.* University Park: Pennsylvania State University Press, 1999.

Clendinnen, Inga. "Yucatec Maya Women and the Spanish Conquest: Role and Ritual in Historical Reconstruction." *Journal of Social History* 15 (Spring 1982): 427–42.

Cline, Sarah. "The Spiritual Conquest Reexamined: Baptism and Christian Marriage in Early Sixteenth-Century Mexico." *Hispanic American Historical Review* 73, no. 3 (1993): 453–80.

Clune, John James. "A Cuban Convent in the Age of Enlightened Reform: The Observant Franciscan Community of Santa Clara of Havana, 1768–1808." *The Americas* 57 (Jan. 2001): 309–28.

Cook, Alexandra, and Noble David. *Good Faith and Truthful Ignorance: A Case of Transatlantic Bigamy.* Durham: Duke University Press, 1991.

Cook, Noble David. *Born to Die: Disease and New World Conquest, 1492–1650.* New York: Cambridge University Press, 1998.

Couturier, Edith. "'For the Greater Service of God,': Opulent Foundations and Women's Philanthropy in Colonial Mexico." In *Lady Bountiful Revisited: Women, Philanthropy, and Power,* edited by Kathleen D. McCarthy. New Brunswick: Rutgers University Press, 1990.

―――. "Women in a Noble Family: The Mexican Counts of Regla, 1750–1830." In *Latin American Women: Historical Perspectives,* edited by Asunción Lavrin, 130–45. Westport: Greenwood Press, 1978.

Curtain, Phillip. *The African Slave Trade.* Madison: University of Wisconsin Press, 1969.

Cypress, Sandra Messinger. *La Malinche in Mexican Literature from History to Myth.* Austin: University of Texas Press, 1991.

Deeds, Susan M. "Double Jeopardy: Indian Women in Jesuit Missions of Nueva Vizcaya." In *Indian Women of Early Mexico,* edited by Susan Schroeder, Stephanie Wood, and Robert Haskett, 255–72. Norman: University of Oklahoma Press, 1997.

Diaz de Castillo Bernal. *The Conquest of New Spain.* New York: Penguin 1986.

Dillard, Heath. *Daughters of the Reconquest: Women in Castilian Town Society, 1100–1300.* New York: Cambridge University Press. 1984.

Doenges, Catherine. "Sources and Speculations Concerning Women's Activity in Provincial Colonial Mexico." *Urban History Workshop Review* 2 (Spring 1994): 17–24.

Dueñas-Vargas, Guiomar. "Gender, Race and Class: Illegitimacy and Family Life in Santafé Nuevo Reino de Granada, 1770–1810." Ph.D diss., University of Texas-Austin, 1995.

Dunn, Alvis E. "A Cry at Daybreak: Death, Disease, and Defense of Community in a Highland Ixil-Mayan Village." *Ethnohistory* 42 (Fall 1995): 595–606.

Erauso, Catalina de. *Lieutenant Nun: Memoir of a Basque Transvestite in the New World.* Boston: Beacon, 1996.

Espejo-Ponce Hunt, and Matthew Restall. "Work, Marriage, and Status: Maya Women of Colonial Yucatan." In *Indian Women of Early Mexico,* edited by Susan Schroeder, Stephanie Wood, and Robert Haskett. Norman: University of Oklahoma Press, 1997.

Etienne Mona, and Eleonore Leacock, eds. *Women and Colonization, Anthropological Perspectives.* New York: Praeger, 1980.

Few, Martha. *Women Who Live Evil Lives: Gender, Religion, and the Politics of Power in Colonial Guatemala.* Austin: University of Texas Press, 2002.

Flusche, Della M., and Eugene H. Korth. *Forgotten Females: Women of African and Indian Descent in Colonial Chile, 1535–1800.* Detroit: Blame Ethridge, 1983.

Gallagher, Ann Miriam. "The Indian Nuns of Mexico City's Monasterio of Corpus Christi, 1724–1821." In *Latin American Women: Historical Perspectives,* edited by Asunción Lavrin, 150–72. Westport: Greenwood Press, 1978.

Garza Carvaja, Federico. *Perceptions of Manliness in Andalucia and México, 1561–1699.* Amsterdam: Amsterdamse Historische Reeks, 2000.

Gauderman, Kimberly. *Women's Lives in Colonial Quito: Gender, law, and Economy in Spanish America.* Austin: University of Texas Press, 2003.

Gillespie, Susan D. *The Aztec Kings: The Construction of Rulership in Mexico History.* Tucson: University of Arizona Press, 1989.

Gosner, Kevin. "Women, Rebellion, and the Moral Economy of Maya Peasants in Colonial Mexico." In *Indian Women of Early Mexico,* edited by Susan Schroeder, Stephanie Wood, and Robert Haskett, 217–30. Norman: University of Oklahoma Press, 1997.

Graziano, Frank. *Wounds of Love: The Mystical Marriage of Saint Rose of Lima.* New York: Oxford University Press, 2004.

Grunberg, Bernard. "The Origins of the Conquistadors of Mexico City." *Hispanic American Historical Review* 74 (1994): 260–73.

Gruzinski, Serge. "The Ashes of Desire: Homosexuality in Mid-Seventeenth-Century New Spain." In *Infamous Desire: Male Homosexuality in Colonial Latin America,* edited by Pete Sigal. Chicago: University of Chicago Press, 2003.

———. "Individualization and Acculturation: Confession among the Nahua of Mexico from the Sixteenth to the Eighteenth Century." In *Sexuality and Marriage in Colonial Latin America,* edited by Asunción Lavrin. Lincoln: University of Nebraska Press, 1989.

Gutierrez, Ramón A. *When Jesus Came, the Corn Mothers Went Away: Marriage Sexuality and Power in New Mexico, 1500–1846.* Stanford: Stanford University Press, 1991.

Guy, Donna, and Thomas E. Sheridan. *Contested Ground: Comparative Frontiers on the Northern and Southern Edges of the Spanish Empire.* Tucson: University of Arizona Press, 1998.

Haskett, Robert. "Activist or Adulteress? The Life and Struggle of Doña Josefa María of Tepoztlan." In *Indian Women of Early Mexico,* edited by Susan Schroeder, Stephanie Wood, and Robert Haskett, 145–64. Norman: University of Oklahoma Press, 1997.

Higgins, Kathleen J. *"Licentious Liberty" in a Brazilian Gold-Mining Region: Slavery, Gender, and Social Control in Eighteenth-Century Sabará, Minas Gerais.* University Park: Pennsylvania State University Press, 1999.

Higgs, David. "Tales of Two Carmelites: Inquisitorial Narratives from Portugal and Brazil." In *Infamous Desire: Male Homosexuality in Colonial Latin America,* edited by Pete Sigal, 152–67. Chicago: University of Chicago Press, 2003.

Himmerich y Valencia, Robert. *The Encomenderos of New Spain, 1521–1555.* Austin: University of Texas Press, 1991.

Holler, Jacqueline. "The Spiritual and Physical Ecstasies of a Sixteenth-Century Beata." In *Colonial Lives: Documents on Latin American History, 1550–1850,* edited by Richard Boyer and Geoffrey Spurling, 77–100. New York: Oxford University Press, 2000.

Horton, Anore. "Constraint, Coercion, and Creation: Women's Migration and Mestizaje in Colonial Spanish America." In *New Perspectives on Women and Migration in Colonial Latin America,* edited by Anore Horton, 47–57. Princeton: Princeton University Press, 2001.

Hunefeld, Christine. *Paying the Price of Freedom: Family and Labor among Lima's Slaves, 1800–1854.* Berkeley: University of California Press, 1994.

Ibsen, Kristine. *Women's Spiritual Autobiography in Colonial Spanish America.* Gainesville: University Press of Florida, 1999.

Johnson, Lyman L. "Dangerous Words, Provocative Gestures, and Violent Acts." In *The Faces of Honor: Sex, Shame, and Violence in Colonial Latin America,* edited by Lyman L.

Johnson and Sonya Lipsett-Rivera. Albuquerque: University of New Mexico Press, 1998.

———, and Sonya Lipsett-Rivera, eds. *The Faces of Honor: Essays on Colonial Latin America.* Albuquerque: University of New Mexico Press, 1998.

Kanter, Deborah E. "Native Female Land Tenure and Its Decline in Mexico, 1750–1900." *Ethnohistory* 42 (Fall 1995): 607–16.

Karttunen, Frances. "Rethinking Malinche." In *Indian Women of Early Mexico,* edited by Susan Schroeder, Stephanie Wood, and Robert Haskett. Norman: University of Oklahoma Press, 1997.

Kellogg, Susan. "From Parallel and Equivalent to Separate but Unequal: Tenochca Mexica Women, 1500–1700." In *Indian Women of Early Mexico,* edited by Susan Schroeder, Stephanie Wood, and Robert Haskett, 123–44. Norman: University of Oklahoma Press, 1997.

———. "Indigenous Testaments of Early-Colonial Mexico City: Testifying to Gender Differences." In *Dead Giveaways: Indigenous Testaments of Colonial Mesoamerica and the Andes,* edited by Susan Kellogg and Matthew Restall, 37–58. Salt Lake City: University of Utah Press, 1998.

———. *Law and the Transformation of Aztec Culture, 1500–1700.* Norman: University of Oklahoma Press, 1995.

———. "The Woman's Room: Some Aspects of Gender Relations in Tenochtitlán in the Late Prehispanic Period." *Ethnohistory* 42, no. 4 (1995): 563–76.

Klein, Cecelia F. "Fighting with Femininity: Gender and War in Aztec Mexico." In *Gender Rhetorics: Postures of Dominance and Submission in History,* edited by Richard Trexler. Binghamton: Medieval and Renaissance Texts and Studies, 1994.

Kordi, Eugene H., and Della M. Flusche. "Dowry and Inheritance in Colonial Spanish America: Peninsular Law and Chilean Practice." *The Americas* 43 (April 1987): 395–410.

Kuznesof, Elizabeth. "A History of Domestic Service in Spanish America, 1492–1980." In *Muchachas No More: Household Workers in Latin America and the Caribbean,* edited by Elsa M. Chaney and Mary Garcia Castro. Philadelphia: Temple University Press, 1989.

Lavrin, Asunción. "Female Religious." In *Cities and Society in Colonial Latin America,* edited by Louisa S. Hoberman and Susan M. Socolow, 165–95. Albuquerque: University of New Mexico Press, 1986.

———. "Indian Brides of Christ: Creating New Spaces for Indigenous Women in New Spain." *Mexican Studies* (Summer 1999): 225–60.

———, ed. *Latin American Women: Historical Perspectives.* Westport: Greenwood Press, 1978.

———. *Sexuality and Marriage in Colonial Latin America.* Lincoln: University of Nebraska Press, 1989.

———. "Sexuality in Colonial Mexico: A Church Dilemma." In *Sexuality and Marriage in Colonial Latin America,* edited by Asunción Lavrin, 47–95. Lincoln: University of Nebraska Press, 1989.

———. "Vida Conventual: Rasgos Históricos." In *Sor Juana y su Mundo: una Mirada Actual,* edited by Sara Poot Herrera, 33–91. Mexico: Universidad del Claustro de Sor Juana, 1995.

———. "Women in Colonial Mexico." In *The Oxford History of Mexico,* edited by Michael C. Meyer and William H. Beezley, 49–75. New York: Oxford University Press, 2000.

———. "Women in Spanish American Colonial Society." In *The Cambridge History of*

Latin America, edited by Leslie Bethell, 321–56. New York: Cambridge University Press, 1984.

———, and Edith Couturier. "Dowries and Wills: A View of Women's Socioeconomic Role in Colonial Guadalajara and Puebla, 1640–1790." *Hispanic American Historical Review* 59 (May 1979): 280–304.

Lewin, Linda. "Natural and Spurious Children in Brazilian Inheritance Law from Colony to Empire: A Methodological Essay." *The Americas* 11 (Jan. 1992): 351–96.

———. *Surprise Heirs I: Illegitimacy, Patrimonial Rights, and Legal Nationalism in Luso Brazilian Inheritance, 1750–1821*. Stanford: Stanford University Press, 2003

Lipsett-Rivera, Sonya. "The Intersection of Rape and Marriage in Late-Colonial and Early National Mexico." *Colonial Latin American Historical Review* 6 (Fall 1997): 559–90.

———. "A Slap in the Face of Honor." In *The Faces of Honor: Sex, Shame, and Violence in Colonial Latin America*, edited by Lyman L. Johnson and Sonya Lipsett-Rivera, 179–200. Albuquerque, University of New Mexico Press, 1998.

Lockhart, James. *The Men of Cajamarca: A Social and Bibliographical Study of the First Conquerors of Peru*. Austin: University of Texas Press, 1972.

———. *Spanish Peru, 1532–1560: A Social History*. Madison: University of Wisconsin Press, 1968.

———, and Enrique Otte, eds. *Letters and People of the Spanish Indies: The Sixteenth Century*. New York: Cambridge University Press, 1976.

Lokken, Paul. "Marriage as Slave Emancipation in Seventeenth-Century Guatemala." *The Americas* 58 (Oct. 2001): 175–200.

Loreto López, Loreta. "The Devil, Women, and the Body in Seventeenth-Century Puebla Convents." *The Americas* 59 (Oct. 2002): 221–34.

Martin, Luis. *Daughters of the Conquistadores: Women of the Viceroyalty of Peru*. Dallas: Southern Methodist University Press, 1983.

Martinez Alier, Verena. *Marriage, Class and Colour in Nineteenth-Century Cuba: A Study of Racial Attitudes and Sexual Values in a Slave Society*. New York: Cambridge University Press, 1974.

McCaa, Robert. "Gustos de los Padres, Inclinaciones de los Novios y Reglas de una Feria Nupcial Colonial: Parral, 1770–1814." *Historia Mexicana* 40, no. 4 (1991): 579–614.

McClintock, Anne. *Imperial Leather: Race, Gender, and Sexuality in the Colonial Contest*. New York: Routledge, 1995.

McKnight, Kathryn Joy. *The Mystic of Tunja: The Writings of Madre Castillo, 1671–1742*. Amherst: University of Massachusetts Press, 1997.

Metcalf, Alida C. "Searching for the Slave Family in Colonial Brazil: A Reconstruction from Sao Paulo." *Journal of Family History* 16, no. 3 (1991): 283–97.

———. "Women and Means: Women and Family Property in Colonial Brazil." *Journal of Social History* 24 (Winter 1990): 277–98.

Mills Kenneth, and William B. Taylor, eds. *Colonial Spanish America: A Documentary History*. Wilmington: Scholarly Resources, 1998.

Morner, Magnus. *Race Mixture in the History of Latin America*. New York: Little, Brown, 1967.

Mott, Luiz. "Crypo-Sodomites in Colonial Brazil. " In *Infamous Desire: Male Homosexuality in Colonial Latin America*, edited by Pete Sigal, 168–96. Chicago: University of Chicago Press, 2003.

Myers, Kathleen Ann. *Neither Saints nor Sinners: Writing the Lives of Women in Spanish America.* New York: Oxford University Press, 2003.

———, and Amanda Powell. *A Wild Country Out in the Garden. The Spiritual Journals of a Colonial Mexican Nun.* Bloomington: Indiana University Press, 1999.

Nash, June. "Aztec Women: The Transition from Status to Class to Empire and Colony." In *Women and Colonization: Anthropological Perspectives,* edited by Mona Etienne and Eleonore Leacock, 134–85. New York: Praeger, 1980.

Nazzari, Muriel. "Concubinage in Colonial Brazil: The Inequalities of Race, Class, and Gender." *Journal of Family History* 21 (April 1996): 107–24.

———. *Disappearance of the Dowry: Women, Families, and Social Change in Sao Paulo, Brazil, 1600–1900.* Stanford: Stanford University Press, 1991.

———. "An Urgent Need to Conceal." In *The Faces of Honor: Sex, Shame, and Violence in Colonial Latin America,* edited by Lyman L. Johnson and Sonya Lipsett-Rivera, 103–26. Albuquerque, University of New Mexico Press, 1998.

Nizza da Silva, Maria Beatriz. "Divorce in Colonial Brazil: The Case of Sao Paulo." In *Sexuality and Marriage in Colonial Latin America,* edited by Asunción Lavrin, 313–40. Lincoln: University of Nebraska Press, 1989.

Offutt, Leslie S. "Women's Voices from the Frontier: San Esteban de Nueva Tlaxcala in the Late Eighteenth Century." In *Indian Women of Early Mexico,* edited by Susan Schroeder, Stephanie Wood, and Robert Haskett. Norman: University of Oklahoma Press, 1997.

Paz, Octavio. *The Labyrinth of Solitude.* New York: Grove Press, 1985.

———. *Sor Juana; or, The Traps of Faith.* Cambridge: Harvard University Press, 1988.

Perry, Mary Elizabeth. "From Convent to Battlefield: Cross-Dressing and Gendering the Self in the New World of Imperial Spain." In *Queer Iberia: Sexualities, Cultures, and Crossing from the Middle Ages to the Renaissance,* edited by Josiah Blackmore and Gregory S. Hutcheson, 394–419. Durham: Duke University Press, 1999.

———. *Gender and Disorder in Early Modern Seville.* Princeton: Princeton University Press, 1990.

Pescador, Javier. "Vanishing Woman: Female Migration and Ethnic Identity in Late-Colonial Mexico City." *Ethnohistory* 42 (Fall 1995): 617–26.

Premo, Bianca. "From the Pockets of Women: The Gendering of the Mita, Migration and Tribute in Colonial Chucuito, Peru." *The Americas* 57 (July 2000): 63–94.

Restall, Matthew, and Pete Sigal. "'May They Not Be Fornicators Equal to These Priests': Postconquest Yucatec Maya Sexual Attitudes." *UCLA Historical Journal* 12 (1992): 91–121.

Restall, Matthew. "Black Conquistadors: Armed Africans in Early Spanish America." *The Americas* 57 (Oct. 2000): 171–206.

———. "'He Wished It in Vain': Subordination and Resistance in Post-Conquest Yucatan." *Ethnohistory* 42 (Fall 1995): 577–94.

———. *The Maya World: Yucatec Culture and Society, 1550–1850.* Stanford: Stanford University Press, 1997

Robertson, Claire. "Africa into the Americas? Slavery and Women, the Family, and the Gender Division of Labor." In *More Than Chattel: Black Women and Slavery in the Americas,* edited by David Barry Gaspar and Darlene Clark Hine. Bloomington: Indiana University Press, 1996.

Russell-Wood, A. J. R. "Female and Family in the Economy and Society of Colonial

Brazil." In *Latin American Women: Historical Perspectives*, edited by Asunción Lavrin, 60–100. Westport: Greenwood Press, 1978.

Salomon, Frank. "Indian Women of Early Colonial Quito as Seen through Their Testaments." *The Americas* 44 (Jan. 1988): 325–41.

Sanchez, Magdalena S. *The Empress, the Queen and the Nun: Women and Power at the Court of Philip III of Spain*. Baltimore: Johns Hopkins University Press, 1998.

Schroeder, Susan. "The Noblewomen of Chalco." *Estudios de Cultura. Náhuatl* 22 (1992): 45–86.

Schurz, William Lyle. *This New World: The Civilization of Latin America*. New York: E. P. Dutton, 1954.

Scott, Joan W. "Gender: A Useful Category of Historical Analysis." *American Historical Review* 91 (Dec. 1986): 1053–75.

Seed, Patricia. *To Love, Honor, and Obey in Colonial Mexico: Conflicts over Marriage Choice, 1574–1821*. Stanford: Stanford University Press, 1988.

Shea, John Gilmary. *Little Pictorial Lives of the Saints*. New York: Benzinger, 1878.

Sigal, Pete. *From Moon Goddesses to Virgins: The Colonization of Yucatecan Maya Sexual Desire*. Austin: University of Texas Press, 2000.

———. "Gendered Power, the Hybrid Self, and Homosexual Desire in Late Colonial Yucatan." In *Infamous Desire: Male Homosexuality in Colonial Latin America*, edited by Pete Sigal, 102–33. Chicago: University of Chicago Press, 2003.

———, ed. *Infamous Desire: Male Homosexuality in Colonial Latin America*. Chicago: University of Chicago Press, 2003.

Silverblatt, Irene. "Lessons of Gender and Ethnohistory in Meso-America." *Ethnohistory* 42 (Fall 1995): 3399–650.

———. *Moon, Sun and Witches: Gender Ideologies and Class in Inca and Colonial Peru*. Princeton: Princeton University Press, 1987.

———. "'The Universe Has Turned Inside Out. . . . There Is No Justice for Us Here': Andean Women under Spanish Rule." In *Women and Colonization, Anthropological Perspectives*, edited by Mona Etienne and Eleanor Leacock, 140–85. New York: Praeger, 1980.

Socolow, Susan M. "Acceptable Partners: Marriage Choice in Colonial Argentina, 1778–1810." In *Sexuality and Marriage in Colonial Latin America*, edited by Asunción Lavrin. Lincoln: University of Nebraska Press, 1989.

———. "Women and Crime: Buenos Aires, 1757–97." *Journal of Latin American Studies* 12 (May 1980): 39–54.

———. "Women and Migration in Colonial Latin America." In Anore Horton, *New Perspectives on Women and Migration in Colonial Latin America*, edited by Anore Horton, 1–20. Princeton: Princeton University Press, 2001.

———. *The Women of Colonial Latin America*. New York: Cambridge University Press, 2000.

———. "Women of the Buenos Aires Frontier 1740–1810 (or, the Gaucho Turned Upside Down)." In *Contested Ground: Comparative Frontiers on the Northern and Southern Edges of the Spanish Empire*, edited by Donna Guy and Thomas E. Sheridan, 67–82. Tucson: University of Arizona Press, 1998.

Soeiro, Susan A. "The Feminine Order in Colonial Bahia, Brazil: Economic, Social, and Demographic Implications, 1677–1800." In *Latin American Women: Historical Perspectives*, edited by Asunción Lavrin, 173–97. Westport: Greenwood Press, 1978.

Sousa, Lisa Mary. "Women and Crime in Colonial Oaxaca: Evidence of Complementary Gender Roles in Mixtec and Zapotec Societies." In *Indian Women of Early Mexico*, edited by Susan Schroeder, Stephanie Wood, and Robert Haskett, 199–216. Norman: University of Oklahoma Press, 1997.

Sponsler, Lucy A. "Women in Spain: Medieval Law versus Epic Literature." *Revista de Eestudios Hispánicos* 7 (Oct. 1973): 427–48.

Spores, Ronald. "Mixteca *Cacicas:* Status, Wealth, and the Political Accommodation of Native Elite Women in Early Colonial Oaxaca." In *Indian Women of Early Mexico*, edited by Susan Schroeder, Stephanie Wood, and Robert Haskett. Norman: University of Oklahoma Press, 1997.

Spurling, Geoffrey. "Honor, Sexuality, and the Colonial Church." In *The Faces of Honor: Sex, Shame, and Violence in Colonial Latin America*, edited by Lyman L. Johnson and Sonya Lipsett-Rivera, 112–29. Albuquerque: University of New Mexico Press, 1998.

———. "Under Investigation for the Abominable Sin: Damian de Morales Stands Accused of Attempting to Seduce Anton de Tierra de Congo." In *Colonial Lives: Documents on Latin American History, 1550–1850*, edited by Richard Boyer and Geoffrey Spurling, 112–29. New York: Oxford University Press, 2000.

Stark, David M. "Discovering the Invisible Puerto Rican Slave Family: Demographic Evidence from the Eighteenth Century." *Journal of Family History* 21 (Oct. 1996): 395–418.

Stavig, Ward. "Political 'Abomination' and Private Reservation: The Nefarious Sin, Homosexuality, and Cultural Values in Colonial Peru." In *Infamous Desire: Male Homosexuality in Colonial Latin America*, edited by Pete Sigal, 134–51. Chicago: University of Chicago Press, 2003.

———. *The World of Tupac Amaru*. Lincoln: University of Nebraska Press, 1999.

Stern, Steve J. *The Secret History of Gender.* Chapel Hill: University of North Carolina Press, 1995.

Sweet, David G., and Gary B. Nash, eds. *Struggle and Survival in Colonial America*. Berkeley: University of California Press, 1981.

Taylor, William. *Drinking, Homicide and Rebellion in Colonial Mexican Villages*. Stanford: Stanford University Press, 1979.

———. *Magistrates of the Sacred: Priests and Parishioners in Eighteenth-Century Mexico*. Stanford: Stanford University Press, 1996.

Trexler, Richard C. "Gender Subordination and Political Hierarchy in Pre-Hispanic America." In *Infamous Desire: Male Homosexuality in Colonial Latin America*, edited by Pete Sigal, 70–101. Chicago: University of Chicago Press, 2003.

———. *Sex and Conquest: Gendered Violence, Political Order, and the European Conquest of the Americas*. Ithaca: Cornell University Press, 1995.

Twinam, Ann. "Honor, Sexuality and Illegitimacy in Colonial Spanish America." In *Sexuality and Marriage in Colonial Latin America*, edited by Asunción Lavrin, 118–55. Lincoln: University of Nebraska Press, 1989.

———. "The Negotiation of Honor." In *The Faces of Honor: Sex, Shame, and Violence in Colonial Latin America*, edited by Lyman L. Johnson and Sonya Lipsett-Rivera, 103–26. Albuquerque: University of New Mexico Press, 1998.

———. *Public Lives, Private Secrets: Gender, Honor, Sexuality and Illegitimacy in Colonial Spanish America*. Stanford: Stanford University Press, 1999.

Van Deusen, Nancy E. *Between the Sacred and the Worldly: The Institutional and Cultural Practice of Recogimiento in Colonial Lima*. Stanford: Stanford University Press, 2002.

———. "Determining the Boundaries of Virtue: The Discourse of *Recogimiento* among

Women in Seventeenth-century Lima." *Journal of Family History* 22 (Oct. 1997): 373–89.

———. "Wife of My Soul and Heart and All My Solace." In *Colonial Lives: Documents on Latin American History 1550–1850*, edited by Richard Boyer and Geoffrey Spurling. New York: Oxford University Press, 2000.

Vega, Garcilaso de la. *Royal Commentaries of the Incas and General History of Peru*. Austin: University of Texas Press, 1966.

Wightman, Ann M. *Indigenous Migration and Social Change: The Forasteros of Cuzco, 1570–1720*. Durham: Duke University Press, 1990.

Wood, Stephanie. "Adopted Saints: Christian Images in Nahua Testaments of Late Colonial Toluca." *The Americas* 47 (Jan. 1991): 259–93.

Zulawski, Ann. *They Eat from Their Labor: Work and Social Change in Colonial Bolivia*. Pittsburgh: Pittsburgh University Press, 1995.

———. "Social Differentiation, Gender, and Ethnicity: Urban Indian Women in Colonial Bolivia, 1640–1725." *Latin American Research Review* 25, no. 2 (1990): 93–114.

6

The History of Women
in the United States to 1865

KATHLEEN BROWN

In this essay I explore what the history of women in the United States might look like from a global perspective. What aspects of women's lives most lend themselves to being studied in a global context? How do global events and forces affect the lives of even the most domestically situated women? Where and how might we trace the consequences of global processes shaping the histories of Euro-American, Native American, and African American women? How do differences in these women's lives reflect different global paths to North America?

Global history seems especially well suited to studying the period in which early modern Europe "discovered" the wider worlds of West Africa, India, and South and North America, and African, Native American, and European people came into regular contact. It is less obvious what a global approach to the early national and antebellum United States might look like, a period for which the internal domestic politics of a nation state rather than global forces have defined historians' approaches. This has been especially true when women are the subjects because their lives have only recently been connected to national politics, let alone those of the world.

Keeping a focus on the period up to the Civil War, this essay moves chronologically and thematically from the point at which Native American women's "global" networks begin to include Europeans to the rise of a Euro-American female population whose labor, consumption of material goods, and participation in print culture made them part of global processes even as they continued to develop ever-stronger ties to local communities. It also examines the paths by which West African women became part of the plantation economies and communities of southern colonies and then analyzes the group of women who would seem least susceptible to being studied from a global perspective—native-born white women whose daily household relations and extra-local concerns reveal identities that are the product of global processes. Finally, it speculates about the ways gender refracts and conditions the experience of and participation in the global. What we learn about women in the United States needs to be placed in the context of how they compare to men of their racial, ethnic, and class position. Global conditions influence the symbolic meanings and lived experiences of gender at even the most local level, just as gender helps define what we consider local and global.

Global Paths, Global Networks

European exploration and trade began along the West African coast in the early fifteenth century, eventually reaching the Atlantic islands, the Caribbean, and the American continents. At each location, European men were emissaries of European culture and the vectors of European interest, followed eventually by settler societies to the Americas that included small numbers of European women. Everywhere they went, European men wrote texts and produced images of native people that rooted their racial and ethnic otherness in gendered bodies and gendered behaviors that appeared unfamiliar to European eyes. Especially in places where the ratio of European men to European women was high—everywhere at first contact, at military outposts, and on the fur-trade frontier—European men circumvented or flagrantly violated religiously informed sexual mores, creating new sexual and racial subcultures.

The demand for labor that accompanied the European desire to extract wealth—metallurgical and agricultural—from new territories became the impetus for coercing the servitude of Native Americans and eventually for transporting West Africans. Initially, much of the transplanted and exploited labor was male, although Native American and West African women were hardly exempt; from the beginning, Europeans clearly expected them to supply agricultural labor and sexual services. Sexual contacts between the men who dominated European explorations and commercial ventures and indigenous women led to demographic changes of different magnitudes throughout the Atlantic basin. Near Portuguese trade outposts on the coast of West Africa and West Central Africa, small populations of mixed-race people testified to European men's liaisons with West African women. In Spanish and French America, mestizo and métis populations arising from European male–indigenous female unions became significant culturally as well as demographically within a few decades after initial contact. With few exceptions—notably that of the English–Native American encounter—the initial contacts between Europeans and people indigenous to the Americas conformed to this pattern of male westward exploration accompanied by sexual intimacy with native women.

NATIVE AMERICAN WOMEN

Before the arrival of Spanish, French, and eventually English explorers, Native American women participated in local agricultural economies that had political and economic ties to Native American groups across the continent. In the complex societies of Mexico and South and Central America, goods from thousands of miles away testify to the political and diplomatic networks that connected the region. Even in North America, home to seven to ten million indigenous people and where economies tended to be more regional and less specialized, long-distance trade brought goods like copper from the Great Lakes to the mound-building cultures of the Ohio and Illinois river valleys as well as to Powhatan Indians in coastal Virginia. In the Southwest, where Spanish conquistadors and clerics attempted to establish a permanent presence, women and men had a distinct division of labor. Among the Pueblo, while men planted and tended crops, women built houses, harvested plants, ground corn, and made pottery. In Cofitachequi, possibly located near Camden, South Carolina, the exploring party of Hernando De Soto encountered an indigenous woman *werowance* (chief) who presented the strangers with gifts of clothing and freshwater pearls before they kidnapped her. In the eastern woodland societies of North America, where English traders and settlers first made sustained contact with Native Americans, women typically planted and tended corn, beans, and squash during the spring and summer; gathered other items of food from the wild; and processed meat and skins provided by male hunters. Throughout the year they manufactured vessels, baskets, kitchen utensils, jewelry, clothing, and other household items; in some cultures they also provided housing materials. Many of these items, including furs, surplus corn, jewelry, baskets, and wampum, were part of an extensive extra-local trade and gift exchange that linked different Indian groups to their neighbors, who might in turn trade with groups even further away.

Native American women supplied labor that was critical not only to daily subsistence but also to the political and diplomatic alliances, the economic networks, and the clan and kin group identities that gave boundaries to different Indian cultures and ensured their survival. Native American women in certain eastern woodland groups such as the Cherokee and the Iroquois had a voice in political and military matters, including the fate of captives, which grew out of their connection to the land and its products. Their management of internal demands for food, shelter, and clothing may thus have grounded their authority to speak about the external pressures and dangers facing their people as well. Among southwestern people, where agricultural production filled a greater proportion of subsistence needs and skilled craftspeople wove and made pottery, women had less political and diplomatic influence and were more likely to play informal diplomatic roles through hospitality.

With the arrival of predominantly male bands of Spaniards, French and English explorers, and religious missionaries, Indian women engaged in a process of creative adaptation that allowed their cultures to make dynamic responses to the newcomers. These adaptations were often a mixture of initiative and coercion, cultural preservation and innovation. This is not to say that men did not engage in similar or at least comparable processes of creative adaptation. Indeed, the situations that brought Native American men and women into contact with European men had important areas of overlap. Trade and hospitality, for example, involved both Indian men and women, although with some differences. While Indian men often assumed roles as traders, warriors, and guides, Indian women were likely to be providers of hospitality, sexual and otherwise, or to become wives and translators.

One important example of that gender dynamic can be found in French Canada, where Indian women provided French coureurs de bois with vital contacts to fur-trading communities. Marrying Indian women was in these early years a desirable means of entering into Indian social and economic networks. Many alliances became long-standing relationships, known as *mariages du pays,* and produced Franco-Indian children poised to mediate the fur trade in the next generation. Elsewhere in North America, women provided sexual hospitality to European guests as they would have done for Indian guests. Women also became unwitting participants, even victims, of Euro-Indian conflicts, as in the Spanish use of kidnapping and hostage-taking in the Southwest.

The exchange of Indian women sometimes became part of the common field of meanings that different European and American groups drew upon to communicate aggression and alliance, as in the initial phase of contact between Spaniards and Indians of the Texas borderlands, where the Spanish presence did not become full-fledged domination for several decades. The Spanish exchange of women for concessions or submission was part of the work of war, but Spaniards also frequently formed permanent sexual unions with Indian women in the Spanish custom of *barragania* (concubinage).[1]

Of all European groups, the English appear to have been the most reluctant to marry Indian wives, but some did have sexual unions with Indian women. Especially in commercial outposts such as the Hudson Bay Company, part of the northern Euro-Indian, fur-trade frontier, English men were as likely to form long-term relationships with Indian women as did their French fur-trading counterparts. For the most part, however, English men's restraint about crossing the cultural divide sexually appears in settlement areas rather than commercial outposts, where relationships with indigenous women promised no immediate advantage and indeed appeared transgressive in light of plans to transport English women and establish English families.

Everywhere in the Americas, epidemics followed the path of European first contacts with Native Americans. Disease wrought the greatest havoc upon Indian cultures and lives, forcing survivors to adapt hastily to the European presence and leaving them poorly equipped to deal with other culture changing conditions like trade and warfare. Massive depopulation caused by diseases like smallpox and influenza disrupted the passage of cultural knowledge across generations, thereby undermining a range of important sites of cultural identity, including religious rituals marking death and promoting religious and physical healing as well as others necessary to daily survival—planting, hunting, and harvesting. Many native women were thrust into the role of being full-time mourners, while others fell victim to disease. Trade and warfare followed quickly on the heels of disease, offering Native Americans opportunities to restructure their relationships with Europeans and Indian allies and also forcing great changes in Indian cultures.

Once larger numbers of European women arrived—in Mexico and Canada and on the eastern coast of North America—the radical potential of religion to transform Indians culturally as well as create venues for Indians and Europeans to engage in culture-making together was realized. Along the French Canadian contact zone, French Jesuits established mission towns but often found that the success of their religious message depended on their ability to use Indian concepts of spirituality to communicate Catholic theology. French Catholic nuns enjoyed particular success converting women and young girls at convent schools designed to spread the faith to indigenous people and serve the needs of transplanted European Catholics.

Investigating why indigenous women turned to Christianity and made it meaningful in their lives reminds us that native people selectively incorporated new religious practices in different ways and for different reasons. Kateri Tekakwitha, the young adopted Iroquois of the mid seventeenth century, provides an example of how native women engaged in creative adaptation to incorporate or even embrace Christianity. Such women were the leading edge of culture change that wed native traditions to selectively adopted spiritual imports. In Tekakwitha's case, Christian spirituality became a source of empowerment for a young native woman poorly equipped to succeed on Iroquois terms. Natalie Zemon Davis has similarly found that Amerindian women of the Northeast—Iroquois, Hurons, and Algonquian-speakers such as Montagnais, Algonquins, Abenakis, and Micmacs—"used the new religion to find a voice beyond that of a shaman's silent assistant, even while Jesuits were teaching them that wives were supposed to obey their husbands." Clearly, Christianity could give marginal native women a new source of authority even as they incorporated it in ways that compromised European missionary goals.[2]

Did most indigenous women welcome Christianity as Tekakwitha and her fellow converts did? Some historians argue persuasively that as guardians of traditions, which included matrilineality, ease of divorce, and female authority within longhouses and kin groups, indigenous women were wary of patriarchal messages of Catholicism that emphasized male leadership of nuclear family households, female subordination, and marital fidelity. In New France, New Spain, and British North America, native women joined the chorus of male voices that considered Christian missionaries to be unwelcome strangers who brought disease and death to native populations.[3]

In addition to the evidence that many women remained staunch traditionalists, there are other reasons why historians need to take the tales of female conversion, told by religious missionaries, with a grain of salt. For the same reasons that we can speak of a "gender frontier"—a powerful site of cultural encounter that called into question the meaning of nature, power, and order for both sides of the encounter—we need to approach European accounts of indigenous women's spiritual and behavioral transformations with a healthy dose of skepticism. Narratives about the transformations of the converted— from a so-called savage appearance to one modeled after European gender roles—provided missionaries with a useful way to communicate the impact of colonization and make an effective appeal for additional investment. One thinks, for example, of the Virginia Company's celebration of Pocahontas's transformation, publicized with an image of the indigenous convert wearing English clothing. There is also the French Jesuit Paul le Jeune's four-pronged plan for converting Indians to Catholicism and Frenchness. His goal was nothing less than a makeover for Indian women and Indian families; Indian women would adopt the manners, behavior, and appearance of pious French women, and Indian families would develop a European family structure (male authority, female fidelity, nuclear family household, and marriage for life). Telling tales of gender roles transformed through conversion was not simply an account of changing indigenous identities but of the power of European capital, religion, and ideas to change the nature of the so-called savage.[4]

In general, European Catholics, including nuns, had the greatest success converting indigenous people, but Protestant missions that included women missionaries also enjoyed some success. The interaction of German Moravians, a Protestant sect, and Pennsylvania Indians is suggestive of this pattern. German Moravian women worked closely with Mahican and Delaware women in mission communities in eighteenth-century Pennsylvania with great success compared to fellow Protestants, whose cooler religiosity resulted in fewer conversions throughout the Americas. The unusual amount of spiritual authority granted Moravian women, including their training as lay ministers, might account for why Moravian missions in Pennsylvania were among the most successful of any Protestant missionary effort in the Northeast. Between 1742 and 1764, Moravians baptized at least 282 Delaware and Mahican women and girls, and many more expressed interest in Christianity. During the same period, according to historian Jane Merritt, 229 men and boys were baptized, for a total of roughly 10 to 20 percent of the native populations of the area. Additional research is needed before historians can determine whether, as the Moravian case suggests, the gender of missionaries was a factor in the success of religious missions to Native Americans.[5]

AFRICAN WOMEN AND THE SLAVE TRADE

Among the migrations of people from Europe and Africa to the Americas, the transportation of enslaved Africans ranks as one of the most significant, demographically, economically, and culturally. That holds true for the history of women and gender. As historian David Eltis has so elegantly noted, before 1800 four out of every five female migrants to the Americas were African. A search for a typical woman, moving along global pathways to the Americas, would point in the direction of African women. The transatlantic slave trade, also an effective mover of men, was by far the most effective mover of women across the Atlantic in the period before 1800.[6]

When we narrow the frame to consider the forced stream of African migrants to British North America only—a much narrower stream than the overall diaspora to the Americas—the picture changes somewhat. By 1775 we can estimate roughly 150,000 female migrants from the British Isles had arrived in British North America, compared to roughly eighty thousand of their West African counterparts. Even if one excludes the growing numbers of Germans who inflated the totals of "white" migrants, West African women composed just over a third of the total migration of women to British North America. Building on Eltis's important observation, it becomes evident that North America differs from the rest of the Americas in the preponderance of European over West African female migrants.[7]

African women first crossed the Atlantic at the hands of Portuguese slavers and Spanish explorers, arriving in the Caribbean, Mexico, Central America, and South America. The impetus for importing African slaves began in the Mediterranean, where early sugar plantations required labor from distant sources to enable the large-scale production of a commodity valuable mainly in distant markets. Even before plantations took hold in the Americas, however, Africans in small numbers (and African women in even smaller numbers) traveled as slaves destined to perform the labor that Europeans had been unable or unwilling to coerce from Native Americans. In Mexico, an enslaved woman might have performed a variety of tasks, including cooking, gardening, and marketing, whereas in Brazil by the late sixteenth and early seventeenth centuries African women were used nearly interchangeably with men to produce and refine sugar for overseas markets. When Spanish conquistadors turned to the North American continent they brought Africans to Florida, where enslaved women engaged in a variety of agricultural tasks that included field labor and raising livestock as well as domestic work such as child care, cooking, laundering, cleaning, sewing, weaving, and midwifery.[8]

From its inception, the transatlantic slave trade bore the stamp of West and Central African participation in multiple global markets for inanimate commodities as well as for enslaved human beings. For centuries before the arrival of Portuguese traders in the 1440s, African merchants and leaders engaged in a lively and profitable trade in gold, spices, cloth, and slaves. Try as they might, Europeans were forced to negotiate with these powerful individuals if they hoped to reap predictable profits from the slave trade. Raiding and coercion of elite Africans who controlled the supply of slaves were ultimately self-defeating. Suppliers kept slaves off the market or offered them to European competitors willing to trade on African terms. There was also the centuries' old market for African slaves to the east—the sub-Saharan trade to Muslim markets—that continued to engage West African suppliers and reap them profits. This latter market featured the highest proportion of female slaves for sale. Of the European nations competing for most favored nation status, the Portuguese triumphed initially and provided most of the slaves to the Americas before the 1620s, followed by a brief period of domination by the Dutch and, eventually, by the successful slaving companies the English and French established at the end of the seventeenth century.[9]

If the slave trade owed part of its dynamic to West and Central African commercial experience, its demography reflected conflicting African and European ideas about female value. In general, African traders preferred to withhold female slaves from the transatlantic market for domestic use within their own societies or for the sub-Saharan trade, where they were highly valued among Muslim buyers. Many West African societies were also reluctant to part with women because of their value as agriculturists and mothers in societies that traced descent matrilineally. In contrast, most Europeans wanted slaves to perform agricultural labor they defined as the purview of adult males.

The unwillingness of sellers to give up women to the transatlantic market and the preference of buyers for adult male slaves combined to skew the sex ratio of slaves transported to the Americas for more than three centuries. Adult men consistently outnumbered adult women forced to cross the Atlantic in the holds of slave ships, and that predominance became more pronounced over time. During the seventeenth century, adult men represented 51 percent of all slaves arriving in the Americas while adult women counted for only 37 percent. By the nineteenth century the sex ratio of arriving adults was more heavily skewed (42 percent to 17 percent), although partially mediated by the presence of boys (25 percent) and girls (12 percent).[10]

Evidence of sex ratios for British North America, although spotty, conforms to the overall pattern of approximately thirty women for every hundred enslaved people arriving in British North American ports until the close of the legal slave trade in 1808. At first, enslaved Africans arrived in Virginia or South Carolina by way of the Caribbean. In Virginia, this meant that by the middle of the seventeenth century the proportion of African men to women was nearly equal, a remarkable fact when one considers the pronounced imbalance in the colony's English population. At century's end, when Virginia began to receive slaves from West Africa directly, the skewed sex ratio of the new arrivals created a significant surplus of enslaved men in the colony, perhaps as great as 180 to every one hundred women. A similar pattern in South Carolina disrupted the achievement of modest natural increase by the colony's Afro-Caribbean enslaved cowherds, woodsmen, and female livestock tenders and gardeners.

Although slave traders for the British southern colonies requested that two-thirds of their cargos be male throughout the eighteenth century, they never quite achieved that goal. Trading with merchants in the Bight of Biafra, Senegambia, and Angola, traders to Virginia accepted female slaves in greater numbers than their target ratio. South Carolina planters were somewhat closer to their target, but their trade with Angola and the Windward Coast similarly resulted in more women than they wanted. Displaying little reluctance, planters from both colonies bought African women and set them to work at agricultural tasks, as they did male slaves. By 1808, the date by which the transatlantic trade was officially closed in the United States, more than half a million enslaved Africans had been imported.[11]

During the seventeenth and early eighteenth centuries, Africans arriving in British North America were likely to be purchased by planters or their agents while still onboard ship or in holding areas, courthouses, or wharves onshore. By the nineteenth century, as northern slave states like Virginia began to supply the rest of the expanding South through the internal slave trade, the slave market became the hub of slave society, the place where planters and their buyers investigated and speculated on slave bodies and where slaves might try to intervene in their own destiny. Typically, buyers were white men who subjected enslaved men and women to humiliating physical examinations, checking their teeth and gums, their breasts, their genitalia, and their feet for evidence of disease and past history. But a few white women also participated in the transaction of information and cash at the slave market, provoking comment from more than one spectator on their lack of female delicacy and modesty, manifested in the ability to subject male slaves to examinations as probing and tactile as those performed by their male counterparts.[12]

Although scholars continue to debate whether newly arrived slaves felt as culturally isolated and alienated from each other as they did from their white captors, it is clear that once in the new world, small numbers of women impeded the rise of African American communities and cultures. This pattern was most extreme in parts of the Caribbean and Brazil, where the killing regime of sugar production inflicted high mortality (and thus family breakup), diminishing the ameliorating effects of enslaved people's formation of families and communities. High mortality also provoked the constant influx of newcomers who reafricanized fledgling creole communities.

In North America, especially in Florida, Virginia, Maryland, and the Carolinas, the demographic damage caused by high mortality and high rates of importation did not last as long as elsewhere in the Americas. By the mid eighteenth century, plantation communities in Virginia and Maryland began to display generational stability and coherence over time—exhibiting what scholars describe as growth by "natural increase"—subject always to the disruption of sale that distinguished the enslaved from their free laboring counterparts. As Jennifer Morgan has shown, however, the term *natural increase* obscures the politics of enslaved women's reproduction, including their reproductive value to their masters even during periods of heavy importation, the process of creolization (in which immigrant populations undergo culture change), and the importance of childbearing for sustaining the humanity of enslaved people. In South Carolina this population increase occurred only by the final decade of the eighteenth century as the large, enslaved populations concentrated on the region's lowcountry rice plantations approached balanced sex ratios.[13]

By the nineteenth century the enslaved population in the United States was reproducing itself, a fact that distinguishes this region from nearly all other New World slave societies, which were characterized by high mortality and continued importation of enslaved laborers from Africa. Indeed, with the official close of the transatlantic trade in 1808, slave traders relied upon this steady growth in population in the Upper South, most notably in Virginia, which became the supplier of slaves to the expanding plantation regime of the lower South and Southwest.

Gender and even motherhood made very little difference in the assignment of labor to slaves until the nineteenth century. Even then the vast majority of enslaved women performed agricultural tasks every bit as strenuous as those of their male counterparts. In Virginia and Maryland they hoed tobacco, with a significant proportion (one-third) entering into domestic labor only in the final quarter of the eighteenth century. In South Carolina, enslaved women in the eighteenth and nineteenth centuries repaired irrigation works, planted rice, tended paddies, harvested the mature rice, and performed the jarring labor of processing the grain with mortar and pestle. By the nineteenth century in the Lower South, enslaved women hoed, planted, and tended cotton, picking it and cleaning it once it was mature.

In all of these regions, white womanhood came with the expectation, although not always the reality, of being released from arduous, unladylike field labor. For white women poor enough to have to perform the work of slaves on a seasonal or occasional basis, reprieve frequently came at the hands of an enslaved woman, hired or purchased to allow the mistress of the house to direct her attentions to labor deemed more appropriate for one of her race. Thus the labor of female slaves became critical not only to agricultural production but also to the deceptive alignment of race and class in the antebellum South.

If different labor systems and ways of defining family lived on in African women's memories and stories, as they most certainly did, then plantation labor in North America jarred not because the work was agricultural or required bending over rows of plant beds for long hours with a hoe but because women generally did not have their own niche for agricultural labor as they did in West Africa. Nor could they easily connect it to a coherent set of domestic and household duties, as they would have done in many West African societies. Rather, in the North American colonies and later in the United States, enslaved women worked at many of the same tasks as their menfolk, with the same tools, in the same stifling weather, and subject to many of the same risks of accident, fatigue, disease, and cruel treatment. In sharp contrast to the West African agricultural labor they might have known, moreover, the work was not exclusive to women but performed by men and women alike, a situation that both sexes might have found disconcerting and perhaps even humiliating.[14]

As a labor system then, slavery appeared to efface many of the gender differences that defined global paths to North America and shaped slave-buyers' calculations about the human commodities they inspected in nineteenth-century slave markets. But that would be a misleading assessment based on a partial definition of the meaning of labor in a slave society. From as early as the seventeenth century, white slaveowners were aware of the challenges that enslaved women's biological reproduction could pose for the emerging legal category of slavery. Early legal definitions of enslavement placed women at the center, making slave status heritable through mothers. In calculating the value of female property, then, slave owners had to consider an enslaved woman's ability to produce new laborers. Although it often went un-recognized, her work caring for other enslaved people, men and children, was also clearly part of the value she added to the plantation labor force.

All of this needed to be balanced against what was, for most enslaved women, their prime value in the eyes of masters: the ability to perform agricultural labor. High infant mortality on rice plantations—reaching nearly 50 percent during the summer season—suggests that planters continued to calculate women's agricultural labor as more valuable than their ability to produce new slaves. By the nineteenth century, with a greater proportion (although still a minority) of enslaved women providing domestic labor, it is possible that planter interest in slave motherhood and the survival of enslaved children might have grown, at least for that portion of the domestic labor force. In general, enslaved African Americans reproduced themselves at greater rates than their slave counterparts elsewhere in the Atlantic Basin. That appears to have occurred as a consequence of a somewhat less brutal agricultural regime (little sugar was produced in North America compared to the Caribbean and South America) and a more healthful climate rather than as a result of better treatment by owners.[15]

EUROPEAN WOMEN AT HOME AND AS COLONISTS

Although students of American history often think of colonial New England as the typical colonial settlement, a global perspective reveals it to be unusual. The relatively equal numbers of men and women to migrate to New England during the 1630s' Great Migration, as it is known to historians, was atypical not only of most European migration to the New World but also of most English migration. Only Providence Island had as balanced a migration stream as New England. Not coincidentally, the Puritan beliefs of Providence Island migrants similarly presented strong motives for family migrations, thus attracting more women to the settlement. More typical of European transatlantic migration than Puritan New England and Providence Island was what used to be called "frontier" societies or "the West." These early settlements were characterized by the maleness of the European presence (true even for New England before it was transformed by the Great Migration of the 1630s), a lack of public institutions transported by the society sponsoring the migration, relatively undeveloped domestic economies, a tendency toward violence, a culture of sexual transgression, and a boomtown atmosphere.[16]

Conversely, New England's religious mission is often seen as unique among colonial settlements, providing a God-fearing foundation for the distinctive religious culture of the modern-day United States. The unusual gender balance of the migrant stream to New England lends some credence to this view of the region's exceptionalism. Most colonies, however, justified their ventures, including their commercial aspirations, with official proclamations of religious motives. Both New Spain and New France, for example, which preceded the New England settlement, justified their presence in the New World with religious mission.

Even confining one's view to British North America, the variety of religious visions and their imprint on colonial settlement patterns was impressive: English Puritans in New England; Dutch Protestants in New York and New Jersey; English Quakers and German Protestants in Pennsylvania; English and Irish Catholics in Maryland; Church of England Protestants in Virginia, the Carolinas, and Georgia; Jews in South Carolina and New York; and pockets of French Huguenots throughout the Colonies. In religiously motivated migrations the gender balance was often much closer to parity than in the migrant population at large. European family migrations like these were also culturally significant beyond their demographic impact.

Among European colonists, household demands traditionally defined both women's labor and their community identity. Women's duties in European and Euro-American households fell roughly into two categories: productive and reproductive labor. Productive labor included making the food and clothing consumed by the household as well as any surplus that might be exchanged or marketed. Reproductive labor centered on the important duties of bearing and rearing children and also included a wide range of services for household members, enabling them to continue being productive laborers in their own rights. Providing food, clean clothes, fresh bed linens, heat, water, a tidy household, and health care all helped to maintain the household labor force of children, servants, and adult men.

Women's household duties tended to make them less concerned with public matters than their menfolk. Household responsibilities, however, sometimes became the justification for women's public activities. Women from nearly all agricultural societies around the world, including Europe, participated in domestic markets for household goods produced by their labor. In the new American colonies the absence of local markets put women's household labor at one remove from public life, at least initially. Traditional production for the market found its earliest expression not only in domestic markets, which took some time to be established, but also in neighborly exchanges of butter, cloth, eggs, and other goods in the northern and midatlantic colonies. In southern colonies, where agriculture focused on staple crops for a global rather than local market, domestic production and local markets were even slower to appear. Female participation in the local economy, which emerged only gradually in North America, linked women to the public sphere of the market rather than to the public sphere of the polity, where men dominated.[17]

Euro-American women's household duties also justified their recourse to the law. Acting as deputy husbands, women might appear in court instead of absent men, a practice tolerated nearly without question during the seventeenth century in New England and the Chesapeake but less commonly during the eighteenth century. As widows with legal guardianship of children and rights to property, women also appeared in court to protect the interests of their families. In northern and southern colonies, however, the eighteenth century marked the growing disappearance of women from courtrooms and the equation of female gentility with privacy. Euro-American women of means would be far more likely to send an attorney or a male representative to court than to appear in person, leaving the courtroom to men, to a handful of less prosperous women, and to women accused of crimes. Even in New England, where populations of African Americans and detribalized Native Americans were relatively small compared to the Chesapeake and the Carolinas, this meant that women appearing in eighteenth-century courts were increasingly likely to be poor and darker-complected.[18]

As the people most intimately involved in the birth process, Euro-American women also played important community roles enforcing moral standards around premarital sex and illegitimate birth. Acting as midwives, some women solicited information from birthing women about the paternity of their illegitimate children, which they then transmitted to the court. Midwives thus played a vital legal role in perpetuating the transmission of property to blood heirs and in protecting the community from the financial support of single mothers and their illegitimate children.[19]

Different motives for migration and the resulting difference in demography led to dramatic differences in the lives of seventeenth-century Euro-American women. In New England, the migration of families and the goal of establishing a religious commonwealth created opportunities for women to enjoy some limited authority in the community. Puritans recognized the important role women played as helpmeets to husbands and as mothers, and they saw the family as the cornerstone of the social order, perhaps to a greater degree than their fellow English Protestants. As long as they met the rigorous standards for female behavior—piety, industry, marital fidelity, and contribution to family and community harmony—Puritan women might enjoy the respect of their community, eventually even playing an important role in enforcing sexual morality among other women.

There appears to have been little flexibility about these standards, however, as many women discovered to their dismay. Aggressive behavior, particularly verbal sparring, unruliness, or disobedience of a father, spouse, minister, or magistrate, might land a woman in court. Postmenopausal women with histories of conflict with their communities, especially those whose relationship to property threatened the family model for the transmission of wealth to male heirs, were the most frequent targets of witchcraft accusations and the most likely of the accused to be convicted. During "outbreaks" of witchcraft accusations, as during the Salem trials of 1692, the profile of the typical witch expanded, and younger women, pious women, and even men were at risk of being accused. Life in Puritan New England best suited women who valued ties to a religious community and had spiritual goals compatible with those prescribed for Puritan women. For women who marched to the beat of a different drummer morally, spiritually, or economically, Puritan New England was a potentially dangerous place to be.[20]

Women's industry and fertility were symbols of and material factors in the New England region's fabled success and prosperity. The skewed demography of the early 1630s soon gave way to unprecedented demographic growth, with families commonly producing upward of seven children. The longevity of New England colonists and the survival of their children combined to make New England the healthiest place in the English-speaking world during the seventeenth century. First-generation settlers could expect to live to a ripe old age: 71.8 if they were men and 70.8 if they were women. In the second generation, men born in New England averaged sixty-four years, and their female counterparts averaged just over sixty-one. Women's lower life expectancy reflected the risks of childbearing. If a New England woman survived its hazards, she had a better chance than her husband of surviving into her seventies.

The phenomenal population growth that characterized the Puritan demographic regime and to which women contributed so signally soon undermined the healthfulness and economic opportunity of the region. Within three generations the grandchildren of migrants had begun to feel the squeeze of land shortages, which in turn encouraged the expansion of the Euro-American population further inland and contributed to rising tensions with local Native Americans. By the eighteenth century, average life spans had begun to fall, and regular cycles of disease, including smallpox, became the rule. By the mid eighteenth century, New England resembled its English counterpart economically, socially, and epidemiologically, and the rise of religious diversity in the region had begun to erode its cultural distinctiveness.

In the southern colonies, life for Euro-American women was considerably different. The biggest differences for most English migrants were the loss of powerful political and religious institutions that enforced social order; skewed sex ratios that diminished the influence of the family (although the ideology of the family as a foundation for social order was still reproduced); a high demand for wives who would provide domestic comforts and establish the bonds of community; and the use of some Euro-American women in tobacco production. Even more pointed were the differences in life and death itself in the southern colonies. During the seventeenth century, the Chesapeake colonies had unprecedentedly high mortality rates, with average life expectancies of thirty-nine years for European and Euro-American women and forty-eight for men.

The low average life span for women reflected the impact of pregnancy on their ability to resist endemic diseases such as malaria. This fact combined with the late age of marriage for women, most of whom arrived as indentured servants in the first half of the century, low birth rates (only three to four surviving children among migrants), and high child mortality (some historians estimate that 40 to 55 percent of children died before their twentieth birthday) to delay the demographic and cultural stability of the region until the end of the century. By 1700 Euro-American sex ratios and mortality rates in the Chesapeake began to look more like those in England and to converge with those in New England. Most of the region's powerful planter families established themselves during this time by making careful matches calculated to consolidate wealth in the form of land and slaves.[21]

Even as Chesapeake lawmakers were struggling to overcome the destabilizing effects of skewed sex ratios and weak family formation, the colony's tobacco planters had begun importing African labor to perform the strenuous field labor. Efforts to secure slave labor in southern colonies like Maryland and Virginia coincided with efforts to encourage white family formation, leading to several legal developments. First, Virginia lawmakers drew distinctions between female populations for whom ideals of domestic labor applied, placing African women in the same tax category as men of all racial and ethnic backgrounds and exempting domestically employed English women from the tax. Second, lawmakers defined slavery as a condition that could be inherited by a child whose mother was a slave. This measure made the paternity of an enslaved woman's child—whether African or English, enslaved or free—irrelevant to the child's legal status.

Third, the colony cracked down on the sexual activity of English and Anglo-American women, setting harsh new punishments for those who bore children fathered by African or Indian men. Finally, at the beginning of the eighteenth century, the Virginia colony tried to define "white" and "black" legally to deal with the discrepancies between appearance, racial categories, and the conditions of freedom and bondage. Increasingly, the stigmas of strenuous agricultural labor and reputed sexual license shifted from poor white women, who had borne both of these as servants in the early seventeenth century, to African American women whose lives as slaves made achieving respectability in Euro-American terms difficult.[22]

In the midatlantic region of North America, the British arrived after other European groups had already made some cultural and material imprint on the landscape and relations with local Native Americans. The British latecomers, moreover, who migrated after 1660, were themselves more diverse religiously than their counterparts to the north or south. In New York, settled first by the Dutch, and in New Jersey and Delaware, where Swedish traders had already set up relationships with local Native Americans, the English grafted their own traditions onto an existing settler culture.

Sometimes the differences between these two waves of European tradition were striking, as in the case of Dutch and English marriage law. Under Dutch law, which was derived from Roman statute rather than common law, a Dutch woman could choose a *usus* marriage in which she retained her legal rights to buy, sell, bequeath property, and make contracts. Within these marriages, property was considered communal and wives were entitled to halves rather than thirds, as in the English tradition. Compared to her English counterpart, who was defined as a *feme covert*, a legal dependent of her husband, a Dutch woman who chose *usus* could engage in business pursuits on nearly equal footing with her husband. With the English takeover of New Netherlands in 1664, Dutch women lost the privileges of usus, with the consequence that the numbers of women appearing in court or on the rolls of merchants and proprietors of small businesses plummeted.[23]

Further south, the presence of English Quakers and German Protestants made for a distinctive mix of religious traditions nearly as diverse as that of New York City. The rich soils of the Delaware and Susquehanna river valleys, moreover, made it possible for farmers in the midatlantic to sustain themselves by growing grain and raising livestock, both for their own consumption and to supply colonies like those in the Caribbean and South Carolina, where staple-crop agriculture dominated.

Both the religious diversity and the suitability of the area for small-scale agriculture shaped the opportunities available to women. Outside of Puritan New England, with its unusually high rates of female literacy, Quaker Pennsylvania had the greatest commitment to educating girls. The Quaker belief in the fundamental equality of souls and the independence of the Women's Meeting, the main body governing the conduct of female Quakers, allowed women more spiritual and social autonomy than in other Protestant faiths. Indeed, Quakers alone among Protestant sects authorized women to become itinerant preachers and writers in their own right, a dispensation that sparked many female "Public Friends" to travel the Atlantic Basin. But compared to Dutch, Puritan, or Chesapeake women, Quaker women had little direct economic control over their households. Rather, their energies were channeled toward nurturing large, tightly knit, and affectionate families and steering young people toward the values and marriage partners that would keep them within the Quaker faith tradition. Some historians have argued that this style of family nurturance, with its emphasis on individual self-discipline and affection, represented the first instance of modern family and childrearing to make an appearance in European North America.[24]

Pennsylvania's settlement near the end of the seventeenth century, at the dawn of an age of commercial expansion, also influenced the legal status of women. Despite the colony's mainly agrarian character, William Penn's concern with making the laws friendly to creditors came at the expense of wives and widows. Pennsylvania wives lacked the protection provided by private examinations in cases where husbands planned to sell dowry property. The laws also privileged the claims of creditors on a deceased man's real estate, no matter what the danger of leaving the widow impoverished, and granted widows only one-third of the surplus after the estate was sold to pay debts. As historian Marylynn Salmon notes, "The Pennsylvania dower policy gave to femes coverts a responsibility equal to their husbands' for repaying family debts, but it did not give them any commensurate power to control the accumulation of those debts." Only Connecticut, a colony whose radical Protestantism also led to reform of the common law, developed laws more injurious to women's dower rights.[25]

Women's Labor and Capital in Global Perspective

Until the dawn of female wage work in textile factories during the 1830s in the United States it might seem pointless to talk about a global approach to American women's labor. Yet even when seemingly confined to their own households, women's labor was part of global patterns of consumption, production, and capital formation. Probably the most signal shift in consumption occurred during the eighteenth century, during what historians describe as a "consumer revolution." In British North America, where per capita incomes topped those in Great Britain by the mid-eighteenth century, women were the main consumers of imported goods like tea, spices, cloth, fashion accessories such as gloves and hats, books (about which more later), and china. Tea became widespread as a marker of gentility, with particular importance for women, who purchased and brewed it, developed the material culture and etiquette for serving it, and centered their sociability around it. Jokes about yokels who did not know how to serve tea—one woman reputedly baked the shredded leaves in a pie—underscored the sense of cosmopolitanism associated with drinking it. When New England men dressed as Indians dumped tea into Boston Harbor in 1775 rather than the imported beverage preferred by men—rum—they were refusing a foreign commodity that their womenfolk had thoroughly incorporated into domestic life. Indeed, even early in the century the association between tea and domestic life was strong. In a humorous 1733

Pennsylvania Gazette commentary on the evils of male gambling and alcohol consumption, an anxious wife named "Patience Teacraft" attested that switching from strong liquor to tea had brought about male redemption.

From the first appearance of markets in British North America, women played a critical role in creating networks of local and regional economic exchange. Indeed, it is not exaggerating to claim that women's productive labor helped to create the economic relationship between urban centers such as Boston, New York, and Philadelphia and the rural hinterlands that supplied them. In the countryside around Philadelphia, to take one example, women found that butter production could be expanded at great profit. By the late eighteenth century, butter makers from neighboring "Butter Belt" counties were hiring additional help in the dairy to produce more butter for market in the city. The technology of butter making and butter storage permitted counties surrounding the city to participate in this market. Rural women reallocated resources like the labor of daughters and the cash needed to pay servants, balancing those needs against the benefits of educating daughters. By the nineteenth century, as class position came to rest on more education, dairymaids were more likely to be hired. Meanwhile, new techniques for mass-producing cheap cloth may have made it more cost-effective for midatlantic farm women to dispense with producing yarn and thread in favor of butter making. The availability of reasonably priced fresh butter in the city likewise made it possible for city-dwellers to reallocate resources and abandon the need to have cows on the premises or devote labor to churning.[26]

Perhaps the best example of the complex relationships among global market forces, shifts in women's productive labor, and the process by which individual households made decisions can be seen in textile production in New England. The industriousness of domestically employed housewives had long been symbolized by the spinning wheel and distaff in England before it became a symbol of female piety and regional prosperity in seventeenth-century New England. By the early eighteenth century, rural New England women were weaving linen, wool, diaper, and other homespun cloth. In Pennsylvania, in contrast, where agriculture thrived, weaving hewed to the British pattern and remained the province of male artisans. As the variety and quality of imported cloth improved throughout the century, however, the consumption of ready-made cloth increased. In wealthy urban households, purchased cloth displaced homespun on the eve of the American Revolution, only to undergo a revival during the war. Yet in New England the end of the war did not mean an end to homespun cloth production. Women in rural households continued to produce homespun cloth for mundane uses and everyday clothes, saving their cash (and their parents' credit) to purchase cloth for special garments and other consumer goods. Young women's textile production also contributed to the household economy by enabling them to supply all or part of their own marriage portions. Even in the decade before the industrial production of cloth began in earnest in New England, women in the region appear to have been intensifying their cloth production at home. Expanding uses for and varieties of textiles thus increased both the production and consumption of cloth. Homespun achieved mythic status as a symbol of New England domestic life during the period in which the transformation to capitalism reconfigured the domestic economy, patterns of consumption, and the value of women's labor.[27]

Women also played important roles in capital accumulation and formation. As early as the eighteenth century, widows with capital helped to fund emerging long-distance trade networks. Although they themselves did not engage in the extensive travel and public activity necessary for this trade, they invested capital in it, enabling trade networks to expand during the eighteenth century. Engaging in productive activities like butter, cloth, or dress making, or providing services like midwifery, women contributed signally to household economies without participating directly in the cash economy. Although debts might be calculated by their cash value and occasionally paid off in currency, payment was more likely to come in the form of livestock, cloth, exchanged labor, or food. Thus, midwife Martha Ballard, the protagonist of Laurel Ulrich's *A Midwife's Tale*, might receive live chickens, pies, or a cooked turkey from a client several weeks or months after the delivery, payments that she carefully noted in her diary.[28]

Although opportunities for wage work as laundresses, spinners, dressmakers, cooks, and dairymaids had always existed, the chance to earn cold, hard cash in exchange for regular employment became more widespread during the 1830s and 1840s when textile factories in Massachusetts began recruiting the members of farm households viewed as most expendable—young women. Farm households were forced to make decisions about the value of daughters' unpaid labor to the farm enterprise, which had fallen on hard times for those with marginally productive land by the nineteenth century, compared to the cash value of seventy-two hours of regular employment in the mills. Farmers' daughters were initially attracted by the chance to make money and avoid strenuous farmwork. Many of these young women were already engaged in textile production to earn their own marriage portions. They came to value the independence that followed from receiving cash payments directly, and many resented having to hand over paychecks to fathers and mothers. The initial motivation for sending daughters into textile factories had little to do with individual preference and independence, however, and more to do with the farm household's strategic allocation of labor and need for cash.

By becoming the first industrial workforce in the United States, the daughters of Yankee farmers brought education, a strong sense of their rights as citizens, and a legacy of political protest in the face of oppression to the textile mills. For most, their stint in the mills would last only a few years but would make an indelible impression on their lives. Native-born factory operatives married later than their still-rural sisters and bore fewer children. They were also more likely to find nonrural mates and live in or near cities. In those respects they anticipated modernity's impact on women as the first generation of industrial employment loosened the grip of an already weakened rural patriarchy.[29]

White women's entry into textile mills in New England was one piece in the larger puzzle of growing global demand for cotton cloth. The other piece was the labor of slaves, including female slaves, on southern cotton plantations. From the Carolinas to Mississippi, cotton became the crop of choice after the invention of the cotton gin in 1792 reduced the labor of separating fiber from seed. Southern cotton supplied textile mills in England as well as in New England. Enslaved laborers produced most of this cotton, although even nonslaveholding yeoman households turned cautiously to producing small amounts. Without the expanded supply and low cost of shipping cotton to northern factories, textile mills could not have produced so much cloth so cheaply. Without the relatively cheap labor of farmer's daughters, the mills would have found it difficult to capitalize the new technology.

As the price of mass-produced cotton fell, manufacturers continued to make profits by reducing their labor costs. Each operative was assigned more machines although her wages remained fixed. Native-born women, who composed 96 percent of operatives in 1836, rebelled against the speed-ups during the 1830s, 1840s, and 1850s and pushed for shorter workdays with limited success. Eventually, they were replaced by Irish immigrants. By the late 1850s, more than half of New England textile factory operatives were Irish. These immigrant workers were older and often married with children. They lacked some of the tools—literacy and a readily applicable political framework—for organizing against their exploitation.[30]

The industrialization of North American textile production and of other traditional female employments combined with the influx of Irish immigrants to transform domestic labor in the northern United States. Both factors could be traced to the larger global process of European industrialization and the demographic and agricultural crisis in Ireland. Along with mass-produced textiles, industrial products like cast-iron cookstoves and milled white flour changed the nature of housewives' labor, contributing to rising standards for the size and variety of wardrobes and the diversity of foods at the table. Such products made it possible for a woman to labor alone without the assistance of family members if her household merely subsisted, or she could delegate work to hired laborers if the household was more prosperous. Yet the rising expectations that accompanied these new products generated new labor, increasing the burdens of laundering and mending delicate but washable cotton fabrics, intensifying the labor required for baking white bread that required yeast, and increasing the number of dishes that could be cooked on the multiple ranges of the cookstove.

Opportunities for wage labor in textile factories or for cash income from the home manufacture of hats, buttons, and gloves drew some native-born white women out of the pool of hired domestic labor, which many saw as stifling to their independence. As foreign-born and African American women increasingly filled the need for domestic labor, their native-born peers began to see such labor as ungenteel in a class sense. New markets for women's labor, shaped in part by industrial technology and the influx of immigrants, thus combined to bring native-born white mistresses and foreign-born domestics together under the same roof. When "Bridget," the generic name native-born employers used to refer to Irish servants, replaced her Yankee forbear, the fast-eroding collective and communal aspects of female labor in the northern and midatlantic states gave way to a class relationship defined by the market. In the intimate spaces of northern bourgeois homes, industrialization and immigration left their marks on labor processes and on the social relations that this domestic labor helped produce. Race, ethnicity, class, and religion, all of which became meaningful categories in the politics of domestic labor in the north, also became important categories in mid-nineteenth-century American politics as nativists helped reshape the national political landscape.[31]

Print Culture

In addition to consuming imported goods like tea and cotton cloth, women in the Colonies and the new American nation participated in global economies as readers of books, newspapers, and magazines. In the intensive reading cultures of the seventeenth century, literate women and men—the vast majority of men and probably nearly 50 percent of all women in New England—read the Bible and a small handful of instructive books over and over again. It was not uncommon for one member of a New England household to read aloud from the Bible or prayer books to others in the group. Many of these seventeenth-century books were imports, published in England, although New England had its own printing houses early in the seventeenth century and dominated North American printing for nearly a century.[32]

During the eighteenth century, as the sources of printed material diversified and increased, women might read newspapers, the execution sermons of criminals, poetry, or English novels. Between 1700 and 1750 most colonies established their own newspapers, which included foreign and commercial news, advertising, and pieces intended to entertain. The homegrown print culture demonstrated its cosmopolitan side by participating in the misogynist humor that could be found in newspapers, magazines, and books on the other side of the Atlantic. Literate men had abundant opportunities for fellowship in a cosmopolitan, transatlantic culture that included Jonathan Swift's graphic accounts of elite women's lax personal hygiene, which appeared in *Gulliver's Travels*, the *Spectator's* satires about women's fashion and manners, fictitious news accounts in which men became the dupes of wily women, and harsh commentaries on women's spending habits and bad influence on the conduct of public affairs.[33]

Despite this seemingly hostile climate, female literacy and female readership grew. By the last quarter of the eighteenth century, literacy approached 100 percent among white New England women, with their white southern sisters lagging behind. Enslaved women, free African American women, and poor women in general did not achieve this rate, even during the nineteenth century.[34] One reason for the growth has to do with the spread of Enlightenment ideas about the importance of education, a trend that was accelerated in North America by the American Revolution. Another reason had to do with the growing supply of reading material targeted for women, a market shift that was itself fed by the rise in female literacy.

As readers of printed matter, literate women could follow news from around the world, most of it filtered through a British imperial lens in eighteenth-century colonial newspapers. By the turn of the century, books advising on appropriate conduct; novels detailing the perils of courtship; and magazines containing serial novels and nonfiction pieces on travel, politics, and exotic "Oriental" cultures in which women were the victims of despotic men all expanded the intellectual horizons of women whose lives might otherwise appear parochial. By the early nineteenth century, many publications targeted female readers by producing small pocketbook editions. Books on household management, health, and childrearing, along with children's books, were also available.

In her study of learned women in the antebellum United States, Mary Kelley found that reading was at the center of many white women's lives, connecting them to the world of ideas, fashion, and learning even after they married and moved to relatively uncosmopolitan surrounds. To a more limited extent, such patterns also seem to have marked white southern women's reading. For them, as for their eighteenth-century forbears, reading was never a solitary pursuit. Women readers exchanged books, recommended favorite works to each other, and discussed what they had read. Reading groups and literary societies provided formal structure for this collective reading experience. Drawing encouragement from the female subjects of their reading—which included the English poet Elizabeth Barrett Browning, the French novelist Germaine de Stael, and the English essayist Hannah More—as well as from other readers, learned women of the nineteenth century departed from domestic expectations to fashion intellectual lives for themselves.[35]

At the same time that women's literary networks created a nineteenth-century female reading culture, women burst onto the literary scene as authors. The phenomenon that Nathaniel Hawthorne decried as "that damned mob of scribbling women" signified the commercial coming of age for women writing for a female audience. From Susanna Rowson's *Charlotte Temple* (1791), the first best-selling novel in the United States, to Susan Warner's *Wide, Wide, World* (1850), which some historians consider the prototype for the concept "bestseller," the literary marketplace included many examples of successful female authorship. Including pirated editions, Rowson's novel had sold nearly forty thousand copies by 1810. One scholar has argued that the hazards of that marketplace, including restrictive publication agreements and the absence of national or international copyright protections, actually worked to the advantage of some female authors, who thrived on the combination of limited male competition, the widespread practice of reprinting without permission, and the need to cultivate a devoted following. Whatever its formula, success brought some women an international readership, as was the case with Harriet Beecher Stowe's *Uncle Tom's Cabin* (1852), a melodramatic account of the plight of fugitive slaves that was eventually translated into twenty languages. Upon meeting Beecher Stowe at the beginning of the Civil War, President Abraham Lincoln allegedly remarked, "So you're the little woman who wrote the book that made this great war."[36]

Most popular nineteenth-century female authors wrote sentimental fiction like that of Harriet Beecher Stowe, with consequences for slaves, Native Americans, and other people of color around that world that scholars continue to debate. The vision of womanhood and of women-in-the-world presented in these domestic novels was not radical, according to literary scholar Nina Baym, but progressive nonetheless. At once validating the domestic focus of women's lives and fostering a sense of individualism that was already becoming a hallmark of the middle class, women's sentimental fiction offered a view of a wider world in which women were capable of acting for good. Even as this message about class stressed a "privately possessive and self-possessive way of being in the world," Baym observes, sentiment helped propel individuals into benevolent activity, forge communal bonds, and define worthy causes. The sentimental novel encouraged political activism through a combination of sympathy, realignment of religious posture in relationship to a benevolent God, and universal application of the notion of legal rights. By evoking the suffering of slaves, antislavery advocates mobilized feeling against slavery as a violation of rights. But several scholars have pointed to sentimentalism's conservative, even destructive, agenda. Defining a narrow range of sexual and domestic behavior that qualified one as fully human, sentimental fiction left out countless others whose suffering, exploitation, and political subordination failed to excite any feeling at all among white middle-class readers.[37]

Perhaps no one illustrates better the type of middle-class "self-possessive" femininity, showcased and unleashed in sentimental literature and the representation of suffering to provoke political activism, than Harriet Jacobs, alias Linda Brent, a woman who escaped slavery to write an account of her experiences. Jacobs's autobiography conformed to the genre of middle-class white woman's sentimental literature even as it detailed sexual coercion, violence, and other threats to female virtue inherent in slavery. In that sense it was like the popular early nineteenth century novels that featured seduction, rape, out-of-wedlock pregnancy, and voyeuristic accounts of life in an "Oriental" harem. Jacobs delivered her life story in a language and format middle-class readers found familiar, even if her particular tale of seduction was not. Her emotional and moral landscape, moreover, reflected that of her audience, even if she was compelled to respond to ugly facts in ways many of her readers would have found repugnant. Jacob's self-presentation had a radical side that was to counter the rising tide of racist caricature, in cartoons and print, and assert that African Americans could possess human dignity—female virtue in particular. But it acquiesced to the project of excluding from civilized humanity the vast majority of slaves, immigrants, Native Americans, Mormons, and people of color, based on their domestic habits and sexual practices.

Although misogynist humor continued to grace the pages of nineteenth-century novels and newspapers, white native-born women escaped some of this scathing wit until they began agitating against slavery in the 1830s or for their own rights in the 1860s. Cartoons depicted white women engaged in sexually suggestive activities, such as dancing, with black men in an effort to discredit so-called negro lovers. Other cartoons lampooned mannish white women invading the halls of government and neglecting their domestic duties.

But those were the exceptions. If fashionable and privileged white women provided the punch line for much eighteenth-century humor, African Americans and the Irish became the butt of jokes during the nineteenth century. Barely recognizable as human and with nearly identical facial features, cartoonish African Americans and Irish, who might be male or female, bore the brunt of what passed for nineteenth-century Anglo-American humor. If literate white men used misogynist humor to exclude women from public life during the expanding consumerism, commerce, and print culture of the eighteenth century, they used racist humor during the period of expanding democratic participation of the first half of the nineteenth century to affirm the exclusiveness of the privileges of whiteness.[38]

Religious Experience

Religious mission and the desire for unfettered religious expression motivated many European migrants to cross the Atlantic to North America. Throughout the period considered in this essay, religious life in British North America continued to be characterized by dissent, episodes of evangelical revival, and a sense of mission, even as it was reshaped by contact with non-Western religious traditions. European, Native American, and African women played key roles in Christianizing the New World throughout the seventeenth, eighteenth, and nineteenth centuries. After the disestablishment of churches following the American Revolution, moreover, female parishioners assumed new importance in the eyes of ministers as the main financial and spiritual support of churches throughout the United States.

Historians often begin the story of religious dissent in British North American with the example of Anne Hutchinson, a dissident from a well-heeled merchant family, who took on the Puritan establishment by questioning clerical authority. Hutchinson believed some clergy were overemphasizing good works and outward behavior at the expense of grace, the intangible but crucial experience of God's goodness believed by Puritans to be necessary for salvation. She held informal reading and teaching sessions attended by women and men at her house, during which she questioned clerical authority and set forth a radical balance of grace and works that gave individuals more spiritual authority.

What has not been noted in telling Hutchinson's tale is that her dissenting posture and the means the clergy used to discredit her—attributing her dissent to Satan, disciplining her for departing from her proper role as a woman, and interpreting her reproductive misfortune as God's sanction against her sinful ways—followed a familiar pattern of religious dissent and its repression in Europe. Like most early seventeenth century dissidents, Hutchinson emphasized the individual's relationship with God at the expense of the clergy. Like her counterparts in Europe, Catholic and Protestant, her charisma gained her a following she was not entitled to by virtue of education or clerical status. As was the case with many European female dissidents, moreover, Puritan clerics tried to silence Hutchinson's challenge by rigorously interpreting biblical injunctions to women to be silent and obey male authority. Failing to break her spirit, Puritan divines called upon Providence to interpret Hutchinson's unfortunately timed miscarriage as a "monstrous" birth, finding it to be a portent of her unnatural behavior and her error. Seen in global perspective, Hutchinson's dissent becomes part of a larger pattern of questioning clerical authority, a pursuit in which women throughout the history of European Christianity played key roles and to which clergy responded by demeaning dissent as female.[39]

In general, New World female religious missionaries and evangelicals tended to be Catholic during the seventeenth century, and their subjects tended to be Native American. The main exceptions were English Quaker "Public Friends," who risked their lives to make their faith known to New England Puritans, beginning in the 1650s, and counted several women among their ranks. Mary Dyer, a young friend of Anne Hutchinson, left Massachusetts after Hutchinson was banished and became a Quaker. Despite the threat of banishment and eventually execution, she returned to the colony to testify to her faith. The colony finally executed her in 1660.

With the end to the Puritan stranglehold over New England churches in 1692 and the rise of evangelical fervor in New Jersey in the 1720s and New England in the 1730s, the religious visibility of Protestant women increased exponentially. Along with children, white and black women were among the most visible participants at religious revivals, where converts wept, wailed, writhed, and fainted as they received God's grace. Throughout the 1740s, 1750s, and 1760s, white women encouraged their menfolk to experience conversion and join churches, and the men did so in record numbers during the first decade of revivals, known to historians as the First Great Awakening.

The First Great Awakening also marked the appearance of full-blown revivals in slave communities throughout the New World, especially in the Caribbean but eventually including the North American mainland. The spread of Christianity throughout the Atlantic Basin owed much to African women's religious zeal, both as converts and as missionaries. Black women infused Christian spirituality with the emotion and immediacy that made it appealing to the enslaved, the downtrodden, and the unlettered. As Sylvia Frey and Betty Wood note, "Conditioned by centuries of training in ecstatic performance, African Americans often inspired and catalyzed revivalism through an intense emotionalism that reflected their belief in the immediate call, the central tenet of the African American understanding of conversion." Women of African descent were especially effective evangelizers when they worked in tandem with white men.[40]

Ecstatic performance of conversion became the hallmark of the eighteenth-century revivals in part because, for the first time, news of the revivals and the number of converts was widely communicated in print and in letters sent across the Atlantic, where the most famous revivalist, George Whitefield, got his start. Women participated actively in this letter-writing effort, spreading news of the revival's success and helping create a truly Atlantic revival culture. Both this and the more visible types of participation in religious revival helped make women

264

the mainstays of North American churches following the American Revolution, when churches were disestablished.[41]

At the turn of the nineteenth century a second major cluster of religious revivals, known as the Second Great Awakening, began first in Virginia, Kentucky, and Tennessee and then in the Northeast. In the South, itinerant evangelical ministers countered white men's initial resistance to their message by compromising on the question of slavery and accepting certain expressions of masculinity and male sociability. In New England, Yankee revivalists began preaching an individualist message of free agency and borrowing from Methodist revival techniques. By the 1830s, the Hudson River Valley had become a hot zone for converts, a disproportionate number of whom were women. For female revival participants, evangelical Christianity went hand in hand with a newly spiritualized approach to domestic life in which mothers, rather than fathers, educated and instilled self-discipline in children.

Spiritualized domesticity was but one component in a cluster of new practices that marked the emerging middle class. Beginning at the end of the eighteenth century and gathering momentum in certain regions in the Northeast by the 1830s, middle-class women began having fewer children. On average, white women nationwide bore nearly seven children in 1800, a figure that declined steadily throughout the century to approximately 3.5 children in 1900. The decline in fertility was even more marked if one examines only middle-class white women in the Northeast. The children in these smaller families received more direct attention from their mothers and better education as a means to prepare their souls for salvation and to help secure their class privileges. Under this new demographic regime, motherhood and childhood became saturated with sentiment and religious purpose, providing a major impetus for the effusion of sentimental novels written and consumed by women during the period.[42]

This matrix of domesticity, evangelical religion, and motherhood also propelled many women into benevolent reform, including missionary activity. Societies to rescue young "fallen" women from prostitution, mission efforts to teach Euro-American domestic arts such as spinning to Native American women, charity relief to poor women and their children, and subsequent antislavery activism all originated in religious impulses to reform and beliefs that society could be perfected if enough Christians chose good over evil. Taken along with the outpouring of sentimental fiction and important domestic rituals like the Thanksgiving feast, the spectrum of female reform activity—what one scholar has dubbed "Manifest Domesticity"—became the domestic partner of Manifest Destiny, the belief that God intended the United States to possess the entire breadth of the North American continent. Amy Kaplan maintains that "'Manifest Domesticity' turned an imperial nation into a home by producing and colonizing specters of the foreign that lurk inside and outside its ever shifting borders."[43] In other words, in the hands of female reformers and the authors of sentimental novels, the task of Christianizing and Americanizing could be accomplished by inculcating middle-class domestic habits in poor women, sexually fallen women, Native American women, African American women brutalized by slavery, and non-Western women victimized by tyrannical men and tradition as well as by combatting male vices.

The range of political possibilities within the world of benevolent reform is nicely exemplified by the life of Catharine Beecher, daughter of the Puritan preacher Lyman Beecher and sister of Harriet Beecher Stowe. Born in 1800, Beecher was a young adult when she became involved in educating girls. She also participated in reform causes such as the protest against Cherokee removal in the mid-1830s, which proved unsuccessful. Beecher, who never married or bore children, focused her efforts thereafter on making domesticity more empowering for women within a narrow program for social change. In keeping with the move toward mechanization and rationalization in industrial workplaces, she developed a scientific approach to household management and explained it in several volumes, including *A Treatise on Domestic Economy*, first published in 1841, and *American Women's Home* (1869). Her ostensible motive in beginning the project was to address the difficulty that middle-class, northern white women had in procuring dependable servants, a problem Beecher attributed to the fluid social structure of the United States compared to England.

The importance of women's domestic role to Beecher's thinking—and her strict interpretation of its limits—became apparent when Sarah and Angelina Grimké, sisters from a prominent Charleston, South Carolina, slaveholding family, began a public-speaking tour in the North to expose the cruelties of slavery. Like the group of Boston ministers who condemned the sisters for addressing "promiscuous" (mixed) assemblies in a pastoral letter of 1837, Beecher was outraged by the potential implications of women engaging in political activity in such a public way. She entered the print debate with a letter that warned women not to cast off domestic life, the only source of their power and influence.

As her female antislavery counterparts began to expand their agenda to include women's rights, Beecher remained wedded to her strict interpretation of domesticity. Seeking in effect to professionalize the role of housewife through a scientific approach to household management, Beecher saw only one paid profession—teaching—as respectable enough for women. Her advocacy on behalf of female teachers, whom she saw as more naturally suited to teaching than men, included establishing teacher's training schools ("normal" schools) throughout the country. In print and through institution-building, Beecher did as much to advance the cause of Manifest Domesticity as any of her antebellum peers.[44]

Although unquestionably engaged in a larger project of American nation-making, some female reform efforts were part of transnational circuits of political activism. American antislavery activists, for instance, were connected to the global effort to end the transatlantic slave trade (which still transported large numbers of enslaved Africans to Cuba and Brazil legally and small numbers to the United States illegally during the nineteenth century) and to abolish the institution. The founding story of the nineteenth-century woman's rights movement illustrates the importance of this global context for American reformers. According to Elizabeth Cady Stanton, the idea for a convention on American woman's rights was born at the World's Anti-Slavery Convention in London in 1840. Lucretia Mott, a seasoned Quaker activist and devotee of Mary Wollstonecraft, the British feminist and political radical, had been selected as a delegate to the convention by the radical Garrisonian wing of the American Anti-Slavery Society but was sidelined by the convention's prohibition on female participation. Stanton, whose husband was also a delegate, sought out Mott, and the two talked at length during their six-week stay. Walking home arm and arm with Mott after the convention had adjourned, Stanton recalled, the two resolved to "hold a convention as soon as we returned home, and form a society to advocate the rights of women." Although likely exaggerated in Stanton's telling, the story is a reminder that nineteenth-century reformers thought of themselves as connected to activists around the world. It also suggests that contact with international political networks might accentuate rather than submerge divisions in tactics and philosophy between radical and conservative American reformers, especially when those divisions concerned the proper work for activist women.[45]

Protestant women were not the only reformers who had global connections. Like their counterparts throughout the Americas, Catholic nuns in North America built institutions that laid the foundations for Euro-American communities in the Midwest, South, and Southwest. They also eased the burdens of urban life for immigrants, the poor, and the sick by providing much-needed social services. In eighteenth- and nineteenth-century Louisiana, French Ursulines inflected colonial race, class, and gender relations with Franco-Catholicism by educating enslaved girls as well as the daughters of an aspiring New Orleans elite. In nineteenth-century Milwaukee, Catholic sisters established the region's first schools, educating Catholics and non-Catholics alike. In New York City, the Sisters of Charity established orphanages, in part to keep Catholic orphans out of the hands of ambitious Protestant reformers. When cholera struck in 1832 and again in 1849, the Sisters of Charity in Baltimore, Washington, Philadelphia, and dozens of smaller cities dutifully nursed the sick, earning the praise of even the most virulently Protestant newspaper editors.

Ultimately, however, charitable services rendered did not deter nativists from venting their hatred of Catholics and their unease over the undomestic character of convent life. Between 1830 and 1860, Catholic communities throughout the Northeast suffered violent attacks and anti-Catholic polemics. For many nativists, the nuns' membership in transnational religious orders outweighed the national consequences of their work establishing hospitals, schools, convents, and networks throughout North America. As the history of nineteenth-century reform reminds us, however, religious organizations with global ambitions, whether Catholic or Protestant, often did the most to build national infrastructures.[46]

Historic Moments: Revolution and Redefinition

Much of the history of women can be told by recounting the gradual changes in the working lives of ordinary women. This type of history emphasizes subtle changes over the long term, in marked contrast to the emphasis of diplomatic, military, or political history on the transformative event. When gender historians try to assess the impact of events like the American Revolution, these two tendencies are placed in tension. A global perspective on the history of American women offers a new way to resolve this tension. How did the consequences of revolution and nation building differ for women in the United States compared to their counterparts in other places in the Atlantic world? How might we assess the significance of the American Revolution differently after placing it in comparative perspective?

One important feature of the American Revolution that made it a markedly different experience for women than the French Revolution was the context of war. Essentially both a civil war and a war for independence that dragged on for eight years, the American Revolution (1775–83) gave some white women a taste of household responsibility and autonomy that many found empowering. Women who entered the war feeling that they could barely cope with running the household alone were by war's end as confident of their own judgments as they had formerly been of their husbands'. This was the privilege of being married to men who owned property. For the wives of poor men who fought, wartime accentuated their dependence by forcing them to follow their men to procure food and shelter. Derogatorily dubbed "camp followers," which suggested a parasitic relationship, itinerant wives actually contributed materially to the comfort of soldiers by nursing the sick, doing laundry, or mending. Wartime might initially have appeared as an opportunity for many enslaved women, who fled to the British in hopes of freedom.

Forced, however, to wait in camps before leaving the North American mainland, many contracted fatal diseases. Others suffered separation from family
members and the disruption of being forcibly removed from a home. The
trauma of war thus defined the initial period of nation-making and provided
a backdrop for subsequent discussions about the meaning of citizenship and
the powers of the federal government.[47]

The consequences of American independence for Native Americans were
remarkably similar to those of colonization on indigenous people throughout the rest of the world. Native Americans lost land to American nationals
eager to push the boundaries of the United States further west and leverage
to missionaries seeking to "civilize" Indians. The devastation of war combined
with new political and economic pressures to compel Native Americans to
change their tactics for dealing with their adversaries. Indigenous gender roles
often came into greater conformity with those of Christian missionaries as a
result of these struggles. The Cherokees, to take one example, tried many of
these new tactics, including culture change, combating American national
power with an indigenous concept of nationhood, and redefining relationships to the land. Cherokee communal values had begun to suffer the encroachments of rising individualism well before the American Revolution as
intensive hunting began to displace agriculture and as the marriages of Cherokee women to European traders placed maternal legacies of clan and kin
affiliations in direct competition with European forms of wealth, prestige, and
education. The eighteenth-century wars precipitated additional changes by
placing young men in new positions of diplomatic and military prominence
and reducing women's ritual connection to warfare. Having suffered devastating losses as a consequence of alliance with the French during the Seven
Years War, the Cherokees sided with the British during the Revolutionary War.
The British were attractive because they had offered the Cherokees some
protection from the encroachments of colonial settlement during the years
between the wars. Such protections were lost, however when the United States
became an independent nation unfettered by imperial policies. In the face
of aggressive U.S. land acquisition, a diminished population of Cherokees
ceded thousands of acres of eastern hunting grounds, fields, and town sites
and relocated further west.

Postwar patterns of residence in isolated homesteads rather than in towns
undermined already weakened kinship systems and traditions of cooperative
female labor. Although they had long valued women's political input and their
roles as caretakers of the land, the Cherokees turned to a model of nationhood early in the nineteenth century that privileged (male) gender over clan
membership. These transformations coincided with the federal government's
new "civilization" project. So-called civilized Cherokees acceded to mission-

ary pressure upon men to abandon hunting for sedentary agriculture and livestock raising. Women took up Euro-American female domestic arts (spinning, sewing, laundering, dairying, and quilting) and saw much of their political influence disappear with the new emphasis on landed property. Protestant missionaries (Moravians, Baptists, and Methodists, among others) also tried to instill bourgeois standards for modesty and sexual chastity in young Cherokee women. Despite the erosion and wholesale transformation of traditional sources of their political influence, a group of vocal Cherokee women joined their men to resist proposed land cessions in 1818 and 1819 and the removal scheme of the 1830s. Women also perpetuated the female art of basket making by adapting it to new raw materials, uses, and commercial opportunities.[48]

Women's historians have typically interpreted the period immediately after the war as a time in which questions about Euro-American women's place in the new nation were raised and then resolved, outside the realm of formal political citizenship, by means of the concept of Republican Motherhood. Emphasizing the responsibility of women to nurture their sons to become good citizens, Republican Motherhood enabled the Founders to balance the competing tensions of a nation of entrepreneurial men, devoted to the pursuit of their own happiness, with the needs of the Republic for unselfish citizens dedicated to the public good. With the moral and intellectual development of its sons in the hands of loving mothers, the Republic would continue to replenish its repository of virtue even as it liberated individual men to pursue their selfish interests. Historian Jan Lewis has amended this emphasis on motherhood to observe that republican wives served the needs of the new nation as much as republican mothers. The cult of motherhood had yet to come into full bloom at the time of the Revolution, Lewis notes, and much of the sentimental fiction of the period focused on the need for women to provide men with educated, moral companionship.[49]

To the limited extent that women were exhorting other women—and being exhorted themselves by ministers and political leaders—to be virtuous mothers in the aftermath of the Revolution, they were following a cultural path already cut by their European sisters. During the second half of the eighteenth century, the appearance of children's books, the critique of aristocratic women in favor of the bourgeoisie, and the advice of doctors to women to nurse their own children produced a new model for moral motherhood in England and France. Its underlying message in England was service to the burgeoning British Empire by providing it with robust, moral citizens. Even the British feminist and political radical Mary Wollstonecraft advocated motherhood as the basis for female citizenship in her *Vindication of the Rights of Women* (1792).

Similar trends could be found in France at mid-century. Jean-Jacques Rousseau castigated women of fashion who abdicated their responsibilities to their children to spend nights out socializing. In his view, public life and virtuous womanhood could not be reconciled. Seen in this context, Republican Motherhood was more the result of timing and revolutionary context than any uniquely American phenomenon. Bourgeois motherhood as cultural ideal made its official debut in the fledgling United States immediately after the Revolution, where it was debated and extolled in the context of new nationhood. From the beginning of its history in North America, then, bourgeois motherhood had an explicitly political content.[50]

The shallow roots of bourgeois motherhood help explain why there was so little debate in the United States, compared to France, on the subject of women's place in the new nation. In France, the rise of the bourgeoisie over several decades and the existence of independent female cultural sites such as the salon enhanced the possibility that women could be considered for citizenship. In the United States, however, such phenomena existed on a smaller scale before the Revolution. Yet as David Shields has shown, women did participate in intellectual and social circles in the colonial and early United States, contributing to a developing notion of wit and literary facility as critical ingredients of the polite world. With the exception of a handful of outspoken women, however, few people in the United States seem to have seriously considered whether women ought to be included among the ranks of citizens. Whereas in France, a serious public debate emerged over how women were to be defined in the new nation, in the United States there was mainly silence. The U.S. Constitutional Convention was marked by heated debate on many subjects, but no debate took place over women's place in the new nation.[51]

Slavery also explains some of the differences between the American and French nation-making processes. The most vociferously patriotic states in the new nation were slaveholding states. These states were not simply societies with slaves, moreover, but slave societies in which slavery anchored key economic, cultural, and political institutions. Whereas in France, debate over the place of women in the new republic was central to definitions of the body politic and slavery a more distant concern, in the United States such debate took place around slavery, involving slaveholders who lived in the slave societies of the American South. (In France, in contrast, most slaves were held in the Caribbean, far from the site of the debates over slavery.) The fissures in the body politic in the United States thus emerged around racial slavery; in France they emerged around gender.

Another piece of the puzzle can be found in the postrevolutionary political climate. Following the most radical phase of the French Revolution, which began in 1793, and fueled by the scandalous XYZ Affair of 1797 in which three French officials agreed to receive American diplomats only if they paid a bribe, the United States entered a period of conservative reaction against French culture and values. One victim of this reaction was Mary Wollstonecraft, whose reputation had been tarnished by the posthumous publication of her love letters, written as she observed the French Revolution. The letters were addressed to an American, Gilbert Imlay, by whom she subsequently bore a child out of wedlock while still in France. Conservatives vilified her in England, and American readers felt obliged to distance themselves from her immoral conduct, although a few brave souls continued to read her book during the nineteenth century. A host of other cultural phenomenon became tarred with the brush of French vice during this period, including women and men of fashion, bath houses (of which there were very few), and private social clubs.[52]

Meanwhile, the political independence of the United States created new possibilities for Euro-American women to participate in public life. Social groups of women and men who wrote poetry, exchanged manuscripts, and met for polite conversation had for many years marked the American version of the French salon in cities such as Philadelphia and New York. This mixed-sex meeting of the minds appears to have continued in these cities as well as in Washington and Boston after the Revolution. In Washington, where women regularly attended the sessions of the Senate and then returned home to discuss politics with men, such gatherings had an overtly political cast. In addition to this more egalitarian discussion, the wives of leading politicians, from the earliest residence of the nation's capital on the muddy bog that became Washington, wielded a type of influence over politics reminiscent of French court women. Dolly Madison was probably the most skilled practitioner of this type of influence, able to advance or check a man's political fortunes with the subtle favor she conveyed upon his wife at balls, banquets, and parties. Female networks and social judgments could thus come to bear on the trajectory of political careers, helping to determine political appointments and alliances. This female public, firmly entrenched in the aristocratic tradition, declined under the austere presidency of Thomas Jefferson and reemerged in new garb during the Madison administration. It retained much of its influence until the so-called Peggy Eaton Affair of 1829 in which Andrew Jackson bucked female opinion to keep a shunned Peggy Eaton, wife of his secretary of war, included in elite Washington social circles.[53]

While literate men and women took pleasure in these rarified worlds of politics and letters, ordinary men and women took to the streets to participate in parades and celebrations. Never isolated from the world of print culture, these popular expressions of patriotism and occupational pride took place in self-conscious relationship to newspaper accounts of similar celebrations in other regions of the country. In dialectic fashion, patriotic displays and the newspaper accounts of them together created the foundation for a popular national identity. For the first few decades after 1790, women and children as well as men seem to have participated in patriotic displays and assemblies, if not as speakers then by wearing political emblems and taking part in parades.

As parades became more formal throughout the first half of the nineteenth century, they focused more on male occupations. Women's participation in them subsequently became symbolic and peripheral, a trend reflected in the waning interest by the 1820s in training girls for public speaking. The wives and daughters of leading men might appear together to meet an honored guest like Lafayette in 1825 or observe a parade from a special balcony, but they had no speaking parts in the festivities. Female allegories of Liberty and Justice, however, were very visible at public celebrations in the form of statuary, banners, plaster figures, or as costumed women. At the fifty-year anniversary celebration of the end of the American Revolution, women waved white handkerchiefs embossed with a poem that paid homage to the sacrifice and suffering of the veterans.[54]

Viewed in this context, many nineteenth-century reforms can be seen as efforts to reappropriate public space to make it safe—morally, at least—for middle-class women. When the New York Female Moral Reform Society published the names of men who patroned brothels and hired a man to read the Bible aloud outside the doors of these establishments, they were not only attempting to reform prostitutes but also contesting the use of urban space for illicit sex. Other reform societies focused on inculcating poor women and children with middle-class values. Significantly, one of the tell-tale signs of poverty and child neglect, in the eyes of these reformers, was the presence of ragged women and children in the streets, gleaning goods from the garbage or trying to make money by hawking food to passersby. Books on conduct and manners, written for middle-class female readers, pointed to concerns about how to negotiate city streets without loss of respectability by offering advice on the proper way to walk down the street or board a trolley.[55]

In a somewhat less literal rendering of the term *public*, one can also see the emerging movement for women's rights as trying to redefine the meaning of citizenship seventy-five years after the Constitutional Convention remained silent on the question of women. If the public sphere in the United States emerged in part through the production of pamphlets on independence and the debates during the Constitutional Convention and subsequent ratification drive, then the women's rights conventions of the 1850s, the speaking tours and referendum campaigns of the 1860s, and invention of new tactics from the 1870s all used the "woman question" to redefine the meaning of that public in relation to the state.

The women and men who gathered at Seneca Falls in 1848 included Quakers and some aggrieved glove makers, people whose religious convictions and participation in new forms of home production gave them a modern rather than traditional sensibility. They deliberately borrowed from the language of the Declaration rather than from the Constitution to claim greater rights for women. In this and subsequent efforts, they stepped out of the cycle of ordinary time—marked by the seasons of domestic labor, childbirth, childrearing, and aging—that marked most women's lives and staged their own transformative event.

Little did they know, however, that the hoped-for transformation in the meanings of "public" and "citizen" would occur at a glacial pace. Glacierlike, it cut a swath through the political landscape, leaving parts of it virtually unchanged. Its path was most dramatic in the North, where urbanization and industrialization had already loosened the claims of community and patriarchal family relations on white middle-class women's energies and political identities. For enslaved African Americans, the global forces of plantation agriculture and staple crop production continued to define women's lives as slavery expanded to new lands. These same global forces pushed Native Americans farther west or relegated them to marginal lands in the East. Fueled by slave-produced cotton and new global markets for cheaply produced factory made goods, northern factories constituted the dominant global force in the lives of working-class women.

It would take a civil war, decades of struggle by a labor movement reluctant to make common cause with female or African American wage-earners, two world wars, and a civil rights movement before that transformative path widened sufficiently to admit women from a variety of class and racial groups. Women still continue to live lives shaped by global forces, although the obscuring lens of nationhood makes it as difficult to recognize the truth of this statement in the present as it has been to trace its influence over the past.[56]

Notes

I am grateful to Thomas Bender, Abby Schrader, Bonnie Smith, and Sandy G. Treadway for their helpful comments on this essay.

1. Sylvia Van Kirk, *"Many Tender Ties": Women in Fur Trade Society, 1670–1870* (Winnipeg, Manitoba: Watson and Dwyer, 1980); Ramon Gutierrez, *When Jesus Came, the Corn Mothers Went Away: Marriage, Sexuality, and Power in New Mexico, 1500–1846* (Stanford: Stanford University Press, 1991); Juliana Barr, *Peace Came in the Form of a Woman: The*

Power Relations of Spanish and Indian Nations in the Early Southwestern Borderlands (Chapel Hill: University of North Carolina Press, 2005); James F. Brooks, *Captives and Cousins: Slavery, Kinship, and Community in the Southwest Borderlands* (Chapel Hill: University of North Carolina Press, 2002).

2. Nancy Shoemaker, ed., *Negotiators of Change* (New York: Routledge, 1995); Natalie Zemon Davis, "Iroquois Women, European Women," in *Women, "Race," and Writing in the Early Modern Period,* ed. Margo Henricks and Patricia Parker (New York: Routledge, 1994), 254; see also Daniel K. Richter, *Facing East from Indian Country: A Native History of Early America* (Cambridge: Harvard University Press, 2001).

3. Gutierrez, *When Jesus Came;* Karen Anderson, *Chain Her by One Foot: The Subjugation of Women in Seventeenth-Century New France* (London: Routledge, 1991); Carol Devens, *Countering Colonization: Native American Women and Great Lakes Missions, 1630–1900* (Berkeley: University of California Press, 1992); Natalie Zemon Davis, *Women on the Margins: Three Seventeenth-Century Lives* (Cambridge: Harvard University Press, 1995), 111–12.

4. Kathleen M. Brown, *Good Wives, Nasty Wenches, and Anxious Patriarchs: Gender, Race and Power in Colonial Virginia* (Chapel Hill: University of North Carolina Press, 1996), ch. 2; Kathleen M. Brown, "In Search of Pocahontas," in *The Human Tradition in Colonial America,* ed. Ian Steele and Nancy Rhoden (Wilmington: Scholarly Resources, 1999), 71–95; James Axtell, *The Invasion Within: The Contest of Cultures in Colonial North America* (New York: Oxford University Press, 1985).

5. Jane T. Merritt, "Cultural Encounters along a Gender Frontier: Mahican, Delaware, and German Women in Eighteenth-Century Pennsylvania," *Pennsylvania History* 67 (Autumn 2000): 502–31.

6. David Eltis, *The Rise of African Slavery in the Americas* (New York: Cambridge University Press, 2000), 97.

7. I have drawn my estimates of the British Isles and West African migration from Bernard Bailyn, *Voyagers to the West: A Passage in the Peopling of America on the Eve of Revolution* (New York: Random House, 1986), 25–26.

8. Jane Landers, *Black Society in Spanish Florida* (Urbana: University of Illinois Press, 1999), 149.

9. John Thornton, *Africa and Africans in the Making of the Atlantic World* (New York: Cambridge University Press, 1992); Barbara Soltow, ed., *Slavery and the Rise of the Atlantic System* (New York: Cambridge University Press, 1991).

10. Herbert S. Klein, *The Atlantic Slave Trade* (New York: Cambridge University Press, 1999), 163; Ira Berlin, *Many Thousands Gone: The First Two Centuries of Slavery in North America* (Cambridge: Harvard University Press, 1998).

11. Berlin, *Many Thousands Gone;* Philip Morgan, *Slave Counterpoint: Black Culture in the Eighteenth-Century Chesapeake and Lowcountry* (Chapel Hill: University of North Carolina Press, 1998), 4, 70; Gregory A. Stiverson and Patrick H. Butler II, eds., "Virginia in 1732: The Travel Journal of William Hugh Grove," *Virginia Magazine of History and Biography* 85 (1977): 31.

12. Jennifer L. Morgan, *Laboring Women: Reproduction and Gender in New World Slavery* (Philadelphia: University of Pennsylvania Press, 2004); Philip Morgan, *Slave Counterpoint;* Walter Johnson, *Soul by Soul: Life Inside the Antebellum Slave Market* (Cambridge: Harvard University Press, 1999).

13. Philip Curtin, *The Rise and Fall of the Plantation Complex: Essays in Atlantic History* (New York: Cambridge University Press, 1990); Klein, *Atlantic Slave Trade;* Thornton,

Africa and Africans; Sidney W. Mintz and Richard Price, *An Anthropological Approach to the Afro-American Past: A Caribbean Perspective* (Philadelphia: Institute for the Study of Human Issues, 1976); Michael A. Gomez, *Exchanging Our Country Marks: The Transformation of African Identities in the Colonial and Antebellum South* (Chapel Hill: University of North Carolina Press, 1998); Philip Morgan, *Slave Counterpoint,* 82–83.

14. Edward Pearson, "'A Countryside Full of Flames': A Reconsideration of the Stono Rebellion and Slave Rebelliousness in the Early Eighteenth-Century South Carolina Lowcountry," *Slavery and Abolition* 17 (Aug. 1996): 22–50; Judith Ann Carney, *Black Rice: The African Origins of Rice Cultivation in the Americas* (Cambridge: Harvard University Press, 2001).

15. Cheryll Ann Cody, "Cycles of Work and of Childbearing," and Richard H. Steckel, "Women, Work, and Health under Plantation Slavery in the United States," in *More Than Chattel: Black Women and Slavery in the Americas,* ed. David Barry Gaspar and Darlene Clark Hine (Bloomington: Indiana University Press, 1996), 43–78; Thornton, *Africa and Africans;* Brown, *Good Wives, Nasty Wenches, and Anxious Patriarchs,* ch. 4.

16. Edmund S. Morgan, *American Slavery, American Freedom: The Ordeal of Colonial Virginia* (New York: W. W. Norton, 1975), 108–30. See also Susan Lee Johnson, *Roaring Camp: The Social World of the California Gold Rush* (New York: W. W. Norton, 2000) for the continuation of this pattern in the nineteenth century.

17. Laurel T. Ulrich, *Good Wives: Image and Reality in the Lives of Women in Northern New England, 1650–1750* (New York: Oxford University Press, 1980); Mary Beth Norton, *Founding Mothers and Fathers: Gendered Power and the Forming of American Society* (New York: Alfred A. Knopf, 1996).

18. Cornelia Hughes Dayton, *Women before the Bar: Gender, Law, and Society in Connecticut, 1639–1789* (Chapel Hill: University of North Carolina Press, 1995); Ruth Wallis Herndon, *Unwelcome Americans: Living on the Margin in Early New England* (Philadelphia: University of Pennsylvania Press, 2001).

19. Ulrich, *Good Wives;* Brown, *Good Wives, Nasty Wenches, and Anxious Patriarchs.*

20. Carole Shammas, *A History of Household Government in America* (Charlottesville: University of Virginia Press, 2002); Jane Kamensky, *Governing the Tongue: The Politics of Speech in Early New England* (New York: Oxford University Press, 1997); Elizabeth Reis, *Damned Women: Sinners and Witches in Puritan New England* (Ithaca: Cornell University Press, 1997); Carol Karlsen, *Devil in the Shape of a Woman: Witchcraft in Colonial New England* (New York: W. W. Norton, 1987).

21. Darrett B. Rutman and Anita H. Rutman, *A Place in Time: Middlesex County, Virginia, 1650–1750* (New York: W. W. Norton, 1984).

22. Brown, *Good Wives, Nasty Wenches, Anxious Patriarchs.*

23. Linda Biemer, *Women and Property in Colonial New York: The Transition from Dutch to English Law, 1643–1727* (Ann Arbor: University of Michigan Research Press, 1983); David E. Narrett, "Men's Wills and Women's Property Rights in Colonial New York," in *Women in the Age of the American Revolution,* ed. Ronald Hoffman and Peter J. Albert (Charlottesville: University Press of Virginia, 1989), 91–133; Deborah A. Rosen, *Courts and Commerce: Gender, Law, and the Market Economy in Colonial New York* (Columbus: Ohio State University Press, 1997); Paula A. Treckel, *To Comfort the Heart: Women in Seventeenth-Century America* (New York: Twayne Publishers, 1996), 154–57.

24. Barry Levy, *Quakers and the American Family: British Settlement in the Delaware Valley* (New York: Oxford University Press, 1988); Rebecca Larson, *Daughters of Light: Quaker Women Preaching and Prophesying in the Colonies and Abroad, 1700–1775* (Chapel Hill: University of North Carolina Press, 2000).

25. Marylynn Salmon, *Women and the Law of Property in Early America* (Chapel Hill: University of North Carolina Press, 1986), 160–68. See also Lisa Wilson, *Life after Death: Widows in Pennsylvania, 1750–1850* (Philadelphia: Temple University Press, 1992) for her argument that Pennsylvania widows had more influence over inheritance than the law would suggest, and Karin Wulf, *Not All Wives: Women of Colonial Philadelphia* (Ithaca: Cornell University Press, 2000).

26. Joan M. Jensen, *Loosening the Bonds: Mid-Atlantic Farm Women, 1750–1850* (New Haven: Yale University Press, 1986).

27. Laurel T. Ulrich, "Wheels, Looms, and the Gender Division of Labor in Eighteenth-Century New England," *William and Mary Quarterly*, 3d ser., no. 55 (1998): 3–38; Laurel T. Ulrich, *The Age of Homespun* (New York: Alfred A. Knopf, 2001); Adrienne D. Hood, *The Weaver's Craft: Cloth, Commerce, and Industry in Early Pennsylvania* (Philadelphia: University of Pennsylvania Press, 2003); Catherine E. Kelly, *In the New England Fashion: Reshaping Women's Lives in the Nineteenth Century* (Ithaca: Cornell University Press, 1999). Cotton homespun production by yeoman wives in South Carolina also offers clues to their role in their households' strategic engagement with both local and global markets. See Stephanie McCurry, *Masters of Small Worlds: Yeoman Households, Gender Relations, and the Political Culture of the Antebellum South Carolina Low Country* (New York: Oxford University Press, 1995), 101–2.

28. Laurel T. Ulrich, *A Midwife's Tale: The Life of Martha Ballard, Based on Her Diary, 1785–1812* (New York: Alfred A. Knopf, 1990).

29. Gloria L. Main, "Gender, Work, and Wages in Colonial New England," *William and Mary Quarterly*, 3d ser., vol. 51 (Jan. 1994): 39–66; Thomas Dublin, introduction to *Farm to Factory: Women's Letters, 1830–1860* (New York: Columbia University Press, 1981), 30–36; Thomas Dublin, *Women at Work: The Transformation of Work and Community in Lowell, Mass., 1826–1850* (New York: Columbia University Press, 1979).

30. Dublin, *Farm to Factory*; McCurry, *Masters of Small Worlds*.

31. Bruce Dorsey, *Reforming Men and Women: Gender in the Antebellum City* (Ithaca: Cornell University Press, 2002), 195–240; William E. Gienapp, *Origins of the Republican Party, 1852–1856* (New York: Oxford University Press, 1989); Ruth Schwartz Cowan, *More Work for Mother: The Ironies of Household Technology from the Open Hearth to the Microwave* (New York: Basic Books, 1983).

32. Kenneth Lockridge, *Literacy in Colonial New England* (New York: W. W. Norton, 1989); E. Jennifer Monaghan, "Literacy Instruction and Gender in Colonial New England," *American Quarterly* 40 (March 1988): 18–41; William Gilmore, *Reading Becomes a Necessity of Life: Material and Cultural Life in Rural New England, 1780–1835* (Knoxville: University of Tennessee Press, 1989); David Hall, "The Uses of Literacy in New England, 1600–1850," in *Printing and Society in Early America*, ed. William Joyce et al. (Worcester: American Antiquarian Society, 1983), 1–47.

33. Charles E. Clark, *The Public Prints: The Newspaper in Anglo-American Culture* (New York: Oxford University Press, 1994).

34. Joel Perlmann and Dennis Shirley, "When Did New England Women Acquire Literacy?" *William and Mary Quarterly*, 3d ser. (Jan. 1991): 50–67.

35. Mary Kelley, "The Making of Learned Women in Antebellum America," *Journal of American History* 83 (Sept. 1996): 401–24; Catherine Kerrison, "The Novel as Teacher: Learning to Be Female in the Early American South," *Journal of Southern History* (Aug. 2003): 513–48.

36. Melissa J. Homestead, "Nineteenth-Century American Women Authors and Literary Property," Ph.D. diss., University of Pennsylvania, 1998.

37. Laura Ewxler, *Tender Violence: Domestic Visions in an Age of U.S. Imperialism* (Chapel Hill: University of North Carolina Press, 2000); Elizabeth Clark, "'The Sacred Rights of the Weak': Pain, Sympathy, and the Culture of Individual Rights in Antebellum America," *Journal of American History* 82, no. 2 (1995): 463–93; Nina Baym, *Woman's Fiction: A Guide to Novels by and about Women in America, 1820–70* (Urbana: University of Illinois Press, 1993), xxii.

38. See Noel Ignatiev, *How the Irish Became White* (New York: Routledge, 1995), but note how the interactions between Irish domestic laborers and their employers never enter into his story. This tale has yet to be told.

39. Sherrin Marshall, ed., *Women in Reformation and Counter-Reformation Europe: Private and Public Worlds* (Bloomington: Indiana University Press, 1989); Marilyn Westerkamp, "Anne Hutchinson, the Puritan Patriarchs, and the Power of the Spirit," in *Human Experience in Colonial America*, ed. Steele and Rhoden, 49–70; Edward Muir and Guido Ruggiero, eds., *Sex and Gender in Historical Perspective* (Baltimore: Johns Hopkins University Press, 1990); Michael P. Winship, *Making Heretics: Militant Protestantism and Free Grace in Massachusetts, 1636–1641* (Princeton: Princeton University Press, 2002).

40. Sylvia R. Frey and Betty Wood, *Come Shouting to Zion: African American Protestantism in the American South and British Caribbean to 1830* (Chapel Hill: University of North Carolina Press, 1998), 109; Jon F. Sensbach, *Rebecca's Revival: Creating Black Christianity in the Atlantic World* (Cambridge: Harvard University Press, 2005).

41. Susan O'Brien, "A Transatlantic Community of Saints," in *Colonial America: Essays in Politics and Social Development*, 4th ed., ed. Stanley N. Katz, John M. Murrin, Douglas Greenberg, et al. (New York: McGraw Hill, 1993), 555–81; Frank Lambert, *"Pedlar in Divinity": George Whitefield and the Transatlantic Revivals* (Princeton: Princeton University Press, 1994).

42. Christina Heyrman, *Southern Cross: The Beginnings of the Bible Belt* (New York: Knopf, 1997); Mary Ryan, *Cradle of the Middle Class: The Family in Oneida County, New York, 1790–1865* (New York: Cambridge University Press, 1981); Susan E. Klepp, "Revolutionary Bodies: Women and the Fertility Transition in the Mid-Atlantic Region, 1760–1820," *Journal of American History* 85 (Dec. 1998): 910–45.

43. Amy Kaplan, "Manifest Domesticity," *American Literature* 70 (Sept. 1998): 581–606.

44. Katherine Sklar, *Catharine Beecher: A Study in American Domesticity* (New York: W. W. Norton, 1983).

45. Elizabeth Cady Stanton, *Eighty Years and More: Reminiscences, 1815–1897* (Boston: Northeastern University Press, 1993), 78–84. For subsequent manifestations of global activist networks, see Daniel T. Rodgers, *Atlantic Crossings: Social Politics in a Progressive Age* (Cambridge: Harvard University Press, 1998).

46. Emily Clark, "'By All The Conduct of Their Lives': A Laywomen's Confraternity in New Orleans, 1730–1744," *William and Mary Quarterly*, 3d ser., vol. 54 (Oct. 1997): 769–94; Florence Jean Deacon, "Handmaids or Autonomous Women? The Charitable Activities, Institution-Building and Communal Relationships of Catholic Sisters in Nineteenth-Century Wisconsin," Ph.D. diss., University of Wisconsin, 1989; Maureen Fitzgerald, *Habits of Compassion: Irish-Catholic Nuns and New York's Welfare System, 1830–1920* (forthcoming); Charles E. Rosenberg, *The Cholera Years: The United States in 1832, 1849, and 1866* (Chicago: University of Chicago Press, 1962), 63–64, 95–96, 139–40. For institution-building in other contexts, see Kathryn Burns, *Colonial Habits: Convents and the Spiritual Economy of Cuzco, Peru* (Durham: Duke University Press, 1999).

47. Linda Kerber, *Women of the Republic: Intellect and Ideology in Revolutionary America* (Chapel Hill: University of North Carolina Press, 1980); Mary Beth Norton, *Liberty's*

Daughters: The Revolutionary Experience of American Women, 1750–1800 (Ithaca: Cornell University Press, 1980); Jacqueline Jones, "Race, Sex, and Self-Evident Truths: The Status of Slave Women during the Era of the American Revolution," in *Women in the Age of the American Revolution,* ed. Ronald Hoffman and Peter J. Albert (Charlottesville: University Press of Virginia, 1989), 293–337; Sylvia R. Frey, *Water from the Rock: Black Resistance in a Revolutionary Age* (Princeton: Princeton University Press, 1991).

48. Michael Adas, "From Settler Colony to Global Hegemon: Integrating the Exceptionalist Narrative of the American Experience into World History," *American Historical Review* 106 (Dec. 2001): 1692–720; Theda Perdue, *Cherokee Women: Gender and Culture Change, 1700–1835* (Lincoln: University of Nebraska Press, 1998); Sarah H. Hill, *Weaving New Worlds: Southeastern Cherokee Women and Their Basketry* (Chapel Hill: University of North Carolina Press, 1997).

49. Kerber, *Women of the Republic;* Norton, *Liberty's Daughters;* Jan Lewis, "The Republican Wife: Virtue and Seduction in the Early Republic," *William and Mary Quarterly,* 3d ser., vol. 44 (Oct. 1987): 689–721.

50. See, for example, Jean Jacques Rousseau, *Emile; or, On Education,* ed. Allan Bloom (New York: HarperCollins, 1979), 44–45. In addition to his emphasis on the duties of the bourgeois mother, Rousseau's theories on education and his explorations of his interior life inspired Wollstonecraft's intellectual and emotional journeys. See also Ruth Perry, "Colonizing the Breast: Sexuality and Maternity in Eighteenth-Century England," *Journal of the History of Sexuality* 2 (Oct. 1991): 204–34.

51. Lewis, "The Republican Wife"; David S. Shields, *Civil Tongues and Polite Letters in British America* (Chapel Hill: University of North Carolina Press, 1997); Catherine La Courreye Blecki and Karin A. Wulf, eds., *Milcah Martha Moore's Book* (University Park: Pennsylvania State University Press, 1997).

52. Susan Branson, *These Fiery Frenchified Dames: Women and Political Culture in Early National Philadelphia* (Philadelphia: University of Pennsylvania Press, 2001).

53. Catherine Allgor, *Parlor Politics: In Which the Ladies of Washington Help Build a City and a Government* (Charlottesville: University Press of Virginia, 2000); Kirsten Wood, "One Woman So Dangerous to Public Morals," *Journal of the Early Republic* 17 (Summer 1997): 237–75.

54. Mary Ryan, *Women in Public: Between Banners and Ballots, 1825–1880* (Baltimore: Johns Hopkins University Press, 1990), 24–26; Simon Newman, *Parades and the Politics of the Street: Festive Culture in the Early American Republic* (Philadelphia: University of Pennsylvania Press, 1997); David Waldstreicher, *In the Midst of Perpetual Fetes: The Making of American Nationalism, 1776–1820* (Chapel Hill: University of North Carolina Press, 1997); Len Travers, *Celebrating the Fourth: Independence Day and the Rites of Nationalism in the Early Republic* (Amherst: University of Massachusetts Press, 1997); Carolyn Eastman, "A Nation of Speechifiers: Oratory, Print, and the Making of a Gendered American Public, 1780–1830," Ph.D. diss., Johns Hopkins University, 2001.

55. Eliza Leslie, "Conduct in the Street," *The Behaviour Book: A Manual for Ladies,* 7th ed. (Philadelphia: Willis P. Hazard, 1857), excerpt reprinted in *Early American Women: A Documentary History, 1600–1900,* ed. Nancy Woloch (Belmont: Wadsworth, 1992), 294–96.

56. Nancy Isenberg, *Sex and Citizenship in Antebellum America* (Chapel Hill: University of North Carolina Press, 1998).

Contributors

JUDITH M. BENNETT is professor of history at the University of North Carolina at Chapel Hill. Her research publications include *Women in the Medieval English Countryside* (1987) and *Ale, Beer, and Brewsters in England* (1996). Her teaching publications include *A Medieval Life: Cecilia Penifader of Brigstock, c. 1297–1344* (1998) and a revision of C. Warren Hollister's *Medieval Europe: A Short History* (2002).

KATHLEEN BROWN is associate professor of history at the University of Pennsylvania, where she teaches comparative women's history and early American history. She is the author of *Good Wives, Nasty Wenches, and Anxious Patriarchs: Gender, Race, and Power in Colonial Virginia* (1996). She is completing a book on the history of cleanliness in the early United States.

BRADY HUGHES taught world history, American foreign policy, and research methods at Hampton University until his retirement in 1990. He received his doctorate from the University of Wisconsin-Madison. He is coauthor, with Sarah S. Hughes, of *Women in World History*, volume 1: *Readings from Prehistory to 1500* (1995), and volume 2: *Readings from 1500 to the Present* (1997).

SARAH SHAVER HUGHES taught world history, comparative global women's history, and U.S. women's history before her retirement from Shippensburg University in 1998. Her doctorate is from the College of William and Mary. Other publications include *Surveyors and Statesmen: Land Measuring in Colonial Virginia* (1979), *Women in World History*, and "Gender at the Base of World History" in *Teaching World History* (1997). In 1979 the Berkshire Conference of Women Historians awarded her its Article Prize.

SUSAN MANN is a professor of history at the University of California, Davis, where she is active in the Cross-Cultural Women's History Program. She is the author of *Precious Records: Women in China's Long Eighteenth Century*, and coeditor of *Under Confucian Eyes: Writings on Gender in Chinese History*. She is writing the history of a nineteenth-century Chinese family whose members included four generations of women writers.

BARBARA N. RAMUSACK is Charles Phelps Taft Professor of History at the University of Cincinnati and has an M.A. and Ph.D. from the University of Michigan. Three Fulbright Fellowships and grants from the American Institute of Indian Studies, the Charles Phelps Taft Fund, the National Endowment for the Humanities, and the Smithsonian Institution have supported her research in India and Britain. She has published numerous articles and essays on the princely states of India and on women in India during the late colonial period. Her more recent publications are *Women in Asia: Restoring Women to History* (1999), coauthored with Sharon Sievers, and *The Princes of India* for *The New Cambridge of India* (2003). Her research is on maternal and infant health in the princely state of Mysore and the neighboring British province of Madras.

BONNIE G. SMITH is Board of Governors Professor of History at Rutgers University. She is author of *Changing Lives: Women in European History since 1700*, *The Gender of History: Men, Women, and Historical Practice,* and other books and articles. She is the editor of *Global Feminisms since 1945,* coeditor of *Gender Meets Disability Studies,* and general editor of *The Oxford Encyclopedia of Women in World History.*

ANN TWINAM is a professor of history at the University of Texas at Austin. Her research centers on colonial Spanish Latin America, focusing on gender, sexuality, illegitimacy, family, and race. Her projects include a monograph on sexuality and illegitimacy in Spain from the fifteenth through the eighteenth centuries and one on the purchase of "whiteness" and racial mobility in the Spanish colonies. Publications include *Public Lives, Private Secrets: Gender, Honor, Sexuality, and Illegitimacy in Colonial Spanish America* (1999), which won the Thomas F. McGann Prize and received honorable mention for the Bolton Prize, and *Miners, Merchants, and Farmers in Colonial Colombia* (1982, 1985), as well as numerous articles. She has been a Woodrow Wilson Fellow, a Tinker Fellow, a Fulbright Scholar in Colombia and Spain, and the recipient of grants from the Ford Foundation and the American Philosophical Society.

Index

abduction, 117, 240, 241
Abel, Richard, 146
Abelard, Peter, 164, 169
abolitionism, 3
abortion, 86, 168–70
Abram, Annie, 140
Aceh, 124
Achaemenid Empire, 21
Adam, 23
adat (local customary law), 123, 130
Adler, Michael, 146
adultery, 37, 39, 41, 74, 151, 215, 218–19
Aelfgyva, 163
African Americans, 2, 251, 264, 266. *See also* slavery and slave trade
agriculture: in ancient civilizations, 14, 16, 26, 106; in ancient Rome, 38; in China, 56–58, 70, 86; in colonial Latin America, 205–8; in India, 26, 106, 110, 116; in Japan, 57; in Korea, 57; in Southeast Asia, 126; in the United States, 240, 241, 244–49, 250, 254–58, 269
Aguilar, Jerónimo de, 202
Ahhotep I, 22
Ahmose, 22
Aisjijah, 130
Akbar, 108, 109
Akhenaten, 22
Akkad, 20
Alexander, 21, 22, 103
Allen, Hope Emily, 164
Altekar, A. S., 25, 26
American Anti-Slavery Society, 267

American Historical Association, Committee on Women Historians, 4
American Revolution, 268–70, 271, 273
Analects, 65
Analects for Women, 76, 77
Ananda, 27
Anataise, 163
ancestor worship, in China, 51
ancient civilizations, 9–46; China, 3, 28–31, 40; comparing women's status in, 39–43; Egypt, 21–23, 36–37; gender roles in, 13–14, 19–39; Greece, 35–37; India, 24–28, 106–7; Israel, 23–24; Japan, 31–34; Mesopotamia, 13, 20–21; production of goods and services in, 14–17; rediscovery of global history and, 10–11; reproductive work in, 13, 17–19, 39; Rome, 17–19, 37–39; social construction of gender in, 11–13; South Asia, 106–7; women's history and, 10–11
Anne, St., 160
Anne of Bohemia, 165
Antal, 107–8
anthropology, 12–13, 43, 103, 213
apprenticeships, 148, 149
archaeology, 12–13, 191
Argentina, 219
Aristotle, 36, 37
Arjun, 102
Around the World in Eighty Days (Verne), 104
art: in China, 68, 75–76; in Medieval Europe, 163–65
Arthashastra, 106–7

283

294

The University of Illinois Press
is a founding member of the
Association of American University Presses.

———————————————————————

University of Illinois Press
1325 South Oak Street
Champaign, IL 61820-6903
www.press.uillinois.edu

Printed by Printforce, United Kingdom